Faith at the Brink

An Autobiography of the Formative Years

INCLUDING

The Epochal Holocaust Period

AND

Historical Perspectives

by Osher M. Lehmann

FAITH AT THE BRINK

First Published 1996
by
Lehmann Books
1097 East Eighth Street
Brooklyn, New York 11230

Second Printing 1997

Copyright © 1996

Library of Congress Catalog Card Number: 96-94455

All rights reserved. No part of this book may be reproduced in any manner whatsoever, including information storage and retrieval, in whole or in part, except for brief contextual quotations in critical articles or reviews, without written permission from the author.

The rights of the copyright holder will be strictly enforced.

Distributed by:
THE JUDAICA PRESS, INC.
123 Ditmas Avenue
Brooklyn, New York 11218
Tel. 718-972-6200

Distributed in Israel, by:
SIFRIATI LTD./A. GITLER BOOKS
10 Hashomer Street
Bnei Brak, 51-361
Tel. 03-579-8187

Distributed in Europe, by:
J. LEHMANN, HEBREW BOOKSELLERS
20 Cambridge Terrace
Gateshead, Tyne and Wear
England NE8, 1RP
Tel. 44-191-490-1692

ISBN: 0-9653098-0-0 (Hard Cover)
ISBN: 0-9653098-1-9 (Soft Cover)

1. Autobiography   2. Holocaust   3. Historical Insights
4. Technological Advancements - Eclectic Perspectives

Designed and Typeset by
SilverGraphics / Brooklyn, New York / 718-645-9722

חסדי ד' כי לא תמנו כי לא כלו רחמיו

*But for the Almighty's kindness
we would have perished,
for His mercies are endless.*
Eichah, 3:22

DEDICATED TO MY DEAR WIFE, RUTH, שתי', who encouraged the documentation of precious memories and whose partnership I cherish in the rebuilding of our people, following the great destruction.

AND TO OUR DEAR CHILDREN AND their budding progenies, נ"י, each of whom, in his or her own right, is a cause for which my survival was merited.

דוד קאהן

ביהמ"ד גבול יעבץ
ברוקלין, נוא יארק

בס"ד

My good friend, R. Oscher Lehmann שי', asked me for a letter of approbation for his sefer which depicts his experiences during the years of "churban Europe". I use the word "sefer", rather than "book", because this memoir does not belong to the realm of the secular. It is rather a sefer of hashkofo - of Jewish weltanschauung - emanating from someone who is a ירא שמים מרבים - an outstanding G-d fearing individual - as well as a scion of one of Israel's illustrious families.

I have read this volume from beginning to end. The narrative gave me the feeling of being with the author throughout his experiences. I felt his anguish which has not abated entirely and was in awe of the honor which he exhibited towards his loving parents.

One can understand the intellectual positions which he takes as one commiserates with a young boy whose idyllic life was ruthlessly interrupted to become filled with strife and turmoil during his formative years.

This is, indeed, a sefer to cry with and to learn from.

May the author with all of Klal Yisroel be blessed with the realization of the Psalmists prayer שמחנו כימות עניתנו שנות ראינו רעה.

Horav David Cohen, Shlita, is Morah D'Asrah in Brooklyn, New York of Beis Hamedrash Gvul Yaabetz.

OHR SOMAYACH
TANENBAUM EDUCATIONAL CENTER

בס"ד

Office of the Dean

One of the great Chassidic Masters is said to have predicted, "In the era preceding the coming of Moshiach, the challenges to faith will be of such great magnitude that to maintain one's faith will be as difficult as climbing bare walls."

"Faith at the Brink," written by my dear brother-in-law, Osher M. Lehmann, is a poignant chronicle of that nigh impossible climb. What is fascinating is the way the author makes that heroic ascent without any apparent struggle.

I have known Reb Osher for close to a half century, first as a fellow mispallel and then as brother-in-law. I cannot remember him ever having spoken a word about the epic events of his early youth - events so cataclysmic that a prophet of the stature of Yirmiyahu would be needed to portray, to bemoan, and to interpret.

Eis Lachashos - V'es Ledaber (Koheles 3,7) - There is a time for silence and a time to speak out." For half a century the author was silent. It was a time of reflection and introspection. A time to absorb the legacy of parents whose bodies were destroyed, but whose spirit has given fresh life to a new generation of Yirei Hashem.

But now is the time to speak out, and to chronicle for future generations what may one day be regarded as a pinnacle of Jewish spiritual attainment: the preservation of faith in the face of incredible adversity.

The Satmar Rebbe ZT"L, upon leaving Eretz Yisroel, was asked by one of his chassidim, whom he should approach for a brocho, now that the Rebbe will be far away. Said the Rebbe, "When you go to shul and see a Jew rolling up his sleeve to don Tefillin and a tattooed number is on his arm, that is the one to ask for a brocho."

The Rebbe was teaching us that a Jew who experienced the ravages of the churban and emerged with his Emunah unscathed - that person is of such elevated stature that he is worthy to bestow blessings on others.

Such is my esteem for my brother-in-law after having read his heart-rending account of the war years.

May he be zoche to witness the Geulah and Techiyas Hamaisim, and be reunited with those Tzaddikim who are the heros of this fascinating work.

19 Sivan, 5756
June 6, 1996

Rabbi Yisroel Rokowsky
Rosh HaYeshiva

Rabbi Yisroel Rokowsky, Shlita, is Rosh HaYeshivah in Monsey, New York of Yeshiva Ohr Somayach

TABLE OF CONTENTS

	PAGE NOS.
Dedication	iii
Approbations	iv
Author's Foreword	xi
Acknowledgments	xvii

Section I – …And A Time To Build
1	Background - Parents	2
2	Growing up in Amsterdam	19
3	Amsterdam Experiences	28

Section II – A Time To Weep…
4	German Refugees	38
5	Barbarians Over the Moat and Dutch Surrender	48
6	Tyranny 1940-1942	51
7	Despotism 1942-1943	56
8	The Prins-Drukarch Family	67
9	First Arrest	73
10	Westerbork Described	79
11	Westerbork – Gateway to the East and West	86
12	Return to Amsterdam	95
13	Return to Westerbork - Way Station to Aryan Lairs	110
14	Bergen Belsen – Daily Encounters	114
15	Bergen Belsen – Challenges and Expectations	112
16	Bergen Belsen – Unusual Events	130
17	No Deals! Farewell to Dad and Mom, A.H.	139
18	Frauenlager – Daily Lives	147
19	Frauenlager – Unusual Events	153
20	Bergen Belsen – Final Days	160
21	Liberation!	164
22	Kazernen	172

	PAGE NOS.

Section III – …And A Time To Gather Stones

23	Return to Holland	182
24	Enschede	186
25	Postwar Tidings	193
26	To England	199
27	At The British Lehmanns	209
28	Noteworthy Experiences	216
29	To New York	223
30	At the Levis	229

Epilogue
Section IV – …And The Almighty Seeks The Oppressed

31	Retrospect	242
32	Epitaph	253
33	Psychosis – German Style	256

Section V – …And A Time to Praise

34	Technological Changes - Eclectic Perspectives	268
35	Appendices – Table of Contents	280
	Appendix A – Four Vignettes of Providential Guidance - Divine Deliverance Sagas	281
	Appendix B – Paternal & Maternal Forebears	292
	Appendix C – The *Chover* Title	326

Section VI – …And A Time To Destroy…

Appendix D – B-17 Flying Fortress Bombers	330
Appendix E – A Sordid German Folk-tale	333

Glossary	335
Bibliography	339

אם אשכחך ירושלים תשכח ימיני
תהלים. קלז:ה

If I forget you, O Yerusholayim, let my right hand forget its skill
Tehillim 137:5

Jews praying at the Kosel Ma'aravi
Reprinted from the Israelit,[21] January 1884

AUTHOR'S FOREWORD

"LEST WE FORGET" IS THE FREQUENTLY HEARD MOTTO. It is now over fifty six years since World War II broke out in Holland and over fifty one years since I last saw my beloved parents in December of 1944. The events that led up to World War II and the happenings that directly touched my life during and following the war are as clear in my memory as if it was yesterday. I frequently relive those occurrences in my mind, and as my subconscious roams through the past, my blood pressure rises and, on occasion, my eyes swell with tears.

I have recorded these memoirs for many reasons: More than five decades have passed during which I painfully was denied the opportunity of according personal honor to my special parents.[a] To redress this deprivation in a minuscule manner, I found solace by giving tribute to many honorable achievements in their short but admirable lives. An additional motive for recording these memories was to preserve the past for the future, in order to remember how Hashem helped and saved us in every

---

a. Shemos 20:12

step of the way over many arduous and eventful years. Furthermore, I would like to eternalize the events for my children, nephews and nieces who have only heard bits and pieces of these accounts. It is important for them to know how thankful a person should be to live in a free society where we don't have to be overly concerned with what the next day will bring.[b] Knowing the extent of real hardship is an important tool in putting our often selfmade daily problems into perspective.

Another purpose of recounting this part of my past is to illustrate the good and benevolent side of our Jewish people and to focus on the chivalrous conduct of my parents. In times of extreme adversity they faced life and death as heroes and as civilized human beings who, with great and unusual faith, courage and bravery, always tried their utmost to protect their brethren. We, their children, certainly have nothing to be ashamed of, and we should be only very proud of their total devotion to our Jewish way of life. On the flip side, once the thin veneer of their enemy's so-called "civilization" blistered away, this account reveals their foes' cruelty and viciousness. It describes how utterly beastly, cowardly, disgusting, greedy and murderous the Germans and their non-German collaborators were.

We cannot forget, however, that there were gentiles who saved and helped Jews. They must be mentioned and given true appreciation. Performing their humanitarian deeds in an environment dominated by vicious and wicked violence produced a most striking contrast and made such benevolent achievements far more exemplary. Their acts of kindness demonstrated that good will existed then and "human free will" was alive and well. Such charitable conduct contradicts the Germans' and their collaborators' claim that they had no choice in refusing to carry out their wanton and evil deeds, which they were "ordered" to expedite.

Living through the turbulent era known as the Holocaust (defined as "a thorough destruction, especially by fire") is an experience many a survivor wants to forget. All who suffered through this "made in Germany" calamity have their own experiences and thoughts that they survived with. Each and every one was exposed to his or her plight in a different setting. Some faced death after untold hardships, others were exposed to physical and/or mental cruelty. None is to be envied.

Among survivors there is great appreciation towards the Almighty for being able to tell their tale. Much is to be learned from the suffering

---

b. Devorim, 28:67

and witnessing of horrors both in coping with distress as well as in preparing oneself for adversity, if that should be possible. Furthermore, one may learn how to place many of these bygones in a rational and orderly perspective. It is my objective to relate as factually as possible, through the eyes and mind of one of the younger survivors still able to do so, from a vantage of some fifty years hence, backgrounds, scenes and happenings as he heard and saw them. To avoid *loshon horah* (bad mouthing), stories with embarrassing moments are not brought. Some passages in this book may be boring, some may be emotional or maudlin but all will be of a personal or historical interest. Derogatory barbs will be reserved for our former tormentors. To understand circumstances, I have elaborated on background information to describe how primitive or advanced people lived in my West European circles at the time. Now a half century after these events, my level of maturity has, of course, changed. That, in turn, has affected my retrospective vision, but only with respect to editorializing and not to the reporting of episodes.

Some of the guidelines used in writing this book are as follows:

Endearing and other suffixes:

- ❖ *O.H.: Olov or Oleho Hasholom* — "peace shall rest on him or her". The farewell of "Go in peace" is used when taking leave from a deceased person.[c] Along a similar vein we are told that a deceased is greeted with expressions of peace in the world to come.[d] Therefore, when mentioning the name of a respected person now deceased we append the wish of *O.H.*, or *A.H. Aleyhem Hasholom* for the plural.

- ❖ *Zatsal:* — Shlomo Hamelech writes "May the remembrance of the righteous be a blessing…"[e] Hence, the abbreviation *"Zatsal"* is frequently added to the name of a prominent deceased person.

- ❖ In these pages mention is made of many venerated people from generations past who are no longer with us. We hereby fervently wish that their mention is a blessing and that their *neshomos* are at peace. In this text, no further suffix follows their names. For contemporaries who are now deceased, the suffix *O.H.* will be limited to their first post-orbit mention in these accounts.

---

c. *Maseches Brochos,* 64a.
d. *Maseches Kesuvos,* 104a, refer also to classical commentaries on Yeshayohu, 57:2.
e. Mishlei, 10:7.

- ❖ The appendage *H.Y.D.: Hashem Yinokeim Domom* — "Hashem will avenge their blood", is herewith indicated in the Foreword for all those who were murdered by the Germans or their accomplices. It is fervently anticipated that the absence of these martyrs will be avenged by the One Who directed mankind not to kill innocent human beings.

- ❖ The above suffixes will not be omitted where textual quotes are brought.

- ❖ The *Torah* directs us to totally obliterate the memory of Amalek, the evil people.[f] In subsequent generations all wicked persons with similar anti-Semitic leanings are broadly banded into this obliteration policy.[g] The abbreviation *Y.S.* is added in this book, following the initial mention of committed German evildoers. *Y.S., "Yemach Shemom"* literally translates to "May his/her/their name be erased".

Idioms and Semantics:

- ❖ *It is my intention not to use the term "lucky" in this book. This decision is based on several definitions provided by the Webster's New Collegiate Dictionary for that adjective, including "happening by chance" and "producing or resulting in good by chance". These are the more common connotations for this frequently used expression of serendipity. We consider all happenings imposed on us to be Providentially guided or "Hashgochah".[h] Describing a matter to be "by chance" is therefore out of consonance with the perspicuity (Anschauung) expected of a believing Jew. On that basis, it would be a misnomer to consider myself lucky, but rather to be extremely fortunate and exceedingly privileged for having survived the war. Deplorably, it is a common semantic error to consider "luck" synonymous to "mazal" which is more appropriately translated as "constellation".*

- ❖ "Tante" v.s. "Aunt" explained: Throughout this book, "Tante" is used in lieu of "Aunt" since that is how our aunts were known and addressed in our Dutch and German language conversations. Note: The German word for "Uncle" is *"Onkel"*. No differentiation was

---

f. Devorim, 25:19.
g. Shemos, 17:16.
h. *Maseches Brochos,* 33b

made in these pages for this noun since the pronunciation for *Onkel* is almost identical to the English Uncle.

- ❖ **In these pages, reference is mostly made to the "Germans" and not to the "Nazis" (National Sozialists) as having initiated and perpetrated wanton acts of violence and lawlessness against humanity and genocide against the Jewish people. The fact was, that the vast majority of the German generation of the Third Reich era, carried out the will of their Nazi government. Therefore, even though most individuals were not card carrying Nazis or Hitler Jugend (Youth) members, the German population, for the most part, did persecute in a most evil, wicked and vicious manner both their indigenous Jews, who formed one percent of Germany's population, and wherever they conquered, Jews and minorities. In the Epilogue, moreover, reference is made to evidence of a lingering consensus of intolerance at both the ruling and legislative levels of government, well into postwar times.**

In reviewing the draft of this book, my dear wife Ruth commented that the text lacks sufficient expressions of emotions. In dwelling on this matter, I concluded that the emotional stress would have been excessive had I expanded on the sentimental aspects of my earlier years. The result would have been no book at all. It is for these reasons that my sister Toni preferred not to talk about grim wartime stories. When I approached my sister Connie to review this book, her response was that she wanted to forget the horrible past and therefore she had blocked most sad memories of that period from her mind. Connie never told her family any gloomy stories and prefers to continue avoiding the recollection of most incidents from these bygone years. I feel, however, that my horrible wartime experiences, should not be forgotten. They are part of my historical recollections and remain a chapter of my eventful life. I was an unsolicited patron to a tragedy named "History In The Making" and involuntarily assigned to a lower balcony box seat.

In reading further through these pages, we can readily understand our daily *brocha* with which we praise Hashem in the *Birchas Hashachar:* *"Asher Bochar Bonu Mikol Ha'Amim",* that indeed we were chosen from all the nations, since judging from some of their actions, or lack thereof, we certainly would not want to emulate them.

Most of these memories picture life under duress versus the relative luxuries to which many of us have now become accustomed. They recall how many did wend their way through an alien and hostile world in those times of misfortune when little went according to their plans.

With Hashem's help and with the assistance of His many good messengers, we did survive and succeed, despite our nomadic lifestyle, having wandered from country to country, language to language, lifestyle to lifestyle and culture to culture in the unstable World War II era and directly beyond those days.

To the One who grants mankind knowledge and teaches us insight, may He give me perception, insight and wisdom to properly convey these memories and cognate matters to paper.

Osher M. Lehmann

ACKNOWLEDGMENTS

FAITH IN HASHEM, ANCESTRAL *ZECHUSIM* AND A PLEASANT disposition are some of the positive attributes and important gear that help a person overcome difficult times. All these traits and more were given to my two sisters and myself by our wonderful parents, *a.h.* Without their constant concern for our physical and spiritual well-being, we would not have been able to maintain our proper faculties or come to grips with the crushing burdens of living in a concentration camp, becoming orphans at a very young age and beginning new lives in foreign lands.

Not commonly considered, but nevertheless a reality, are the *zechusim* of the generations to come, for whom we are a link in the chain of existence.[a] Therefore, retroactively, those who have descended from my family and those of my sisters' (Grunhut and Rubinstein), by their daily good deeds, give justification to our having emerged unscathed.

In 1940, our uncles and aunts, with their respective children, lived in Eretz Yisroel, England, Germany and the United States, while my

---

[a]. Shemos, 2:12, Rashi there and *Maseches Bova Kamma,* 38a,b.

parents and family lived in Holland. Unfortunately, my father's oldest sister, Emmy (Lehmann) Sutin was deported in the early 1940's from Mainz, Germany to Theresienstadt, Czechoslovakia and was never heard from again. Following our liberation in 1945, no family members remained in Germany and Holland, and the major burden of responsibility for the well-being of the Dutch Lehmann children was borne by my uncle and aunt Mr. and Mrs. Michael and Alice Levi of New York and our aunt, Mrs. Resi Lehmann of England (my mother's sisters). They took upon themselves the task of assuring our extrication from continental Europe at the earliest possible opportunity and orchestrating our arrival in New York. Without their joint efforts, we would have been left to the whims of numerous well-meaning Dutch relief organizations, whose track record in providing for a fully orthodox Jewish upbringing were frequently weak to non-existent. We are therefore very grateful to these giants of *chesed.*

A half-hearted acknowledgment of appreciation must also go to the Allied governments and the leadership of their armed forces, under the supreme command of General Dwight D. Eisenhower, for liberating us in the nick of time (see chapter on liberation). It is not a full-hearted gratitude, since it was the lack of statesmanship of the world leaders in their policies of appeasement from 1933 to 1940 that allowed Germany the opportunity to invade and subjugate most of Europe. Furthermore, the subsequent and immediate goal of the Allied governments in conquering Germany was not to aid or liberate the Jews or other oppressed minorities, but simply to eliminate armed enemy opposition and ultimately to restore law and order. It is further noted that the Allied tacticians did not modify their military or political strategies one iota to liberate prisoners. Millions of lives were deemed expendable and lost as a result of these non-policies.

Much recognition and gratitude must be given to many members of most European national resistance groups and to the rank and file of the Allied armed forces, who displayed exceptional patriotism, valor and selflessness in resisting and battling the Third *Reich* and their accomplices. It was a daunting task, to say the least, and many made the ultimate sacrifice. They too, however, had their own agenda, and it did not include saving the Jews from extinction.

Much appreciation also goes to various family members and friends for assistance rendered in making this book a reality. Salient observations raised by my son Yisroel (Marcus), my daughter Chanaly Fischer and my son-in-law Shlomo Pesach (Robert) Kassai were all addressed. Without the fast and accurate typing of my daughter, Sarah Kassai, this work would still be at square one. Frequently, I would proofread a section and find typed into the text, "Dad, what happened when…?" Her questions helped embellish the narratives on matters considered obvious to myself. On occasion, the phone would ring late in the evening. "Dad, isn't the following too harsh?" Sarah would ask. "Do you want people to read this?" This led to further reflection which, in fact, enhanced the quality of this book.

I am thankful to Professor Meir Lehman for his informative comments on the two chapters involving the British Lehmann branch. Jacob Levi's comments on the chapter devoted to his parents and Abraham Levi's comments on the book as a whole are also much appreciated.

Much indebtedness is due to Joshua Goldschmidt, my Swiss son-in-law, who faxed us many valuable observations and performed our German language spell-check.

I am also grateful to Mrs. Rachel Prins of Rechovot for her fine-tuning of the chapter on her family's wartime experiences. Thanks also goes to Rabbi Chaim Mordechai Wainkranz for making available his encyclopedic knowledge of the Talmud.

I would also like to thank Rabbi David Cohen, my *Morah D'Asrah,* for taking the time to read my manuscript from cover to cover and for providing accurate insights and valuable comments. I am appreciative, too, for Rabbi David Cohen's encouragement to have my book published.

My daughter-in-law, Sara Lehmann, has done a magnificent job of professionally editing this text. She took a fresh look at my writing and made it more palatable and reader-friendly.

Rabbi Shimon Hook deftly buttoned up my memoirs by proficiently applying his editing skills. He was indeed a friend in *deed.*

I very much cherish and am delighted with the comments received from my two sisters, Mrs. Toni Grunhut of Kew Gardens, New York and Mrs. Connie Rubinstein of Yerusholayim, Eretz Yisroel. They, too, suffered through the same camps and hardships as I did, and similarly travelled from Holland to England and then to the U.S.A. They are respectively four and three years my senior, and their input resulted in some ten additional pages to this book on subject matter they would have preferred not to discuss or remember.

To be totally factual was not an easy task. Therefore the comments I received from many friends and family members greatly contributed towards the authentication process of this work.

The graphical and textual aspects of this book were greatly enhanced by the sophisticated professionalism of SilverGraphics. Their high caliber workmanship and first rate skills have helped give *Faith at the Brink* a special niche in contemporary Judaic Libraries and placed it on par with works produced by the great publishing houses.

Finally, I must give overwhelming thanks to Hashem for my *Aishes Chayil* and homemaker, Ruth (Rokowsky) *shetichyeh*, who has given me comfort and a special meaning in life, and who has helped me rebuild my world after the great destruction of the early 1940's. As a result of our numerous discussions, additional thoughts were pulled from my subconscious mind, which helped shape this book. Ruth grew up in America, in a home imbued with Jewish renaissance, where she witnessed her parents' involvement in *Hatzolah* work with many European refugees. Her parents, Meir Rokowsky o.h., and, l.b., Rachel Rokowsky *shetichyeh*, deserve praise for raising wonderful children and for playing key roles in many communal organizations and important *mosdos* in the American Jewish desert of the early 1940's. They deserve special credit for co-establishing the Beth Jacob School of Boro Park in New York, which, in fifty years, has grown from three students to well over eighteen hundred students. Describing their worthy accomplishments could fill several voluminous books.

May it be the will of the Almighty that we, the Jewish People, who have emerged from the sad epoch of *Hasteir Astier Ponai* — "I will indeed hide My face,"[b] — may now enter the dynamic era of *Nachamu Nachamu Ami, Yomar Elokeichem* — "Comfort, comfort My people! will Hashem say."[c] I pray that all debts for our generation's and for past generation's sins be fully settled, absolved and paid off in full.

Osher M. Lehmann
Brooklyn, New York

Adar 5756/February 1996

---

b. Devorim, 31:18.
c. Yeshayohu, 40:1.

Section One

...AND A TIME TO BUILD.
(KOHELES 3,3)

Chapter One

BACKGROUND

R ABBI JOSE SAID: "APPLY YOURSELF TO STUDY TORAH FOR *it is not yours by inheritance.*"ᵃ

Horav Meir Lehmann, my great grandfather, explained this teaching[18] in an interesting manner:

Material goods may fall into one's lap without any effort on the part of the recipient. However, becoming imbued with the spirit and knowledge of *Torah* requires major exertions. In fact, this endeavor starts already with a person's parents. "Why should our child be involved with Jewish studies? What benefit will he or she reap from this later in life?" Unfortunately, that is how many parents have undermined the non-material well-being of their offspring and deprived them of our people's biggest treasure. For that reason, youngsters must start early in life, to labor at becoming acquainted with our *Torah* heritage. But, as milk and wine will

---

a. *Pirkei Avos,* 2:17.

last longer in clean containers, so will the knowledge of our *Torah* also require pure receptacles. It is the constant vigilance of the individual in avoiding iniquities and inappropriate companions that guarantees the stored knowledge to surely remain unspoiled. The fact that former generations were dedicated to Torah in no way implies that we, their descendants, will again be another generation of spiritual heirs and have non-material bliss delivered to us on a silver platter. The above interpretation of the *Mishnah* is not considered a contradiction to another *Ma'amar Chazal,* which teaches that *Torah* will remain in a family once it is truly practiced by three consecutive generations.[b] The latter only guarantees that their descendants will welcome the *Torah* as a treasured guest. Careful mastering of its lofty ideals will, however, be required to convince the *Torah* to remain and continue to linger.

My family was endowed with ancestry and relatives of the highest caliber. My family's labor and goal are to continue in their lofty ways. The difficult world that framed our constant struggles, especially prior to and during World War II, proved to be as arduous an obstacle course as earlier infamous trials and tribulations alas experienced by our forebears over the last two thousand years. To explain the courage and salvations we witnessed in recent years, it is necessary to meet some of our family patriarchs and matriarchs of the recent past in whose merits we bask. For interesting details on my paternal and maternal forebears, please refer to Appendix B.

PARENTS
Meir and Chana Lehmann

MY FATHER WAS BORN ON 17 SHEVAT, 5653 (1893) IN MAINZ, Germany. He was the fifth child and second son of six children. His namesake was his grandfather, being the first grandson to be born after Horav Meir Lehmann passed away. Father grew up in Mainz and, as was to be expected, attended the Mainz *Yeshivah* established by his late grandfather.

---

b. *Maseches Bova Metzia* 85a.

While my father grew up in Germany, the continent was seething politically below the surface, as has been the case during most of the last two thousand years of recorded European history. Europe, a section of the Eurasian continent, has another country, culture and monetary system just about every two hundred miles in any direction that one travels. There is hardly a country in Europe that doesn't have two or more well established languages each with its own culture, cuisine and historical roots.

At the turn of the twentieth century, there were dark clouds over the land. Militarism seemed to be the way of life, and governments were inept at peacemaking and greedy for their neighbor's wealth and

Father's birth certificate issued in Mainz, Germany, February 3, 1893

turf. Germany, especially, was no exception. It was a country that loved war, and its cultural folk heroes rose to fame mostly in battle lore.

Father was born during the reign of Kaiser Wilhelm II (1859-1941) who ascended the Imperial throne in the year 1888. The Kaiser commanded great international respect and Wilhelm knew how to assert his Imperial rank. One example was the Kaiser's visit of state, in the year 1898, to the walled city of Yerusholayim. Despite the fact that this Prussian monarch was not a Moslem, it was significant that the Ottomans accorded him the royal red-carpet treatment. In a friendly "gesture" towards the Kaiser the Turkish sultan demolished a thirty seven foot wide section of the magnificent city wall, directly to the south of the Jaffa gate. This enabled the horse drawn royal coach to avoid awkward maneuvering through the circuitous passageway within the gate tower. That breach in the old city's fortifications still exists one hundred years later. Two decades after Wilhelm's visit, Germany's monarchy came to an abrupt end and this high and mighty potentate was deposed and exiled.

Several years prior to World War I, the Kaiser had already mobilized German military forces so that he could defend his *Reich* at the earliest sign of any outside provocation. To that end, my father was drafted into the German army in March of the year 1912. He was nineteen years old. Being of above average intelligence, father was sent for officer training. He remained in uniform for one and a half years, until September 1913, and was assigned to the Kaiser's 87th infantry regiment.

World War I broke out on August 1, 1914, which coincided with *Tisha B'Av,* the ninth day of the Jewish month of Av. It is noteworthy that the war began on this sad day of the Jewish calendar. The significance of *Tisha B'Av* dates back to the year of our people's exodus from Egypt.[c] It was to this calendar date that the twelve tribes accorded a dubious prominence when they showed their unworthiness to enter Eretz Yisroel, and thus, it was decreed on Tisha B'Av that many of them would succumb in the desert. Both holy temples in Yerusholayim were subsequently destroyed on *Tisha B'Av,* and on that date in the year 1492, King Ferdinand and Queen Isabella chose to expel the Jews from Spain. World War I, which was the precursor of World War II, began on that day; thus the Holocaust as well had its roots on *Tisha B'Av.*

The Kaiser's army mobilization that followed the declaration of World War I required Father to be back in uniform by August 4, 1914. He

---

c. *Maseches Taanis,* 29a.

remained with the Kaiser's fighting forces until the end of World War I, November 11, 1918, which was Armistice Day. Almost eighty years later that truce date is still celebrated in the United States and is known as Veteran's Day.

Father held the rank of *Vize Feldwebel* in a field communications group, which is the equivalent of Assistant Sergeant Major or Master Sergeant.

His unit was initially on the eastern front in Poland, south of Breslau, Germany. In the year 1917, towards the war's end, with the start of the Russian Communist revolution and the entrance of the United States into the conflict, his unit was reassigned from Poland to northwestern France, near Albert. While in the army, Father received several citations and was even wounded. However, his injuries were apparently insufficient to permit departure from his unit.

Despite Father's heroism he never neglected his *Yiddishkeit* and observed all religious laws as was humanly possible. His sister, Tante Sophie, once told me with tears in her eyes, that when his Company was cut off by the enemy and food was scarce, the men slaughtered and ate their horses. My Father, however, despite his severe hunger would have nothing to do with that horsemeat.

Many Jews served in the army of Kaiser Wilhelm II. Interestingly, on Father's military record, his religion is described as *mosaisch* (Moses' religion) and not as *juedisch* (Jewish). Some historical perspective is needed to understand the rationale for classifying Jewish servicemen in this manner.

Towards the end of the eighteenth century a political movement dawned that eventually led to granting Jews equal rights. This offer of increased freedom was conditioned on the assumption that Jews would relinquish all their distinctiveness. Allowing entry into the gentile society as equals led to a rapid decadence in Torah values and resulted in reduced Jewish identity. Increased assimilation followed and ultimately led to the growth of the Jewish reform movement. Greater emphasis on identity as a German rapidly replaced Jewish distinctiveness. The highest priority of such Jews became their drive for full acceptance in German society. Spin-offs of this new attitude were attenuating or even dropping many sacred vestiges of their Jewish beliefs and practices.

Dr. David Kranzler, the historian, observed: "to avoid standing out in any way from the rest of society, the reformers were anxious to emphasize

Zentralnachweiseamt
für Kriegerverluste und Kriegergräber
Büro für Kriegsstammrollen
Nr. St XVIII 179 L 43

Berlin SW 68, den 30. Juli 1943
Lindenstraße 37
Fernsprecher 17 51 46

Bei Rückfragen ist diese Bescheinigung beizufügen

Militär-Dienstzeitbescheinigung*)

über den __Vizefeldwebel Markus L e h m a n n__,

geboren am __3. 2. 1893__ in __Mainz__

1. Dienstverhältnisse:
   a) vor dem Kriege: __25.3.1912-19.9.1913 b.3.Komp.Inf.Regt.87.__

   b) nach Eintritt der Mobilmachung:
   __4. 8.1914 z. Ers.Batl.Inf.Regt.168,__
   __25. 8.1914 " 9.Komp.Reserve=Inf.Regt.221,__
   __23. 1.1918 " 1.Komp.Reserve=Inf.Regt.221,__
   __3. 5.1918 verwundet bei der Truppe verblieben,__

   Entlassungstag nicht festgestellt, nachgewiesen bis 31.10.1918.

2. Gefechtshandlungen oder Aufenthalt im Kriegsgebiet:

   (Anordnungsgemäß erfolgt für jedes Jahr nur Angabe einer Kampfhandlung oder eines zweimonatigen Aufenthalts)

1914:	Vom 18.12.1914 bis 8.1.1915
1915:	Schlacht an der Rawka-Bzura;
1916:	Vom 1.9.1916 bis 19.5.1917
1917:	Stellungskämpfe an der Bystrzyca;
1918:	5.7.-5.10.Kämpfe zwischen Arras und Albert;

3. Beförderungen: __19.9.1913 Gefreiter;25.8.1914 Unteroffizier;9.11.1915 Vizefeldwebel.__

4. Orden: __16.2.1916 Eisernes Kreuz zweiter Klasse;5.10.1917 Hess. Tapferkeitsmedaille;16.8.1918 Hess.Kriegsehrenzeichen__
5. Bemerkungen: __in Eisen;25.7.1918 Verwundeten Abzeichen in Schwarz.__
   __Religion: mosaisch.__

Vorstehende Angaben stimmen mit der Kriegs-Rangliste-Stammrolle Bd. Nr. __3122/1705__ überein.

*) Militärpässe werden bestimmungsgemäß nicht mehr ausgestellt.

Military record of Father's service before and during World War I.
The World War II Berlin archives office added the swastika seal

their *German* identity at the expense of their *Jewishness*. One of the manifestations of this new perspective was their preference to have all co-religionists identified as Germans of the *Mosaic* persuasion rather than as *German Jews*. The label *Jewish* connoted too distinctive a lifestyle and implied a conduct considered to be distasteful to some non-Jews. The tragic result was however that the more that Jews tried to act like Germans, the more the Germans resented them."

Avrohom Yaakov Finkel, author of classical Judaica works, noted that using the *Mosaic* adjective in qualifying our religion was done solely for purposes of denigrating our faith. Its usage implied the Jewish belief to be not Divinely inspired but merely being a creed with its supposed founder's namesake.

The German army of World War I had Jewish chaplains, who not only assisted the Jewish soldiers but also helped the local Jews in Poland and France. Realizing that the troops had to remain at the front for *Pesach,* the Frankfurt am Main community printed a special *Hagadah* edition in the year 5676 (1916) for the troops at the battle front. The German language title page states in part:

> *Mit treuen Heimatgruessen, zum Feste ueberreicht von der Freien Vereinigung fuer die Interessen des Orthodoxen Judentums E.V. [Eingetragener Verein] in Frankfurt am Main, im Kriegsjahr 5676.*

> Translation:
> With faithful greetings from back home, presented in honor of the festival, from the Free Association for the Interests of Orthodox Jewry Corp., in Frankfurt am Main, in the war year 5676.

The association which sponsored this Hagadah was described by Horav Shimon Schwab, *Zatsal,* as the forerunner of the current Agudath Yisroel. It served as the umbrella organization for furthering the interests of Orthodox Jews, including the needs of those in military uniform. An interesting footnote was related to me by the historian, Dr. David Kranzler: "The subject Association was originally founded in 1885 by Horav Samson R. Hirsch. Subsequently, this group was incorporated into the Agudah when the latter was founded in 1912. The Agudah was, however, an international organization, which included members in the combative countries of Poland and Russia. To display their patriotism, the German Jews reverted back to their organization's title as originally designated in 1885."

V. Pfarr. Lehmann 9/22

Mit treuen Heimatgrüßen

zum Feste überreicht

von der

Freien Vereinigung für die Interessen des orth. Judentums E. V.

in Frankfurt a. M.

im Kriegsjahr 5676.

„Eine Nacht des Gottesschutzes war es, sie herauszuführen aus Ägyptens Land,
sie bleibt eine Nacht, Gott geweiht, eine Nacht der Hut für alle Söhne Israels, für ihre Nachkommen."
(II. B. M. 12, 42.)

סדר

הגדה של פסח לשני ימים

Erzählung

von dem Auszuge Israels aus Ägypten

an den beiden ersten Pesachabenden.

übersetzt von

W. Heidenheim.

Neue, verbesserte, illustrierte Ausgabe.

Frankfurt a. M. (Bockenheim.)

Druck und Verlag von M. Lehrberger & Co.

1914.

*Title page of Hagadah which was presented to Imperial German servicemen during World War I.
Note the rank, name and company number in the upper righthand corner (V.fldw Lehmann 9/221)*

*A company of Imperial German soldiers in Koslow, Poland in the year 1915.
Father is the fifth person from the right.
Notice the country house with the thatched straw roofing.*

It must be realized that Jewish soldiers were fighting for each of the combatants involved in those World War I hostilities. This affected our family, e.g. Germany was fighting against both England and Russia. Father had a first cousin living in London named Selina Sassoon (Prins) who was very much involved with the British war effort. Similarly, he had first cousins from his maternal side, the Rabinowitz family, who may have been fighting for the Russian cause. To place all this in a proper perspective, one could refer to the original German language *Lehmann Hagadah* [20] where,[d] it is found that Horav Meir Lehmann, living in Imperial Germany, exhorts nationals of different countries to serve their respective governments faithfully. There was, however, one major stipulation: Jews of these countries were to be treated justly and as equals to all fellow citizens, with no discrimination.

---

d. page 54.

Jewish Servicemen in the Imperial German Army during the Franco-Prussian War (1870-1871) conducting Yom Kippur services around an open Sefer Torah, outside the French city of Metz, October 1870. Reprinted from the Israelit, [21] September 1895.

Horav Meir Lehmann writes:

> ...There is no contradiction between the request of Jacob's sons to Pharaoh to "settle" (personally) *yeishvuh* in Egypt and his sons' request to "sojourn" *lohgur* in the land (i.e. to "temporarily" dwell in Egypt).[e] The explanation being, that during the period of their stay, they will whole-heartedly accept and perform the civic duties of their host country, to share the fortunes of the state with other inhabitants of the land, to strive for the happiness of their adopted fatherland and to attempt to preserve it from any evil...We shall look upon our stay in your (Pharaoh's) country as temporary only, for we cling to the hope of returning one day to the Promised Land; but we shall dwell in the land of Goshen under your rule, and as faithful subjects, we shall not try to avoid our duties as citizens to this country.

> After eighteen centuries, we find ourselves in a similar situation. Our sanctuary is in ruins, the Jewish State was destroyed and the children of Israel are scattered over practically the entire globe. Although we have not abandoned hope that G-d will again gather together the scattered remnants of our People and return them to the land of our Fathers, nevertheless until then we are entirely a part of the country in which we live, we are part of its people and active in its state government. We German Jews are Germans at heart. Our ancestors, and now ourselves have lived for over a thousand years in this large and beautiful land. German is our mother tongue. Its traditions, its customs and the characteristic traits of the German peoples are also ours. We are loyal subjects of our Princes and our Kaiser. We respect our fellow Germans as we do our Jewish bothers and sisters. The welfare of our Fatherland, in good and bad times, is our concern as much as it is of all the other segments of the population. We stand prepared to protect and defend this precious Fatherland with life and limb... Not only in these days when there are proper and just laws which assure our citizens' political rights... All these are obligations to G-d and should be natural to us.

> Just as the Jews act in Germany, so do Jews conduct themselves in a similar fashion in Austria, Hungary, Russia, France, England, the Netherlands, Denmark, Sweden, Turkey, America and all other countries where descendants of Jacob reside...

---

e. Breishis, 47:4

The above discussion on apparent dual loyalties was written in the year 1888. This was significantly prior to the exacerbation of German anti-Semitism, which commenced in the year 1933 and which was officially condoned, and finally became the established government policy. It is for this reason that English and Hebrew translations of the *Lehmann Hagadah* omit this section, despite its apparent relevance and validity.

Being in the army was the first real occasion when Father was exposed to the non-Jewish German population. Father was now presented with a first hand look at the make-up of the typical contemporary German soldier. He was disenchanted with their lack of correct character, intolerance, excessive vulgarism and base non-values. All these traits he considered as latent and systemic flaws. This was not the country where he wanted to raise a family.

Father in Officer's uniform prior to World War I

Therefore, in the year 1919, father decided to leave his parent's home, his family and his friends and move to Amsterdam in the Netherlands. There he had an uncle, Maurits Prins, a brother in law of his father through marriage with Tante Emma (Lehmann) Prins. Uncle Maurits was in the diamond business and was happy to teach the trade to his nephew. While in Amsterdam, Father made many friends and met several fellow expatriates, including his future brother-in-law, Michael Levi, who immigrated to Amsterdam from Frankfurt am Main in the early twenties.

IN 1972, RUTH AND I VISITED OUR AUNT, TANTE SOPHIE (LEHMANN) Tscherniak, an older sister of Father's, who lived in Tel Aviv. After spending an hour of talking and catching up on many family news items, my aunt said that she must tell us of a dream that she had over thirty years ago. All six siblings, including herself, were asked to indicate one

in diesem Lande sind wir gekommen, denn es ist keine Weide für das Vieh, das deinen Dienern gehört, denn schwer ist der Hunger im Lande Kenaan; und

מִרְעֶה לַצֹּאן אֲשֶׁר לַעֲבָדֶיךָ כִּי כָבֵד הָרָעָב בְּאֶרֶץ כְּנָעַן וְעַתָּה יֵשְׁבוּ־נָא עֲבָדֶיךָ בְּאֶרֶץ

Die Worte der heiligen Schrift וגר שם „und er hielt sich dort auf" bedürfen der Erklärung. Bekanntlich währte der Aufenthalt der Kinder Israel in Mizrajim 210 Jahre. Jakob selbst kam als hochbetagter Greis nach Mizrajim, um den Rest seines Lebens dort zu verbringen. Warum wählt also die heilige Schrift den Ausdruck ויגר „und er hielt sich vorübergehend auf?" Es hätte doch heißen sollen: וישב שם „und er ließ sich dort dauernd nieder." Daraus lernen wir, daß es Jakobs Absicht nicht war, seine Nachkommen dauernd ihren Aufenthalt in Mizrajim nehmen zu lassen; er wollte vielmehr, daß sie sich stets dessen bewußt bleiben sollten, daß sie einst in das gelobte Land zurückkehren würden, wie ja auch Gott zu Jakob gesprochen: „Ich werde mit dir hinabziehen nach Mizrajim, und ich werde dich wieder heraufführen." — Zum Beweise führt der Baal Hagadah die Worte der Brüder Josephs an, die sie zu Pharao sprachen: לגור בארץ באנו „uns vorübergehend aufzuhalten in diesem Lande sind wir gekommen." — Schon die alten Erklärer der Hagadah werfen die Frage auf, weshalb hier der ganze Vers herbeigezogen wird; es hätte doch genügt, die Worte anzuführen, die wir soeben wiedergegeben haben. Wenn wir jedoch den Vers genau betrachten, so werden wir in ihm einen Widerspruch finden. Wir haben dargelegt, daß das Zeitwort גור einen vorübergehenden Aufenthalt bedeutet, während ישב eine dauernde Niederlassung bezeichnet. So erklären auch unsere Weisen den Vers: 1. B. M., K. 37, V. 1): וישב יעקב בארץ מגורי אביו, ביקש יעקב לישב בשלוה, קפץ עליו רוגזו של יוסף. Jakob wollte sich dauernd niederlassen in dem Lande des Aufenthaltes seines Vaters; da kamen über ihn die traurigen Ereignisse, die sich an die Geschichte Josephs knüpften, und er mußte den Gedanken, schon damals von dem gelobten Lande dauernd Besitz zu nehmen, aufgeben. — Wenn nun dem so ist, wie können die Söhne Jakobs zu Pharao sprechen: לגור בארץ באנו וגו' ועתה ישבו נא עבדיך בארץ גושן „Vorübergehend uns aufzuhalten im Lande sind wir gekommen, und nun mögen sich dauernd niederlassen deine Diener im Lande Goschen!"

Es scheint hierin ein Widerspruch zu liegen, in der Tat aber sind die hier gewählten Ausdrücke vollkommen sachentsprechend. Es ist damit die eigentümliche Lage angedeutet, in der sich unsere Väter damals befanden, und in der wir uns heute seit länger als achtzehn Jahrhunderten wiederum befinden. Unsere Väter sollten zwar 210 Jahre lang in Mizrajim bleiben, sie sollten aber nicht die Hoffnung aufgeben, in das gelobte Land zurückzukehren. Infolgedessen durften sie ihren Aufenthalt in Mizrajim, und sollte er auch Jahrhunderte dauern, nur als einen vorübergehenden betrachten; zugleich aber wollten sie während der Zeit ihres Aufenthaltes dem gastlichen Lande, das sie aufgenommen, ganz und voll angehören, alle bürgerlichen Pflichten erfüllen, das Wohl und Wehe des Staates mit den übrigen Bewohnern des Landes teilen, für das Glück ihres angenommenen Vaterlandes streben und jedes Unheil von ihm abzuwenden suchen. Deshalb sprachen sie zu Pharao: Wir werden zwar unsern Aufenthalt in deinem Lande stets nur als einen vorübergehenden betrachten, wir werden die Hoffnung aufrecht erhalten, dereinst in das gelobte Land zurückzukehren; aber wir werden wohnen im Lande Goschen als getreue Untertanen deiner Herrschermacht, und wir werden uns keiner Pflicht als Bürger dieses Landes entziehen.

Auch wir, die späten Nachkommen, befinden uns seit länger als achtzehnhundert Jahren in ähnlicher Lage. Zerstört ist unser Heiligtum, vernichtet das jüdische Staatswesen, und die Kinder Israel sind fast über den ganzen Erdboden zerstreut. Wiewohl wir nun die Hoffnung nicht aufgeben, daß Gott einst die Zerstreuten wieder sammeln und uns zurückführen wird in das Land unserer Väter, gehören wir doch bis dahin ganz und voll dem Lande, dem Volke, dem Staate an, in dem wir wohnen. Wir deutschen Juden sind Deutsche in unserem innersten Wesen. Seit länger als tausend Jahren wohnen unsere Voreltern, wohnen wir in diesem großen und schönen Lande. Die deutsche Sprache ist unsere Muttersprache; die Sitten, Gewohnheiten, Charaktereigentümlichkeiten des deutschen Volkes sind auch die unserigen. Wir sind getreue Untertanen unserer Fürsten und unseres Kaisers; wir lieben unsere deutschen Volksgenossen gleich unseren Brüdern; des Vaterlandes Wohl und Wehe liegt uns gerade so am Herzen wie allen anderen deutschen Volksstämmen; wir sind bereit, mit Gut und Blut dieses teure Vaterland zu verteidigen und zu schützen. Das alles ist uns ebenso sehr Pflicht gegen Gott wie natürliches Empfinden. Man liebt sein Vaterland wie man seine Eltern liebt. Nicht allein jetzt, da eine gute und gerechte Gesetzgebung uns die bürgerlichen und politischen Rechte sichert, sondern auch in den früheren Zeiten, da unsere Voreltern unendlich viel gelitten, waren die Juden stets von der heißesten Liebe zum Vaterland durchdrungen. Geradeso wie in Deutschland verhielten und verhalten sich die Israeliten in Österreich, Ungarn, Rußland, Frankreich, England, in den Niederlanden, in Dänemark, Schweden, in der Türkei, in

54

Page 54 of the German language Lehmann Hagadah,[20] part of which was omitted from the Hebrew and English Editions'

Father and Mother departing on a Lufthansa flight, July 4, 1928.

major wish that each had. This is how she described everyone's response: The oldest son, Julian, editor of the German-Jewish weekly *Der Israelitise Familien Blatt*, wanted the opportunity to write more and better articles. Her older sister Emmy, wished that people would read more so her husband Hillel Sutin could be more successful in expanding their book business. As for herself, my aunt, Tante Sophie wanted the German population to drink more tea thereby improving her husband's tea import business. Her younger sister, Martha wished her husband Sholom Hildesheimer to be able to devote more time to studying and to have bright Talmudic students. The youngest brother Fritz, who was a medical doctor, wanted more challenging patients. When it came to Father's turn he simply requested to be able to assist his parents in Mainz in whatever was possible, such as sending large food parcels from Amsterdam and meeting their other needs. In the 1920's, Germany had an incredible rate of inflation, thereby making food and other goods scarce and extremely expensive. Simple items such as a loaf of bread could cost millions and later billions of Marks! Father's desire to help others was beyond reproach. Our aunt had high regard for her three brothers and two sisters but found my father's response to be exemplary.

OVER THE YEARS, FATHER TRAVELLED BACK TO MAINZ ON various occasions to visit his parents. One such trip was by way of the Lufthansa Airline on July 4, 1928.

My father married my mother in Frankfurt am Main on Sunday, 14 Elul, 5687 (1927). The city of Frankfurt is located along the river Main, hence its designation "Frankfurt am Main". It is differentiated that way from the another German town Frankfurt an der Oder, which was established along the Oder river. Rabbi Moshe Schreiber, more commonly known as the Chasam Sofer (1762-1839), was born in Frankfurt am Main. He once referred affectionately to his native city as "one of a kind in the Jewish World". The city was home to many former and contemporary luminaries. These include the author of the Yalkut Shimoni, the Chasam Sofer's teacher Rabbi Nosson Adler, the Sheloh, the Haflo'oh, the Pnei Yehoshua, Horav Samson Rafael Hirsch, etc. On the secular end of the Jewish spectrum, Baron Meyer Amschel Rothschild (1744-1812), the starter of the great Rothschild dynasty, a great philanthropist and supporter of Orthodox Jewish causes gave Frankfurt am Main prominence in the financial world.

Mother was born on 23 Av, 5660 (1900) in Frankfurt am Main. She was the second oldest of four children. Her education was at the *Hoehere Maedchenschule der Syn.-Gem. Israelitische Religionsgesellschaft zu Frankfurt am Main* (High School for Girls of the Orthodox Jewish Congregation). Mother was an exemplary student there. I possess several books, which have certificates pasted to their inside covers stating that the books were presented as a sign of exceptional satisfaction by teachers at class promotions. One such book, *The Book of Jirmejah* with commentary by Rabbi Dr. Joseph Breuer, was presented on April 3, 1916. A second book, presented on April 3, 1917, was titled *Chorev, Discussions Regarding Israel's Duties in the Diaspora, Especially for Israel's Thinking Youth and Young Ladies,* by Rabbi Samson Raphael Hirsch.

To the best of my knowledge, Mother, following her graduation, joined her father's office staff where she assisted by taking over many of grandfather's business responsibilities while also being his personal secretary. Grandfather David Wallerstein was frequently referred to by his friends as the "Papier Wallerstein", since he sold paper products for commercial use.

[In 1991, Ruth and I visited a first cousin of my mother, the late Kurt Stern, in Haifa. He told us that mother was a capable and accomplished typist who had typed his thesis, which he had written in the early 1920's "It was typed in record time," he remembered. This was a noteworthy accolade considering that it was made regarding an era that predated the development of electric typewriters and electronic word processors.]

As a young lady, Mother always envisioned raising a family with her personal touch. To this end she attended local cooking and baking courses, so that the kitchen would be her own domain. More important, to ensure the building of a flourishing and vibrant Jewish home, Mother's principles dictated that raising children be a full time occupation. She rejected the institution of a *kinderfraulein* (nanny), which was so prevalent in those years, and maintained these values after marriage, despite the luxury of having had full-time sleep-in help.

The first years that Mother lived in Amsterdam, following her marriage, were spent getting acclimated to her new surroundings and language. She conversed in German with her parents and friends and later with my sisters and myself, until the time that we started school. "Secrets" between our parents were discussed in English.

Our parent's marriage was a happy one. They shared a great mutual respect for one another. Their marriage lasted almost eighteen years, at which time they succumbed to the murderous acts of the nefarious German beasts.

Father was an active member of the nearby *shul* on Gerard Doustraat. The *shul* was a modest, quaint brick structure dating back to the 1890's. It was on a narrow side street where each house was built against a neighboring building. Thus, there were no gardens or alleys. In fact, by walking down the block, one would hardly imagine that behind its drab, unobtrusive facade stood a large beautiful *shul*. I remember its decorum being dignified and yet warm and friendly. On one occasion, father received a personal printed invitation from the *shul* to attend the inauguration of a newly written *Sefer Torah*. The invitation was accompanied by a special ten page booklet for the ceremony. The card read in part (translation from Dutch):

> Entry Card for Mr. M. Lehmann to the ceremonial inauguration of a new *Sefer Torah* at the Synagogue on Gerard Doustraat on Sunday 29 Nissan, 5690/April 27, 1930, at 3 P.M. The doors of the Synagogue will open at 2:30 P.M. and close by 3 P.M. Attendee's formal dress code to include a top hat.

VEREENIGING תשועת ישראל

TOEGANGSKAART

VOOR <u>DEN HEER</u> *M. Lehmann*
~~MW.~~

TOT DE PLECHTIGE INWIJDING VAN EEN NIEUW
ספר תורה TER SYNAGOGE GERARD DOUSTRAAT
OP ZONDAG $\frac{\text{29 NISSAN 5690}}{\text{27 APRIL 1930}}$ 'S MIDDAGS TE 3 UUR

VOOR HET BESTUUR,

S. LOOPUIT, VOORZITTER
E. ASSCHER EZN. SECRETARIS

DE DEUREN DER SYNAGOGE WORDEN TE 2.30 UUR GEOPEND EN TE 8 UUR GESLOTEN.   VISITETOILET MET HOOGEN HOED VERZOCHT

DEZE KAART IS STRIKT PERSOONLIJK.

A personal invitation for Father to attend inauguration of a Sefer Torah at the Gerard Doustraat shul.

My parents were anxious to relinquish their German nationality. In the Netherlands this procedure involved passing all the prerequisite requirements and then, like other qualified candidates for Dutch citizenship they were listed on a special parliamentary bill, which upon passage was signed into law by Queen Wilhelmina.

Chapter Two

GROWING UP IN AMSTERDAM

THE ERA OF THE 1930'S WAS THE DAWN OF OUR CURRENT technological lifestyle. Air conditioners had not yet been developed, and most mothers gave birth at home. It was into this mode of living that I was born.

My date of birth was 25 Tamuz, 5693 (1933). The summer days were long in northern Europe, and it didn't get dark till ten o'clock in the evening. When I arrived at three o'clock that Wednesday afternoon, Amsterdam was a steamy hot city. To cool things down a bit on the third floor at Hemonylaan 5, the midwife hung wet towels over the wrought iron window guards of the double casement windows. The bris took place in the second floor living room.

My given name was inherited from our paternal grandfather, *Hachover* Osher Lehmann, who passed away in Mainz, Germany on 25 Tishrei, 5689 (1928). My Dutch middle name, Maurits, was given in appreciation to Father's uncle, Maurits (Moishe Meir) Prins, who had taken father into his diamond business in the year 1919 and taught him that trade. Uncle Maurits died on 12 Cheshvan, 5693 (1932) in Amsterdam.

The early years of my life were relatively uneventful compared to later years, though not wholly uninteresting. At the age of one and a half I fell while running on a highly polished parquet floor in a carpet and mat store. The *Roentgen* (x-rays) showed a cracked knee cap. For the next four to five weeks, I crawled around the house with a large plaster cast on my leg. Following recovery, Dr. Blok came to the house to remove the cast, where he labored to cut it away as I lay on the first floor dining room table. He became so exhausted from that task that he needed a drink of alcohol; a no-no for medical doctors.

Our house at Hemonylaan 5 was in a middle class neighborhood. Attached on both sides (row house), it was built of brick walls and was probably no wider than fifteen feet by perhaps thirty feet long, excluding the rear extension which housed the stairways *(trappenhuis)*. This was considered an above average sized home in pre-war Holland. There are many fond memories from this home that I still cherish. To the best of my knowledge, the house still exists.

The first floor front room of the house was our den and weekday dining room. We read books there, did our school homework, played games and ate weekday meals at the large center table. It was the room with the telephone (telephone No. 23625). Prior to *Shabbos* and *Yom Tov* we disconnected our telephone wall-jack. Residential telephones were relatively new and therefore our uncle and aunt, the Levis, took an additional precaution to avoid unintentional slip-ups. Below their directory phone listing was printed in abbreviated form: *Zaterdag en Israelitisen feestdagen geen gehoor.* (translation: no response on Saturdays and Jewish holidays)

I remember once sitting around the supper table while Father showed us a small glassine tissue paper package of diamonds that he had brought from the office for business purposes. When one of the tiny diamonds fell on the carpet, we all searched for it and fortunately the stone was found.

My sisters and I had many friends who would frequently come to join us and spend pleasant times in this room and the adjoining long corridor. For privacy and security, the two front windows had folding, interior, solid wooden shutters, which would be closed at night. The den also had a trap door in the floor for the watermain shutoff valve, watermeter, sewer house-trap and crawl space (refer to a later chapter for significance).

Behind the front room was the wardrobe (guest walk-in closet) followed by the kitchen. Along one wall of the kitchen were a counter and overhead cabinets with framed glass doors where the weekday dishes and pantry items were stored. On the opposite wall were the kitchen sink and

The Levis' listing in the Amsterdam telephone directory for the year 1939 (contributed by Abraham A. Levi, Monsey, N.Y.)

open-counter space. To wash dishes, we utilized a moveable center table, which had two large and deep, steel pullout drawers with white enamel finish. In one of these drawers we put the dirty dishes over which was poured hot water from the sink. After the dishes soaked for a while they were washed in their soaking water and then rinsed in the second drawer. This allowed us to conserve both hot and cold water. Other equipment in the kitchen included a four burner gas range with an oven below, a one door electric refrigerator with a small freezer compartment large enough for two ice cube trays and a kerosene fueled countertop hot plate. Interestingly enough, while iceboxes were extensively used in Western countries in lieu of refrigerators, they were not known in this part of Holland!

[In some respects Holland was more advanced than America: The first and only icebox that I saw and used was in the town of Hunter, New York (in the Catskill mountains). It was there that my cousin Abraham (Bram) Levi and I stayed with the Norbert Greunebaum family in July of 1948. Their son and our good friend, Joseph, subsequently became a *Musmach* of Yeshiva Torah Vodaath in Brooklyn. In recent years, he has been known as Dr. Greunebaum, Professor of Physics at Brooklyn College. In August of that year, it was the turn for the Levis to take over their apartment, and Bram and I remained in Hunter to complete a very pleasant summer, despite the primitive accommodations.]

In the year 1940, I distinctly recall seeing our old and worn wooden kitchen floor being covered by a terrazo finish, which is a mechanically polished, thin concrete floor that contains a specially colored stone aggregate. The floor was installed by Italian speaking craftsmen. [The above detailed description of our kitchen is given solely to illustrate that in the 1930's, except for the way we washed dishes, our living standards matched fairly closely those currently practiced in the West.]

Our backyard was small but ample enough to contain a little grassy area, a bicycle shed built by our carpenters, the Reusinks, and the coal storage bin. In the far corner were two beautiful lilac trees with pink and purple flowers. A wooden board fence, five foot high and covered with ivy, surrounded the entire area.

Central heating by use of radiators was practically unknown in this part of town. Accordingly, there were two heavy, iron coal stoves that were enclosed and recessed into the fireplaces, one in the first floor den and the other in the second floor living room. Small mica windows made it possible to observe the glowing coal. The bedrooms were unheated. Warm water bottles of all types were usually used in the deep winter to warm us below the freezing woolen blankets. The winters were intensely cold so that the water pipes in our lavatory frequently froze and burst as a result of the extremely frigid temperatures.

Our *succah* was originally built and, in later years, annually reconstructed by our carpenter and his sons on the rear porch off the second floor dining room. The wooden wall and roof panels were stored in the attic, and these were lowered with block and tackle hoists from the fourth floor. My sisters and I spent many enjoyable hours decorating and furnishing the *succah*.

For *Pesach* we took down the custom made plywood kitchen table and counter covers from the attic. These were also made by the Reusinks. The *Pesach* dishes were stored in the *Pesach* kitchen cabinet with an inventory sheet attached to the door. Every year, Mother updated this itemized list.

To accommodate the moving process, most old houses had a large, permanent, horizontal wooden hoist (ridge) beam projecting from a front attic dormer window. Block and tackle (pulleys) were then attached to this beam, and crates and furniture were raised and lowered by rope rather than by having them lugged up the narrow indoor stairways. These wooden hoist beams were sawn off during the severe fuel shortage in the winter of 1944-45. (Refer to a later chapter for details.)

Last Minute Pesach Cleaning Drawn by B. Picart (1663-1733) Reprinted from the Israelit, [21] April 1889

In April of 1935, Mother's older sister, Mrs. Resi Lehmann became a widow when her husband, died of pneumonia. In those days there were no antibiotics to treat this common lung disease. The family lived in London, and their six children ranged in age from one to almost twelve years old. Our aunt was a lady of valor and courage, who raised a generation of Jewish leaders and activists, each one special and a pride to our people. Being a single head of household, made raising her family a difficult task, but with the financial help of Mr. Sussman, her husband's junior partner in the jewelry business, and help from the Almighty, she did a remarkable job.

In July of 1937, Mother visited her sister in London. At that time, traveling from Holland to England was expensive and not the quick journey it is today. However, children below four years of age traveled at no charge. Thus, two weeks prior to my fourth birthday, I accompanied Mother to England for two fascinating weeks. To this day, my sister Connie is still disappointed that she did not join us. We traveled by night boat from the Dutch port, Hoek van Holland, literally translated, the "Corner of Holland". I still remember the dozens of large crates of strawberries at the dock which were being exported to England. Our cabin was above the water line, and in the morning, after crossing the English channel we gazed out of the porthole at Harwich and saw the many small seaplanes anchored to their mooring in the harbor waters.

The most memorable sights in London that I recall were the large elephants and the elephant rides at the world famous London Zoo. The Amsterdam *"Artis"* (zoo) lagged far behind in the variety of its animals and the size of its grounds.

Our parents were known for their gracious hospitality, and our home on Hemonylaan was a pleasant stopping point for many friends and family who visited us from out of town. They included uncles, aunts, nephews, nieces and first and second cousins. For longer stays, a room would be rented down the block on Hemonylaan, and all meals were sumptuously prepared and served by Mother in our house. Some relatives even joined us in Zandvoort on the Noordzee (Northsea) during the summer, which was always a special treat for both the host and the hosted.

Medical science of the 1930's left much to be desired. According to our doctor, my tonsils were excessively enlarged, and he decided they should be cut (not removed). I was about seven years old when we went by taxi to the doctor's office for the procedure. My arms were strapped to the arm rests of a high chair since anesthesia was not used. The doctor reached into my throat with a pair of sharp edged tongs and pinched off part of my tonsils! As for dentists, their crudeness then was more or less the same. Dental drills were slow, noisy and vibrated everything they touched. Fortunately, I never had any teeth extracted in those years.

The city of Amsterdam was advanced in the field of recycling its collected garbage. Once a week, a horse drawn cart passed along the street. A man rang the doorbell and collected a prepared pail of wet kitchen garbage consisting of food waste which was subsequently fed to pigs at a local farm. In the winter, Mother would serve the shivering garbage collector a much appreciated hot drink. The dry garbage was collected separately by a truck, which had special accommodations for dumping equipment at its rear. Our specially designed metal garbage pails would hook onto the truck's dumper hooks and were easily tipped up, thereby neatly discharging their contents into the rear of the truck. Filled garbage pails were not left in the street. Before the collection truck drove down each block, a sanitation worker with a very large rotating wooden rattler walked down the street to notify all persons on the block to bring their garbage pails to the sidewalk. Loose, blowing garbage was not found in Amsterdam.

The milk we purchased was milked under the supervision of the Jewish community. In this way it was assured to be *Cholov Yisroel*. The manner of delivery to the home was by way of several large metal milk cans mounted on top of a well varnished street pushcart that had stainless steel and polished brass trim. These cans had a spigot at their base, and the can covers were sealed shut with a special tag affixed by the *Rabbinate* at the filling station. Each purchase was measured by a liter sized cup, and the milk was placed directly into the buyer's cooking pot. Homogenized and pasteurized milk was not yet in vogue, and therefore before consuming the milk, it had to be boiled and allowed to cool in the refrigerator. To keep the milk from boiling over and spilling, a round, curved porcelain stone was placed in the milkpot. The creamy thick skin that formed on the cooled milk was coveted by some and despised by others.

Preserves such as strawberry jam were not available at the grocery store. These items were all homemade. Every household saved small and medium sized glass jars during the year. Then, in the early summer, a pushcart vendor passed through the street loaded with huge baskets of sweet, deep red colored strawberries. The man pushing the cart yelled out *"Aardbijen Mevrouw, Aardbijen Mevrouw,..."* ("Strawberries Madam,

Strawberries Madam,...") Housewives then came out and bought their annual supply of strawberries. After the fruit was cleaned, Mother added water, pectin and a little sugar and boiled several large pots of this delectable jam. This event became an annual harvest celebration and ritual. The glass jars were filled to within a half inch of their tops and, while still hot, were covered tightly by cellophane held in place by a rubber band. As the hot air cooled, the cellophane was pulled in to form a concave shaped, hermetic seal. These jars were then stored without refrigeration in a cool closet, and lasted for most of the year until the next *Pesach*.

The Netherlands is a country that is internationally famous for its horticulture. Like many West Europeans, Father was also a flower connoisseur and very much appreciated the large variety of domestic flowers. He even won several prizes in our school contest for growing flowers from special Hyacinth bulbs. During the year, we always had fresh cut flowers in the living room and dining room. These flowers were bought in honor of *Shabbos* and lasted from *Erev Shabbos* to *Erev Shabbos*. It was a daily routine for Mother to carefully change the water, trim the stems and rearrange the flowers in their vases. Artificial flowers were not acceptable.

In the absence of radiators and central heating, we used a small kerosene burner to heat our grandmother's ice cold bedroom when she was bedridden. On occasion, the bathroom also had a small kerosene stove to prevent the plumbing from freezing. To keep food warm or simmering, Mother used a kerosene based hot plate in the kitchen. The kerosene for all this was purchased from pushcart vendors.

Electrical appliances made their first serious debut in the late 1930's. Father was determined to make life easier for Mother, so he purchased state of the art home appliances at the "cutting edge" of industrial progress. These included a washing machine with manual wringer rollers mounted on top, a vacuum cleaner and a mix-master for the kitchen with special juicing attachments for grapes and tomatoes. With this modern equipment Father made delicious grape juice (called *Most*) in season, which was then stored in our small cool cellar for use on *Shabbos*.

I remember when carpets were still slung over the backyard laundry line and the dust removed by pounding, slapping and swatting, using large, braided cane beaters. Before the washing machine era, laundry was soaked in the bathtub and then agitated by being scrubbed and rubbed up and down on a wooden washboard covered by corrugated sheet metal.

Amsterdam was known for its sparse automobile count and its moderate number of horsedrawn carriages. Most people commuted to work by bicycle. Everyone in our family had bicycles which were kept in the backyard shed. On Sundays the whole family cycled through some of the older and more deserted sections of the city. One unavoidable topographical feature was the small bridge which is at every street that intersects with a *"gracht"* (canal). These bridges were very old and had a noticeable hump, so as to provide clearance for the barge traffic. Mother was not the type to speed and when the bridge was higher than usual, she would walk her bicycle on the far side down the slope, while we patiently waited in the distance. Riding across the Amsterdam trolley tracks was an art. There was many a time that my narrow bicycle tire was caught in the flangeway of one of these rails, thereby throwing me off balance and causing a bicycle spill.

For additional exercise, we children used to visit the father of my friend Freddie, who lived down the block at Hemonylaan 15. Mr. van der Woude was a professional sports trainer and physical therapist. His entire first floor was crammed with the latest gym equipment of the 1930's, and it was fascinating to use some of this sophisticated gear.

To help with the domestic work, a non-Jewish charwoman, Mrs. van Renen, came to our house once a week. During the winter, her daughter Marrie came on *Shabbos* morning to add coal to the coalstoves and remove the night's ashes. Thermostats and automatic heating controls did not yet exist. From the *Halachic* viewpoint, all persons are considered as ailing in matters of inadequate creature comforts during the heating season. Therefore, a non-Jewish person may be requested to service a stove on Shabbos on a regular basis.[a] Manipulating a stove by banking the coals overnight and adjusting the damper openings so as to control the rate of combustion is an art that has been lost on recent generations. The North Sea oil and natural gas deposits have since been discovered and coal is now relegated to industrial and nostalgic use.

---

a. *Mishnah Berurah,* 276:5,40.

Chapter Three
AMSTERDAM EXPERIENCES

MANY PARTS OF HOLLAND HAVE LOW ELEVATIONS AND high ground water tables. As a result, there is a proliferation of natural and man-made waterways. Amsterdam, especially its older sections, has many canals, all of which are connected to the Amstel River. That waterway was not far from our house. The north European winters were bitter cold, and after an extensive period of cold weather, the river and canals became covered with a thick layer of ice. On Sundays in January and February, we took walks on the ice, and my sisters even went ice skating in those areas where the snow had been cleared. In the winter, the elementary schools frequently dismissed the upper classes for *"ijs-vrij"* (dismissed for ice) in the afternoons. The sole purpose for this time off was to allow the students to skate on the frozen waterways.

The Herman Elte School was located at Ostadestraat 103, near the Zwelingstraat, perhaps a fifteen minute walk from home. We were allowed to take our *autoped* (scooter) to school, as there were hardly any automobiles on the road.

I remember scooting to school with my sister and myself standing on the scooter board, my sister Connie holding onto my shoulders while I steered the handlebars. We used our left leg in unison to propel ourselves. On occasion, there would be a slow horsedrawn carriage next to us on the van Woustraat. Then we would hold on for a free hitch. During the noon hour we always returned home to eat the main meal of the day, a European custom. Frequently, I took the scooter to Professor Tulpstraat 2, which was in the opposite direction from school. There I picked up Father from the office. This always meant that I could then stand on the scooter with both legs since Father pushed me home.

During the summer we spent most of our time on the shores of the North Sea at the town of Zandvoort, which was a small seaside resort town where many Jews vacationed to escape the city heat. The town had a *shul* and many apartments and cottages for rent. The weekdays were spent mostly at the exceptionally wide ocean beach, which is clean and has a fine grain, light brown sand. Frequently, one would see groups of bicycles and tandems riding on the firm surf-wetted beach sand. Behind the beach were wide stretches of dunes where sheep grazed and soccer teams practiced. On occasion, summertime ocean waves were able to reach five feet high, but that was the exception.

Father did not go mixed swimming, i.e. swim or sunbathe with the opposite gender. Accordingly, he went early in the morning to the beach for swimming purposes when everything was fairly deserted. Traveling to Zandvoort from Amsterdam by train took about half an hour which enabled Father to commute daily. In the summer of 1940, our parents rented the house at 26 Doctor Johan Cornelius Metzgerstraat. Starting in 1941, access to the coast was blocked because of German fear of an Allied invasion. All beaches and dunes were subsequently land mined. When Ruth and I visited the town of Zandvoort in 1988, we found this house to be the only building on that street still remaining from the pre-war years. Today, there are new high-rise buildings overlooking the ocean and most single family village houses were replaced. The *shul* was, as expected, destroyed by the Germans. Directly to the south was the seaside resort of Scheveningen, where many Jews also spent their summers.

In the 1930's, the institutions of playgroup, pre-kindergarten and kindergarten did not yet exist. There was really little need for preschooling, since most mothers did not leave their homes to go to work. To expose us children to a head-start program, we were enrolled in a non-denominational Montessori school's pre-1A class in lieu of kindergarten.

from left to right: My sisters Toni, Connie, our cousin Erika and Oscar. Class photo at the Herman Elte School, May 1941.

It was named Wilhelmina Caterina School or nicknamed the "W.C." School. The philosophy of Montessori was that the student can be occupied with any subject in the school curriculum at any time of the day for as long as he or she wanted. For children in my group, that meant they could do arithmetic, learn to tie shoe-laces or polish brass door knobs, etc. whenever and for however long they wished. My year and a half (1938-39) in the Montessori school went by quickly, and I learned a lot. [In the year 1988, while in Holland, I wanted to show Ruth the school building. Of course, the school had moved and the new, young superintendent in charge of maintaining the building knew nothing of what I was referring to. I felt like Chonie Hamagal [a] waking up after fifty years.]

The Herman Elte School was the most popular Jewish elementary school in Amsterdam. By the time I entered school, it had already been in existence for at least fifty years. Led by the principal Mr. Stibbe, nicknamed Mr. Stipje, we received a relatively good mix of religious and secular education. Unfortunately, I only attended the first two years in full and the third year in part, since our family was then arrested and deported.

---

a. *Maseches Taanith* 23a.

All teachers were of a top caliber, and the students were, for the most part, very bright. I was not scholastically near the top of my class. [After the war, despite having missed two years of schooling and having changed languages from Dutch to English and switched schools and curriculums from Holland to England and then to America, I landed up near the top of the class. Subsequently in Engineering College, I was deferred from the military draft for four years (1951-55) during the Korean conflict by being on the Dean's list for all eight semesters. This meant being academically in the top ten percent of the class. During the ensuing years of 1955-61, I continued to be draft exempt due to my involvement in engineering design projects for the national defense and NATO (North Atlantic Treaty Organization). Frequently, I surmise that had my Dutch classmates survived and competed against me scholastically, I certainly would not have been near that class' top. The pre-war Jewish schools in Amsterdam fostered academic excellence.]

In Holland, there are some Jewish customs that differ from those found elsewhere. In *shul*, after the Torah is read, it is rolled up and wrapped with a *mappah* as in most other *Ashkenazic* communities. The difference, however, is that a young boy is assigned the additional task of holding the upper end of the *Torah's Atzei Chaim*. This makes it easier for the one holding the Torah at the bottom of the *Atzei Chaim* while the *mappah* is being wound around the *Sefer Torah* five or six times. This extra *kibbud* is named *"Eitz Chaim"*.

I had joined father in *shul* on *Shabbos* mornings probably since the age of three. When I was five years old, I was given the honor of *Eitz Chaim* - my first *mitzvah* involving the *Sefer Torah*. It was an extremely emotional occasion, and I cried throughout the two minutes that were spent up on the *bimah*.

During the weekdays, our *shul* had an established early morning *Shacharis davening*, which I attended with Father on a fairly regular basis. Since the number of men attending were not as many as on *Shabbos*, the *minyan* met in a smaller rear room, which was actually a permanent *succah* structure. For security, a non-Jewish man was assigned to the main entrance to screen all attendees. During the war, this person became a prime source of clandestine international news since he had apparent communication with the world beyond our borders and shores and had a brother who lived in England.

International flights in the 1930's were limited both in number and in the distances that could be traveled. It was only during the late 1930's and afterwards, during World War II, that the Atlantic could be crossed by commercial and military aircraft on a regular basis. But even then, the flights were slow and the distances relatively short. Planes usually stopped for refueling at Shannon, Ireland and at Gander, New Foundland. Other stopovers were also pressed into service.

Father traveled a considerable amount for his business. Being in the diamond business meant that his destinations were mainly Antwerp, Belgium and London, England. Once, during the mid-1930's, he became the talk of the town. On that occasion, he had breakfast in Amsterdam, flew to London for business dealings, where he had lunch, and then returned by plane to Amsterdam in time for supper at home! In former years, this would have involved a boat trip both ways and an absence from home of at least one and a half to two days. From these business trips, Father even had time to bring back special treats for the family - cheese cake from the Grozhinsky bakery of London and mints from Antwerp.

My paternal grandfather's sister, Emma Prins (Lehmann), moved from Mainz, Germany to Holland when she married in 1882. For many years she lived in Amsterdam at 26 Sarphatistraat. I remember her when she was already widowed and in her eighties, with most of her eight children living overseas. We enjoyed visiting her every *Shabbos* afternoon. Tante Emma who was very frail and extremely hard of hearing still lived like an aristocrat. She always did much reminiscing, bringing back many family memories to our parents. Despite her handicaps she was extraordinarily personable and charismatic, and a friendly smile was her trademark.

In those days, electronic battery operated hearing aids did not exist. Our great-aunt did however have several "earhorns", which were hand-held non-electric instruments and consisted of a thin rigid tube that was inserted into the ear. A palm-sized metal framed box was secured to the tube's base and speaking towards such a box would amplify the sound to the hearing impaired.

YOM TOV IN PRE-DEPORTATION AMSTERDAM WAS ALWAYS special. It was a city where perhaps one out of nine persons was Jewish in a population of close to nine hundred thousand. For *Pesach* we took out our special dishes and silver, some of which dated back several generations. Our *sedorim* were held in a regal manner in the second floor rear room, which was the *Shabbos* dining room. We discussed the Hagadah at length and sang the same *nigunim* that our forefathers must have sung for hundreds of years. Father repeated many of the explanations and stories found in the Hagadah of Horav Meir (Marcus) Lehmann, his grandfather and namesake.

We celebrated *Succos* by eating in a large, beautifully decorated *succah* built on the balcony (porch) off the *Shabbos* dining room. A layer of thick evergreen pine branches was used for *schach,* which gave the *succah* a delightful pine scent and ambience. There was ample room for the family, as well as a limited number of guests. On days when we had many guests, the ladies used to eat on the dining room side of the porch's double French doors. In Holland, the weather is already quite cool in September and October, but the thick, wooden paneled *succah* walls kept the bone chilling winds out. We did, however, wear sweaters and jackets. Prior to leaving the *succah,* we lowered the two-hinged *succah* roof panels, which were raised during *succah* use and whose vertical movement was controlled from within the *succah* by ropes and pulleys. The *succah* size was probably six foot by nine foot (2 meters by 3 meters).

Simchas Torah was a very special day on the calendar and the *shul* became the center of attraction. It was a time when dozens of children showed up whom I did not recognize or see the remaining weeks of the year. For the children who attended *shul* regularly during the year, candy bars and white and brown chocolate bars were handed out by many individuals. I always came home with a large box of these goodies, which usually lasted until *Pesach.*

For *Simchas Torah,* mother used to order several dozen bags of carefully chosen candies from Mr. Duizend, the grocery owner, to distribute to the children in *shul.* Mr. Duizend's grocery was around the corner from our house, on Jan Steenstraat. The grocer was a kind and friendly old man, with a long white beard. He knew how to please his young customers and always gave free samples of chocolate and old, aromatic hard Dutch cheese (*oudbelegen kaas*). The cheese was sliced on the counter from wedges cut from a large circular cheese "wheel". Following the consumption of aged, hard cheese, we waited six hours before eating meat products. Therefore, Mr. Duizend always required parental permission before we youngsters were treated with cheese samples.

On *Shavuos,* our house was always full of flowers. For the occasion, our *shul* on Gerard Doustraat was decorated with flowers and potted plants, including small palm trees. We enjoyed special homemade cheese cake and other dairy dishes during the day, and learning went on through the night. In later years, when the *shul* was not open at night for security purposes, I remember Father going to the home of Mr. and Mrs. Wechsler to study the entire night with his friends and then *daven* early in the morning at sunrise. In this part of Northern Europe, along with daylight savings time, dawn came very early (around 3 A.M.), since Amsterdam is at 52° north latitude and 5° east longitude.

Besides attending *shul* twice daily, Father also attended *shiurim* and was involved in Jewish organizations. In *shul,* in front of the "Almemmar" *(bimah),* there was a special row of five or six seats reserved for *"Parneisim".* These were men who were among the *shul's* directors. Father sat in one of these seats on Friday nights. Since the entire city of Amsterdam had an *eruv,* Father was able to carry his golden pocket watch to *shul.* I can still picture him standing at his Parness seat with his pocket watch in hand, the watch lid in its open position and Father giving the signal to start davening *Minchah* at the exact time when scheduled.

To display dignity at *shul,* Father wore a "cylinder", which was a top hat with a six inch high cloth covered cardboard cylinder, and had an oval cross section above the hat's brim. The hat's color was black and was the type of head covering worn in those years throughout Western Europe and Japan for formal affairs, including affairs of State, weddings, etc. To avoid attracting attention in the streets, these furnishings were stored in the *shul's* rear dressing room, and those who wore them arrived a few minutes before the *Shabbos davening* in order to change from their street attire. The walk to *shul* was only about five minutes, but it meant walking through the Albert Cuypstraat, which is a very busy outdoor market street that extends for several city blocks. One also had to pass the horse stables of the Boesch coal company.

On *Shabbos* morning, Mother and the girls would attend *shul.* Mother, too, was active in the Jewish community. Her activities involved helping the needy and serving on school boards. I remember joining Mother on several occasions when she visited the Pallasheh School, a school for Jewish children. There she was accorded special respect by the staff.

MOTHER WAS A LADY WHO KEPT UP WITH THE TIMES AND ALL technological developments involving the home. Her style of dress was, however, discreet and very modest. She did not wear fur, neither a fur coat, scarf, hat or muff. The latter was a fur sleeve hung over the chest to serve as a handwarmer. She also wore no makeup. Her ears had been pierced as a young girl, but she decided at an early age not to wear earrings. Mother covered her hair at all times so as to maintain her style of modesty in the dress code.[b] At home, she usually wore a kerchief (*tiechel*) or turban over her hair. For *Shabbos,* special occasions and outdoors, Mother wore a *sheitel* (wig). On summer vacations at the North Sea, Mother's hair was covered at all times by a kerchief or, when in the water, by a bathing cap. Mother's *sheitel* was simple, and when a three inch wide "curl" of hair was added to the bottom of the back neckline, all her friends came to admire it. Our parents had many friends, and to the best of my knowledge, all of Mother's friends were attired with similarly modest clothing.

My Mother's mother, *Oma* Wallerstein, became a widow on 20 Tamuz, 5694 (1934), when our grandfather, David Wallerstein, *o.h.,* passed away. Sometime thereafter, Grandmother moved into our home.

After living with us for several years, Grandmother slowly became afflicted by a crippling case of arthritis. Nurses were retained to attend to her needs around the clock once she became bedridden. Our Grandmother's ability to fight her chronic disease worsened during the wartime years when the assortment of food was mostly limited to staples, with very little out of season fresh fruit. The extremely limited variety of foods which were available in the 1930's, and the even more restricted selections during the war years, were nowhere near the broad assortment presently available. There are now many types of both plain and exotic fruits and vegetables in plentiful supply the year round. The predominance of refined foods, such as white flour and white sugar products, along with the lack of fresh farm produce, all had their negative effects on her deteriorating health. The cold and damp Dutch winters combined with poorly heated and uninsulated homes also contributed to her deterioration.

Being Grandmother's only daughter in Holland during the 1940's, Mother had the strenuous task of being the sole person to attend to Grandmother's needs. Grandmother was often in steady pain, which put a great mental strain on Mother. Doctors frequently visited the house, and nurses attended to Grandmother around the clock for several years. In the absence of any available or known medication, morphine injections were resorted to. It was an emotionally taxing situation on the family. For Mother it was a labor of love.

---

b. *Shulchon Aruch O. Ch.* 75, *E. HaE.* 21 and 115.

The winter of 1941-42 was extremely harsh. I remember how the wild ducks came during that period to the city streets to scrounge for food. I used to feed them the dirty crusts that we cut off the edges of hard Dutch cheese. In return, the ducks left behind some beautiful colorful feathers which I added to my other collections.

One cold morning Father came down from *Oma's* room and asked for some of my smaller feathers. I wondered why those feathers were needed from my carefully guarded collection. We had woolen blankets and used no down feathers for either blankets or pillows. Then I found out that these small duck feathers were placed under Grandmother's nose to determine whether she was still breathing.

Grandmother passed away in our house in the year 1942. The *Tahara* was in her bedroom, and the funeral was held in our house. The institution of "funeral homes" did not yet exist. It was a cold, overcast and dreary day when I joined the funeral procession at Diemen. Grandmother passed away well over a year prior to our deportation. She was thus spared untold agonies and was given a proper burial next to Grandfather at Diemen, outside Amsterdam.

Thus ended the era of our Wallerstein grandparents. They had much to be proud of, having lived useful and productive lives. All of their four children were fully observant Jews, each active in their own communities. Their fifteen grandchildren are all alive today (1996) and are also fully observant and active Orthodox Jews.

Mother's sister, Tante Alice, once told me that many of the Orthodox Jewish girls in Frankfurt am Main were considered *"Minnich"*, which is the Jewish German word for *"Parve"*. In other words, the direction of their devoutness had much to do with whom they married. In the Wallerstein family, their oldest daughter, showed great concern for her siblings in encouraging them to associate with and marry sincere and committed Jews. It was an age when, unfortunately, assimilation and intermarriage became widespread. In an era when large segments of some of the finest Jewish communities were lost to their great heritage, much credit must be given to families that remained committed to Orthodox Jewish ideals. In our family, much praise goes to our valiant aunt, Tante Resi, a true stalwart of the Wallerstein kin. Until her passing at a ripe old age of 89, she maintained close contact with all her family, even with the many great-nieces and great-nephews. To this third generation, her love, grace, devotion and involvement was almost an institution the likes of which are seldom found in our modern and complacent societies.

Section Two

A TIME TO WEEP...
(KOHELES 3,4)

Chapter Four

GERMAN REFUGEES

THE 1930'S WERE TURBULENT YEARS FROM WHOSE CAULDRONS of political struggles were forged new world orders. The outcome of these conflicts were both scientific and political quantum leaps of incredible magnitudes. Rivers of ink have since been harnessed to write a multitude of books on this era in general, and in particular concerning the Holocaust.

The roots to this dark, tear drenched page in our recent history lead back to ongoings well over three millenniums ago. In recent history, events took a decisive turn for the worse, when in March of 1933 Adolf Hitler, Y.S., a political neophyte, won a critical vote to become dictator chancellor of Germany. After the final vote count was tallied, his giddy, reveling followers in the *Reichstag* (German Parliament in Berlin) whooped in unparliamentary conduct and broke out into spontaneous song to applaud that victory. Their true colors shone forth, and a respectable institution, its reputation tarnished, was transposed into a menagerie. The words to their melodious marching song included the following:

...Wenn das Judenblut vom Messer spritzt, dann geht's den Deutschen gut...

Translation:

...When Jewish blood spurts from the dagger, then will it go well with the Germans...

In the great legislative hall of the *Reichstag,* these words rang in harmony, sung by a group of mutated parliamentarians, who were the democratically elected legislators, members of the German government. The decent world was stunned. Those ebullient and rowdy hoodlums had thus bared and flaunted their hidden claws and fangs. Overnight, these men had brought the institution of the prestigious *Reichstag* into disrepute. Immediately, ominous forebodings began casting long shadows over a peaceful world. The democratic process, as practiced in Germany, was shown to be seriously flawed. Diversity among the German population was no longer respected.

These so-called parliamentarians were Prussian miscreants and parasites of German society who were allowed to surface in a quiescent manner, as a direct result of a weak League of Nations, an indifferent Neville Chamberlain (British Prime Minister who was a renowned appeaser) and a splintered German electorate. They were villains on the threshold of turning global politics into chaos and sending the world teetering in hitherto unknown proportions and directions. Consequential international instabilities were the watershed which triggered unprecedented arms races. Resulting domino effects were: escalated norms in battlefield fury, ability to cause vast devastation remote from the front lines and large scale conflagrations between opposing alliances. The ensuing mass destruction was referred to as *World War II.*

Using modern methods of mass dissemination, the new German government known as the Third *Reich* (Third Regime), sponsored numerous seminars to teach recruited SS men and women the basics of barbarism, how to become zealous beasts while serving the *Vaterland* (Fatherland). Brains and talent were not required. The only prerequisites to such courses were being an Aryan, in good physical condition and having no conscience. The seminars' alumni were true ambassadors to their *perfect countrymen,* pushing the definition of perfect to new realms of arrogance. With little or no on the job training, these academicians became the brute monsters who staffed the concentration camps.

GERMAN JEWRY DIDN'T KNOW WHAT HIT THEM. FIRST SLOWLY, and then decidedly, Jewish refugees streamed out of the land they had revered for over a thousand years. Beneath a seemingly placid surface, the waters of hatred were roiling. The urgency to their exodus came on the sixteenth of *Mar Cheshvan*, 5699, (November 9, 1938), when the Germans organized their evil forces and destroyed most German and Austrian *shuls* in one night. The German code name for this operation was *"Kristallnacht"* (Crystal Night, i.e. the night with an unambiguous, crystal clear message or alternately, the broken glass of the *shuls* and of the Jewish owned shops). Countless *Sifrei Torah* and other *seforim* were burned, Jewish homes and stores were broken into and most Jewish men between the ages of sixteen and sixty were arrested and imprisoned in concentration camps. Although some of those arrested were later released, that date went down as a day of infamy. It was the signal for all Jews to depart their *Vaterland,* even if this meant leaving most possessions behind.

[As if to smother a fifty one year-old calendar inequity, the breakup of the famous Russian built "Berlin Wall" was scheduled for November 9 of 1989. The "coincidence" in calendar dates was not an auspicious accident, and I prefer to mourn what happened in 1938 rather than celebrate the 1989 reunification of Berlin.]

German Jews had been declared as persona non-grata or non-citizens and became therefore stateless. Passports belonging to German Jews became worthless and obtaining exit visas was extremely difficult. Despite all handicaps, Jews departed by the tens of thousands. For many, it literally meant torture at the borders, railroad stations and harbors. The Germans shaved off beards so brutally that cheeks were injured. They extracted teeth from the elderly refugees to obtain gold from their fillings and false teeth. These inhuman acts were done at the railroad stations by non-dentists and took less than five minutes per person. Novocaine was not used. [Note: Porcelain teeth and porcelain teeth implants had not yet been developed.] Property taken along by the emigrants was confiscated if it exceeded a certain amount. Men were turned back for trumped up technicalities, etc. The harassment of the refugees was intended to spread the word that the Germans were no "push-overs". The virulence of the anti-Jewish sentiments, a staple of the German people, gave further urgency and impetus for Jews to emigrate from Germany, posthaste.

During the early 1950's, I joined a Malbim *Shiur* in Boro Park conducted by the late Mr. Siegfried Strauss, *o.h.* He had been a World

EXPELLED! (Deja-vu) by G. Knorr.
Note the raised arm on the semaphore post - an indication of the Railroad company's complicity in this act of bunishment. Reprinted from the Israelit,[21] March 1893

War I veteran of the Kaiser's army and knew how rough military life could be. During the turbulent 1930's, he was arrested and incarcerated in the infamous Buchenwald Concentration Camp. One of the stories he recounted concerned the only water they had to drink was rain water dripping from the barracks' roofs. He and his family were fortunate to have obtained visas to America, where they arrived in 1939. Once the war broke out, there were no further releases from these camps.

HILLEL STATED:

...don't state anything which (you think) won't be heard because eventually it will be heard... [a]

The Swiss government is known to pride itself for being neutral in all its international dealings. It now appears that the Swiss sullied their image and were not that impartial after all. In fact, they gave some handy tips to the Berlin government on how to implement their anti-Jewish policies. This Swiss character defect, which surfaced in the year 1938, was not generally known until some fifty-five years later. It was on June 3, 1994, when the prestigious *Wall Street Journal,* with a daily international circulation of several million copies, ran a front page feature article on this sad story. The report described how in the year 1994, a non-Jewish former local Swiss police chief was still refused a posthumous pardon by the Swiss for the 'crime' of saving Jewish refugees some fifty-six years past. He died twenty-two years ago in poverty after being stripped of his pension. The report reads in part:

> "Born in 1891, Mr. Grueninger worked as a teacher before joining the St. Gallen police. When Hitler marched into Austria in 1938, sparking an exodus of Jews, Switzerland reacted swiftly. It introduced visa requirements for the refugees, closed its borders and asked German authorities to put a special mark in Jews' passports so they could be identified easily. The Nazis eagerly complied.
>
> Mr. Grueninger, then the *canton* police chief, argued against such measures with colleagues from elsewhere in Switzerland, saying they were inhuman and would lead to uncontrollable illegal immigration. Then, unable to prevent the restrictive new rules from being introduced, he did what he could to encourage illegal

---

a. *Pirkei Avos,* 2:5.

immigration himself. Among other things, he altered refugees' papers to make it seem that they had arrived before the borders were officially closed. Nobody knows how many people Mr. Grueninger saved, but the total is in the hundreds, perhaps thousands."

I remember when the Joseph Magnus family, good friends of our parents drove up to our house in November 1937, after traveling by night train from Hamburg, Germany. Their taxi was loaded down with boxes, and small crates were tied down to the car's roof and rear rack. Most of their belongings were left behind. During the early 1940's, Mr. and Mrs. Magnus and their three sons were sent to the Dutch internment camp of Westerbork and from there to Theresienstadt, a concentration camp in Czechoslovakia. [They survived the war, and today, their families live in Amsterdam where we visited them in 1988.]

Father's oldest brother and his family, Mr. and Mrs. Julian and Else Lehmann lived in Hamburg, Germany with their two daughters, Thea (Mrs. Thea Loewy, Elizabeth, New Jersey) and Erika (Mrs. Erika Weilburg, Melbourne, Australia). As the political situation grew bleaker, they were fortunate in being able to obtain visas to America, not an easy feat. Uncle Julian wrote to a distant relative in America named Herbert H. Lehman. Subsequently, it was through the kind efforts of New York States' Governor Herbert H. Lehman (1932-1942) that the visas became available. In the late 40's, the former governor was elected by his state to the United States Congress as a Senator (1949-1956). In order to expedite matters, the Hamburg Lehmanns first stopped off in England and from there they had planned to continue across the Atlantic. To facilitate their traveling, our cousin Erika departed first from Hamburg and was sent to us on a temporary basis, she arrived at our house in November of 1938. The plan was for our cousin to join her family again once they were safely in England.

The policy of the United States government during the 1930's and early 1940's made entry into the States extremely difficult for most European Jews. A condescending State Department used every dirty trick in the book to camouflage and implement their anti-Semitism. *The New York Times*,[b] reported the following sad and morally corrupt state of official Washington affairs during those years:

---

b. April 6, 1994, page C-18.

>...a particular villain of this account is Assistant Secretary of State Breckenridge Long, who is blamed for exaggerating security concerns in order to keep refugees out. His technique is revealed by a memorandum he wrote in 1940: 'We can delay and effectively stop for a temporary period of indefinite length the number of immigrants into the United States. We could do this by simply advising our consuls to put every obstacle in the way, which would postpone and postpone and postpone the granting of visas...

By and large, European Jews were left to their own wits and devices to leave the continent. Those who entered the United States immediately prior to World War II arrived despite the State Department's anti-Jewish policies, and not thanks to their magnanimity. Methods of leaving Europe included traveling via one of several friendly Central and South American countries. Many of these countries were extremely accommodating in providing both passports and visas. The Netherlands Antilles (N.A.) didn't even require visas and almost anyone was welcome. It was thanks to the Dutch Caribbean island of Curacao (N.A.), that the Mirrer and Kamenitzer *Yeshivas* were able to escape from Vilna, Lithuania in the nick of time. They were, however, unable to reach their destination, and while en route to Curacao, these *Yeshiva* groups spent the war years in Shanghai, China and in Siberia, the Soviet Union respectively. (See Appendix A). United States entry visas were frequently obtained by means of *"protectia"* (pull).

ENGLAND HAD A MILITARY ALLIANCE WITH POLAND, AND when Germany invaded its eastern neighbor in September, 1939, the British, as Polish allies, declared war on the belligerent Germans. Due to extensive red tape, bureaucratic bungling and the breakdown in the international peace, our Hamburg cousin was stuck in Holland. Erika was born on September 7, 1930, two months after my sister Connie. Some "adjustment" was made in the official records regarding her age, and for the next five years Erika became a year younger and was considered one of the (Amsterdam) Lehmann siblings. This meant that whenever we were arrested or freed from detention, Erika came right along, without raising any eyebrows.

Erika was eight years old when she joined us. I still remember waking up one morning and, lo and behold, I had a new sister! Our German born cousin learned Dutch very quickly and attended the same schools we did. During the first few years she was extremely homesick for her family, and

I remember Mother comforting her during her frequent crying spells. After the war, Erika was happily reunited with her mother and sister in London. In 1943, her father *o.h.* had, unfortunately, passed away in England on the 26th of Adar. This, of course, became known to Erika only after the war. Our uncle had succumbed to the side effects of over-exertion while doing more than his share for the war effort.

As will be described in a later chapter, many German refugees who had no visas were detained in Westerbork. This camp had been established by the Dutch government in northeastern Holland prior to the war. Unfortunately, the Germans converted it during the war into a transition camp for deportees from Holland to Germany, Austria, Czechoslovakia and Poland.

Those Jews who remained in Germany were never heard from again. The Germans systematically transported their fellow citizens to such extermination camps as Auschwitz. The fact that these people had lived for generations as productive members of German society meant absolutely nothing to this nation harboring hate and ensconcing a full spectrum of blood thirsty creeds.

Some details of my father-in-law's heroic and courageous activities while rescuing hundreds of persecuted Jews are described in a *Memorial Journal* published by the family on his first *Yahrzeit*.[16] [In the year 1992, my mother-in-law received a phone call from an elderly couple who had been one of those personally rescued in 1940 and who had gone directly to Eretz Yisroel. In an emotional tribute, they expressed their great appreciation for having been personally rescued by my father-in-law. At the time of that phone call, they already had fifty-two descendants!]

My father and father in law both placed their lives in jeopardy so that many others would survive. (Refer to later chapters.) They were hewn from a generation that produced martyrs and heroes possessing superhuman courage and bravery — a mettle breed of giants practicing true benevolence and compassion, the likes of whom society has not witnessed in recent years.

THE BERLIN GOVERNMENT'S POLICY OF DISCRIMINATION and bigotry was counter productive to their war efforts and became the start of its own undoing. Not only were their top advisors extensively preoccupied with time consuming activities of hate mongering and propaganda, but the lot of the average German citizen was not improved as had been promised. The government's target was their highly motivated and productive local Jewish population, numbering in excess of six hundred thousand persons. The latter were mostly engaged in material pursuits, and their output was far out of proportion to their one percent of Germany's population. For example, twenty-five percent of the coveted Nobel prizes awarded to Germany went to Jews.

Albert Einstein, the winner of the 1921 Nobel Physics prize, was one of many who fled his native Germany. Einstein's arrival in the United States became its gain. His work with and the eventual success of the United States nuclear research and development program was pivotal in attaining the August, 1945 victory over Imperial Japan and avoiding thereby perhaps an additional million American military casualties. Einstein's personal involvement cannot be minimized. In the year 1939, President Franklin D. Roosevelt expressed a total disinterest in the potential of uranium, both for its military and civilian applications. Numerous attempts at persuasion always fell on deaf ears. Following this impasse, Albert Einstein sent a personal letter to the White House regarding the strategic importance of atomic energy. Roosevelt made an immediate and complete about-face by approving the needed funding for commencing a modest nuclear research program. This was the start of the historic "Manhattan (Nuclear Research) Project". Almost six years after Einstein interceded with the President mankind detonated its first nuclear explosion in the New Mexico desert. Hashem creates His relief in anticipation of an affliction.[d]

In governmental avocations, such as teachers and judges, German Jews far exceeded their one percent. Their numbers in the professions, such as doctors, accountants and lawyers, were also considerably out of proportion to the general population. To Germany's detriment this talent that it desperately needed in peacetime to succeed was either ruthlessly exiled or senselessly murdered.

In the early 1930's, Hitler wanted to highlight the large Jewish involvement in the local retail trade. The government therefore decreed that partly or wholly Jewish owned stores be closed for one day. It was ironical that the day designated was to be on a *Shabbos*. In the large metropolis of Berlin, the result was that practically all large stores were shuttered. Reform Jews who always wanted to act like the Gentiles were not exempt. This rude awakening quickly revealed to those reformers that their desecration of the *Shabbos* and many other sacred laws did not win them any friends, merits or privileges.

---

c. *Maseches Megillah,* 13b.

Over the years I have noted that during times when Jews were permitted to pursue their Divine calling in a free environment, their country experienced improved material and non-material prosperity. Conversely, those countries restricting and persecuting their Jewish population experienced a steady decline in their standard of living. Germany was an extreme example of this phenomena.[d]

IN CERTAIN ASPECTS JEWRY'S EXPULSION FROM GERMANY HAD elements with an unusual historical parallel. Following the exodus of our ancestors from the Egyptian "iron crucible", some thirty three centuries ago, rabblers were still reminiscing about the fish and vegetables in the "good old country".[e]

In a similar fashion, it is interesting, but not novel to note that many refugees from Germany in the U.S. did not look upon their former country with disdain. In the late 1940's, I was hurt to hear that on the streets of New York, there were German refugees who extolled the virtues of their native land: "But by us in Germany…!", *(Aber bei uns in Deutschland…!):* the river Rhine was more beautiful than the Hudson river; or a particular appliance was built better, *(bei uns wurde das besser gemacht!);* or protocol was maintained *(Ordnung muss sein!),* etc. To these remarks we can unfortunately say the words from *Koheles*;[f] There is nothing new beneath the sun!

Recently, Leon Magnus, our friend from Amsterdam, reminisced about my grandmother *Oma* Wallerstein and the first lesson she had taught him when he was eleven years old. It was on the day following his immigration from Germany, in November of 1937, that he saw the Amsterdam trams for the first time and commented to my grandmother, *"Die Strassenbahnen in Hamburg sind viel schoener."* ("The trolleys of Hamburg are much nicer.") My grandmother responded, "You might be correct, but as a guest in someone's house or as a visitor in another country, such comments are not appropriate." Grandmother's words remained a timeless lesson to Leon, which he taught to his chilren, grandchildren and many an immigrant over a span of half a century.

---

d. Refer to commentary by Horav S. R. Hirsch on Breishis, 12:3.
e. Bamidbor, 11:5.
f. Koheles, 1:9.

Chapter Five

BARBARIANS OVER THE MOAT AND DUTCH SURRENDER

THE LAWFUL AMBITIONS OF CIVILIZED NATIONS WERE appropriately articulated by the English jurist Sir William Blackstone (1723-1780) when he stated the maxim: "Law is the embodiment of the moral sentiment of the people."

In the Dutch capital city of The Hague (Den Haag) such judicial ambitions manifested themselves in the affirmative as evidenced by the seating of various renowned arbitration and justice organizations that fostered international peace. These were the Permanent Court of Arbitration, established by The Hague Conference of 1899 and the Permanent Court of International Justice, established in 1920. The latter was the predecessor for the International Court of Justice, popularly known as the World Court. All these Hague courts were used internationally to mediate, arbitrate, settle disputes and to promote disarmament. These courts of law were internationally recognized and used successfully and extensively by many countries from around the globe. All such establishments were testaments to the Dutch commitment in maintaining a neutral stance and symbolized their feelings of responsibility towards promoting world peace through law and order rather than by the use of force.

During World War I, Dutch neutrality was honored by all belligerents, including imperial Germany. Following that war, Germany's deposed Kaiser Wilhelm II even fled to Holland and stayed in the town of Doorn, where he died in the year 1941. When Europe was preparing for war during the 1930's, Holland also built up its military forces. Nevertheless, the Dutch people had no appetite to fight and again declared to the world their intention of remaining neutral in any possible upcoming military conflict.

There were many differences in the military hardware which was available in the 1930's as compared to that of the year 1914. The entire science of warfare had advanced from the new trench warfare developed during World War I, to the subsequent development and use of armored vehicles, such as tanks and personnel carriers, and deadly military attack fighter planes and bombers. These sophisticated weapons had been tested and refined during the recent Spanish Civil War, whose main purpose appeared, in retrospect, to have been for designing and testing new weapons of mass devastation.

Another major difference between the two world wars, from the Dutch viewpoint, was the French Maginot line. This was the heavily fortified French frontier shared with Germany. Any German military advance across that border would be short-lived, since ground and aerial fortifications were built for a depth of many miles inland. The French considered themselves invulnerable to all possible attempts at German incursions. France, however, made a major blunder and left its northerly border with their sympathetic Belgian neighbor unprotected. German strategists analyzed their foe's proverbial forests rather than scrutinizing its trees. This led to the discovery of gaping chinks in the Norman armor. To realize overall objectives, the Germans made an end run around the French ramparts, violated Dutch neutrality and proceeded to invade the Benelux (Belgium, the Netherlands and Luxemburg) countries, thereby enabling their panzer (armored) divisions to skirt the Maginot line and pierce France through its unprotected northern underbelly.

When Hashem wants a country to be vanquished, its state-of-the-art strategies and its sophisticated arsenals at the cutting-edge of science are all in vain, as we learn from Yeshayohu;[a] "(Hashem) turns wise men feeble minded and makes their knowledge foolish."

---

a. 44:25.

With swift modern planes and tanks, Germany occupied France in a matter of a few weeks, and while all French cannons were firmly bolted down and concreted in place to face Germany, the scurrilous Huns strode in with ease behind these fixed emplacements!

The Dutch also erred in underestimating the large fifth column in their midst, those treacherous *Bund* collaborators, who betrayed Holland. Furthermore, the country was unprepared for the insane cruelty of the German military. As a result, Holland capitulated and unconditionally surrendered within eight days following initiation of German hostilities.

Germany declared war on its tiny neighbor, the Netherlands, on the evening of May 10, 1940. There was no match between the Dutch army of four hundred thousand and the strong German army of over ten million troops. The Dutch, however, were prepared to fight. They also expected the French army to come north through Belgium and help beat off the barbaric hordes from the east. One of the Dutch Army strategies was to blow up several important bridges crossing the wide Maas and Rhine rivers which would then keep the invading army at bay behind broad 'natural' water filled 'moats'. The Germans, however were prepared for this plan and came across these bridges in trucks with Dutch military markings, driven by German soldiers wearing Dutch army uniforms! Once on the opposite river bank, the enemy had the bridge in their possession and ready for use. German soldiers also parachuted to many other strategic locations, wearing Dutch army uniforms. Realizing the German propensity for fraud, road blocks were established by the Dutch, and all soldiers and civilians were asked to pronounce the name of the seaside resort town along the North Sea, which is south of Zandvoort. If they could not properly pronounce the name "Scheveningen", they were arrested and suspected as German spies.

Rotterdam was a thriving port city along the shores of the Rhine river where it flows into the North Sea. The Germans gave the Dutch an ultimatum to surrender or that strategic port city would be smashed to oblivion. Two hours prior to their deadline, German fighter bombers viciously attacked its business district and port areas killing thirty thousand civilians! Unleashing this *Blitzkrieg* (lightening war) attack was part of Germany's well orchestrated terror-war tactic and was "the straw" that broke the Dutch resolve to resist these brutal assailants.

Chapter Six

TYRANNY 1940-1942

Following the Dutch surrender, there was initially very little difference in the pattern of our daily lives. After several months our lifestyles began to steadily decline towards the austere. The United States was not yet involved in the war and so there was mail between Holland and America. Correspondence was censored and always arrived with a censor stamp containing the swastika emblem.

To cross the Atlantic Ocean by ship became very hazardous, since numerous German predator submarines prowled the high seas and coastlines to torpedo almost any neutral friend or foe they found. Political relations between the United States and Germany were becoming more and more rancorous. Hardly a week passed that Dutch newspapers were not full of screaming headlines and front-page photos showing sinking ships and rescued people clinging to life boats, rafts and floating debris.

In the first year of German occupation, an adequate supply of domestically grown food was available and there were very few civilian restrictions. Subtropical foods, such as bananas, were no longer available, but

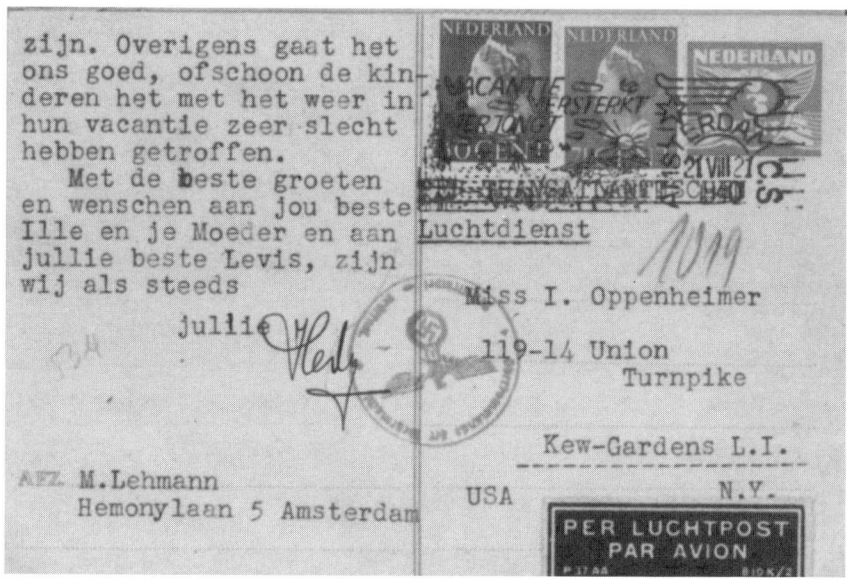

Airmail postcard written by Mother and mailed to the USA on August 22, 1940 using the (exiled) Dutch crown princess Juliana postage stamps, note the German censor stamp

oranges were imported from Spain. I remember German soldiers bathing on the North Sea beach at Zandvoort, mixing with the Dutch population. Public swimming pools in Amsterdam were also used jointly by German soldiers and the local Dutch populace.

Following the Japanese sneak attack against Pearl Harbor on December 7, 1941, America officially joined the fray by declaring war on Japan and its infamous ally, Germany. It now became truly a "World" War.

By now, the Germans tightened their grip on Holland. The entire North Sea coast, along with its beaches and dunes, became off limits. All beaches were heavily mined to prevent an invasion from England. [After the war, I saw a news movie showing German prisoners of war who were given the task of clearing these mines. Once these prisoners declared the area mine-free, they locked arms at low tide and jogged down the beaches and dunes to demonstrate the thoroughness of their efforts. Some did not survive this test.]

When summer approached, our parents wanted us to be away from the hustle and bustle of the hot city. With Zandvoort incorporated into the German coastal defenses, it was no longer possible to enjoy the beautiful North Sea shore and its serene rolling dunes. For part of the summer of 1941, Father and Mother rented a small house in the village of

Bussum, near Hilversum, which is a half hour train ride from Amsterdam. Around that time, Grandmother Wallerstein's health had taken a turn for the worse and Mother was very much preoccupied with helping out as much as possible. Despite the full time nursing help, Mother was busy around the clock. The result was that we four children were frequently alone with the mother's helper during the week. Our parents then joined us for *Shabbos*. We enjoyed much of the outdoors and did extensive bicycle riding through the countryside. Holland's topography has shallow contours and is ideal for bicycling relatively long distances.

AFTER TWO YEARS OF OCCUPATION, THE GERMANS FELT adequately confident and commenced to extend their hegemony over the Dutch vocabulary. In Amsterdam there were few traffic lights. At a busy intersection, for example that of the Ceintuurbaan and the van Woustraat, a traffic policeman would stand in the middle of the intersection. In his hand was a two meter high post, supported on the ground, with a horizontal board at its top. On that board was painted in large block letters the word "STOP". This 'T' shaped post was then rotated ninety degrees to permit alternate flow of traffic. I used that intersection daily to ride to school on our scooter. One day, I saw that the word "STOP" was changed to the German *"HALT"*.

In Germany, the Government initiated Germanization fever had reached its peak during the late 30's and early 40's when English words became taboo. Thus, previously used common expressions such as "telephone" became *"Fernsprecher"* (distance-speaker), "television" became *"Fernseher"* (distance see-er) and "automobile" became *"Kraftwagen"* (power-wagon), etc.

The Dutch currency remained the *Gulden* (Guilder) during German occupation, but all gold, silver, nickel and brass coins were changed to a substitute legal tender. Guilders and larger denominations were converted to paper money, while the smaller values were changed to hard lightweight shiny coins. [I saved some of these metallic looking coins. Looking at them 45 years later, I found that the larger denomination had transformed to cardboard discs.]

Food became scarce even though Holland was, in the prewar days an agricultural commodity exporter, especially of dairy and vegetables products. The Germans, however, pillaged most of the harvest as well as many herds of cattle. As a result, rationing cards and coupons were introduced, and a black market for food products quickly developed.

Gasoline became in short supply, and horses slowly came back into use. Horses even pulled trucks with their engines removed. Coal which heated most city houses also became scarce and very expensive.

FROM THE ONSET OF WORLD WAR II, THE GERMANS STARTED losing various battles, the most notable of which occurred in the late summer of 1940 and was appropriately named the Battle of Britain. This campaign consisted of aerial combat between the Spitfire fighter planes of the Royal Air Force and the Messerschmidt fighter planes of the *Luftwaffe*. Both aircraft models were spinoffs of the frenzied arms race of the mid 30's. The action took place over the span of several days at the end of which the Germans had lost in excess of nine hundred of their planes over southern England. Planes and parachutes literally rained down on the countryside. Prime Minister Winston Churchill of Britain, in his now famous speech, stated that "never in the field of human conflict was so much owed by so many to so few".

People all over occupied Europe got their world news from the B.B.C. (British Broadcasting Corporation). It was untainted and free of German propaganda. To crush anti-German morale boosters, all regular and shortwave radios had to be surrendered to the Authorities, and new radios could be purchased, which were made to exclusively tune into a local station. After this, we were only permitted to listen to Radio Hilversum, a station near Amsterdam. Despite all German efforts, however, there were many Dutch people who maintained a secret shortwave radio to listen to BBC's daily news. Those who were caught were arrested.

The Germans realized the strategic importance of England and made no secret of their eagerness to invade and capture that country as well. Though all European radio stations were state owned and therefore had no commercials, between programs, however, one could always hear a German army choir sing:

> *"Und wir fahren*
> *Und wir fahren*
> *Und wir fahren nach Engeland!"*

Translation:
> "and we will travel
> and we will travel
> and we will travel to England!"

"Man has many schemes in his mind, but the counsel of Hashem will prevail".[a] Whenever I look at an atlas, I always marvel at that large offshore European island named Great Britain. When Hashem planned and created the world, He surely must have planted the British Isles off the continent of Europe instead of attaching them with a landbridge, all for the purpose of keeping the murderous German armies at bay.

The Dutch fifth column, which had collaborated with the invading Germans, were now in the open and their members were known as the NSB - *Nationaal Socialist Bund*. They had parades and frequently wore armbands with the letters "NSB". It was a hateful and hated group. Persons who we never suspected of being pro-Nazi turned out to be members of the NSB. I remember a friendly Mr. Van Duin in Zandvoort who had a large ocean beach concession stand. All of a sudden, the word spread that he was an NSB. He had, indeed, become a changed and openly wicked person.

Once my sister Connie and I took a walk in Amsterdam to the vicinity of the *Concert Gebouw* (the main concert hall). There was an NSB parade in progress. They were in a close lock step formation, mimicking the German goosestep march by raising their legs up high and straight forward while swinging their arms sideways. Most marchers were in their forties and fifties, many wore eye glasses, which was considered a sign of aging, and they seemed to me ill suited for such a strenuous activity. But it was their way to show allegiance to the Germans. They were like mindless robots, displaying no individuality and following their piper. May their fate parallel that of the legendary pied tragedians from the medieval German town of Hamelin.[b]

---

a. Mishlei, 19:21.
b. Refer to Appendix E.

Chapter Seven
DESPOTISM 1942-1943

THE WRITERS OF THE UNITED STATES CONSTITUTION envisioned well over two hundred years ago a scenario in which persecution of individuals by an abusive or corrupt government could be a real prospect. For that reason they added the famous ten amendments known as the Bill of Rights. The first amendment showing such foresight in regard to religious persecution states in part:

> "Congress shall make no law respecting an establishment of religion, or prohibiting the free exercise thereof;..."

Thus Church and State had no affiliations. This was not the case in most European countries. In Holland, for example, the state licensed and fully paid teachers to teach all secular subjects in the Jewish day schools. Jews could not be married or buried without being registered at the local *Rabinaat* (Jewish Religious Council). With the various detailed records of names and addresses readily available from the Jewish organizations, it was easy for the Germans to trace down most Jewish men, women and children. Subsequently, even persons who had Jewish sounding names were in trouble with the German Authorities.

Disappearing and hiding among the Gentile population (known as *"ondergedoken"*, literally translated "to duck under") required sophisticated changes in personal identification papers, in addition to the full cooperation of some heroic non-Jewish sympathizers and neighbors who would arrange for the disappearance.

Slowly but surely, and as early as the year 1941, anti-Jewish laws were enacted. Initially, our use of public transportation was curtailed. Jews were prohibited from traveling between cities and using city trolleys. Subsequently, all Jewish owned bicycles were confiscated and had to be turned in, as they were by far the most popular means of conveyance. Automobiles were also blacklisted, but, since practically no one owned an automobile, this restriction had little impact.

We turned in an old bicycle at the Gallery, on the Sarphatistraat, to show in a token manner that we complied with the law. The rest of our bikes were hidden at the Greco music shop across the street. In those days, all bicycles had a license number, which was embossed on a small thin metal plate. That "license plate" was then affixed to the bike by curling it around and securing it to a frame on the handle bar post. The issuance of such I.D. numbers meant that the authorities were well informed of the existence of all bicycles.

THEREAFTER, JEWS HAD TO WEAR A YELLOW COLORED CLOTH hexagram star on all outer garments, sewn over the heart. In this way, all Jews could be identified when outdoors. The star looked like the Star of David and had the black colored letters *JOOD,* Dutch for 'Jew', in its center. These stars were sold to the Jewish population in large uncut sheets. The yellow star worn in each German occupied country spelled "Jew" in their native language. When the Danish Jews were required to wear the identifying star, many gentiles, including their king, Christian X, also wore the star in protest. This successfully negated the German plan for stigmatizing and singling out the Danish Jews.

The letters on the star were supposed to resemble Hebrew style lettering.

The yellow dye of these stars ran onto the parent cloth when they got wet in the rain or laundry. To remedy that, we first washed the uncut, thin sheet of cotton stars in vinegar. It was part of German audacity that not only was it mandated that we should wear these senseless yellow signs but we were expected to sponsor their hate campaign as well. [To this date, I keep one of my old yellow stars in my bank's safe deposit box. Each time I see it, I am forcefully reminded of the persecution the hated

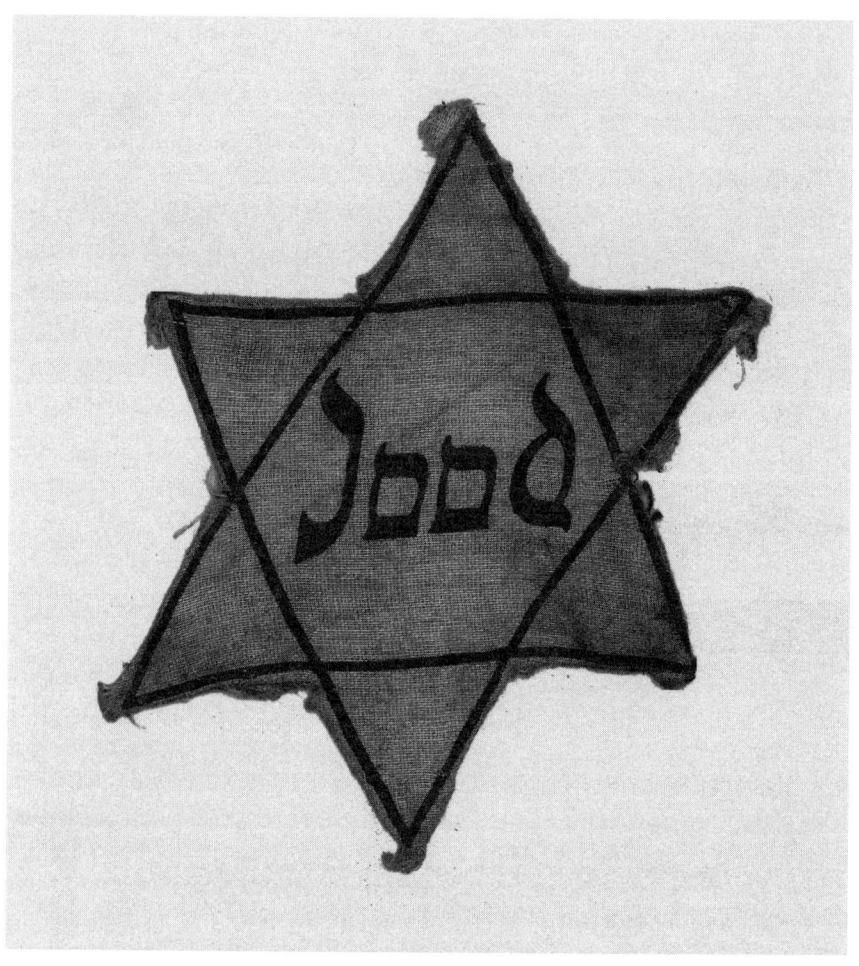

This was the yellow star which I salvaged from my jacket while in the Bergen Belsen Frauenlager.

Germans perpetrated, and of how a so-called highly civilized nation allowed itself to become so gullible as to accept their invective filled national propaganda and be mesmerized by their cruel and senseless government. Third world governments do not single out their minorities in such a manner: how much less was it expected from supposedly advanced industrialized nations.]

The next restriction on Jews was to limit access to various commercial establishments. All the better and larger stores had large printed posters openly displayed in their windows or mounted on their glass doors, which read:

VOOR JODEN VERBODEN

Translation: Forbidden to Jews

As was the case with all restrictions, there were decent non-Jewish persons who disagreed with this hate policy. Such store keepers would place these signs in an inconspicuous, partially hidden location. A city inspector was once sent to post such a sign. Outside the store was a long line of customers waiting to purchase needed food supplies. The inspector stood at the end of the queue rather than walk into the store and create havoc.

The Dutch underground was alive and active. It made sure that the NSB and their German cronies would not have an easy time. As a result of these efforts, many German troops were bogged down behind the fighting front. Unfortunately, there were double agent spies as well. On one occasion, such a traitor was on his way to the *Gestapo* to deliver an extensive list of underground members. While approaching the Amsterdam H.Q. the mole was intercepted and decapitated in the street, thus many deserving heroes were saved from torture and certain death. The *Gestapo's* instinctive and impetuous knee-jerk reaction was to take with the least hesitation several residential houses on the block of their headquarters and destroy them by tossing in a boxfull of hand grenades.

When Jews had to appear at the *Gestapo* Headquarters on the Euterpestraat, they had to follow protocol. At the front desk they were required to remain a step away from the counter and take a deep bow before they spoke. The language was to be in German, and the personal pronoun of *"du"* for a peer could not be used. They could only use *"sie"*, i.e. they could only use the formal "thou" and not the informal "you".

The name "Euterpestraat" in Amsterdam received such a bad connotation because of the *Gestapo* Headquarters that the street's name was changed after the war to the "Gerrit van der Veenstraat", after a Dutch underground fighter, who was presumably killed in action.

On one occasion, a Jew, who was a World War I German Army veteran, came to *Gestapo* Headquarters and showed the military medals that he had earned. He expected to be exempted from deportation and other harsh anti-Semitic edicts in return for having fought and risked his life for Germany. To his amazement, he was denied all requests. Thereupon, the man threw his medals down in anger. He was forced to pick up all his trophies and apologize to the arrogant, uncouth clerk.

DURING THE NIGHT, BEAMS OF LIGHT PIERCED THE DARK skies over Amsterdam. These were search lights probing for Allied war planes. I doubt if any such searches were successful, but as a young boy I remember they looked impressive.

One bright sunny spring day, my sisters, cousin and myself went on an outing. We took a small ferry boat across the Amsterdam harbor, the IJ (pronounced ay). Along the sides of the ferry boat, there was a raised narrow walkway overlooking the center of the boat, which was depressed, and presumably meant for vehicles. We stood on the walkway and I remember a German officer with his flat-topped light green colored uniform cap standing below us. The cap's top was slightly curved upward toward the shiny black front visor and was immaculately clean. The officer was studying a map of the harbor. My sister Connie was standing next to me and, typical of her courage, she released a string of saliva from her lips to see how low she could get it without touching the officer's cap below. Just before reaching the point of no return, she retracted her saliva and we all breathed a sigh of relief. [It was this type of courage that my sister transmitted in later years to her children and children-in-law in coping with various dangers while living in Eretz Yisroel.] We were scared but also proud of our daring sister.

Food shortages became worse with each year. The Dutch had a lot of pet dogs. With the serious food scarcity, pets could no longer be fed. I remember going on one of my many long walks through Amsterdam and observing numerous floating dog carcasses along the bulkhead line of the Amstel river. They had been drowned by their owners and abandoned.

Electricity came in short supply because the generating plants had difficulty obtaining scarce coal supplies. To cope with this shortage, I observed many houses from whose top floor projected a large pole with a small propeller at its tip. These were miniature electrical wind generators.

Jews were no longer permitted to possess silver or other precious metals. Accordingly, we had our carpenter Mr. Reusink and his sons, place most of our silver inside a large crate below our ground-floor front room, in the rear of the crawl space. The crate was then covered with stones and soil so it would be inconspicuous to any curious intruder or crude metal detector. A token amount of *placebo* silver was handed over to the authorities to demonstrate our compliance with their divestment decree.

When we saw that many Jews were arrested and deported, we requested Mr. Reusink to crate and take away many other valuable household items such as linens, crystal, etc. All these were hidden in his woodwork shop. The Reusinks risked their freedom and their lives to help us, showing appreciation to the many years that my parents patronized their services. With their positive assistance, they cast negative votes against the prejudicial policies of the occupational Dutch puppet government.

Even though residential neighborhoods of Amsterdam were never bombed by the Allies, reconnaissance fly-overs did take place. Every time a plane flew over the city or its harbor, air raid sirens would sound. The initial alarm sounded like a wavy tone and at the end of the air raid period the all-clear alarm, a steady uniform sound was heard. For purposes of protecting individuals during such air raids, the city built above ground air raid shelters. Initially, these consisted of a single long narrow passage, which was covered with thick layers of earth and sand. The entire structure was then camouflaged by growing grass and weeds on the outer surface. Subsequently, some of these shelters were replaced with above ground all-concrete shelters. To enter these, one would have to crawl on one's hands and knees because of the low height clearance at the entrance. None of these shelters, however were used, and they appeared to be only for show. Their capacity to hold people was extremely limited and they would only have been adequate to protect a very small fraction of a percent of the population. One such concrete shelter was constructed around the corner from our block, on Hemonystraat. That shelter was of average size and had a potential occupancy for perhaps twenty-five persons.

IN RETRIBUTION FOR SOME LABOR UNREST DURING THE early Forties, the Germans looked for able bodied Jewish boys in their late teens to go to Germany and work in labor camps. Around thirty to forty local Jewish boys were arrested for this purpose. They were crowded into and made to sit inside one of the air raid shelters for many hours with their hands above their heads. Thereafter, they were shipped off to an infamous concentration camp named Mauthausen in Austria. There, they reportedly worked and succumbed to the harsh conditions. About a year later, in 1942, their families each received an urn with the individual's ashes inside for local burial. This was the only time that I know of that the Germans thought of accommodating the families of deceased captives. However, when the urns were opened, they were found to be filled with plain earth. *The boys were never heard from again.*

In Amsterdam, there was a sephardic *Weeshuis* (Orphan home) for young and middle teenage Jewish girls. Most of these were girls who had arrived from Germany just prior to the war to be temporarily sheltered and raised in an orphanage. The girls were able to leave Germany, since children below a particular age did not require a passport. For *Shabbos,* we frequently had some of these children as guests. I remember some of their names as being Esther Zuntz and Yetta. Esther, we discovered, was a first cousin of my cousin Erika. The girls were friendly and of good character and became friends with my sisters and cousin. When the deportations began, the cowardly Germans made the helpless residents of this orphanage one of the first targets. *The girls were never heard from again.*

In the early 1940's, we had a mother's helper named Lotte Bachrach. Lotte and her family had arrived from Germany, and both Lotte and our parents were satisfied with the arrangements of mutual help. She was in her late teens. By the beginning of 1943, the Germans had already made a significant dent in the Dutch Jewish population. One day Lotte and many other young persons her age received notice to report to Centraal Station for deportation to the East. Efforts were made to intercede with the *Joodsche Raad* (Jewish Council) to rescind the order. All attempts were in vain. Lotte's train did not stop in Westerbork or Vught but went directly to Germany or Poland. It was another example of the cowardly Germans preying on the weak. *Lotte was not heard from again.*

It was early in the year of 1943 and spring was in the air when we were joined for our weekday lunch by a visitor. Berthold Rothstein, a widower and a brother-in-law of my uncle Michael, had stopped in, and we sat down in the first floor front room to a delicious dairy meal that Mother had prepared. As we were eating and talking, the doorbell rang. Everybody's first reaction was to quickly remove all dishes from the table which had food from the Black Market. Accordingly, the eggs and cheese were rushed out of the dining room into some closet.

Father went to answer the front door. It was the Dutch Secret Police, the S.D. or *Sicherheits Dienst*. Our guest was on their wanted list and they were anxiously looking for him. The S.D.s had followed him in the street to our house. Several S.D.s were waiting outside. The gentleman was taken into custody and accompanied to the nearby local police station on the corner of Gerard Doustraat and Stadhouderskade. There he was questioned on what he knew regarding other Jews in hiding, his own hiding place and the Gentiles who were providing secret shelter. When they received unsatisfactory answers, pails of water were thrown over his head to force revelations. Of course, those inquisitors barked up the wrong tree. No decent person would ever betray anyone, Gentile or Jew, even if that meant risking one's own life. To these police collaborators, Berthold Rothstein remained reticent. *He was never heard from again.*

TO KEEP OUR HEADS UP, THE DUTCH DID INTRODUCE SOME occasional humor into the sad daily events. The Germans had a famous General who was the Commander of their North African Corps. His name was Field Marshal Erwin Rommel, known among the Allies as the "Desert Fox" and by his compatriots as *"der Wuestenfuchs"*. His first major downfall was the battle of El Alamein, seventy miles west of Alexandria, Egypt, which he lost to the Allies on November 5, 1942. Tens of thousands of soldiers were killed in that battle, which was probably the largest tank and armored vehicle battle the world ever saw. To this day, the British maintain the sprawling military cemetery near that battle ground.

Rommel's armies had been racing eastward along the Mediterranean coastline, looking to the Suez Canal as their next prize target. Two hundred miles west of the canal the Axis armies were literally stopped dead in their tracks. Strategically, the battle of El Alamein stemmed the Axis (Axis = Berlin-Rome Alliance) advance and was the beginning of the end for Hitler and Mussolini in their North African campaign. They had reached an area that was less than four hundred airmiles from Yerusholayim. The *Yishuv* in Eretz Yisroel was greatly relieved. Rommel's retreat also fulfilled a response given in the 1930's by Rabbi Yisroel Meir Kagan, known as the Chofetz Chaim. The latter was asked where Polish Jews should flee. His reply was to Eretz Yisroel, because it is written in Yeshayohu,[a]; "…they will not hurt nor destroy in all of Eretz Yisroel, saith Hashem." (Refer there too to the classical commentaries.)

As a result of the rapid and complete routing of the German and Italian forces in North Africa, and subsequent strategic losses in Normandy, France, Hitler summoned Rommel to return to Germany. According to historians, Hitler was convinced that Rommel was implicated in the plot to assassinate him. Because Rommel was a national hero, the option of suicide rather than disgrace was granted. Once in Germany, he was given, according to an unofficial Dutch version, a revolver with one bullet – he committed suicide.

---

a. 11: 9 and 65:25.

In the Dutch language, the word *"rommel"* means "rubbish" and slogans were painted on Dutch city walls, graffiti style, that read:

Rommel is en blijft de beste Duitse soldaat
Juxtaposed translation:
The best German soldier is and remains rubbish *(Rommel)*

The Italians under Mussolini had been fighting alongside the Germans. But unlike the Germans, the Italian soldiers were not particularly interested in this war. Many of the Italians surrendered to the Allies when they could. This prompted Prime Minister Winston Churchill of Great Britain to report to the world that the Allies had captured Italian prisoners of war "by the acre".

German propaganda minimized and played down any and all Allied military achievements. One of the songs that became popular in Holland was:

De hemel is zo groot en de aarde is zo klein,
daar boven in de hemel vliegt een Engelse piloot...
...een koe en een ei in een kippetje."

Translation:

The sky is so huge and the earth is so small,
above in the sky flies an English pilot ...
(all that was damaged by the aerial bombardment was)
a cow and an egg in a chicken's womb.

TO SOLICIT BETTER TREATMENT BY THE GERMAN OCCUPATION forces, Father requested, in the summer of 1943, a confirmation of his World War I German military record. The response was dated July 30, 1943. It describes, twenty five years later, in the greatest detail the dates of his army service both prior to and during World War I.[b] Despite the detailed account of Berlin's confirmation regarding his military service, there was no reprieve of any edicts that limited his civil liberties.

After most of the Dutch Jews were deported, and our presence in Amsterdam was questioned, we were given by the Germans Certificates of Presence Approvals *(Aufenthaltsbewilligung)* issued by the Central Authority for Jewish Immigration, Amsterdam. It was dated October 18, 1943 and stated that:

---
b. Refer to Chapter 1.

```
Zentralstelle für jüdische           Amsterdam, den  18. Oktober 1943   194
Auswanderung Amsterdam                     Adama van Scheltemaplein 1
B. Nr.                                     Fernruf: 98005, 98006, 29577

                                                              Nr. 189  D

              A u f e n t h a l t s b e w i l l i g u n g

   Der Jude //////////  Markus  L e h m a n n
   geboren am   3.2.1893            in
   wohnhaft     Amsterdam      Strasse   Hemonylaan 5
   Persoonsbewijs Nr.  A 35/618117
   erhält die Genehmigung, sich bis auf weiteres frei in Amsterdam
   zu bewegen.

                              I.A.
                              [signature]
                              SS-Hauptsturmführer
```

*Certificate permitting Father to reside in Amsterdam,
October 18, 1943*

The Jew, Markus Lehmann, born February 3, 1893 residing at Hemonylaan 5, Amsterdam, I.D. No... is granted approval, until further notice, to move freely throughout the city of Amsterdam. Signed by: *S.S. Hauptsturmfuehrer.*

This was a case that demonstrated the audacity of the non-Dutch, Germans who authorized Dutch citizens to live in a city where they had resided as far back as 1919. These aliens now took over the Dutch Immigration office. Of course, all this was in complete violation of the Geneva Convention of War.

```
Zentralstelle für jüdische          Amsterdam, den  18. Oktober 1943   194......
Auswanderung  Amsterdam                    Adama van Scheltemaplein 1
                                           Fernruf: 98005, 98006, 29577
B. Nr. ......................................
                                                                  Nr. 190  D

              A u f e n t h a l t s b e w i l l i g u n g

        /Herr/ /Frau/ /  die Jüdin   Hedwig Lehmann-Wallerstein

        geboren am   18.8.1900          in

        wohnhaft    Amsterdam         Strasse   Hemonylaan 5

        Persoonsbewijs Nr. A 35/614255

        erhält die Genehmigung, sich bis auf weiteres frei in Amsterdam
        zu bewegen.

                                   I.A.
                                   a. d. [signature]
                                   SS-Hauptsturmführer
```

Certificate permitting Mother to reside in Amsterdam
October 18, 1943

Chapter Eight
THE PRINS-DRUKARCH FAMILY

THE JEWISH DAY SCHOOL THAT WE ATTENDED IN AMSTERDAM had limited resources in teaching the full spectrum of religious subjects despite its excellent staff and curriculum. To assure that all Jewish subjects taught would remain with us, our parents arranged for a tutor to come to the house and study with all four of us children on an individual basis. The tutor, Miss Rachel Drukarch, had a good religious background and was very knowledgeable. After several years she married Rabbi Prins who then became my tutor. Thanks to Rabbi Prins, I knew how to *lain* from the *Torah* and *Megillah* (Esther) by the age of eight. [After the war, in England, I was able to teach myself the Bar Mitzvah *Sedrah* using the Dutch *Nigun,* which is not quite identical to that used by Jews from Germany or other countries.]

The Prins family lived on the upper floor of a three story building at Weesperzyde 63, approximately twenty minutes walk from our house. Frequently, I went to their home to study. After each session, Rabbi Prins would read to me, in German, a half or full chapter from a Lehmann story written by my illustrious great grandfather, Horav Meir Lehmann. On weekday mornings, Rabbi Prins would often *daven* at our *minyan* on the Gerard Doustraat.

WHEN THE GERMANS BEGAN ARRESTING AND DEPORTING Jews from Amsterdam en masse, their *modus operandi* was to close off areas and deport Jews based on their location and district within the city.

The day before *Rosh Hashonoh* of 1943, Rabbi Prins came to our early morning weekday *minyan*. There he received information that his neighborhood had been blocked off and was now under curfew, for the purpose of rounding up the local Jewish population. Rabbi Prins stayed in our *shul* most of the day, while his wife, her two brothers and their wives were at home. These relatives were in hiding from the Germans and had their bedrooms in the attic of the Prins apartment. When their doorbell rang, Mrs. Prins had a choice of opening to the arresting officer or not answering the door and keeping it locked. A locked door would almost surely be bashed in, which in turn ran the risk of having the four hidden persons discovered. Mrs. Prins therefore sacrificed herself for the sake of the four others, and, with nerves of steel, opened her front door.

A German officer stood at their main entrance way to arrest the family. The German asked Mrs. Prins who else was at home, and she responded that she was the only one in the apartment. The officer then looked at the long, straight narrow stairway leading from the street's entrance to the top floor apartment, and apparently in a hurry, didn't bother going upstairs. Mrs. Prins' brothers and sisters-in-law thus remained undetected and were saved, eventually surviving the war. Mrs. Prins bade good bye to a friendly non-Jewish neighbor and handed him a note to pass to an acquaintance familiar with the whereabouts of another brother's family in hiding. Mrs. Prins' brother was thus able to guide the two couples in the attic to a safe location.

With her *rucksack* (knapsack), Mrs. Prins was taken to the city's main railroad terminal, Centraal Station. The station was a large, European style building with many passenger train platforms interspersed with train tracks. Restaurants and shops were along the sides of the end platforms. At the station, Mrs. Prins met numerous other Jews who were also arrested for their religious affiliation. The arrestees were directed to a long string of cattle cars awaiting them along one of the station's platforms. There were no commuters or other travelers in the station besides the uniformed Germans and the Jews.

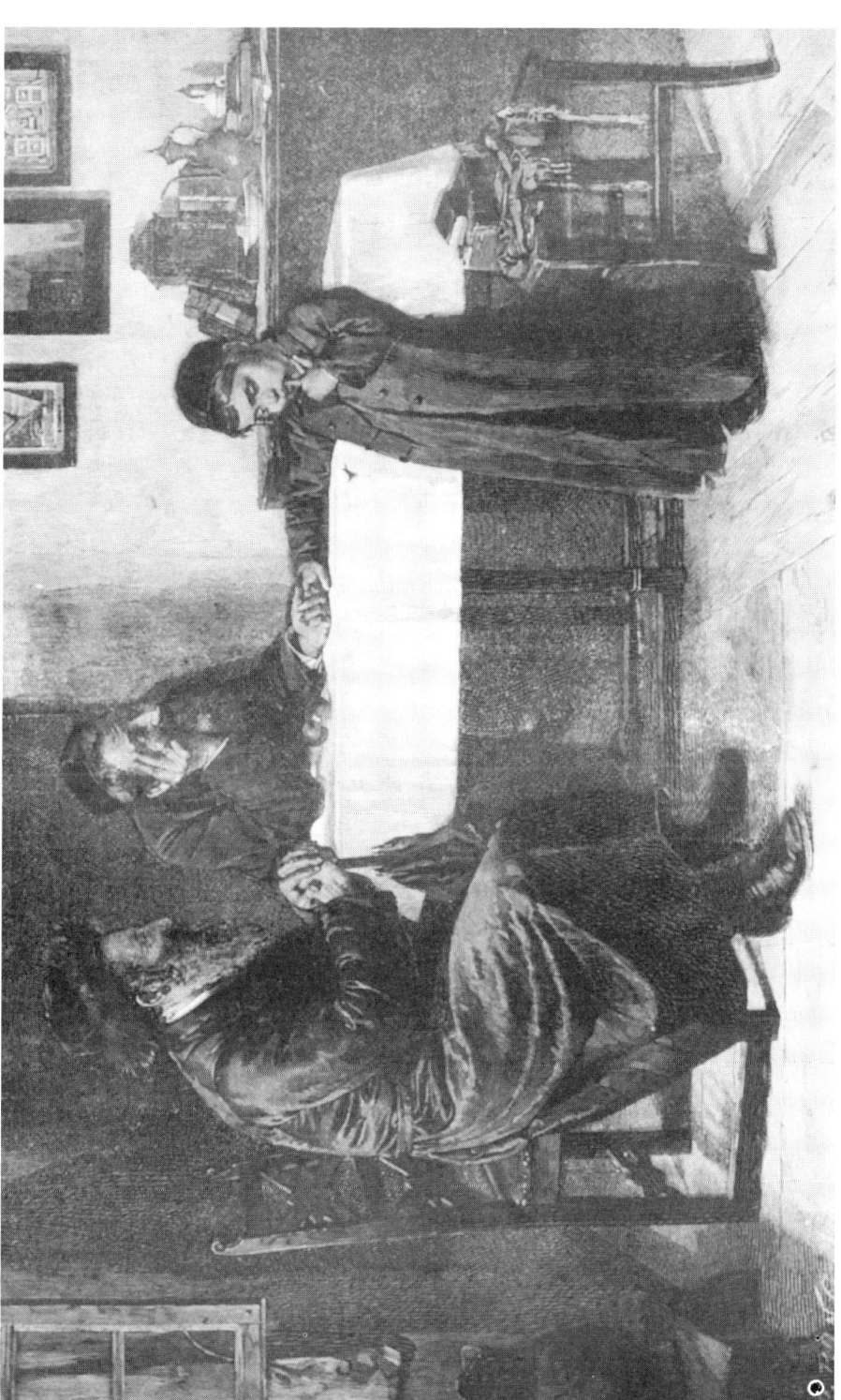

Question Time – verkoer   by J. Kaufmann   Reprinted from the Israelit, [21 March 1895]

Mrs. Prins shoved her *rucksack* into the railroad car. She rebuffed the general mood of despair and resignation that pervaded the atmosphere and told a niece of hers that she had no intention of boarding the train. The niece was therefore at liberty to take anything she found in her aunt's *rucksack*. Mrs. Prins then removed the yellow star from her coat, and the seconds passed like hours as she contemplated her next move.

Determined not to become another statistic, Mrs. Prins entered a small trackside restaurant with an air of confidence. No one questioned her, and she figured that there was nothing to lose. The worst that could happen was that she would be kicked out and thrown on the train. Inside the restaurant Mrs. Prins found Germans eating and drinking at the tables. She summoned a waiter and requested to be assigned a job in the kitchen. The waiter did not utter a word, but took Mrs. Prins along, provided an apron and asked her to cut up fruits and vegetables. The waiter then brought this food to his German customers.

At dusk, the train started to move and slowly pulled out with its pathetic load of prisoners. Immediately thereafter, the kind waiter came to Mrs. Prins to accompany her to the street. She was his "girlfriend" who had come to help for the day. Mrs. Prins thanked the waiter who had risked his freedom and life to be a gallant rescuer. Once outside, she was a citizen who was now persona non-grata and was no longer permitted to reside in Amsterdam.

MRS. PRINS WAS CAREFUL TO HIDE HER IDENTITY, AND SHE and Rabbi Prins were reunited at the clandestine home of her brother. With the help of some friendly Dutch, the Prins family obtained "alternate" identification papers. The lady who had several months earlier hidden their one and a half-year-old daughter Betty was now bold enough to rent for the Prins' an apartment in her own name. A special feature of this dwelling was that it had entrances from two distinct and separate sides. It was located at Fokke Simonszstraat 80 and was along a *gracht* (canal) in an older section of Amsterdam. Thereafter, the Prins family was able to disappear from the general daily scene. In all, there were seven occupants in that apartment. They included Rabbi Prins' elderly father, who had a long white beard, a sure giveaway of his identity, Rabbi and Mrs. Prins and the two brothers with their respective wives who had been hidden in the attic.

With Hashem's help, they remained several years at their new location, undetected and unscathed. Even though their survival was a miracle, they did not rely on miracles. The door to one room was replaced by a bookcase on hinges – a perfect camouflage. In that room, several persons slept and spent a good part of each day, thus remaining unobserved. On one occasion, the elderly father was sitting in the hallway, learning from a *sefer* when something fell down from the neighbor's house and broke a skylight glass pane right next to him. Fortunately he was not hurt and, despite being visible through the break, he and his family remained undetected.

Before *Rosh Hashonoh,* the Prins family practiced blowing the *shofar.* To assure that the sound would not reach the street, they practiced with one person standing at the alley entrance along the street's sidewalk, while a second person blew inside. Of course, there was no *minyan* but the *mitzvah* of *shofar* can be fulfilled without a quorum as well.[a]

I remember one day when Mrs. Prins came to our house and received from Mother some dishes and cutlery to start their new home. It must be realized that both money and the ability to purchase household items in wartime were extremely limited.

ONE OF RABBI PRINS' MANY SPECIALITIES WAS HIS KNOWLEDGE of the Jewish calendar. After the everyday Jewish community life came to a halt, common things such as a *luach,* which most of us take for granted, were no longer available. Rabbi Prins developed a calendar for the year 5704 (1943-1944). It contained all the relevant information including the *zemanim* (time for lighting candles, etc.) for Amsterdam. The calendar was typed in Dutch and Hebrew, was photographed for distribution and handbound in a hardcover volume.

Needless to say, the calendar came in extremely handy, first in Westerbork and then in Bergen Belsen. May the *zechus* of this project, along with all his other endeavors, be a *Meilitz Yoshor* for his *neshomah.*

After the war, my cousin Erika stayed for several weeks with the Prins family in their inconspicuous apartment while waiting for her English visa papers to be issued. Those documents would allow Erika to finally travel to England and rejoin her mother, Tante Else after seven long years of separation.

Several years after Amsterdam was liberated, the Prins family moved to Rechovot, Eretz Yisroel where they established a Jewish High School known as Tichon Datieh and a *shul,* Mercaz Avrohom. As of 1996, both the school and the *shul* are in active use. Mrs. Prins, a great grandmother several times over, lives as a widow nearby. Mrs. Prins' son is now the *Rav* in his father's *shul* and also *Rosh HaYeshivah* at Yeshivas HaDarom.

---

a. *Mishnah Berurah,* 689:5,15.

1943 DECEMBER	ח ת ש"י מבת	5704 TEIWEIS		1944 JANUARI	ח ת ש"י שבט	5704 SJEWAT	
	מולד Maandagvoormiddag 2 uur 30 2/9 min.				מולד Dinsdagnamiddag 3 uur 14 5/18 min.		
	28 Dinsd 1	יום ז' דחנוכה ב דרח			26 Woensd 1		ראש חדש
	29 Woensd 2	חנוכת המזבח			27 Donderd 2		
	30 Donderd 3			ing. 5.00	28 Vrijdag 3		בא
ing. 4.30	31 Vrijdag 4			uitg. 6.07	29 Zat שבת 4		
JAN uitg.5.27	1 Zat שבת 5	ויגש			30 Zondag 5		
1944	2 Zondag 6				31 Maand 6		
	3 Maand 7			FEBRUARI	1 Dinsd 7		
	4 Dinsd 8				2 Woensd 8		
	5 Woensd 9				3 Donderd 9		
uitg. 5.32	6 Dond 10	עשרה בטבת		ing. 5.15	4 Vrijdag 10		בשלח
ing. 4.30	7 Vrijdag 11	תקופה 's mo.5.10		uitg. 6.19	5 Zat שבת 11		
uitg. 5.34	8 Zat שבת 12	ויחי			6 Zond 12		
	9 Zond 13				7 Maand 13		
	10 Maand 14	שובבים ת"ת			8 Dins 14		
	11 Dinsd 15				9 Woensd 15		ר"ח לאילנות
	12 Woensd 16				10 Dond 16		
	13 Dond 17			ing. 5.30	11 Vrijdag 17		יתרו
ing. 4.45	14 Vrijdag 18			uitg. 6.31	12 Zat שבת 18		
uitg. 5.44	15 Zat שבת 19	שמות			13 Zondag 19		
	16 Zondag 20				14 Maand 20		
	17 Maand 21				15 Dinsd 21		
	18 Dinsd 22				16 Woensd 22		
	19 Woensd 23				17 Donderd 23		
	20 Dond 24			ing. 5.45	18 Vrijd 24		
ing. 5.00	21 Vrijdag 25			uitg. 6.43	19 Zat שבת 25		משפטים פ' שקלים
uitg. 5.55	22 Zat שבת 26	וארא			20 Zondag 26		
	23 Zondag 27				21 Maand 27		
	24 Maand 28				22 Dinsd 28		
uitg. 6.--	25 Dinsd 29	י"כ קטן ערב ר"ח		uitg. 6.51	23 Woensd 29		י"כ קטן ערב ר"ח
					24 Dond. 30		יום א' דראש חדש

Luach pages for Teves and Shevat, 5704, prepared by Rabbi Prins for Amsterdam, Holland

Chapter Nine

FIRST ARREST

FROM MY EARLIEST YEARS ON, I WAS INCULCATED WITH the premise that government was vested with the powers of disrupting civilian freedom only for purposes of national security and separating the criminal element from a peaceful society.[a] Now, at a tender young age, I was experiencing firsthand the dichotomy of a fascistic *modus operandi* versus our Common civil laws, as promulgated over seven centuries ago in the English Magna Carta (1215 C.E.), and since emulated by the regimes of most western nations including that of the (vanquished) Dutch government. That seven hundred year old declaration of civil rights states in part:

> "...no man can be arrested, imprisoned, deprived of his property, outlawed, exiled, or in anyway destroyed except by legal judgment of his peers or by the law of the land..."

It was a late spring day in the city of Amsterdam when the Dutch puppet government decreed that my family's curtailed liberties now be

---

a. refer to *Pirkei Avos*, 3:2.

totally terminated. Our being taken into custody was not on account of any illegal activity but solely because of our religious affiliation.

Many neighborhoods of Amsterdam had already been emptied of their known Jewish inhabitants during previous months and weeks. With the German penchant for thoroughness, however, they had not forgotten us. The hatemongers merely moved methodically through the city, ultimately taking away over one hundred thousand of our city's Jewish neighbors.

My parents knew that the inevitable day would arrive, and we had prepared very large, canvas shoulder bags, which bulged with the barest of necessities. We also took one or two small suitcases that could be easily carried. The items packed included a little food for traveling, light summer clothing, a small blanket, candles for Friday night, some *seforim* and some cutlery but no dishes. This luggage was prepared and lay for several weeks in the first floor den. On a few occasions, it was unpacked and then repacked after a false alarm.

ON JUNE 6, 1943, THE FIRST CITYWIDE CURFEW WAS ANNOUNCED. No person, except those authorized, were permitted to leave their homes. It was a long day. The wooden shutters of the first floor den were closed, and our "luggage" was prepared and ready in that first floor front room. We spent the rest of the day either in the kitchen or upstairs. Then, in the late afternoon, around five o'clock, I looked out the second floor living room window and saw several German soldiers with guns slung over their shoulders about one hundred feet away, pacing back and forth at the entrance to our street, i.e. the intersection of Hemonylaan and van Woustraat was now sealed off. About a minute later a *Gestapo* officer rang our door bell. These Germans were real "heroes" in arresting a Jewish couple with four young children. May they and their like rot in their living and dead graves![b]

After a few minutes, our parents, my sisters Toni and Connie, my cousin Erika and I left. I was nine years old at the time, but I remember the scene vividly. We walked with our luggage along the sidewalk, accompanied by a soldier. I wanted to walk alongside one of my parents as I usually did but was told to walk single file. A few neighbors who had small balconies stood silently as we walked by, others watched from windows. It was a silent march. We made a right turn into Hemonystraat

---

b. Yeshayohu, 66:24.

and then continued walking to the Ceintuurbaan, all the time being joined by additional persons arrested from nearby side streets. It mattered not whether a person was an observant Jew or not, all who were found were arrested. Even the intermarried Jews and those who only had one Jewish grandparent were taken away. All this was done to make the city and the country *"Judenrein",* literally "clean of Jews". (In 1993, in the Balkan sectarian conflict between Bosnians, Croatians and Serbs, this would be termed "ethnic cleansing". A historical footnote: the Bosnian and Croatian Moslems were masters of intolerance and competed with the German army in butchering and murdering their fellow Yugoslavian Jews. On the other hand, the Greek Orthodox Serbs accommodated the Jews and considered the Germans as their common enemy.) The luggage began to feel gradually heavier from the walk. We finally reached the Ceintuurbaan, where a trolley was waiting to take us to the Centraal Station, the largest railroad station in Amsterdam. Since there was a curfew, no other *trams* (trolleys) were operating except for these which were pressed into service by the Gestapo for deportation purposes.

Jews had not been permitted to ride trolleys for already several months, and so this trolley ride brought back some memories. Amsterdam had no busses in its public transportation system. The trolley took us over the Amstel River and let us off at the railroad station. There we met up with many hundreds, probably several thousand, fellow arrestees. Our common destination was a Dutch camp named Westerbork, near the city of Zwolle, in the northeasterly Dutch province of Drenthe. By train, it was an overnight ride of some eight hours.

OUR TRAIN WAS WAITING INSIDE THE STATION. IT WAS NOT THE kind of car one normally travels in. Instead, the Germans had prepared a huge string of boxcars, or as we correctly termed them *veewagens* (cattle-cars). They contained no partitions, no seats or benches, no lights, no toilet, no carpets, no fans or air conditioning and no windows, just a sliding side door. For a toilet there was one pail. Once on board with our luggage, the sliding door was closed, with six inches remaining open for "ventilation" on this warm spring night. It was crowded inside, and there was no room to lay down for the night, just enough to sit on one's own luggage. I insisted on occupying the spot in front of that slit opening so as to watch the railroad and the country side. I claimed that due to travel restrictions for Jews I hadn't traveled on trains for so long and now wanted to make up for that loss and peek outside. [Hashem must have paid special attention to those words, which was not a *Tefillah,* because years later I worked as a Construction and Design

Engineer for an urban railroad some four thousand miles away, The New York City Transit Authority, for thirty full and interesting years, 1962-92.] Traveling during the early summer in a crowded box car without the basics of human comfort is something never to be forgotten. Alas, many, many of my co-travelers did not make it to see the freedom that some of us survivors now enjoy. May the organizers and implementers of these inhuman transports experience the fate of all their charges who never returned to see liberty and partake in the pursuit of happiness.

German greed for Jewish property and hatred of Jewish blood was so intense that they ordered *Train-Consists* from Amsterdam, which were assembled with extra cars so as to form a much longer train than the Dutch railroads commonly accommodate. This enabled the envious Germans to flaunt their innate burning desires and deport many more Jews at one time. The normal single steam locomotive was inadequate to pull our train. Accordingly, a second locomotive had to be assigned to push the aft end of our transport. This created havoc when the train started to move, since the individual boxcar couplers were extremely crude mechanical, non-electrical devices and the locomotives were not coordinated. The result was a pronounced forward lurch that was quickly followed by a sudden recoil. This in turn led to a lot of bouncing and pummeling of us travelers inside the cars – back and forth, till the locomotives became synchronized, following which the train moved smoothly. There were no poles or overhead grab-bars to hold onto as we bounced around inside this windowless boxcar. We only had the inboard surface of the rough wooden wallboards to support ourselves. Our train traveled relatively slowly through the countryside, leaving behind the city we had loved so much.

These costly deportation actions were mandated by the Berlin government and implemented under the auspices of the cruel *Rijks Commissaris* (Governor – General of occupied Holland) the Austrian Nazi Dr. Arthur Seyss Inquart *Y.S.* (1940-45) and his parsimonious stooges in the Dutch puppet government. Deportation operations and internment activities were funded from the proceeds of the sale of confiscated Jewish owned assets.

The use of box type railroad cars for our cross-country trip was for the sole purpose of humiliation and degradation. The passengers ranged from infants to the old and invalid, men, women and children, rich and poor – they were all herded into the same type cars. The mean oppressor's efforts were, however, futile in that our self respect and human values were

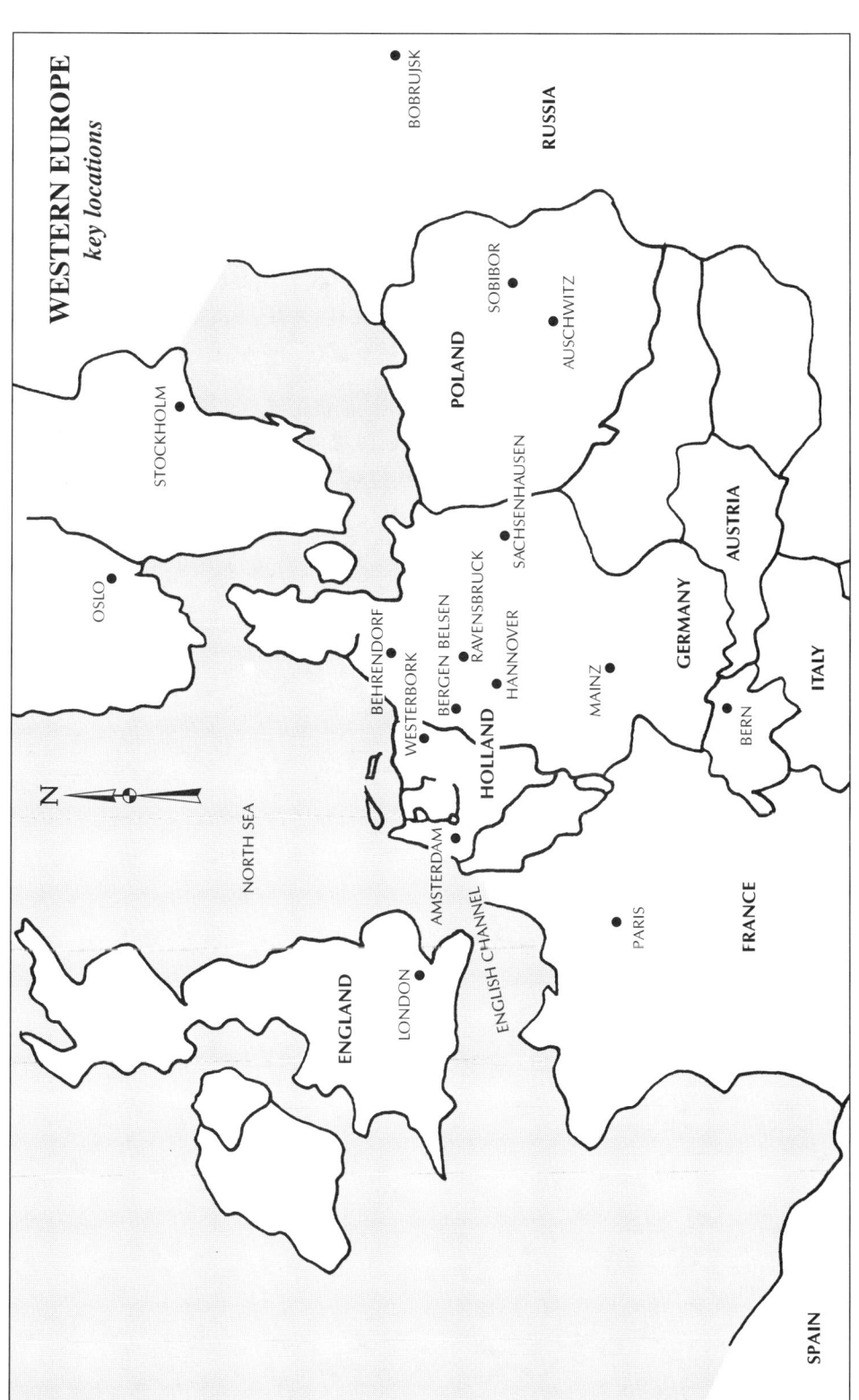

maintained and our dignity was not destroyed. To the contrary, the stress under duress brought out the best in most of these people, who now helped each other, where humanly possible. Unfortunately, there were individuals to whom this type of harassment and crisis brought out their negative traits, but among the observant Jews I did not note this phenomenon.

Early the next morning, on June 7, 1943, we arrived in Westerbork, tired, worn and hungry, ready to face a new world and new experiences.

I NOW COMPLETED MY FIRST LESSON IN "GERMAN BIGOTRY". The Amsterdam experience taught me that not all humans are capable of respecting their fellow beings. Now, in Westerbork I was to be enrolled in a follow-up course, titled "German Pathological Brutality", where I was to learn firsthand, how our Jewish people were locked in a bitter conflict with the scum of the western world. I was to find out that the Germans were a nation "...who had no consideration for the aged and showed no favor to the young...".[c] Their principles were diametrically opposite to our Judaic creed. Germany was a state whose de facto dictum was: destroy non-Aryan society, exploit the weak, revile human diversity and emulate Sodom. Our foe was obsessed with intolerance, vile hatred, greed, cruelty and arrogance – murder and genocide were their ultimate goals.

---

c. Devorim, 28:50.

Chapter Ten
WESTERBORK DESCRIBED

AFTER A LONG NIGHT OF TRAVELING, OUR TRAIN FINALLY pulled into the Dutch internment camp of Westerbork. The camp was located not far from the German border. All rail traffic to Westerbork went via the Zwolle railroad switching yards.

Prior to World War II, Westerbork had been established by the Dutch government as a temporary location for German immigrants who fled oppression but had no visas to stay in Holland. When the German government cancelled citizenship privileges to most of their Jewish population in the 1930's, many German emigrants became stateless, i.e. without valid passports. Some of these people found a temporary home in Westerbork until a visa to America or to England could be obtained. A large number of these Jewish refugees were still in Westerbork when we arrived. They were housed in one story wooden barracks, subdivided into two or three room apartments with a small kitchenette and lavatory. Most of these units had a very small vegetable garden planted in front.

For most Dutch Jews who were arrested by the Germans there were generally two temporary internment camp stops in Holland, prior to being sent further to Germany or Poland. These were Westerbork in the northeast and Vught in the southern province of Limburg, just north of the Belgian border. Of these two camps, Vught was the lesser humane.

A friend who had been transferred from Vught to Westerbork once came to visit us. His hair was cut very short and an electric shaver had been passed down the middle of his head so that he had one long swath, 3 cm wide, without any hair from his forehead to the back of the neck.

To accommodate the additional thousands of Jews arriving in Westerbork, a whole series of new one story wooden barracks had been constructed. These buildings were long and narrow with men sleeping in one half of each barrack and women and children in the other half. There were no interior partitions for privacy.

The barracks were of inferior quality construction. Lighting was extremely poor, with only one single seventy-five watt, open light bulb for perhaps every ten feet, mounted along the barrack center on the roof truss' bottom chord. I recall that on one moderately windy day, the entire roof blew off our barrack, leaving the interior entirely exposed. Apparently, the wrong size, spacing and type of nails had been used to secure the pitched roof's wooden board sheathing.

TYPICALLY, BEDS WERE STEEL FRAMED TRIPLE DECKERS WITH rough narrow mattresses, each mattress supported by a coarse wire mesh. There were no boards below these mattresses. Two people slept on each mattress. In each half of the barracks there were four long rows of side by side beds down the length of the barrack with perhaps sixty triple deckers in each row. Open corridors consisted of a total of two narrow aisles per barrack, or one aisle between each two rows of beds, down the length of the building. They posed genuine fire hazards. The barrack's width was probably thirty feet.

One six foot long plain wooden table, with two simple wooden benches and a window at each table, were available throughout the barracks for every five or six triple decker beds. The shortage of table seating meant that many had to sit on their beds instead. For a taller person, this meant sitting slouched since there was not much headroom between beds. There was no room to store personal belongings. Instead, items were stored either below the bottom bed, below or on top of the middle mattress, and for those "fortunate" enough to occupy the top bed, there was storage available within the exposed triangular wooden roof trusses.

Each end of these barracks had one toilet and one sink. For additional toilets, one had to go outdoors to small wooden buildings housing multiple toilets represented by ten or so large holes in a sitting board above a deep pit. To take showers one would have to go to the camp's central bathhouse. Bathtubs did not exist at Westerbork.

With the exception of food, fuel and basic raw materials, the camp was generally self-supporting in that it generated its own electricity, had its own central kitchen, medical laboratory, store rooms, working places and a few small class rooms. There was even a small jail which could house as many as ten persons. Of course, the needs of all Westerbork prisoners were kept at a very modest level. There were no houses of worship nor any recreational facilities.

The electrical power generating station was coal fired and was also the sole source of hot water. I remember once carrying a full pail of scorching hot water to Mother. On the way, I knocked my leg against the pail causing it to splash. Thereafter, I had for many months a large blister scar below my right knee.

The camp's kitchen provided all the staple food for the large barrack population. Hot food was picked up for each barrack in large metal urns that were carried by two people, each holding one side handle. Coffee was delivered the same way. Of course, this was not real coffee, only *"koffie surogaat"* (imitation coffee), which had the color of coffee and was hot. Occasionally, one would fish out of the coffee urn an old boiled hat.

Once the food arrived at the barracks, it was dished out to everyone who lined up with their plate, large bowl or pot. I remember many a time carrying a brimming full plate or pot of hot watery food to the family through the crowded aisles and yelling repeatedly *"Pas op! flekkenwater!"* ("Watch out! dirty stain water!").

The medical laboratory had many windows in its one story building, and one could watch from outdoors as tubes carried liquids from one glass container to another. There were also many racks of test tubes which to a youngster looked very impressive.

The camp's supplies were kept in the store rooms. Naturally, these supplies were exceedingly limited even while demand for them was great. Management of this aspect of the camp was handled by the original German-Jewish refugees who had inhabited the camp since pre-war days. To obtain anything usually required some *"protectia"*. (My sister

Toni worked in one of these store rooms during our second stay at Westerbork.)

WESTERBORK HAD LARGE RECYCLING FACTORIES. WHEN fighter planes were shot down, the fuselage and wings were sent to this camp and all components were separated, e.g. copper, aluminum, plastic, etc. There was a story told of one camp inmate who had found a roll of candies in one of these fighter cockpits. After taking one candy he noted that he couldn't sleep at night. Upon further investigation, it had become evident that the candy was really an anti-sleep pill for the pilot.

Old batteries were also taken apart at these factories. This was hazardous work because the workers would inhale excessive amounts of ammonia gas. As an antidote, the laborers were permitted a larger ration of milk. Unfortunately, with the war food shortages, that milk supplement was totally inadequate. Another item being dismantled there and recycled were radio parts. As previously mentioned, the Germans did not want citizens of occupied lands to listen to the B.B.C., and so most radios with the regular and short-wave bands were surrendered to the authorities. These units were then taken apart and many of their components shipped to Westerbork. I remember rummaging through a large pile of capacitors outside one of these factories and "salvaging" a few for my own collection. Taking them apart meant unwinding many layers of oily waxed paper and then finding some thin shiny sheets of bright copper.

THE SMALL CLASSROOMS WERE COMPLETELY INADEQUATE for the camp's occupants and so the majority of the children did not attend any school. Most teaching that did occur was voluntary. There were adult education groups, such as *shiurim,* and also tutors for children of concerned parents. Naturally, the lack of discipline at these few classrooms made any efficient learning process impractical.

THOUGH EVERY CAMP INMATE WAS IN FACT A PRISONER OF THE Germans, they were more or less free except during working hours, to roam the camp grounds. A small group of these inmates were prisoners found to have violated some petty camp rule, these were sent to the tiny camp jail. Both the administration of the jail and the policing of the camp's perimeter security fence were handled by the Dutch police known as *Marechaussees* (the U.S. equivalent to State Troopers). They, in turn, were under the command of a *Nazi Kommandant* who walked around on crutches since he had one wooden stick leg. Policing of the general camp grounds was the responsibility of *Kapos* who were Jewish and, unfortunately, did not always have the highest ethical standards.

Another but very small group of camp inmates were confined to their barrack, which happened to have been directly adjacent and behind ours. Their barrack was surrounded by a six foot high barbed wire fence and had a small courtyard within that fencing. The occupants of that barrack wore, unlike other inmates, special striped prison garb with a large white letter "S" sewn onto the back of their clothing. They were allowed "fresh air" and "exercise" once a day, for a short period of time, by walking single file in a circle within their courtyard, their hands behind their backs. The "S" on their clothing stood for *"Straf"*, meaning "punishment". Their crime was that they had been *"ondergedoken"*, i.e. "had been in hiding", so as to avoid being arrested for being Jewish. Many such persons had been arrested as a result of informers who were paid a couple of Guilders for each individual they reported. The usual fate of these special inmates was to be placed onboard the next available train heading east to either Auschwitz or Sobibor.

Some Dutch churches must have dabbled in an unloading process and indulged in their own style of ethnic cleansing by providing the authorities access to lists of converted persons within their ranks. There was a large barrack which was dedicated to inmates who had defected from Judaism (baptized). This group included even priests, pastors and nuns. All were of Jewish parents or grandparents! None of these persons wore church related garments in the camp.

JEWISH PRE-WAR HOLLAND WAS PLAGUED BY EXTENSIVE problems of assimilation. Even among the observant Jews, I could sense a degree of undesirable secularization by their modes of dress, entertainment and attitude towards leisure time. The persecutions of World War II did bring many back to a more observant posture. On the other hand, there were too many who had no desire, time or ability to even try to understand the root of their grueling hardships and suffering.

[An analogy to a possible cause of these tragic sufferings could be our realization that just as it is the experienced navigator at the helm, and not the rudder, that steers the ship through stormy waters, so must we recognize that without Hashem having removed His protective umbrella, i.e. *Haster Ponim*,[a] the Germans could never have inflicted their extensive harm. May it be the will of the Almighty to spare the generations to come from such superhuman tests. Our sanctification of His Name should be channeled through serving Hashem "with gladness",[b] rather than

---

a. Devorim, 32:20
b. Tehillim, 100:2

considering it too onerous a task to thus serve our Creator, and thereby removing the "gladness and joyfulness" component from our service.[c]

OUTSIDE OF THE BARRACKS THERE WERE NO BENCHES OR tables to form sitting areas. There certainly were no playgrounds or playing fields. Thus, there were essentially no large open areas for recreation, only the relatively narrow spaces between the barracks. Of the few larger areas available, there was one site behind the classrooms that was used to spread out the sewage, pulled up by the pail full, from below the latrines. These pails were called "honey buckets", and with the dysentery, diarrhea, etc., one can imagine the stench of these areas and the unfortunate persons who were occupied with that task. The sewage was not aerated or neutralized by chemicals.

ALONG THE CENTER OF THE CAMP WAS A SINGLE RAILROAD track and the only paved roadway was adjacent thereto. The day prior to each transport's departure, a long string of cattle cars would be delivered and would remain standing on the track overnight. I remember once seeing an unusual sight. On the floor of one such empty box car was a large hollow concrete cube with approximately 2 foot wide sides, 4 inch thick walls and two adjoining sides missing. In retrospect, I assume that this was a prefabricated chimney cap for a gas chamber at Auschwitz. This was based on a conversation I had a year later with a Polish lady at Bergen Belsen who claimed to have climbed up such a chimney to escape from inside a gas chamber. May whoever designed, fabricated and provided that concrete cap meet an ugly fate with all the pains and misfortunes he richly deserves.

On the morning of a transport's parting, the process of assembling the pitiable travelers began. Early in the morning, when one could usually not hear what was being said ten feet away because of the incessant din, the person in charge of each barrack would start to summon those who were listed to report to the train. The announcer stood at the barrack's center, where he or she could now be heard even one hundred feet away. One could almost hear a pin drop. Surprisingly, I found there to be little commiseration and the negative reactions of those being called were very limited. Only the persons going to the train were allowed outside the barrack. Once the train pulled out, the "all clear" camp siren sounded, and life for the remaining prisoners continued as before. Even though the train may have taken two to three thousand persons, it didn't take long for word to pass around between barracks as to who was sent away.

---

c. Devorim, 28:47

The vast majority of the Dutch Jews who were deported to the East were sent to either Auschwitz or to Sobibor, both were death camps in Polish territory. Auschwitz (Oswiecim) was located between the cities of Krakow and Katowice, and Sobibor was near the city of Lublin. These two camps were due east of Amsterdam by a distance of seven hundred and eight hundred and fifty miles respectively. The existence of Auschwitz, and to a lesser extent Sobibor, were known in Holland and in many other parts of Europe as well. Deportees leaving Westerbork usually knew their destination. The presence of gas chambers at Auschwitz and similar equipment at Sobibor was also known to many. What was not known was the German policy regarding who would be gassed. However, when deportees were told that their next stop was to be Bergen Belsen, Germany or Theresienstadt, Czechoslovakia, then there would be a certain sense of relief as neither of these concentration camps were reputed to have sophisticated extermination facilities, such as gas chambers.

THE WORLD BEYOND CONTINENTAL EUROPE ALSO KNEW OF German extermination activities at many sites. To this end, the Allied Command was requested to bomb the railroad bridges leading to those concentration camps. Unfortunately, that was **NEVER** done. It was always claimed by the high command that diverting bombers for such destroy missions would mean delaying other war efforts, and that removing vital support duties from the front line troops could be hazardous. Postponing scheduled bombing missions and weakening troop support missions were not considered to be justified. Lengthy discussions and numerous requests could not sway the Allied generals.

Of course, it must be realized that some bombing missions were scrapped due to poor visibility of targets caused by low cloud cover. In such instances the bombers went in search of secondary ground targets. Railroads leading to Auschwitz and their like were not considered secondary targets. Allied intelligence also claimed that the supposed extermination activities were unfounded. It was a sorry case of bureaucracy and red tape being harnessed by the British and American Air Force Generals to deny assistance. The Allied hierarchy recanted their myopic viewpoints very quickly once these death camps were liberated and tales of horror shocked the world.

Chapter Eleven

WESTERBORK - GATEWAY TO THE EAST AND WEST

Westerbork also had a commissary. The only annoyance was that it sold totally useless items, ranging from small, manual cigarette rolling machines for making one's own cigarettes to fancy long stemmed clay pipes to blow soap bubbles. Apparently, it was another effort by the Germans to unload useless merchandise and collect whatever currency they could get ahold of with the least effort. Only official camp tender was allowed as cash to purchase these worthless wares, or to pay for other camp services, and so Dutch civilian money was exchanged for Westerbork camp money. In fiduciary parlance, this currency was the epitome of fiat money.

THE GERMANS VENTED THEIR HATRED NOT ONLY AGAINST JEWS, but against many other non-Aryans as well. Even some non-stereotype Aryans, like Germans who were terminally and gravely ill or those who were in mental institutions, were put to death by their intolerant

German Fiat Money, replica of Westerbork paper money. Note: 100 cents equals one Guilder. Aerial view of Westerbork appeared on the face of each denomination.

"fearless", "heroic" and "gallant" fratricidal medical doctors and staffs. After all, a German must be perfect. (Refer to the Epilogue for details.)

All *Sigeuners* (Gypsies) residing in Holland were given their marching orders and instructed to report to Westerbork. These people had an itinerant lifestyle and resided mostly in horse drawn, mobile house carriages, spoke their own language and had their own (non) standards of sanitation. I remember one day when many of these carriages appeared and lined up outside camp while the gypsies entered Westerbork. These people were dirty and infested with lice and fleas.

The first job was to clean and steam their clothing, while they took hot showers in the camp's central bathhouse. Note: Clothes "steaming" was not for the purpose of pressing and ironing, but to kill the fleas and lice which could be carriers of disease. Subsequently, these Gypsies disappeared on the next transport to Auschwitz while their deserted carriages stood outside camp as a stark monument of another cowardly German hit and run campaign on a group of unarmed civilians.

THE CAMP WAS SURROUNDED BY A FIVE FOOT HIGH, BARBED wire security fence. An approximately six foot wide by possibly four foot deep empty moat was on the inside of this fence. Dotting this perimeter fence on the outside were watchtowers some fifteen feet tall. These were manned by Dutch *Marechaussee* Police officers. To assure that no camp inmate would escape, the young able bodied men and women prisoners had the task of chopping down all shrubs, bushes and trees outside the camp within the perimeter fence's vicinity.

The Dutch did have some feelings of compassion, and on one occasion, all children from ages seven to thirteen were allowed to go outside the camp for approximately three hours to play in the open fields. We were carefully counted as we exited the camp and later again when we returned. This show of kindness was never repeated, probably due to a reprimand by the German camp commander.

Communication with the outside world was practically nil. There were no telephones and there was little mail; however, some people did receive small food packages. I remember how there was a (friendly) yell from nearby, when someone in our barrack discovered a written note at the bottom of a jar of jam that had been received through the mail.

Some further Westerbork memories:

UPON OUR ARRIVAL AT THE CAMP, WE WENT TO A SMALL hall where everyone was registered and then assigned to a barrack. The registration took place at a very large "U" shaped table-layout by young lady typists. They were camp prisoners who typed relevant information with confiscated office typewriters, stolen by the Germans. Following our arrival at the assigned barrack, everyone would negotiate which bed to use, which level of bed, i.e. bottom, middle or top, and who would share a bed with who. I remember how Father, slept on the table in the men's section because he did not want to share his bed with another person. Coming from middle class comfort in Amsterdam to subhuman camp conditions, after traveling all night in cramped cattle cars, was a real shock.

Despite the inhumane treatment, the vast majority did not succumb and lower their moral and ethical standards. For example, I remember hearing the son of the *Noord Holland* (North-Holland) Chief Rabbi Onderwyzer give regular *Mishnayis Shiurim* to a group of men while sitting among the beds in the men's section. Despite shortages of clothing and laundry problems, people wore clean, untorn clothing. There was comraderie to the fullest extent, with people helping each other wherever possible. It was a case of adversity bringing out the best in most persons. The contrast between us and those who put us in the camp was most pronounced. The latter, the scum of humanity, used deceit, lies, foul language, deprivation, hard labor, torture, death, hunger and disease as their daily tools.

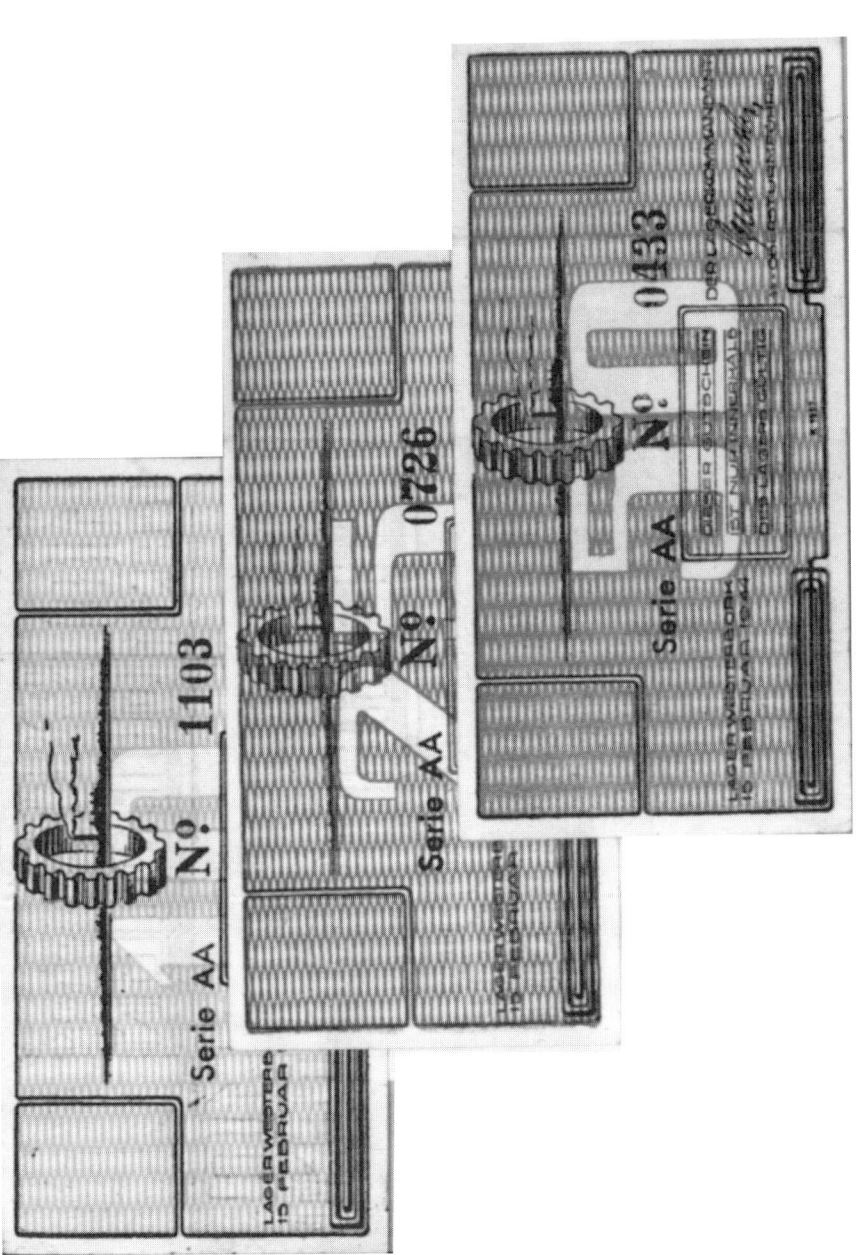

Westerbork paper money – back side of bills. Note the gear, which was intended to give the camp an industrial reputation. Printed in German, this 'legal' tender states: Voucher only valid within the camp (Westerbork). Signed by: Der Lagerkommandant, S.S. Obersturmfuehrer (rank) Y.S.

While at Westerbork, I met my good friend and former neighbor Freddie several times. Freddie van der Woude, along with his older brother Loetje, older sister Dina and their parents were in a barrack somewhat distant from ours. We played and enjoyed good times together despite the camp setting. We also did a lot of walking and talking. Freddie was very involved in the friendly "war games" that the boys of our age were practicing in his part of the camp. The "hostilities" were replete with homemade bunkers in the peat and sandy soils, captured prisoners and lookouts. Had Freddie survived, I believe he would have been an excellent candidate for some high military position in either Holland, NATO or Israel.

One day, after a train pulled out for Auschwitz and the siren sounded the all clear, we discovered all the van der Woudes were missing. Mother tried to console me by saying that they were probably all gassed to death in the cattle car without having to exit and put up with the hardships of Auschwitz. Such was the conversation between mother and son. As I recall this, some fifty-three years later, my eyes still swell with tears.

It has been said that the Germans chose eastern European countries such as Poland for their mass extermination camps because of the anti-Semitism of the local population. Without the latter's collaboration, they could not have achieved their grisly goals.

NOTE: DEATH BY GASSING SHOULD NOT BE CONSIDERED AN easy death. In Bergen Belsen I spoke to persons who were Auschwitz "alumni". They had seen bodies still moving as they were being cremated, after being removed from the gas chambers. It was said that the Germans used two different gasses to murder their victims. In later months, they ran out of numbing gas, thereby making the murdering process more painful.[a] *The New York Times*[b] reported, that when some ninety-seven thousand persons were gassed to death by the exhaust of a truck engine: "there were special instructions for emptying the trucks (of bodies) after each round of killings, because this could be, detrimental to the health, and morale of the (German) SS men. In a letter to Rauff – a Colonel in the elite SS, an SS officer, speaking of morale, said that the victims' contorted faces were a very ugly sight." It is noteworthy to mention that the trucks used for the murdering were disguised with large red cross emblems!

---

a. Devorim, 32:25.
b. September 5, 1972, page 11.

BY THE SUMMER OF 1943, THE GERMANS STILL EXPECTED TO win the war. Their major military setbacks were yet to come, and the sadistic German war machine wanted to upgrade its deadly arsenal. The Germans had many surprises up their bloodsoaked sleeves. These included research and development of:

(a) the airplane jet engine, which would allow a plane to travel much faster than the heretofore propeller driven planes;

(b) nuclear energy, which could lead to devastating atomic bombs. (It should be noted that Germany had a very active nuclear research program starting as early as the mid-1930's which preceded the U.S. Manhattan project by at least five years. Otto Hahn and Fritz Strassmann had then conducted extensive nuclear fission experiments in their laboratories, which resulted in significant discoveries. With Divine Providence, the Germans were stymied in their nuclear development efforts and did not enjoy the fruits of that work.)

(c) air to air rockets, which would permit their fighter planes to shoot down bombers without the use of anti-aircraft guns or fighter plane machine guns;

(d) surface to surface flying bombs known as rockets, which would relieve airplanes from delivering lethal loads. (Here, they had already proven their technical ability by launching the V-1 and V-2 rockets from German-occupied France to London and its suburbs.)

(e) gasoline production from coal by the "cracking" process. This was very important, since coal was plentiful and nearby. Oil wells were in distant and vulnerable or inaccessible countries like Rumania, Iraq, Iran and North Africa. Without gasoline and oil, all modern military ventures would quickly come to a screeching halt.

REALIZING AND IMPLEMENTING SOME OF THEIR EVIL RESEARCH and development plans demanded production of precise fitting machinery parts which, in turn, necessitated special machining of mechanism components. Very accurate metal cutting by the use of diamond tipped cutting tools would aid in this not so distant but yet to be developed strategic war campaign. Amsterdam was one of the large diamond centers with many experts in that field. Most of the diamond cutters and experts were Jewish and were now in Westerbork or about to be rounded up and sent there.

Consequently, members of the Amsterdam diamond establishment and their families were given a reprieve so as to facilitate German war

Wiesenthal Asks Extradition of SS Colonel in Killings

Special to The New York Times

VIENNA, Sept. 4 — Simon Wiesenthal, the man who tracked down Adolf Eichmann, has appealed to the Chilean President, Salvador Allende Gossens, to extradite a German, alleged to be a major war criminal, who has lived in Chile since 1961.

In a letter sent to Dr. Allende by diplomatic courier last week and made available to the press today, Mr. Wiesenthal submitted what he termed evidence that Walter Herman Julius Rauff, a former colonel in the SS, or Elite Guard, had been responsible for the murder of at least 97,000 people in so-called gas trucks.

Mr. Wiesenthal, who heads the Jewish Documentation Center here, has made a career of tracking Nazi war criminals. His organization is sponsored by the Federation of Jews Persecuted by the Nazi Regime.

A warrant for Rauff's arrest has been issued in West Germany. The public prosecutor in Osnabrück asked for Rauff's extradition from Chile in 1963, when Rauff's whereabouts first became known. However, the Chilean Supreme Court turned down the request at the time.

The method of slaying in trucks, which were disguised with Red Cross emblems, was reportedly devised and perfected by Rauff. Exhaust fumes were channeled into the sealed interior of the trucks, killing about 50 persons at a time by suffocation in 15 to 20 minutes.

The systematic killings, mostly of Jews, took place mainly in 1941 and 1942 before Hitler's extermination camps were ready for use. The trucks were used in Byelorussia, the Ukraine, Poland and Yugoslavia.

Rauff, now 66, was a section chief in the Reich security office in Berlin, which dealt with the mass extermination of Jews. Eichmann, too, had his office here.

The figure of 97,000 victims is mentioned in a secret report by Rauff dated July 5, 1942. The document said that since December, 1941, "97,000 have been processed" without a technical hitch.

There were special instructions for emptying the trucks after each round of killing, because this could be "detrimental to the health" and morale of the SS men. In a letter to Rauff, an SS officer, speaking of morale, said that the victims' contorted faces were a very ugly sight.

Novel Calls Jews the Only Targets of Nazi Killings

By RAYMOND H. ANDERSON
Special to The New York Times

MOSCOW, Aug. 24—A quarter of a century after German troops murdered tens of thousands of Jews at Babi Yar, a ravine in Kiev, a harsh and detailed description of the massacre has been published for Soviet readers.

In a documentary novel about the mass executions in September, 1941, a Soviet writer, Anatoly Kuznetsov, rebuts a contention, advanced here when Nikita S. Khrushchev was Premier, that the victims at Babi Yar included not only Jews but also Ukrainians and Russians.

Mr. Kuznetsov emphasizes that the Germans intended to execute only Jews. He adds that a few Ukrainians and Russians were shot as a result of confusion or because the Germans feared that they had seen too much to be released.

The first part of the documentary novel, titled "Babi Yar," is printed in the latest issue of Yunost, a Soviet youth magazine, which appeared on the newsstands today.

Mr. Kuznetsov was 12 years old when the Germans occupied Kiev, his home town, on Sept. 21, 1941. A week later, all of Kiev's Jews were ordered to assemble at its northern edge. Most of them believed that they were to be resettled in another area away from the war zone. The sound of machine guns echoing from Babi Yar dispelled

Continued on Page 9, Column 3

Two of thousands of articles on German atrocities which appeared in daily newspapers

STAND ON BABI YAR ALTERED IN SOVIET

Continued From Page 1, Col. 8

the illusion. The slaughter went on for two days.

Mr. Kuznetsov's account of the massacre reflects a new attitude here about the Babi Yar atrocities. Five years ago, Yevgeny Yevtushenko, the Soviet poet, was denounced for a poem that was dedicated to the Jewish victims and criticized the absence of a monument at the site.

Mr. Yevtushenko was assailed for suggesting that lingering anti-Semitism in the Soviet Union was the reason that the authorities had not permitted the erection of a monument to the Jews. Critics of Mr. Yevtushenko said a monument only to Jews would be inappropriate on the ground that Russians and Ukrainians had also been among the victims. The poet was compelled to revise his poem.

Although the massacre at Babi Yar has been widely discussed in the West, little has been written about it here. The Great Soviet Encyclopedia says laconically that "195,000 peaceful citizens" were shot there by the Germans.

Until a few years ago, Western visitors to Kiev encountered resistance from Soviet official guides when they asked to go to Babi Yar. Recently, this reluctance has been moderated. Last month, American rabbis were permitted to conduct a memorial service at the site, which is now surrounded by apartment houses. Kiev officials say that a memorial to the Babi Yar victims will be raised soon.

Some Welcomed Germans

Mr. Kuznetsov, in describing the entry of German troops into Kiev, acknowledges that some of the older residents, hostile to the Bolshevik regime, welcomed the invaders with traditional offerings of bread and salt.

The writer depicts widespread looting of stores and apartments until the Germans imposed the death penalty for such acts.

The first days of the occupation passed quietly, Mr. Kuznetsov relates, and some of Kiev's citizens were beginning to agree with those who had welcomed the Germans as liberators.

The first sign of the coming terrorism, the writer says, was the appearance of posters playing on Ukrainian nationalist sentiments. They said, "Jews, Poles and Russians are the worst enemies of the Ukraine."

Then, on Sept. 28, announcements were put up throughout Kiev ordering "all the Jews of Kiev and its surroundings" to assemble the following day near Babi Yar at 8 A.M. The announcement instructed Jews to bring their documents, money, valuables and warm clothing.

"Any Jew who does not comply with this order and is apprehended in another area will be shot," the announcement warned.

Long before dawn the next day, the streets of Kiev were filled with thousands of Jews, carrying babies and bundles of possessions and helping the old and feeble to reach Babi Yar before the deadline, Mr. Kuznetsov wrote.

Rumors swept through the crowd that execution awaited the Jews, but most of them expected to be put on trains and removed from the combat area.

"There's a war going on," one Jew explained to quiet the more nervous people, Mr. Kuznetsov said. "They are taking us away from here to quieter areas."

"But why just the Jews?" someone asked.

"Well, because the Jews are related to the Germans, so they decided to evacuate the Jews first."

They Were Shot in the Back

At the edge of Babi Yar, related Mr. Kuznetsov, who tagged along part of the way at the rear of the crowd, German troops with machine guns checked documents. Jews were passed through the cordon. Ukrainians or Russians accompanying Jewish friends were turned back.

As the staccato sound of machine guns broke through the morning air, the Jews realized that they were being herded to death.

German troops and Ukrainian policemen collaborating with the occupants forced the Jews to undress and move to the edge of long pits. There squads of machine-gunners shot them in the back.

One Jewish woman, Dina pronincheva, now working in the Kiev Puppet Theater, escaped the bullets and managed to crawl out of the grave at night.

Years later, she told Mr. Kuznetsov of the Germans' initial efforts to sort out Ukrainians and Russians.

"Sit over there with those people," a policeman told her when she denied that she was Jewish. "We are shooting just Jews and those people will be allowed to leave."

However, the woman said, a German officer came along and said: "Shoot all of them immediately. If one of them gets out of here and spreads the word in the city, not a single Jew will show up tomorrow."

efforts. The Germans realized the importance of not destroying the infrastructure of this important manufacturing industry. And so it was that all the families of those involved in the Dutch diamond industry were returned from Westerbork to Amsterdam on July 17, 1943.

It was already dark and late in the evening of July 16, 1943 despite the long summer daylight hours in northern Holland. All those involved gathered in a small building next to the camp's railroad track, along with their meager luggage. The countdown started. All persons permitted to return to Amsterdam were called by name from the roll call. At the end of the list there was a sigh of relief as all present had heard themselves mentioned. We boarded the short train, consisting of ordinary passenger cars, and took off into the silent dark. We had to pinch ourselves to believe that Westerbork was behind and the next stop would be Amsterdam! While thousands of unfortunates had headed eastward, and many of these recent deportees were no longer alive, we were now headed west to Amsterdam to a limited freedom.

That evening of July 16, 1943 was Friday night, and we had to travel on *Shabbos*. Even though we were being released from Westerbork, it was nevertheless considered a matter of *Pikuach Nefesh* or "life threatening", since remaining behind could have led to our demise. The traveling was therefore not considered a violation of the *Shabbos* laws.

Chapter Twelve
RETURN TO AMSTERDAM

OUR TRAIN PULLED INTO AMSTERDAM'S LARGE Centraal Station, and we were informed that an air raid was in progress. Apparently, there had been some air activity over the city harbor known as *"het IJ"* (the Egg), named thus due to its egg shaped layout. Along its shores were many important ship-related installations, hence the air raid. Returning to Amsterdam was no panacea, but I preferred getting caught in a minor local air raid than being back at Westerbork. After a long time the 'all clear' alarm sounded, following which we left the railroad terminal and traveled to our house at Hemonylaan 5 (Zuid) in an open truck. Good things don't always come easy and the final leg of our trip home became another lesson of *Pikuach Nefesh*.

July 17, 1943 was a *Shabbos* and I remember there having been a discussion at the station on how we, who had just been freed from camp, could travel home without violating the *Shabbos*. However, following the 'all clear' siren, we could neither remain in the railroad terminal, nor on the street with the possibility of another air raid. Therefore, due to life threatening circumstances and the urgency of making it to a safe area, the use of a motor vehicle was condoned and the *Shabbos* law was not considered to have been desecrated.

When we returned home, we found that the inside of our house had been plundered. What was movable had either been stolen or just moved to check if something was hidden behind it. The ransackers had made toilets out of several rooms, and many carpets were filthy, torn and no longer salvageable. The first and second floor's heavy iron fireplaces, where we burned coal, had been pulled out of the wall and left in the middle of the room. Many personal items such as clothing, dishes, clocks, wall paintings, etc. were all missing. Despite these setbacks, we were happy to be home again.

Mrs. van Renen, our charlady, helped tremendously in the cleanup operation. While this tidying up was in progress we dormed at the old *Nederlandse Israelietiese Ziekenhuis* (Dutch Jewish Hospital), known as the NIZ, which was located along the *Nieuwe Keizersgracht* near the *Weesperstraat*. This was one of three Jewish hospitals that existed in Amsterdam at that time. We slept in ward rooms that had many beds but no partitions. The hospital had practically no patients since they had all been deported. The small but mostly Jewish staff was kind and friendly and the facilities were clean. The food was tasty and nutritious. We even had clean bed linens. Coming from Westerbork where we had no linens, nothing was taken for granted.

Being in the diamond industry, Father had thought he was relatively safe and had considered it unlikely that he would be deported to Westerbork in the first place. It was because of this assumed security and because many synagogues had been ransacked and robbed of their contents, that it was decided by the remaining leaders of our *shul* on the Gerard Doustraat to transfer *shul* valuables to our house. This included seven *Sifrei Torah* and some associated silver pieces. Upon our return, we found the silver stolen and the *Sifrei Torah* all over the house, including on the floor.

With the help of friends and some neighbors, we slowly returned to our old routine. Our house was made habitable, and the *Sifrei Torah* were returned to the *shul,* as it appeared that the Germans had overlooked that place of worship or more likely were unaware of its existence in the first place.

STORES SELLING SECOND-HAND GOODS APPEARED TO BE DOING a flourishing land-office business. Many items removed from homes of deported Jews found their way to these establishments. One such shop across the street from the Sarphatipark, proudly displayed such wares in their window. We recognized our *Shabbos* dishes and an old black-marble mantel piece clock.

After registering our shock, we went to the local police, whom we asked to assist us in retrieving these stolen items. They were accommodating but did ask for proof of ownership. The dishes were returned when we brought them a plate with a matching pattern. These dishes were part of a service for twenty-four which our maternal grandparents received for their wedding some fifty years earlier. We had to think a little harder to produce evidence of ownership for the clock. Then my sister Toni remembered that she had made a scrap book, which was still in the house. In it, she had sketched the clock with some of its unique features. This was drawn several years earlier under the guidance of our grandmother. Fortunately, the police accepted this as proof and the clock was restored to our possession.

A S THE WAR PROGRESSED, IT TOOK ITS TOLL ON AVAILABLE civilian supplies. By now, the chronic shortage of food was starting to affect everyone. Shopping became an arduous task and sometimes involved long trips to other parts of the city. To complicate matters, we had to wear our 'rank and file I.D. badge', the yellow star. In addition, the public trolley was off-limits to Jews. All this necessitated private transportation, but we had no cars, and even if we did, there was no gasoline to buy. Using bicycles was also no longer a viable option as these had been confiscated (or hidden) long ago. The only remaining mode of transportation was our old trusty *autoped* (scooter). It had two spoked wheel hubs with probably two inch wide, rubber balloon type, air filled tires. The job was left to me, and I would scoot all over the city with a shopping bag hung from the handle bars, picking up groceries for Mother from distant stores.

Synthetic rubber manufacture was still a fledgling industry in its infancy of development, and this material was not yet available for civilian use. Regular natural rubber had been imported from the plantations of Malaya (today the Federation of Malaysia) in southeast Asia and from Brazil in South America. This critical raw material source was therefore not accessible to Europe during the war years. Consequently, since the Germans had taken over all local rubber and rubber repair supplies for their war effort, it became impossible to replace or repair the scooter's rubber tires. After the tires were worn and torn, I had to scoot on the steel rims of the wheels. It must be realized that many of Amsterdam's roadways were paved with cobblestone or ordinary baked clay bricks set in sand, all of which produce a bumpy and noisy ride without the tires' air cushion. These roadway bumps subsequently wore down and cracked the front steel rim so that it became slightly helical in profile. I can still hear myself riding alongside the *"grachten"* (city canals) on the cobblestone pavement, clicking along on the cracked rim. I really got total use out of that scooter until its final demise.

With most of Amsterdam's Jews either deported or in hiding, it became more difficult to conduct school classes. The regular elementary school that I had attended was within five minutes by scooter or fifteen minutes on foot. But most of the staff and student body were gone. This pattern was repeated at other Jewish elementary schools as well. Accordingly, the remaining parents got together and combined resources so that all students would attend only one day school. The site chosen was a building which, in former years, housed a local *Talmud Torah*. The commute for us was over thirty minutes each way. The Dutch ate their main meal (dinner) at noontime. Therefore, I came home around twelve o'clock, had dinner and usually did some distant shopping for Mother at Klerekopers, after which I returned to school again in the early afternoon.

On my way to shop at Klerekopers in the Jordaan section of Amsterdam, I passed an open street market at the Damrak, an old and lower class section of the city. As a result of the war, there was tension in the air. It didn't take much for a loud argument to get started. Then a whole crowd would gather around and heated epithets filled the air. Unfortunately, on such occasions, the new vogue was frequently Jew bashing. Vilifying Jews caused the entire scene to become extremely ugly and made it totally undesirable for me to linger around and listen.

A S THE CITY "AUTHORITIES" BECAME CONCERNED ABOUT night-time air raids, a whole new industry came into being. All windows from which indoor electric lights could be detected after dark, now had to be furnished with opaque pull-down shades or solid shutters. In addition, a permanent wooden cap had to be installed over the edges of the pull down shades along the full window height and both ends so that no light would escape from along the sides, top or bottom. Street lights were also turned off, and flashlights could only show one small pencil size hole at the center of its lens. Furthermore, apartment hallway lights, in cases where such hallways had no window shades, required the use of special pencil hole type, "blacked out" light bulbs. That meant that the light bulb was covered with opaque black paint with a small dot of exposed glass at the bottom allowing light to shine through. All these night-time restrictions were strictly enforced by air raid wardens who patrolled the streets.

FUEL BECAME VERY SCARCE AS WELL. HOLLAND WAS BLESSED with plenty of coal mines in the south of the country, but, just like food, much of the coal production was pillaged by the Germans for their own consumption. Our house was heated by two coal burning fireplaces. The coal type used was anthracite, a very dense, hard coal that burns slowly and glows while emitting heat for hours. On the opposite side of the coal quality spectrum there exists a soft bituminous coal, which is smoky, messy and burns quickly, thereby requiring frequent firechamber refills and ash removals. The high pollution factor of this cheap coal was not even considered.

Behind our house was a huge wooden one story high silo type coal bin structure, which was filled once a year before the heating season. The coal men used to parade through our first floor corridor at delivery time, each carrying on their shoulder a large sack full of coal. Then they climbed a ladder in the backyard and dumped their load into the top of the bin until it was full. To remove the coal involved shoveling into and filling a small pail from a narrow hatchway at the bin's base. As the war progressed, it became more and more difficult to purchase any coal on the open market. I remember one black market man coming to sell a few bags of coal, which was to be of anthracite quality. After delivery, it was discovered to have been the low quality soft coal. It was a major disappointment but still better than being in the cold.

Availability of gasoline was now exclusively for German military vehicle use. The Allied strategists made it a priority to destroy Axis fuel dumps, refineries and gasoline manufacturing (coal cracking) plants. These operations were so successful that by war's end the Germans had insufficient fuel to both train their replacement fighter pilots and to fly fighter plane missions. Despite propaganda to the contrary, German fighter pilots, the bullies of the *Blitzkrieg,* had a very high casualty rate, due in part to superior Allied morale, training and equipment. Accordingly, there was an ever increasing demand for newly trained German pilots.

Forty years earlier, following development of the automobile, people called these new vehicles, "horseless carriages". Now it became a common sight to see a truck without its engine, and the former "horseless" carriage being pulled by a horse! Passenger cars with huge wooden frames mounted on their roofs were also common sights. Within those frames were large canvas containers of cooking gas to power the engine. The gas was not compressed, and one could see the canvas rippling in the wind. (It should be noted that local, north European natural gas from gas wells was not yet discovered; instead all cooking gas was the byproduct of the manufacture of coke from coal.)

F OOD WAS RATIONED AND IN VERY SCANT SUPPLY. AS IN MOST countries, there existed a black market where, for a premium price, "supplementary rations" could be obtained. Unfortunately, many could not afford this extra expense and, for those who went into hiding, the whole matter of sustenance, especially without income or a ration card, became a major burden. To alleviate this problem, I remember how one or two men used to come to our front door on a daily basis. Mother was prepared and handed them each a neatly wrapped, thick, nutritious sandwich made with love and care which then quickly disappeared into a large pocket. Few, if any, words were exchanged at this pickup, but I am sure that the food was much appreciated by their recipients as was evidenced by daily returns for refills.

Basic medical supplies were also in short supply. I remember one occasion when the word went out that certain Jews in a camp needed bandages, cottonwool and the like. A collection center was set up in the Mulo Jewish High School. No questions were asked. Mother took at least half of our own supply and sent it over. Whether all materials collected ever reached their intended destination is unknown, but we did our part. In cases as these, the Germans would frequently intercept relief supplies and either not permit their delivery or confiscate them for their own use.

M UCH MUST HAVE BEEN KNOWN TO MOTHER REGARDING the immediate and bleak outlook for Jews in Europe in general and for us in particular. Every day brought new problems and new restrictions. The constant pressure of negative news could have unnerved the strongest person. People went into hiding, some went to prison, others were deported to camps, thousands were murdered by all different methods, many lost their jobs, there were shortages of all kinds, etc. One day as I entered the kitchen, Mother was standing in front of the gas range stirring a pot of soup. I was shocked to see her weeping quietly with streaming tears. It was not usual for her to act this way. When I asked why she was crying, she remained silent. In retrospect, it is a wonder that I didn't see such visible outbreaks of her

Trial by Jury at Cleve – When Germany had equality and practiced civility. Presenting closing arguments at a closely watched, high profile murder trial. The Jury found the Jewish defendant to be innocent of all charges. (State vs. Buschhoff) Reprinted from the Israelit, [21] July 1892

feelings on a daily basis. Mother was an emotionally strong person with a vibrant personality and staunch convictions. She had full trust in Hashem; whatever would happen to us would be accepted by Mother, as decreed by the Almighty.

ONE OF MY WAR TIME HOBBIES WAS TO COLLECT PIECES OF shrapnel *(granaten)*. These were small pieces of steel, usually twisted and odd shaped, which came from exploded *flak* (acronym for: *Flieger Abwehrkanonen)* or anti-aircraft shells. My whole piggy bank overflowed with these relics of war. To obtain them, I spent hours searching the street gutters and scouring roof tops and gutters of our block. This was possible since the roofs were flat and the houses were all attached (row houses). The excitement of finding one such small metal fragment was the equivalent in those days to an American boy getting a special baseball card or a Superman comic book.

MOTHER MUST HAVE KNOWN OR FELT THAT OUR DAYS IN Amsterdam were numbered. To assure proper attire for the coming winter and summer, we went to a famous department store in downtown Amsterdam named Maison de Bonneterie. Despite their short supply in every clothing department, we nevertheless came home with our basic needs covered. It was this clothing that took me all the way through Westerbork, Bergen Belsen, Liberation, Holland and then England.

My sister Connie told me of the following sad and touching incident which she clearly recalls. She frequently joined Mother on Wednesday afternoons to go to downtown Amsterdam for shopping. Such trips usually included a stop at Maison de Bonneterie. The store's sales staff knew Mother very well as she was a frequent customer. They always greeted her in an exceptionally friendly way. On one particular day, however, when Mother and my sister entered the store, there were no greetings, no warm smiles and no sales persons came forth to assist. Finally, one sales lady took them to the street and, abashed, pointed to a small printed sign in the large showcase window. The sign read, *"VOOR JODEN VERBODEN"*, i.e the store was now off limits to Jews. The lady apologetically stated that she had been forced to display the sign.

For those persons not able to find their clothing needs in a store due to the ever dwindling supplies, tailors and seamstresses developed a new enterprise. Men's old suits and lady's used dresses were cut down, taken apart, recut and redesigned into boy's pants and jackets and girl's skirts and dresses. Torn socks were never thrown away but were darned.

Russian Jewish Cobbler – Reprinted from the Israelit,[21] August 1891.

To assure availability of shoe leather for soles and heels, people purchased large sheets of leather when these were still available. They would then cut off the necessary sized piece at home and bring it to the shoemaker along with their shoes to be re-soled. Rubber heels and soles were hardly used in the early 1940's. Later on, shoes were no longer left overnight for repairs, for if the shoemaker were arrested then the shoes would be lost.

AS THE SIMPLE DAILY ROUTINES BECAME MORE DIFFICULT, I perceived the notion that I was witnessing a passing phase in our lives. As a result, it became a constant preoccupation of mine to more carefully observe my parents' distinctive nuances, how they looked, acted, reacted, what they did, what went on in *shul,* the *nigunim,* etc. It was my intention to never forget our surroundings of that time and how my dear parents adapted themselves to them.

As time went on, there seemed to be little possibility of escaping the fate of the rest of Dutch Jewry. Immigration to Palestine was always a dream. The first step required was the acquisition of *Palestina Papieren* (visa). The British, who governed Palestine, wanted to placate the local Arabs and hence did not accommodate this process. Accordingly, not too many such papers were issued. On August 13, 1943, the Dutch Red Cross issued a perfunctory but useless memo to Father, which stated that Palestine Papers were applied for and that "prospects are good". However, of the 150,000 Dutch Jews, perhaps 250 persons benefitted from such papers during the war. (Refer to a later chapter)

YOM KIPPUR 1943, WAS AN UNFORGETTABLE OCCASION. We davened in the house of Dr. Seligman Ph.D, rather than in *shul,* which would have been almost empty. Dr. Seligman was a very knowledgeable person who had frequently given *droshos* in our *shul* on *Shabbos* morning. He was also a teacher at my oldest sister's school, the *Joodse HBS (Hogere Burger School)* or Jewish High School, and he was famous for his father's collection of Judaica books. This was the school that was attended by Anne Frank of diary fame. Even the Germans knew of his extensive library and one sad day they drove up with a large truck to cart away his entire collection. [On *Succos,* 5753, Mr. and Mrs. Charles Bendheim of New York organized a large and memorable Prins family gathering in *Yerusholayim.* It was hosted by Else Bendheim, a great granddaughter of Liepman Prins[2]. There, for the first time in fifty years, I met the widow of Dr. Seligman o.h. She related how the Germans took

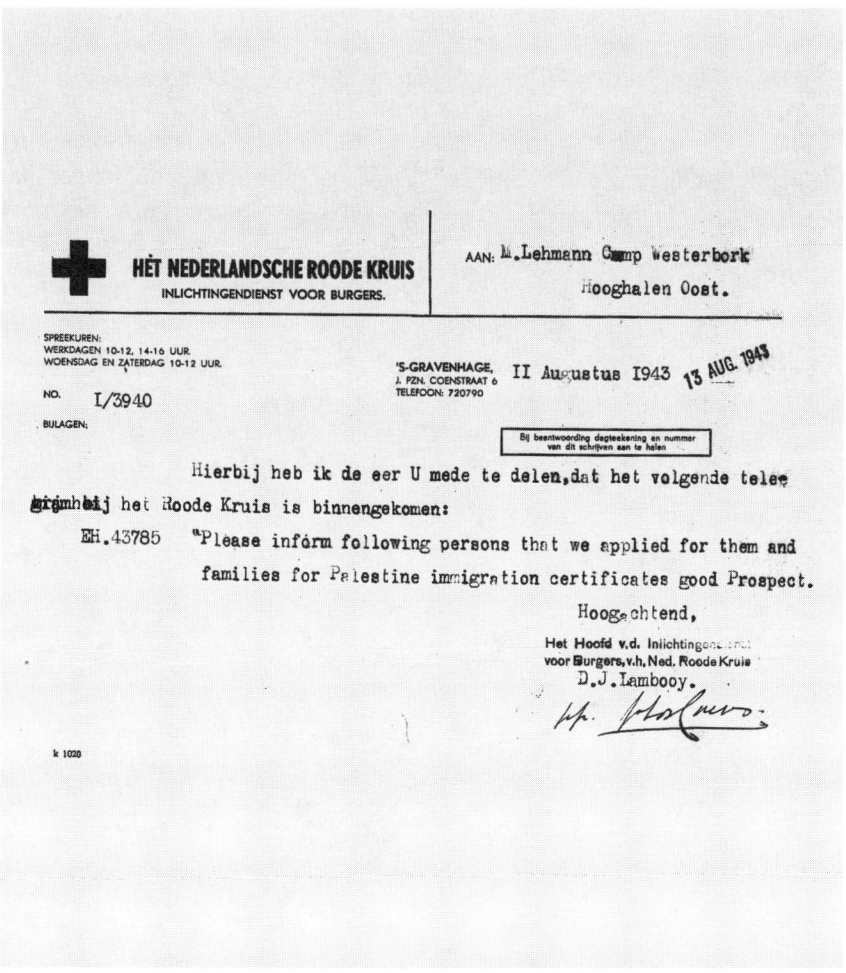

*Communication sent to Westerbork, August 13, 1943
in reference to application for Palestine papers.*

their family to the Theresienstadt Concentration Camp for the purpose of cataloging his own stolen library. Many of his valuable books were looted and lost in this greedy book heist. In Amsterdam, I still remember the Seligman *succah* which used a woven mat for *schach*. This was an unusual feature as such man-made coverings may not be used for *schach* except in cases where the mat is dedicated solely for that purpose.[a]

That *Yom Kippur* night we came in from the cold stark street to a well lighted, warm library-living room, a real contrast and welcome. Albeit the prospect that this *Yom Kippur minyan* might be our last in Amsterdam, for

---

a. *Mishna Berurah,* 629:6,17

*Kiddush Levonah, Sanctification of the Moon.
Reprinted from the Israelit,[21] September 1898*

the foreseeable future was not lost on us and made the entire scene extremely emotional. Alas!, we already had many brethren who were now our Heavenly advocates. After *Maariv*, father even got the *kibbud* of reciting one of the *Shirei Yichud*. When we walked home afterwards, the streetlights were off and house lights were blacked out, but Hashem saw to it that we had plenty of light from His bright moon in the cool crisp clear sky. Walking through older sections of the city was not easy, considering that most of the *grachten* have no safety railings along their banks. (It should be noted that all *grachten* are flanked by street pavements up to the water's edge on one or both of their sides.) As we walked on the cobblestone roadway late that night, there was an eerie silence except for the jingling bells on a horse's neck from a distant horsedrawn carriage. The hundred to four hundred year old houses alongside the moonlit *grachten* and cobblestone streets lent a medieval storybook touch to that memorable night. To me it appeared as a scene come to life from the middle ages.

That *Succos* we had our regular *succah* assembled on our second floor back porch. As in previous years, Mr. Reusink and his sons lowered the heavy panels by hoist from the fourth floor attic to the porch below. After the *Chag,* they disassembled all panels and neatly returned everything to the attic – never to be used again.

OUR RETURN FROM WESTERBORK WAS SHORTLIVED. ON the night of November 17, 1943, when we were all in bed and fast asleep, the doorbell rang. Our parents knew who it was. They opened up to a *Gestapo* officer and a Dutch S.D. *(Sicherheits Dienst)* or "security officer". We were told to get dressed and depart with them. Just like the nocturnal predators of the wild stalk their prey after dark, so too did the sadistic *Gestapo* develop a reputation of pouncing on their victims during the night time. The S.D.s were nothing more than amateur sleuths who sold their conscience for a paltry six Guilders for every Jew they managed to arrest.

It was Wednesday, and because of the many uncertainties, Mother had already baked an assortment of cakes for *Shabbos.* Some of this cake was intended to be given away to those who had no *Shabbos* food.

To give us time to dress and get ready, Mother took the *Gestapo* officer to the kitchen and gave him several pieces of homemade *Streusel cake,* which he readily ate. My bedroom was on the third floor and, on the way down, I stopped at the second floor living room. There, Father had his large glass doored bookcase. I opened the wooden side door and took a pocketsize, leather bound *siddur*. It was a Dutch Roedelheim edition printed in 1907. Not to leave home without a *siddur* was very important to me. By this time, Father was standing there also and with his usual patience gave me moral support. I asked for permission to take the *siddur* which was, of course, readily granted. Then we discussed what else to take. Father suggested that I take the *Lehmann Hagadah* which I had received as a present from the widow of Mr. Meir HaLevi Goldschmidt, o.h. (The *Lehmann Hagadah* has a lengthy commentary, which was started by my great grandfather Horav Meir Lehmann and was completed posthumously by my grandfather *Hachover* Osher Lehmann. The commentary was in German and is replete with *Hashkofah, Medroshim* and other *Chazal* [20]. It is suitable for year round study and reading enjoyment.)

I carried these two *seforim* with me wherever I went in those years, from barrack to barrack, from camp to camp and from country to country.

Being encumbered by toting this additional and not insignificant burden was never a serious consideration. The Hagadah was more important to me than most of the other items that I carried. This Hagadah which accompanied me through Bergen Belsen I have proudly used on every *Pesach* since my liberation. Over the years I have read and studied its commentary from cover to cover. Every time I use it, I am reminded of that *Hagadah's* journey, starting with the memorable conversation with Father in front of our Amsterdam bookcase, on that dreadfully dark night, and how Hashem delivered me from the cruel German bondage. The *Hagadah's* commentary by my great grandfather remains to me a constant and visible sign of *zechus avos*. The teachings ensconced within this magnum opus is an enduring testimony to our family's lofty Judaic goals and Torah values.

The *siddur* was used frequently by myself in both Westerbork and Bergen Belsen. [Forty-eight years later, I attended the *chassenah* of our niece, Shiffy Rubinstein, in Yerusholayim in May of 1991. This occasion was a family milestone, as Shiffy was the second to the last grandchild of my parents to get married. I took along that pocket *siddur*, and standing by the *Kosel Ma'aravi*, I opened the *siddur* to the second *Brocha* of the *Shemona Esrei* where it reads:

> Who is like You O Master of mighty deeds, and who is comparable to You, O King Who causes death and restores life and causes salvation to grow.

I held this page tight against the large stones. The persons around me must have thought this action a bit odd, but it brought back many thoughts and much appreciation. With tear-stained eyes, I gave thanks to the *Rebono Shel Olam* for answering my *tefillos,* many from these pages, in our People's darkest hours. *"MiPi Ollalim VeYonakim Yosadeto Oz".* From the mouths of children and sucklings hast Thou founded might."[b]

I often wonder how, with a *Gestapo* officer and a Dutch S.D. thug downstairs, my father and I were able to stand calmly before a bookcase and discuss what *seforim* I should take. Of course, all books had to be hand-carried along with everything else that we planned to take with us. There were no movers or car trunks to put in another box, suitcase or knapsack.

THIS TIME, I DID NOT RETURN TO HEMONYLAAN 5 UNTIL AFTER the war and then only as a young orphan. At ten years old I was already exposed to what others fortunately haven't experienced in a lifetime. Alas, much more was to come. We walked in the dark, down Hemonylaan to Hemonystraat, then to the Sarphatistraat and over the Amstel River bridge to an old abandoned theater building. There, the Gestapo officer and S.D. left us off. Inside, we met many of the other members of the *Diamant Groep* (Diamond Group). After several hours, the men were released but the women and children were sent back to Westerbork. Thus at the age of ten I had the dubious distinction of having been arrested twice – for non-criminal, non-offenses.

We traveled by railroad passenger car to Westerbork, while Father went back to the house to take out whatever he could salvage. Unfortunately, Father was too careworn and unprepared. As a result, he took mostly what he thought of at the spur of the moment. He walked out of the house in the pitch dark with such things as towels, linens, etc., whatever he could carry. It was not a moment too soon, for as he left and closed the door behind him he saw a horde of a dozen S.D.'s converging on the house, each with their own pencilpoint flashlight. These scavengers had one thing in mind – to do what they knew best, to loot, plunder and prey on the weak.

WHILE ALONE IN AMSTERDAM, FATHER WAS FREQUENTLY invited to eat with the Joseph Strauss family, later of Brooklyn, New York. (In January of 1994, I met his widow, Mrs. Lola Strauss at a *chassenah* of Yaakov Finkel's granddaughter. She related how Father, along with Mr. Braunschweig of Switzerland, ate all *Shabbos* meals at their home. The Strauss family was able to remain in Amsterdam by claiming Swiss citizenship.)

---

b. Tehillim, 8:3

Chapter Thirteen

RETURN TO WESTERBORK – WAY STATION TO ARYAN LAIRS

OUR SECOND STAY IN WESTERBORK LASTED SEVEN months and took us through the cold winter of 1943-1944. With Father in the city, we children and Mother became literally hostages, satisfying the German guarantee that their prize would not disappear from sight.

By the time we arrived in Westerbork, the population of the camp had dwindled significantly due to the constant deportations to Germany, Czechoslovakia and Poland. As a result, we stayed in a large public barrack only for a short time and then were transferred to a barrack with small apartments, which offered more privacy. We shared this unit with the Joseph Werner family, whom we knew well from Amsterdam and later from the Amsterdam suburb of Soesdyk, where they resided in the early 1940's.

I also remember the family Kruskal living in one of these camp apartments. They were there since the start of the war, and Mrs. Kruskal had been a good friend of Mother from the days when she lived in Frankfurt am Main. With Father in Amsterdam, we were often invited to the Kruskals for a Friday night meal. The food was more or less the low quality camp food but, the warm and friendly *Shabbos* ambience was most memorable.

A medium sized circus tent that was able to accommodate three to four hundred persons had been erected to alleviate a possible camp population explosion. Deportations of prisoners, however, kept up with new arrivals and, the tent was therefore used instead for non-dormitory functions. Children met there for group singing, listening to stories, presenting plays and also for some studying. The adults also had many gatherings in that tent.

My sister Toni reminded me of a distinctive Friday evening *davening* at the tent *minyan*. Many of the participants sensed this *Shabbos* to be their last one in Holland before being sent to an extermination camp like Auschwitz. The *davening* was a moving experience, full of heart wrenching *tefillos* and earnest passions, begging Hashem to remember in His wrath His capricious and wayward children with kindness and life. Those impassioned supplications and streams of tears were surely borne in haste by the *mallachim* to the Almighty to beseech and plead for annulment of all evil decrees.

When *Pesach* arrived, *Pesach* products were hardly available. *Matzos* could not be baked and food was in short supply. To meet the needs of the hour, special permission was granted by the *Rabbonim* in 1944 to eat legumes (beans, peas and lentils) on *Pesach*. It is noted that while *Ashkenazim* do not eat legumes or their derivatives on *Pesach,* the *Sephardic* community allows its consumption. Due to the crushing effect of the war, an exclusive exception was made for the *Pesach* of 1944.

FATHER WAS PERMITTED TO VISIT WESTERBORK SEVERAL TIMES during these seven months. Each time he came from Amsterdam was a major celebration. Seeing him again, talking with him, eating and walking with him all had special significance. He would update us on all world politics, which he heard from listening to his highly illegal BBC shortwave news programs. We also heard the latest saga of the German preoccupation with the diamond industry. Of course, Father would bring along all kinds of food and other items which one could not obtain in the camp. Each such visit was for approximately three or four days.

MEETING THE SHOE REQUIREMENTS OF ALL WESTERBORK inhabitants was a major task. There were no camp shoe stores and no shoemakers and, even if there were, there would have been no shoes or leather to meet all needs. Despite the fact that Holland was known for its dairy products and multitudes of cattle herds, there was a large deficit of milk, cheese, meat and leather, since the Germans had plundered most of these products. To meet this footwear challenge, many of us at camp were issued *klompen.* These were shoes carved of light weight pine wood. My regular leather shoes were put away and henceforth I wore only *klompen.* Initially, these wooden shoes were extremely uncomfortable, but by using a little newspaper for padding and allowing the feet to get used to this punishment one got around very well. *Klompen* are not flexible, as regular shoes are, but for purposes of walking on unpaved paths and roads, they are much warmer and dryer, especially in the winter. Unfortunately, I had to turn in these *klompen* when we departed for Bergen Belsen.

As in previous months, the ranks of the Westerborkers were constantly thinned by deportations. No distinction was made for age or physical condition. I remember one transport that was headed for Bergen Belsen. As I watched the train, two men suddenly passed by carrying a stretcher with an old lady. After they passed, I realized that the person being carried was none other than Grandfather's sister, Tante Emma Prins who was by now probably eighty-three years old. Here was a lady who could only walk with difficulty, was hard of hearing and extremely frail but was not permitted to live out her years in Holland.

Allied air activity was constantly on the rise. Unfortunately, casualties did exist on the Allied side. On one occasion, I remember how an Allied bomber plane was crippled and lost altitude. It limped over the camp at a height of perhaps two hundred feet. Several hours later, the word around camp was that one of the airmen was captured and was now tied to the camp fence. My friends and I got to see him from a distance of perhaps three hundred feet. Even though we ourselves were prisoners, we were concerned about this man's safety. Despite the fact that Germany was a co-signer of the Geneva Convention on Prisoners of War, they were known not to abide by it. After the war, it became general knowledge that the Germans executed numerous Allied prisoners of war, especially if they were found to be Jewish.

WE SURVIVED THE WINTER OF 1943-1944, AND NOW IT was our turn to be deported to the East. Father, and, most of his colleagues arrived in Westerbork from Amsterdam on May 18, 1944. On May 19, 1944 we departed for Bergen Belsen. We said goodbye to the few remaining acquaintances and friends still in camp and boarded the 93rd transport to depart from Westerbork. The train we rode in had passenger cars with individual cabins. On board were a total of two hundred and thirty eight souls, most of whom were never to return.

The Germans sent a total of ninety nine transport trains from Westerbork to the East, during the twenty six month period from July 15, 1942 to September 13, 1944. These trains each carried a passenger load of as few as one hundred and one victims and as many as three thousand and seventeen crammed prisoners. Most trains consisted of cattle cars, unheated in the bitter cold winters and uncooled in the scorching hot summers.

In *Yesoepar Lahdor* [7]a *(Let Coming Generations be Told)* are listed details of those sad Westerbork transports and their Aryan lair destinations. Following is a summary:

No. of Transports	Destination	No. of deported persons
65	Auschwitz	57,800
17	Sobibor	34,313
7	Theresienstadt	4,771
8	Bergen Belsen	3,724
Total No. of persons sent from Westerbork		**100,608**

These 100,608 abducted civilians were mostly Jewish, and the vast majority of these prisoners never returned. The total pre-war Jewish population of Holland was approximately 150,000 persons. Thus, two out of three Dutch Jews were deported by way of Westerbork. As previously mentioned, there were other points of departure and routes of deportation from Holland as well. Alas, those were the years when I was taught firsthand the meaning of Yirmiyohu's heartrending lamentation: "My eyes shed streams of water on account of the devastation of my people."b

The last transport to Sobibor departed Westerbork on July 20, 1943, following which there was a prisoner uprising in that mass murder camp. The last transport that left Westerbork for Auschwitz was on September 3, 1944. Soon thereafter, that infamous death camp was evacuated in front of the advancing Red army. The Soviet troops liberated Auschwitz on January 27, 1945.

---

a. page 110.
b. Eichah, 3:48.

Chapter Fourteen

BERGEN BELSEN – DAILY ENCOUNTERS

THE TRAIN RIDE TO BERGEN BELSEN WAS AN INTERESTING one. As we crossed the German border, a different kind of architecture came into view. The country houses seemed bigger and the pitched roofs were much higher. Some roofs had two levels of dormers, something I had not seen in Holland. At one point, when the train stopped to change locomotives, probably near the German border, we asked some soldiers walking alongside the train to give us water from a trackside manual water pump. They gave it to us grudgingly, and then told us we weren't permitted to take any pens or pencils with us. "All must be relinquished, and anyone caught with such writing instruments would be shot." We did not take them seriously and only a token number of pens and pencils were handed over. The soldiers were satisfied with their small booty and the journey continued about an hour later without incident.

While en route, our train briefly stopped at a local railroad station. On the track right next to us, along the next station platform, was a trainload of young German soldiers in their late teens or early twenties, who were probably on their way to the fighting front. After they realized we were Jewish, they made some of the most hateful and disgusting gestures I had ever seen.

Bergen Belsen is in the northwest region of Germany, near the city of Hannover. The camp did not have its own railroad station but used the station of the neighboring town of Celle.

Interestingly enough, my Grandmother Emma (Oppenheimer) Wallerstein was born in Celle and grew up in Hannover. [In fact, I have one of her *Machzorim* where she wrote in her beautiful script EMMA OPPENHEIMER – HANNOVER, LANGELAUBE 36. It was customary in her times to write the city before the street address.]

THIS WAS THE FIRST TIME I STEPPED ON GERMAN SOIL. MY feelings were ambivalent. On the one hand, this land was home to our ancestors for at least the last fourteen hundred years, where they grew and prospered physically and spiritually. The *realpolitik,* however, was that Berlin's national goals went awry, we were kidnapped from another land and this generation of Germans had mutated to a nation of murderers and thieves.

As we got off the train, we saw a group of men working on the station platform. One waved to us and we recognized him. It was Bob Posen – our second cousin and a grandson of my great-aunt Emma Prins. He later died at Bergen Belsen of malnutrition due to hard labor. The modus operandi of the Germans was to force their prisoners to perform manual labor that was unreasonable and physically taxing and not commensurate with the persons' food allowance or physical condition. In Bergen Belsen, this work included digging, breaking stones, chopping wood, cutting and carrying wood, etc. As a result, many succumbed and died of exhaustion, malnutrition and disease.

From Celle to Bergen Belsen we were driven in the back of an open truck with a German soldier standing guard, his gun slung over the shoulder. We drove through the countryside where everything was green and sunny. What a pity, I thought to waste nature's beauty on these Germans.

We arrived at Bergen Belsen on May 19, 1944. As we entered the Dutch section of the camp, we disembarked on the large open center grounds used for *"Appell"* (roll call). A large group of children, aged seven to thirteen, stood at a distance, giving us the once over and checking out these new arrivals.

It is now necessary to describe Bergen Belsen so that the reader will understand our handicaps in this concentration camp and under what subhuman conditions we were made to live. The criminal German people treated us as outlaws and provided facilities unfit for humans.

Bergen Belsen Described:

AT THE TIME OF ARRIVAL, THE CAMP WAS OFFICIALLY KNOWN as an *"Austauschlager"* or "exchange camp". There was one paved center roadway through the camp and various compounds alongside accessing to this road. Each compound had its own classification of prisoners. Initially, ours consisted of only Dutch speaking Jews. With the exception of those in our Diamond Group, most, if not all, other prisoners in our compound had passports and papers from neutral countries, e.g. Uruguay, Honduras, Ecuador, etc. Further down the road, in another compound, was a group of Americans who must have been stranded in Germany when the war broke out and were now considered aliens. A third compound consisted of men, who were the only prisoners dressed in striped prison garb with their hair shaved off. Their background was unknown. In a fourth compound were Russian prisoners of war. As time progressed, additional compounds were added, e.g. the *"Frauenlager"* (Women's Camp) where there were mostly Russian, Yugoslavian, Hungarian and other east European women, almost all of whom were Jewish. In addition, as new prisoners arrived, the Dutch speaking camp was given more barracks to house Albanians and some North African Jews from the Libyan city of Benghazi.

At the far end of the camp's main road stood a small brick house with a thirty foot tall brick chimney alongside. That was known as the crematorium. It was operated by two men who lived there and who were not permitted to communicate with anyone. In their spare time, they made brooms by tying up dried, thin stalks of heath vegetation. These brooms were then dumped at night over our fence and those of other compounds to sweep the barrack floors.

Next along the road was the camp kitchen. There were actually several kitchens throughout the camp; this one served our Dutch compound. It was administered by an SS officer and workers were from our section of the camp. Uncle Max Finkel and his son Jackie (Yaakov) were among these workers.

A little further down from the kitchen, alongside the main road, stood very tall gallows. It was a wood frame consisting of two high square posts and a header beam across their top. The ground all around this frame was paved in concrete. I never saw the gallows in use. However, its mere sight prominently displayed at the camp's center, added to the unpleasant atmosphere.

Towards the entrance gates of the camp and near the Russian prisoner of war compound, was the bathhouse. To designate this structure as a bathhouse is a misnomer, as it only had showers for washing purposes. For the duration of our stay in the Dutch compound, we showered every six or eight weeks.

Beyond the camp gates were storerooms. These contained regular supplies required to operate a camp. After Liberation, these store houses were found to be bursting full of canned food and other packaged food supplies shipped by the Red Cross from Portugal. While the prisoners were starving and dying of malnutrition and disease, the sadistic Germans kept this food from being distributed. This was a typical German S.O.P. (Standard Operating Procedure).

Aside from the above fenced off compounds and buildings, the camp had many other facilities, including a bakery for making the camp's bread, a truck service area, soldier barracks and officer *"Kazernen"* (barracks), a shooting practice range, etc.

Around each compound were six foot high barbed wire fences, with the wire strung vertically and horizontally between wooden posts. A low single wire electric fence followed by a double barbed wire fence surrounded the entire camp perimeter, with barbed wire coils between these double fences. Guard towers were located at uniform intervals along the outside fence. A beautiful thick pine tree forest lay beyond this security perimeter.

The barracks were squalid, flimsy and austere one story wooden structures. At the center of each barrack were long trough type sinks with cold water only and lavatories. All washing facilities were located within a concrete and brick structure and below a wooden roof. The beds were of a triple decker type constructed of wooden or metal frames and provided with dust producing rough mattresses. The beds were closely spaced with one person per bed. An eating and sitting area was set up in our barrack between the men's and women's sections. Our barrack was directly adjacent to the *Appell* grounds where the daily roll-calls were conducted.

Bergen Belsen landscape sketch of a remote corner of our compound. I drew this sketch in camp at age eleven. Shown are other compounds in rear left and rear right, a latrine, a low electric fence in front of an intracamp security fence and a guard tower.

As in Westerbork, the Bergen Belsen double and triple decker beds had no ladders or sideboards. The bedframes and mattresses had to be used as ladder rungs for climbing, a situation not conducive for friendly relations. In addition, there were no boards below the mattresses, thereby allowing for a good measure of dust to fall on the lower beds every time someone stirred above. The mattresses were probably filled with wood shavings and/or some straw. Mattress covers consisted of a coarsely woven, rough, low quality cloth material.

Daily Routine:

EVERYONE IN OUR COMPOUND WAS COUNTED EVERY SINGLE morning. This was to make sure no one had escaped. For this purpose, there was a large open, unpaved flat area, void of any vegetation, called the *Appell* grounds (roll-call area). Here, all persons were lined up according to their barracks, the men of each barrack in one group and then the women of that barrack in the next group. Following a short gap of some six feet a group from the next barrack gathered in a similar fashion. We lined up in three rows with the tallest in the rear and the shortest in the front row. An SS officer, by the name of Otto, did all the counting. We nicknamed him Napoleon because like his namesake he frequently tucked his right hand between his jacket buttons. To set the mood these despised SS officers wore a silver colored skull and bones brooch on their uniforms' collar. The groups formed a giant circle around the *Appell* grounds. Each group was required to stand at attention when its turn came to be counted. Since Mother spoke fluent German, while most others only spoke Dutch, it became her task to accompany SS Officer Mueller (nicknamed *"der rote Mueller"* since he was a redhead) to the barracks to count the sick, the handicapped, aged and the invalid inmates who could not possibly make it to *Appell*.

More often than not, the totals didn't jibe and the counting started all over again. On such occasions, we had to stand around for at least an additional hour, at which time Father would reminisce of the old times with his parents and grandparents and of his World War I experiences. On days when the count checked out, everyone would breathe a sigh of relief and we were dismissed to return to our barracks. I remember the cold winter days of late 1944. We stood in the biting cold air, typical for northern Europe, with thin, inadequate clothing. My toes, fingers and ears really suffered. When I returned to the barracks, I would take off my shoes and sit on a wooden bench warming my aching toes with my aching cold fingers and hands.

Cleanliness and neatness had to be maintained in the barracks. For this reason a German SS officer would visit the barracks daily to check up. To the German non-Jews, it was improper for a male to be indoors with his head covered by a cap or hat. Thus, when such a SS S.O.B. officer would enter, the person in charge of the barrack would say in a loud voice:

"Achtung!, Muetzen Ab! (Attention!, Hats Off!)

We then had to stand at attention with our hats or caps in our hand as this uncouth German lowlife walked around to check up.

Those officers were the most rude and ambrageous individuals one can imagine. It is not that these Germans were ignorant on matters of etiquette, since for themselves they expected to be addressed by the use of the German language's formal personal pronoun *"sie"* (thou) instead of the informal *"du"* (you). For simple and minor matters they yelled, spouted and barked at us with vitriolic hatred. Some sample expletives were: *"Du Sau Jude!", "Du Schwein Jude!", "Du verfluchter Jude!", "Du Hund Jude!",* etc. ("You sow Jew!", "You pig Jew!", "You cursed Jew!", "You dog Jew!", etc.) [To this day, I am reminded of a dog's bark when I remember their shouts and find myself imitating those despicable hoodlums by barking like a dog. When we sing *Mo'oz Tzur* on *Chanuka,* the first stanza mentions how Hashem saved us from the "barking" oppressor. The Germans took their cue from these ancient tyrants; may their fate be the same!]

The thick pine tree forest outside the camp had its own secrets. On some days, one heard the staccato sounds of machine gun fire coming from within the forest to the rear of the camp. At the same time, in an open clearing next to that forest German soldiers were seen throwing objects over long distances. The official version was that all this was practice at machine gunning and hand grenade throwing. Seemingly unconnected with this was an interesting phenomenon. On some mornings, at the corner fence of our compound facing the crematorium chimney, there lay a pile of shoes against the fence's inboard side. There were so many shoes that they formed a wedged shaped pile that was the height of the fence by about eight feet in width and extending perhaps six feet away from the fences' base. This amounted to a few hundred pairs of shoes per occasion, tossed over the fence during the night, probably by the two men who lived at the crematorium. The shoes in question were men's over the ankle type and brown in color. The Russian prisoners of war, whom the Germans hated profusely, were disappearing from camp at the same time. By liberation only a handful of Russian soldiers remained.

From the book, *To My Dear Children*,[9]a regarding the ten meter (thirty three feet) deep hole Max Finkel helped dig, he wrote: "…after the war it became clear that the (33 foot deep) hole instead of a sewage plant, actually was a mass grave into which the bodies of the dead were cast each day."

Accordingly, putting all bits of information together, it appears that the machine gun sounds we heard were not military practice sessions but mass murder in progress. The shoes must have been "salvaged" before the victims were buried. Prisoners of war do not carry spare shoes. These shoes were subsequently disassembled by persons in our camp[9]b and then "recycled" for German use.

---

a. page 140
b. page 142

Chapter Fifteen
BERGEN BELSEN – CHALLENGES AND EXPECTATIONS

THE FOOD WAS PREPARED IN THE CAMP'S KITCHEN JUST across the main road outside our compound. The food's quality and quantity were wholly inadequate, the results of wartime scarcity and German unwillingness to be accommodating to their prisoners. The bread, also known as *"kuch,"* was a small, rectangular shaped, dark brown colored bread, which probably contained more ground-up legumes, i.e. peas and beans than wheat flour. After the daily ration of bread was picked up by several of each barrack's occupants, it was sliced by placing a tape measure along its top. Everyone received approximately two and a half centimeters (one inch) of bread. Other food frequently consisted of watery soup containing diced turnip cubes, sometimes pumpkin soup *(kuerbis)*, spinach, cooked potatoes, etc. Each of these represented a "meal". On one occasion, I remember the spinach being full of small white colored worms. It obviously had not been cleaned prior to cooking. At that time, the camp's *Kommandant*

(Commander) was Adolf Haas. He was a relatively reasonable person, and when he received complaints of the wormy spinach, he had all the spinach recalled, and subsequently new food was prepared and distributed.

The European war theatre had fronts along its western, eastern and southern approaches. Within less than three weeks after arriving at Bergen Belsen, fighting on the Western front commenced. That starting date was code named D-Day and occurred on June 6, 1944 with the Allied invasion at the Normandy beaches in northwestern France. The logistics of this invasion were unprecedented. In the initial twenty four hours, a well equipped fighting force of no less than one hundred and fifty six thousand men were ferried across the thirty mile wide English Channel. There were so many ships that some Allied pilots described the scene thusly; "you could have walked across the Channel". Then there was the southerly front where the Allies had already cleaned out the Axis troops from north Africa and were now wending their way northward along the Italian peninsula. Since the Germans no longer trusted the Italian army, all fighting was taken over by the German troops. In eastern Europe, the Germans were bogged down in Russia, Poland, the Baltic States, Hungary, Bulgaria, Yugoslavia, Rumania, Greece, the Balkan states, etc. For the Germans, this part of the fighting became a nightmare, a bottomless pit that drained their reserves and energies. Fatalities in the Slavic states were enormous, and it was therefore considered a punishment for a German to be assigned to the "Eastern Front".

Word must have gotten out that *Kommandant* Haas was reasonable to his Jewish prisoners. Soon thereafter, he was reassigned to the "Eastern Front". After an interim camp commander, *Kommandant* Haas was replaced by an animal of a German with a capital "A" whose name was Josef Kramer. May all those of his kind never know happiness. Kramer stayed on until Bergen Belsen was liberated by the Allied forces. After that, he was known in the international press as "the Beast of Belsen". He was convicted for war atrocities at Hamelin, Germany and hanged by the Allies on December 13, 1945.

On occasion, our Dutch compound was "treated" to food specials, none of which were particularly gastro-friendly or complementary to the palate and colon. These included a large truck load of canned red beets, limburger cheese and *blutwurst* (sausage made of blood).

On one or two occasions I recall that the Germans distributed to each prisoner a small, light green colored soap bar. Before complimenting this magnanimity, let me explain that the soap had such a high coarse sand

> **BELSEN,** bel'zən, was a notorious concentration camp in Hitler's Germany. It was situated in the village of Belsen (population, 1961, 166), now in the West German state of Lower Saxony. Like others of its kind, the camp contained a large proportion of Jewish prisoners, many of whom were murdered. When the survivors—over 50,000 sick and starving—were liberated by the British army on April 15, 1945, 10,000 unburied corpses were found. Soon afterward some 13,000 others died from malnutrition, disease, and the effects of torture. On Dec. 13, 1945, 11 persons convicted of atrocities at the Belsen and Auschwitz camps were hanged at Hameln.

From Encyclopedia Americana, 1993 Edition
Copyright 1993 by Grolier Incorporated. Reprinted by permission [8]

content that it was practically useless. One could not use it to scrub one's hands.

There was absolutely no possibility of purchasing any food from the outside, there were no vegetable gardens – not even weeds or trees – and the only source of food was the camp's kitchen, which was supervised by an SS officer. Anyone caught smuggling food from the kitchen to the camp was in mortal danger. Mother, did, on occasion, go to the kitchen to cut and peel carrots and on her return was able to smuggle out some small pieces of raw carrots in her apron pockets.

As previously mentioned, Bergen Belsen was an *"Austauschlager"* (exchange camp) and there were two groups of prisoners who made it out of camp to safety.

In the summer of 1944, the Germans wanted to repatriate a group of several hundred ethnic Germans living in Palestine (now Israel). To permit their return to Germany the Germans had to agree to exchange these persons with an equal number of Jewish prisoners. In Bergen Belsen, there were many who qualified, according to German imposed parameters. To my knowledge, they had to have a *Palestina Papier* (Palestine papers - i.e. a visa) and they could not be of military age. As a result, approximately two hundred and fifty persons came into question. They included many of our friends and relatives, including Rabbi and Mrs. Eliezer Dunner with daughter Margot, Rabbi and Mrs. Tall, Mr. and Mrs. Jacob Oxeman, the Kruskaal family, etc. Since most of these persons were either old or had young children, permission was granted for Rabbi Dunner's son, Sally Dunner, M.D. to accompany the group, despite the fact that he was of military age. The group went by train and traveled via Turkey, a neutral country, to Palestine.

The second group of Jews released from Bergen Belsen came from Hungary and were known as the Kasztner Transport. [Note: many poignant details on the Kasztner Transport and a scathing critique on the methods employed by Dr. Kasztner in implementing the group's release may be found in Ben Hecht's book *Perfidy*[11]]. These men, women and children were temporarily housed in barracks in a newly formed compound next to ours. Prior to the group's arrival, a barbed wire fence was hastily erected between our two compounds so that there would be no communication between us. To enforce that silence, the Germans posted sentries on our side of the fence who were supposed to keep the two groups apart and incommunicado. In the late summer of 1944, the Germans were running short of manpower and were forced to draft men into military uniform who were in their late fifties and early sixties. One of these sentries was such a person. He was skinny and old and his face looked more like a living skull. We nicknamed him Don Quixote after the well-known Seventeenth century Spanish hero of Cervantes' famous satire. Don Quixote was the horseman who did "battle" with phantom windmills. The Hungarian Jews numbered close to sixteen hundred persons. In later years we discovered that this group included the famous Rabbi Joel Teitelbaum, known as the Satmarer Rebbe. Also in the group were Mr. and Mrs. Chaim (Edmund) Stern with their children, Willie, Alfred and Tezza (Stephanie). Refer to Appendix A for an experience of a related family Stern.

One day, while standing outside our barrack, I looked through the fence to the camp road as I did on many days. There, down the road, at the far side of our compound appeared a quiet human sea of people streaming on foot, from their compound towards the camp's exit. The group's destination was the neutral country of Switzerland. Following their crossing of the Swiss border, they were interned near the city of Montreux until after the war.

My dear wife's uncle and aunt, the late Mr. and Mrs. Moses and Recha Bollag lived in Montreux with their nine children. Despite impositions by the Swiss authorities, the Bollag family was able to be of significant assistance to many of these expatriates.

While wandering around camp I once happened to come upon a group of twenty-five children of my age. They were standing in three neat rows and were being guided and taught by a young man to sing various Jewish songs. Uninvited, I took my spot alongside the middle row and joined in the singing. They were from several barracks and would meet on occasion to sing, a sort of "camp" glee club. I remember one time when we met at the back of the camp in a large open area, perhaps one hundred yards from and in open view of one of the guard towers. One of the songs we sang was extremely fitting:

> O, Hashem of Vengeance *(Keil Nekomos Hashem)*
> All Mighty Hashem Shine Forth
> Raise Thyself
> O, Judge of the Earth
> Bring a Recompense upon the Arrogant![a]

We repeated these two *Pesukim* many times over and over, as they were appropriate and underscored to us the timelessness of *Tenach*. Despite being incarcerated in a distant and unfriendly environment, many prisoners did keep their heads high and most were reluctant to despair. The young man who organized the group singing deserves great credit for his devotion and sense of duty in fostering *Emunah* and spreading cheer.

There were many learned and good people in our Dutch compound, including a Mr. and Mrs. Asscher. Mr. Asscher was an elderly man, frail, very learned and a good *Baal Midos*. In better times, he occupied the *Parness* seat in our *shul* on the Gerard Doustraat. To be a *Parness* in a congregation required all kinds of worthy attributes, including a knowledge of learning, honesty, helpfulness, daily attendance, etc. Being assigned the title of *Parness* was a great honor. Our parents saw that Mr. Asscher possessed many good virtues and they noted how he was burdened under the yoke of the cursed Germans. And so a deal was struck – my parents would give him several carefully saved cans of sardines which we had brought along from Holland. In exchange, Mr. Asscher would study with me several hours a week. Mr. Asscher's lessons were inspiring and appropriately chosen. He taught me how Yosef instilled trust in our

---

a. Tehillim, 94:1 and 2

Talmudstudien bei Nacht.

...ובהם נהגה יומם ולילה...
...and you shall study the Torah by day and by night...
By: Sacher Musoch. Reprinted from the Israelit,[21] May 1894

ancestors long ago in the *Golus* of Egypt when he told them: *"Pokoud Yifkoud Elokim Eschem,* Hashem will surely consider you again!"[b] Mr. Asscher also studied with me *Parshas Beshalach* which includes the *Shierah*[c]. His words were reminiscent of similar hopes expressed by Yosef in Egypt and he taught how we, too, will survive from amongst the *"Mayim Rabbim"*, i.e. the oppressing nations; Hashem will surely extricate us from this German bondage![d]

The Asschers were eligible to be exchanged to Palestine but they declined, feeling that they were not strong and healthy enough to make the strenuous journey. In their consideration for others, they wanted a more able couple to benefit from the exchange privilege! To the best of my knowledge, they did not survive the war.

---

b. Breishis, 50:25
c. Shemos, 13:17
d. Refer to Tehillim, 144:7, *Metsudas Dovid* and *Malbim* ad. loc.

WHILE STILL IN HOLLAND, WHEN WE WERE INFORMED THAT our next stop would be Bergen Belsen, Father filled several suitcases in Amsterdam with all kinds of canned food provisions, including condensed milk, canned meat, sardines (tuna fish and salmon were not canned in those days), etc. To heat up some of these foods, one could purchase in a pharmacy small, aspirin size, white colored medication tablets to be used for "fuel". When these tablets were burned below a small pot, they actually brought the contents to a hot temperature. Thus we took along several large glass jars of such "medicine tablets". Plastic containers did not yet exist. This private food and fuel supply served as a lifesaving supplement to our camp food. It was used very sparingly and lasted for approximately half a year.

The camp food was meager, of low nutritional value and certainly inadequate for growing children. To alleviate this situation, young children and children with special needs were granted a milk ration. Starting on October 10, 1944, a large metal milk can was delivered daily to our compound. Those with a milk authorization ticket got one small cup per child. The milk had so much skimmed off that it appeared watery and had a very slight blueish tint. Our ticket was originally for my sister Connie but was subsequently expanded to *"4 Kinder"* (four children). It expired December 15, 1944.

In New York, our uncle and aunt, the Levis, were informed by the Oxemans, who had been in the *Palestina* exchange deal, about our whereabouts. They made all sorts of efforts to help us. Portugal was able to remain a neutral European nation and, through its policy of assistance, Red Cross food packages were sent. The Levis also made a strong effort for us to receive Palestine Papers. On two occasions we were notified that food had arrived for us from Portugal. We had to report to a particular shack in the camp, where an SS officer gave us <u>one</u> small can of sardines, which we then had to open in front of him. This was to ascertain that nothing was being smuggled into camp. The bulk of these relief packages and most of the package's contents never reached us.

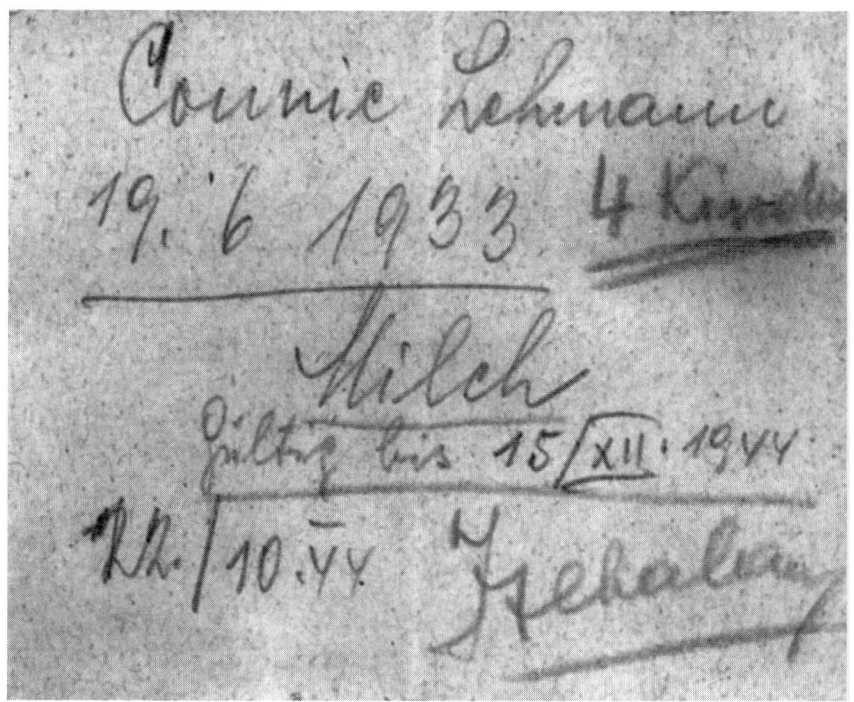

A camp milk ticket. My sister Connie's birthdate is off by three years, it was probably 'adjusted' so she would qualify.

Chapter Sixteen
BERGEN BELSEN – UNUSUAL EVENTS

WORLD WAR II WAS A CONFLICT FREQUENTLY MARKED by outbreaks of *"Quid Pro Quo"*, meaning "Tit for Tat" or "Something for something". The Germans blasted off their V-1 and V-2 rockets (V=Victory) across the English Channel to indiscriminately bombard and destroy South Eastern England. Their main target was metropolitan London and its large civilian population. However, areas in the London suburbs were not spared. German bombing became so intense and dangerous that hundreds of thousands of civilians were relocated to remote inland areas of forty to one hundred miles from London, and even beyond.

When the Allies bombed German targets, using their numerous squadrons of B-17 and B-24 flying fortresses, their aerial bombardment was retaliation in kind. The British manned squadrons adopted a "carpet bombing" policy while the American bombers conducted pinpoint bombings. When a squadron of perhaps twenty British bombers flew over a German city, they would close their formation and fly as near to each other as possible and then open their bomb-bays simultaneously.

Needless to say, this carpet bombing approach wiped out entire neighborhoods in many German cities and caused tremendous losses in human lives.

Another policy of the British was to discharge their entire bomb cargo prior to leaving German airspace, despite obscured primary and secondary ground targets. In contrast, the American flyers dropped their leftover bombs into the North Sea so as to minimize civilian casualties. It is my personal opinion that the Germans were worthy of every bit of this British "air mail". It was communicating with the enemy in their own language of violence.

While confined in Bergen Belsen, we heard practically no background motor or machine noises. There was no vehicular motor traffic to speak of and the nearest town was several miles away. There was practically total silence within the camp except for machine gun fire, barking Germans and, on many occasions, the air raid sirens. When these sirens sounded we all had to seek cover in our barracks. At such times, we witnessed the epic fly-over of hundreds of Allied aircraft, embarked on their large scale seek and destroy missions. The sound of the approaching bombers could be compared to being in an out of town area on a quiet Sunday morning and biking towards a gasoline driven lawn-mower, the motor sound of which being initially very faint and gradually getting louder and louder. When the bombers finally arrived, there appeared over the green, forested horizon, squadron after squadron of bombers, flying very high in the sky. We saw mighty armadas of airships steadily droning and plodding by in the clear blue skies. The formation of each twenty plane squadron, as seen from the ground, was diamond shaped with one plane in the lead. To provide protection against enemy fighter planes, these "combat box formations" (diamond shaped squadrons) had a huge vertical profile that measured nine hundred feet between the top and bottom plane within each squadron.[26] From the planes' wakes would come white colored vapor streams as their engine exhaust gasses condensated into the cold upper atmosphere. Circling around these planes at a much faster speed were small Allied fighter planes that could only be seen as an occasional bright light in the blue sky when the sunlight reflected off one of their body elements. The bombers were propeller driven, since jet engined planes did not yet exist, and they traveled at a steady speed. This aviation "parade" sometimes lasted for several hours. It was one of the most beautiful sights one can imagine. These planes were headed for some large German targets and we had front seat views. This was the new horseless cavalry to the rescue! Since Germany was overwhelmed by

Allied military pressures, they no longer retaliated with anti-aircraft fire nor were there any more German fighter planes rising to challenge these bombers. Besides that, Germany was extremely short on gasoline and therefore had to carefully conserve its dwindling supply. Accordingly, German fighter planes were mostly limited to protecting their big cities, e.g. Berlin, Leipzig, Hamburg, Bremen, Stuttgard, etc. The day following these fly-bys, one would usually hear, through the grapevine, what the target city had been.

These state of the art "flying machines" represented almost the entire technology of the new era in aerial warfare. To appreciate the B-17s requires some background knowledge of their physical parameters and their achievements. B-17s were unique to World War II and the whole fleet became obsolete by 1946.[a]

Harbeh schluchim yesh laMokom, the Almighty has many messengers to accomplish His wishes. Looking back, it is apparent that the Allied airforces were one of the arrows in His quiver, which were targeted to destroy the German scourge. The Germans were the originators of unprovoked aerial tyranny through their *Blitzkrieg* and V-rockets. Now they were repaid in kind! "By the very thing wherein they transgressed presumptuously was punishment brought upon them." [b]

Radar (Radio Detection and Ranging) came into full and effective use towards the end of World War II. To thwart the effective use of radar, the Allied planes dropped overboard bundles of thin short aluminum confetti so as to confound any possible use of radar directed anti-aircraft fire. At Bergen Belsen we received our share of this special thin shredded aluminum.

On one occasion, I remember picking up a small piece of printed paper thrown from the planes. Unfortunately, not only was it a torn portion of a page, but it was in English, while we only knew Dutch.

FOUR MONTHS AFTER WE ARRIVED IN BERGEN BELSEN, THE final group of Dutch Jews arrived. They were the last contingent of the Diamond Group and included some of the biggest names in the business, including the family Asscher. Part of their "luggage" consisted of medical appliances to equip a camp hospital. This medical gear was immediately confiscated by the Germans.

TANTE EMMA PRINS, WAS A WIDOW NOW IN HER EIGHTIES AND the Germans, in their greedy zeal, had deported this aged lady. As

---
a. Refer to Appendix D for more details.
b. Shemos, 18:11

wheelchairs were not available, the lady was carried on a stretcher each time she was taken to a new location. Her final destination was Bergen Belsen. Here she was helpless and bedbound. Being deported, caused her frailty and hearing handicap to worsen. Her daughter and son-in-law, the Posens, took care of her as much as camp conditions permitted. Finally, on June 12, 1944, this aged prisoner passed away. Tante Emma Prins *o.h.*, the daughter of Horav Meir Lehmann, was eighty four years old, she was one of the oldest prisoners of the camp. Those German heroes must have gleed when this frail and helpless octogenarian inmate succumbed to the pressures of their spartan life.

It was still during a stage when few persons had died in our Dutch compound that this prominent senior prisoner passed away. Father, who was her nephew, tried very hard to have her body buried rather than cremated. The Germans, however, refused. It was the only occasion that I remember that someone in camp had a *levaya*. Her body was placed in a simple wooden coffin and placed on a crude, four-wheeled horse drawn carriage. A German soldier sat on the driver's seat to direct the horse, while a small group of us walked behind, up to the compound's gate. Whether her body was placed in a mass grave or cremated was unknown. For several days, I watched the crematorium's chimney for signs of smoke but never noticed any.

IN OUR BARRACK, UNFORTUNATELY, NOT ALL OCCUPANTS WERE observant Jews but Father and his colleagues were able to assemble an adequate *minyan* for all important occasions.

Several years ago, my sister Connie was given by an acquaintance in Yerusholayim a copy of a certificate that was penned in a fine calligraphy in Bergen Belsen. The certificate designated a Reb Eliezer ben Reb Uri de Puy of our barrack No. 17 to be the *Choson* Torah and Reb Uri ben Aharon de Puy to be *Choson Breishis*. This small document, written in plain language, describes the plight of the prisoners and is a glowing testimony to the tenacious loyalty accorded to the Torah and to Yiddishkeit, despite the crushing assaults on our dignity. It is another rare glimpse that confirms our parents' involvement in the maintenance of our orthodox ways under bleak Holocaust conditions.

The English translation of the Hebrew text:

"For Torah and For Testimony

We the undersigned hereby testify that on the festival of *Simchas*

> לתורה ולתעודה
>
> אנחנו חתומי מטה מעידים בזה · שבחג שמחת התורה שעבר
> ר' אלעזר בן ר' אורי דע פוי נבחר להיות לחתן תורה בצריף י"ז
> במחנה ברגען בלזען כאשר היינו שם סגורים ואנוסים · והחתן בראשית
> היה ר' אורי בן כה"ה אהרן דע פוי · השם ישמרם מכל רע ויגיע אותם
> למחוז חפצם לחיים ולשלום ולבריאות בב"א אמן
>
> כ"ד תשרי אסרו חג · ברגען בעלזען תשה לפ"ק

*Certificate of Choson Torah and Choson Breishis,
Barrack 17, Succos 5705 at Bergen Belsen*

Torah, which just ended, Reb Eliezer the son of Reb Uri de Puy was chosen to be *Choson Torah* in barrack 17 at the camp of Bergen Belsen where we are imprisoned and oppressed. And the *Choson Breishis* was Reb Uri the son of his honor Aharon de Puy. May Hashem protect them from all evil and let them attain the realization of their desires for life and for peace and for health, speedily and in our days, *Omein*. 24 Tishri, *Isru Chag,* Bergen Belsen, 5705. signed:

> *Aharon Yakov the son of his honor Naftoli HaLevi Duizend
> Meir the son of, Rosh Hakohol, Osher Lehmann (my father).
> Shlomo the son of Yaakov HaLevi de Welde."*

Alas, we had no *succah* in the camp and no *Sefer Torah* in our barrack, but that did not deter the spirited from celebrating one of the major milestones in our calendar.

THE GERMANS WERE VERY ANXIOUS TO SET UP A DIAMOND cutting industry in Bergen Belsen. To arrange that they had assembled as many Dutch Jewish diamond experts and cutters as they could find and lodged them in our barrack No. 17. Of course, handling diamonds requires that one's hands and fingers be free of blemishes. Accordingly, all men in the "Diamond Group" were exempt from physical work including kitchen work, wood cutting in the forest and digging ditches and pits, etc.

To arrange the details and logistics of this proposed gem industry, the Germans transported diamond cutting machines from Amsterdam to Bergen Belsen and frequently an industry "expert" would arrive from Berlin to discuss details (Mr. Sickinger, et. al.). These discussions were held in the *Kommandant's* office. Father, being knowledgeable on the subject of diamonds and fluent in speaking German, was one of three or four representatives from our group to sit in on these meetings.

Consensus was always reconfirmed prior to such high-level meetings. Thus, most Diamond Group members and their spouses met in the barrack's sitting area the day before, to discuss details. Prior to such gatherings the children were sent outdoors or were already asleep and were thus not privy to these deliberations. Judging from Father's harmonious rapport with all members of the group, it is apparent to me that no differences in approach existed, especially regarding matters of resisting German demands. It was however exceedingly difficult for the negotiating team to confront the Germans in a firm but polite manner while simultaneously attempting to stall off the seemingly inevitable day of reckoning.

The first camp *Kommandant*, Haas, who fell into German displeasure and was subsequently reassigned, was an obese fellow and a prolific cigar smoker. He used to offer Father a cigar at these meetings. Father, being an ardent anti-smoker politely declined. One must realize that tobacco products in the camp were a non-renewable resource, and many men would have given almost anything to get their hands on a cigar. One can imagine the wrath that Father received from fellow prisoners when his refusal of the cigar offer became known.

THE ONLY RUNNING COLD WATER WAS IN THE LAVATORY section of our barrack. There were no baths or showers and there certainly was no hot water. In addition, these wooden barracks were flimsily built with no insulation, the window glass was only single pane and there were four small pot belly stoves for winter use in a structure that was well over four hundred foot in length. It is therefore apparent that washing oneself in the winter with cold water under these conditions was not very advisable.

Near the entrance to the camp, contiguous to a Russian prisoner of war compound, was the one story brick structure which housed the showers. While waiting on line in the bath-house courtyard, I still recall peeking through the wooden board fence and getting my first glimpse of Russian officers in uniform as they milled around outside their barrack. The bath-house consisted of two large rooms plus the boiler room where the hot water was produced. In one room were some two dozen shower heads pointing down from the high ceiling, which allowed a group of perhaps forty or fifty persons to shower together while standing naked next to each other. This room had large fixed windows made up of small glass panes for the upper four feet of wall. Next to the shower room was an enclosed area where we placed our clothing on movable racks. Once the doors to this dressing room were closed and the showering was in progress, the clothing was exposed to intense dry heat so as to kill any fleas or lice that might have been on the clothing. People used to bring their blankets there as well to de-flea them. Of course, the Germans had to place their own fly in the ointment. The entire process was under the direction of an *Aufseherin* (German S.S. woman soldier). When the men finished their showers and, standing there in the nude, the sauna room doors were opened and the *Aufseherin* would wheel to the door our clothing racks. From their facial expressions, these women revealed their low background.

As is typical with the Germans, they couldn't make things convenient and comfortable. They scheduled some showers in the middle of the night! When we left our compound at night to walk to the shower area the men would walk in groups and when we returned groups of women departed for the showers. In West European circles, there was a custom which I did not observe among other persons. Many spouses had an individualized signature whistle consisting of a combination of three to eight musical notes. This way husbands and wives could easily call each other without having to shout out names. For the night-out escapade, the whistle communication method worked well. All participants were told that our destination was the camp bath house in a remote part of the grounds. Considering the fact that the Germans were masters in deceit, there was always the possibility of us being victims of devious tactics. Indeed there was no guarantee that we would be headed for the showers once we left our compound gate. A safe return to our barracks was also not assured. When, in the starlit night, the showered group met the outgoing group, one could hear dozens of different sounding call whistles. It was a relief to know who had safely returned. These showers became off-limits upon our eviction from the Dutch compound.

ADDITIONAL WOODEN BARRACKS WERE CONSTANTLY BEING built. The lavatories, at their center, were constructed of brick and concrete. For the latter the Germans imported a few masons from a nearby town to perform the brickwork. Of course, no person from camp was permitted to communicate with these outsiders. After all, we were dangerous persons! I enjoyed watching the bricklayers with a friend. Once, an SS Officer in charge threw a chunk of brick at us to make sure we maintained our respectable distance.

THERE WERE MANY CHILDREN IN THE DUTCH COMPOUND, but there was no formal schooling whatsoever. By September of 1945, I had actually missed two years of formal classroom schooling. As an example of the extreme dedication of some of these Dutch prisoners, it must be realized that the only things we had in camp were those items which we had physically carried, i.e. food, blankets, summer and winter clothing, medical supplies, candles, etc. It must also be noted that suitcases in those days were not equipped with wheels. Imagine our great surprise, when a group of fifteen children were invited to join a one hour a day Hebrew class and each was presented with a blank school notebook to take notes! Someone must have carried less food so as to be able to carry this school material that was to be used by others!

Hitler, as well as many other fascist leaders, was known for his long rhetorics. These were filled with harangue, punctuated with hate and of course loaded with empty promises. During the war, his oratory was carefully analyzed for points of German weakness and hints of policy changes to come. I recall a day in late 1944 when all the camp guards were anticipating Hitler to deliver a major radio address. The German war effort was not progressing as had been expected, and the mere hint of a major speech aroused anxieties and uneasiness in these empty headed punks. When Hitler finally came on the air, every SS soldier in every guard tower was listening. During these speeches, no SS officers were found walking around. Along with several friends, I walked as near as possible to a watchtower during that speech to hear Hitler yell. However, the guard kept the volume low and nothing was heard. Later it became known that the subject of the address was a national pep talk exhorting Germans not to yield to foreign pressures, despite major military setbacks.

Air raids consisted of Allied armed forces fighting the Germans. Obviously, we were therefore in no significant danger should such air raids occur. Nevertheless, the Germans made the Dutch prisoners dig deep trenches in the open spaces between the barracks so that we could jump in and be "protected" in the event of a strafing aircraft. A soldier would walk between the barracks holding the leg of a "T" shaped stick that had two nails sticking out. He would then score on the hard sandy ground two parallel wavy lines approximately eighteen inches apart. These would then be the outlines of the walls for the proposed trenches. After they were neatly dug to a depth of some four feet, they were again backfilled. It was a work program designed solely to harass the prisoners.

Chapter Seventeen

NO DEALS!
FAREWELL TO DAD & MOM, A.H.

MONTHS OF NEGOTIATIONS AND DISCUSSIONS WERE spent between the Germans and members of the *Diamant Groep* regarding the establishment of a diamond industry in Bergen Belsen. Obviously, such an undertaking would be of great help to the German war effort. An added bonus would be that such a facility would not be subject to aerial attack since concentration camps were not targets for Allied bombing missions. The bold inmates however stood fast, they were courageous and adamant and refused to acquiesce. In their desperation, the surrealistic Germans even offered us apartments instead of the spartan barracks, if only we would collaborate. Eventually attempts to drag out the discussions were no longer successful and the Germans lost all patience. To the bitter end, the group remained united and to their credit they spurned all *modi vivendi*. The denouement became clear, our differences were irreconcilable; no deals would be struck. The Germans realized that we would not aid or abet our tormentors and the negotiators returned to Berlin.

Soon thereafter, a young SS officer showed up outside our barrack. He had curly blond hair and a loud mouth. Several of our barrack's leading occupants were requested to step out to talk with him, or rather for him to talk to them. He informed them that shortly all men, women and children of the *Diamant Groep* would be relocated and taken out of the Dutch compound. Furthermore, he stated that the adults would be *"ein Steinwurf entfernt"* — "relocated by a stone's throw". In addition, the men were not to take anything along except the barest minimum. This could be interpreted in several ways, including that the men would be summarily lined up and shot.

Following that "bombshell" news, my parents requested friends and family to drop in at our barrack to say farewell. [On *Succos*, 5753 (1992) we visited Mrs. Liesje Joshua in Bayit Vegan, Yerusholayim. She was Mother's age and they had been good friends since childhood. Mrs. Joshua described how someone had come to her barrack that day in Bergen Belsen and had requested her to come visit Mr. and Mrs. Lehmann for the purpose of bidding farewell to their friends. No one had anticipated this departure, and Mrs. Joshua described how shocked she was.]

FATHER TOOK A SMALL *RUCKSACK* (KNAPSACK) AND, IN A dejected mood filled it with a few personal items, e.g. underwear and a shirt. He wore his regular European style navy blue woolen beret for a hat. He did not take his *tefillin,* his electric shaver, food or significant clothing. We walked Father to the compound's gate where other men of the Diamond Group had already assembled. Father placed his two hands on each of my sister's heads and then on mine, *benched* each of us and kissed us good bye. He then walked out the compound's gate to the camp's main roadway. There Father stood within earshot, his back to us, waiting for the other men to follow. The distance between myself and Father was perhaps sixty feet. Not knowing when I would see Father again, I wanted to give one more farewell. I loudly called to Father,

"PAAAA-PIEEEEE!"

But Father did not turn around. Mother was standing next to me and told me to call a bit louder for perhaps he didn't hear me. I then called once more, at the top of my lungs,

"PAAAAA-PIEEEEEE!!"

This time Father turned around slowly. Everyone looked at Father and me. I seemed to be the only son interested in his Father or perhaps the only youngster who dared to call to his Father in front of the German officers. I waved to Father and he waved back with difficulty. His face had a forced smile and I sensed Father's emotional strain. The whole scene made an indelible impression on me. It was one of those moments that I frequently thought of but never discussed with anyone.

THE MEN WALKED OFF TOWARDS THE CAMP GATE accompanied by the curly haired, blond young SS officer. The next day we were told that the women and children of the Diamond Group were also to leave the Dutch compound. We each packed one or two carrying pieces. The ladies were directed to take all the luggage including those belonging to the children. The women were to go by truck and the children would then follow on foot. We, therefore, expected to see our mothers down the road. Mother apparently expected differently and so she instructed, in my presence, that my sister Connie should take care of me in her absence. Connie was closer to my age than my older sister and therefore was more likely to remain together with me. After waiting a while longer, we walked towards the camp's gate.

It was cold in that early evening on December 5, 1944. Before the main camp gate we were told to wait another half an hour. While waiting, my sister Toni and I went into the guard quarters next to the gate to warm up. There we saw a pitcher of milk being kept warm on a pot belly stove. In German, my sister asked from a young soldier who was busy at his desk with some paper work for permission to drink the milk. He agreed and we had our first glass of whole milk in probably a year.

Finally, we proceeded to the truck garage and there, on the floor, was all the luggage belonging to us children. After picking out our pieces we realized what the cunning Germans had done to us. They had separated the mothers from their children without permitting them to hug and kiss each other goodbye. It was a case of the astute Germans not wanting to be bothered with an emotional farewell.

It was a difficult period of adjustment that followed. We were very attached to our parents and respected them, the love between us was mutual. Many of our waking hours had been together and now our parents were gone. ***Forever!*** No one knew what lay in store for either our parents or ourselves. Communication between prisoners at different camps did not exist. We did have high hopes of meeting again. In fact, we only learned officially of Mother's passing after arriving in England. Regarding Father's fate, we had been told in 1945 to expect the worst. However, in the absence of an official document, I had not given up on seeing Father again until perhaps six or seven years following the war's end.

OUR PARENTS AND THEIR COLLEAGUES WERE COGNIZANT OF the possible dire consequences in their dealings with the treacherous foe. These heroes were well aware that their lives and those of their loved ones were endangered. Those men and women also realized that they could now do their share to win the war against Germany. Denying the German war machine important and strategic industrial tools was a rare opportunity that certainly would impact upon further research and production efforts. Therefore, it would have been folly to cooperate with the killer enemy. Like loyal soldiers in battle they considered the general welfare to be paramount and allowed their lives to be jeopardized so others would be protected from untold calamities. They were tested by Hashem in a way that few of us are, and they passed with banners flying. In retrospect, it is evident that, unfortunately, it was decreed from above that many would die a martyr's death. May the Almighty avenge our parent's blood and that of their colleagues and may the deeds of these heroic righteous people be a merit to them and to all their dear ones who survived. We look forward to meeting their *Neshomos* after a hundred and twenty years.

IN THE *BENCHING* AFTER OUR MEALS, THE FIRST *BROCHO* WAS authored by *Moshe Rabeinu*. It describes how "...we have never lacked food and (request) that we may never lack food...". There are thus envisioned circumstances under which starvation and famine can occur, and we hope not to be part of that specter of deprival. A review of *Tenach* will reveal various occasions when famines took place and fatalities resulted. To understand the cause and effect of such periods in our history, the classical commentaries, the *Talmud* and the *Medroshim* thereon must be studied. Rabbi Yosef learned:[a] "Once permission has been granted to the Destroyer, then he does not distinguish between righteous and wicked. Moreover, he even begins with the righteous at the outset...". Our parents perished from lack of proper and adequate food and the resulting malnutrition. (Refer to later chapters.) There are any number of reasons why their succumbing to those deprivations could have been decreed; the answers are only known in Heaven. Refer also to Talmud Yerushalmi *Yoma*,[b] which infers that the death of the righteous is an

---

a. *Maseches Bova Kamma*, 60a
b. 1:1

atonement for our people. In view of the above *Chazal,* one can possibly approach an understanding of how some of our best were taken from this world.

In retrospect, the choice of our parents not to depart Europe prior to the war was apparently part of a Divine plan to enable Father to act as a key participant in resisting the Germans. It certainly was a task for which the average person is not cut out for or prepared. Considering German accommodations to and patience with our group is positive evidence that our skills had strategic importance. Accordingly, I consider the Diamond Group's defiance a resounding success.

ONCE OUR LUGGAGE WAS COLLECTED, WE CHILDREN OF THE Diamond Group were now directed to a different section of Bergen Belsen known as the *Frauenlager* (Women's camp). My sister Connie remembers the name of this compound to have been the *Frauenstraflager* or Women's Penal Camp. We were all assigned to a very large room in one of the barracks. There were triple decker beds on both sides of the room and a few tables along the center. We then unpacked our luggage. In my canvas bag were two communications from Mother. One was a long, two page hand-written letter carefully explaining many of the problems leading to our family's separation. Unfortunately, and to my great consternation that letter was lost. A second note from Mother was written on the back of our milk authorization ticket. [That note is kept in my safe deposit box at a local bank in New York. Every time I open the box I dwell on the note's content and shed a tear. The note serves as a very effective reminder that we lived through some extremely difficult times and that we must be thankful to Hashem for whatever we have. When reading it, I am always reminded of Mother's strong convictions and her bond and love for us children.] It reads as follows:

"Blijven jullie vroom
wij zien elkaar terug.
Gd zegen jullie,
Tante Metas, Liesjes,
Bondies alle Soeps.
Blijven jullie sterk
jullie Moeder"

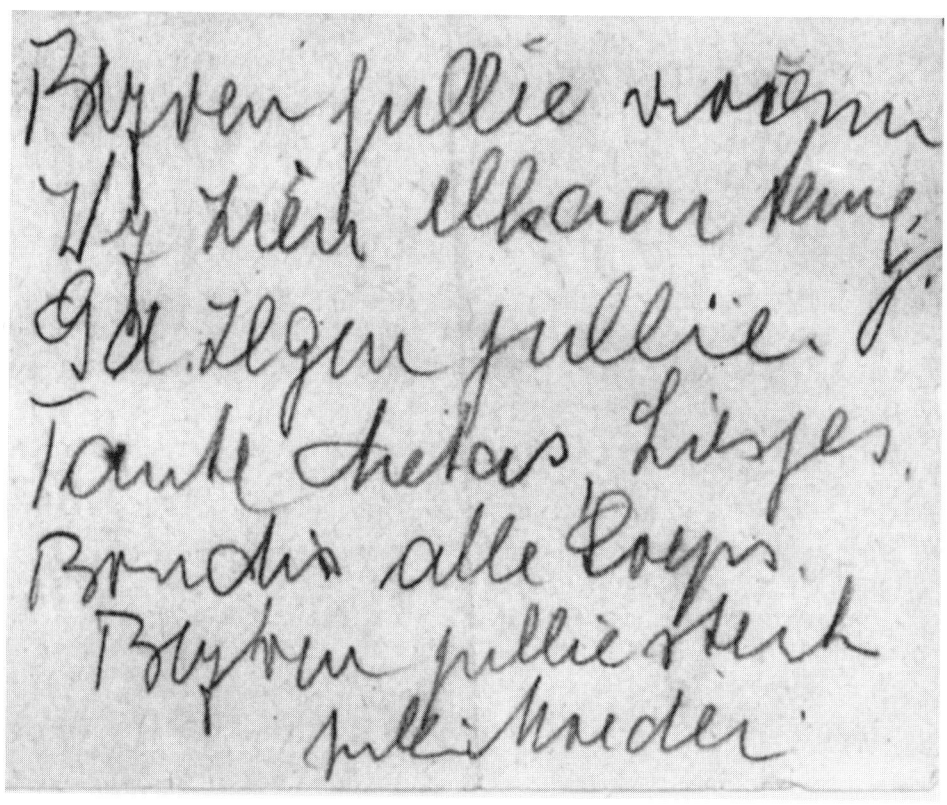

Mother's Goodbye note - de facto Tzavo'oh

(translation from Dutch)
"Remain faithful (observant Jews)
we will see each other again.
May G-d bless all of you,
Aunt Meta (and husband-Posen), Liesje (and children-Joshua),
Bondi (family), the entire Soep (family).
remain strong.
your Mother"

The names in the note were of some of the close friends and relatives we left behind. Apparently, Mother thought we would return to our Dutch compound and then friends would look after us. Since we were now assigned to a different section of Bergen Belsen, it was not possible to convey to them the contents of Mother's note. The families referred to were Meta Posen, the daughter of our great aunt, Tante Emma, and her husband Eli, our friends Liesje Joshua and her three children, Karen, Jacob and Henry, the Bondi family who were second cousins and our friends the Soep family. To the best of my knowledge, of the above, only the Joshua family and some of the Soep family survived the war.

Father's months of difficult and patient negotiations and the carefully worded letter and stirring note of Mother, calmly written, beautifully drafted, logically sequenced and wholly without signs of fright or panic, are all noble epitaphs that left indelible and searing marks on all of us.

Mother's expressions of *brochos* and concern were an outpouring of true maternal love. The word "love" was not used and would have been redundant. Under the circumstances, this was the optimum and most ideal message possible. To the best of my knowledge, our parents were the only ones in the Diamond Group to have both been that involved in the negotiations and to have communicated with their children to the extensive degree in which they did. These parent-child relations were of great significance, considering that the entire scene was superimposed on a setting fraught with frustrations and perils.

The "stone's throw" distance that described our parent's upcoming relocation turned out to be completely inaccurate and instead was as follows:

Father: 150 miles eastward
Mother: 150 miles to the north

For a nation as obsessed with punctiliousness and exactitude as the Germans are, this blatant lie was just one more example of their deceptive and cruel practices.

[Forty eight years later, as I was sitting in my doctor's office at the Mount Sinai Medical Center in Manhattan for an annual medical checkup, the doctor started preparing my arm for a routine blood pressure test. He then inquired casually if my parents were still living. I told him that they had been killed during World War II. My blood pressure was then found to be exceptionally high. Realizing that it was our discussion that caused the elevated pressure, the conversation was changed to a pleasant topic and several minutes later a new reading showed a normal pressure. This is to illustrate how the murder of my parents so many years ago has not been forgotten through the passage of time.]

My parent's travail and torment have produced within myself a permanent scar for which there is no healing and to which I desire no cure. Those who want to forget and to forgive the agonies perpetrated on our people and on the world by a generation of barbarians have in my opinion very convoluted values of life.

I, on the other hand, shall always remember that my parents' efforts are perpetuated in more ways than one: their sacrifices allowed us to be here, to tell their story, to learn from their experiences and to continue their tasks.

A personal plea:

> *Ribono Shel Olam,* when Your world was desecrated and ravaged by a profane and arrogant nation, the members of the Diamond Group united to risk their lives and thereby sanctified Your Name. May it be Your Will to sanctify Your Name on those who venerated Your sacredness. In the merit of these sanctifiers may You (continue to) bring salvation and true Jewish *nachas* upon all their progenies.

THE ALMIGHTY HAS MANY MESSENGERS AT HIS DISPOSAL. Following the separation of our group's adults and children, a new survival scheme emerged. With Divine Providence, we children became the pawns in an exchange-program discussion with Great Britain, via the good offices of the Swiss government. That transfer deal between England and Germany never materialized but Germany's Foreign Minister Joachim von Ribbentrop *Y.S.* directed the *Gestapo* to save certain Jewish children at Bergen Belsen. The children "had to be spared for the time being, in the event that the British accept the arrangement."[c]

---

c. Source: *Martyrdom and Resistance,* vol. 22 - No. 2, page 14.

Chapter Eighteen
FRAUENLAGER – DAILY LIVES

THE *FRAUENLAGER*, AS THE NAME IMPLIES, WAS A CAMP compound which housed mostly women and a few children. These youths probably amounted to less than a half percent of that camp's occupants. Of those children, perhaps one third were boys. The *Frauenlager* was a section of Bergen Belsen that was completely separated from all the other compounds. It differed in many respects. There were overcrowded barracks, poor sanitary conditions, no showers or baths and the women were mainly Hungarian. Other nationalities included a sprinkling of Russian, Yugoslavian, Rumanian, Greek and Dutch. There were some Gypsies as well, several of these groups were more neglected than others.

Many of the Hungarian women were sole survivors of their respective families, their husbands and children having been wiped out by the murderous Germans. Whenever these prisoners saw our small group of children, they were always amazed and exclaimed each time: "*nem lehet, jyerekek!*" Literally translated, these words mean: "not possible, children!", i.e. it is unbelievable to see surviving children!

KEEPING ORDER IN THIS COMPOUND WERE *"KAPOS"* OR *KAMP* (camp) Police. These were Jewish prisoners who disciplined fellow prisoners for petty offenses. Needless to say, they were thoroughly disliked as they had no business adding to the German imposed hardships. I remember walking around camp one day and seeing a lady on her knees with a large raw turnip in each hand at shoulder level – palms up. Her face showed signs of distress from the physical anguish and mental torture. She was forced to remain in that position for several hours by a *Kapo*.

In a society where life is sacred and killing is the ultimate in criminality, it is incredible that Germans were engaged in mass murder. In some camps, the *Kapos* were actually accused of aiding and abetting the Germans in their acts of homicide. An example of *Kapo* complicity is said to have taken place in Auschwitz. When a large transport of deportees arrived at Auschwitz, the hapless families were separated into groups of the weak, the men, the women and the children. Children were usually doomed by the next day, following their arrival. These children were placed overnight in a separate barrack. They were given no food or water. Food was in short supply and a dryer body cremates more easily. On occasion, such a barrack held as many as fourteen hundred poor souls. *Kapos* were placed in charge to assure that no child escape from the building. If the next day's count did not agree, the *Kapos* were then substituted for the missing children and sent along to the gas chamber.

Stories are told by the Weitzener Rav about parents who bribed *Kapos* to have their child extricated from a group of condemned-to-die children. To make up the resulting deficiency in the head count, a *Kapo* would grab a substitute child that had been hidden by its parents in another barrack. Thus, a grisly exchange of children took place.[25a]

[Our son-in-law, Simon Fischer, from Melbourne, Australia, reported that some of these *ex-Kapos* live at the other end of that city, away from the Jewish neighborhoods. They feel and are ostracized, and rightfully so.]

The Germans apparently did not particularly care for the *Kapo* mentality either. A story is told that the Warsaw Ghetto had some three hundred Jewish policemen *(Gepos)*. These men survived the systematic and cruel eviction process that the SS conducted when moving some four hundred thousand persons to extermination camps in only a few weeks' time. The *Gepos* must have done their share in assisting in this task. Their work was completed when the Ghetto was empty, destroyed and systematically burned down. The SS Commander then gathered all *Gepos* and thanked them for their dedication. When that commanding vulture finished his talk, German soldiers stepped forward and machine gunned to death the entire Ghetto Police force!

The institution of *"Kapos"* in our Dutch compound did not exist, either because it was not needed or because the Dutch Jews refused to act as *Kapos*. I remember a commotion one night after the lights were already off. A man had walked in from another barrack. He wore socks over his shoes to muffle his footsteps on the hollow rough wooden floor and was caught in the act of taking a few items from under someone's mattress. Immediately, ten men including Father got up, caught the intruder and "interrogated" him. They lit a candle and sat at a table for at least one hour before letting him go. The incident was, of course, not reported to the Germans.

UNLIKE THE DUTCH COMPOUND, WHICH WAS BARE OF TREES and vegetation, the *Frauenlager* did have many evergreen trees and weeded green areas. It appeared that this section of camp had been reclaimed from the forest in a hurry. We were fortunate that the winter of 1944-1945 had relatively little snow here.

Sleeping accommodations varied. One barrack that I saw had deep wooden shelves, perhaps eight feet wide, one on top of the other, to form four layers. These warehouse style lodgings were used for sleeping quarters in lieu of individual beds.

Our initial quarters consisted of a barrack that housed all the children of the Diamond Group. In all, we were approximately forty to fifty children. The Germans placed three Jewish women, who were in their early to middle twenties, in charge of our group. *Schwester* Lubah, as she was known, (Mrs. Lubah Fredericks, North Miami Beach, Florida) oversaw the whole children's group operation. In the German language, *Schwester* literally means "sister" but is generally used to mean "nurse"; Lubah was neither. To me she appeared to be short and on the heavy side, when compared to the other emaciated prisoners, and her voice was much louder than I was accustomed to. She spoke both Polish and German. Most of the prisoners had tales of woe and *Schwester* Lubah was no exception. After her arrest in Poland, the Germans had her two-year-old son thrown into a large fire! Now she was alone, without husband or child.

ON THE FIFTIETH ANNIVERSARY OF OUR LIBERATION FROM Bergen Belsen, *Schwester* Lubah was honored in Amsterdam and presented with the Royal Silver Medal. It was in recognition for her courage, valor, devotion and loyalty to her young Dutch charges. A well deserved tribute. She showed kindness, worked hard and above all kept us out of all sorts of life threatening and non-life threatening troubles. In recent years, Mrs. Lubah Fredericks has been affectionately dubbed the "Angel of Belsen".

Hermina, the second lady in charge was also of Polish background. She had been transferred to Bergen Belsen from Auschwitz. At Auschwitz, she had been able to escape from the gas chambers TWICE! Once, by hiding in the truck underneath a mattress, the second time by climbing up the chimney. The latter story fits in well with the hollow concrete cube, which I saw on the empty train in Westerbork. As previously mentioned, the concrete was probably to cover a gas chamber chimney. We heard many Auschwitz stories from this lady. My cousin and I were among the few Dutch children who understood German and therefore we got a greater share of those horror stories.

Food was picked up from the camp's own kitchen by some of the older children in our group who were perhaps two to three years my senior. To and from the kitchen, these children walked, single file, under the direction of one of the ladies in charge. We younger children were strictly forbidden to leave the vicinity of the barrack. In fact, we were especially cautioned not to go to the kitchen. One day, two boys my age and I decided to go to the kitchen to beg for some raw potatoes. We were starving and didn't care if the potatoes were not cooked. We started out very optimistic, but upon reaching the kitchen we were turned back by a gauntlet of somewhat obese looking lady workers, and that was before we even got to the potato section. Coming back to our barrack, we were confronted by *Schwester* Lubah who gave us a tongue lashing. Then, in front of all the other children, she took off our belts, pulled down our pants and gave us a token lashing on our buttocks. That was our last trip to the kitchen. (We did get our belts back.)

The children were divided according to age. Those who were approximately fourteen years and older were housed in a different barrack than the younger ones. Accordingly, my cousin and I were in the younger group where we were wards of *Schwester* Luba et. al. until we returned to Holland following our liberation. Among the children there was camaraderie and a spirit of tolerance. I don't remember any fights or quarrels despite our lack of games, books, schooling, amusements and adequate space.

Being in separate barracks meant that I did not see much of my sisters, perhaps only once every two or three weeks. However, I devised a way to maintain contact with them, as follows: Despite our meager diets, I did not eat the occasional chunk of half raw meat that would be in my turnip soup. Rather than throw out the meat, I placed it in a small glass jar, which would be picked up by one of my sister's friends. This friend apparently had some reason for being at the hospital barrack that was near us, and so she was in the "neighborhood". The meat did not spoil since it was winter and the barracks were scantily heated. Through this friend we were able to pass news to each other on a weekly basis.

Our barrack was subdivided into various sections. We children had three large rooms — one for eating, one for sleeping and one room where we whiled away our time. The women in charge had their own smaller room. My bed was a double decker bed, of which I occupied the upper unit and my cousin Erika the lower bed.

AN INTERIOR BARRACK PARTITION NEXT TO MY BED WAS A thin wall enclosing an area known as the maternity ward. There, expectant mothers would come when they went into labor. To the best of my knowledge, none of their babies survived. In fact, we would occasionally see a dead newborn baby at the bottom of a deep pit behind the maternity ward. During the night, one could hear the groaning of the women in labor through the thin partition. The sound that was heard throughout the quiet night was "Yoy...Yoy...Yoy...".

In front of our barrack was a hard unpaved road perhaps nine feet wide. This road led to another barrack further down known as the "hospital". Alas, there was no medicine, no medical equipment, no hospital beds and no medical authority in this facility. It was a one way street. The semi-conscious and the seriously ill were carried or rolled to the hospital barrack. The Germans made absolutely no effort to help the patients. I remember on one occasion watching some camp prisoners pushing along a makeshift stretcher on wheels. Just as they were in front of our barrack, the sick lady being transported fell off onto the hard, icy ground. In other words, there was no competent staff to attend to the sick and dying.

Once the sick died, their bodies were temporarily placed into a small brick house in front of our barrack. From there, the bodies were removed either to a crematorium or to a mass grave outside camp. Towards January of 1945, prisoners were dying at such a rapid rate that the brick house could no longer accommodate their bodies. Accordingly, the dead bodies were neatly stacked along the roadway, three or four high. When that area filled up, another neat row of dead bodies, stacked like firewood, was started behind the first row. The bodies were laid perpendicular to the roadway, with the feet in front. Hundreds and hundreds of emaciated, naked, female bodies piled face up, right near our children's barracks.

Fortunately, there were no flies or vermin to aggravate the situation. These women had died of hard work, delivery-room labor, starvation, malnutrition, disease and above all of no medical care. The body count increased right up to the day of liberation and beyond.

The cries of these women, along with those of millions of other victims of German atrocities must have ascended to the Almighty's throne. The German beast's doom was sealed, the days of the Third *Reich,* which was designed by its fascist founders to last for "a thousand years", were numbered (12 years total). Their downfall and capitulation was only a matter of a few more months.

It was a long, cold and rough winter for us prisoners, but with help from above, some fortunate souls did pull through this nightmare and we have very much to be grateful for.

Chapter Nineteen

FRAUENLAGER – UNUSUAL EVENTS

TOWARDS THE END OF DECEMBER 1944, TWO *AUFSEHERINNEN* (German S.S. Women) placed a small x-mas tree in our barrack with several small cookies below the tree. Whether these cookies were real, edible or of wood, nobody knows since they remained untouched until they were removed a week later. That tree certainly was out of place and no one was interested in it.

In early 1945, a group of ten to fifteen young Russian speaking girls arrived at our barrack. Their ages ranged from perhaps seven to fourteen years old. Since they knew no Dutch or German and we spoke no Russian, communication between us was very limited. Their background remains completely obscure to me. I would, however, assume that their parents were prominent persons in the Russian hierarchy and that is why they were saved and sent to Bergen Belsen. [Forty-two years later, in the late 1980's, President Ronald Reagan (1981-1989) hosted the Soviet Premier Mikhail Gorbachev and his wife at the White House. A newspaper account of that state visit contained photographs, which included the first Soviet lady. To me there appeared to be a striking resemblance in the facial expression and appearance of Mrs. Raisa Gorbachev and that of the youngest Russian girl in our children's group, who was also named Raisa.]

With these additional Russian children, our facilities became far more cramped. Up to now we slept two to a bed, with one head at each end. I remember giving up my bed to the Russian children and having to sleep on one mattress with three other boys, sardine style, i.e. two heads at each end. The mattresses were of cheap quality, made of thin canvas filled with a combination of straw and wood shavings, not exactly conducive to dust free, soft luxury. The beds were narrow to begin with and this new imposition brought great discomfort.

One night, we heard a lot of commotion and shooting outside the barrack. From the perimeter guard towers powerful spotlights pinpointed one site within the camp's exterior security fence. The next morning, it was clear that their target had been a prisoner who tried to escape. The escapee's body was draped over the coiled barbed wire between the double perimeter security fence. This whole scene took place approximately two hundred feet from our barrack. To extricate the mangled body required the efforts of half a dozen persons for several hours.

THE NOTORIOUS AUSCHWITZ CAMP IN POLAND HAD BEEN closed by the Germans ahead of the advancing Soviet (Red) armies. Rather than abandon the remaining prisoners to the approaching Russians and grant those poor souls their freedom, the Germans decided to remove the remaining living prisoners and bring many to Bergen Belsen. One of the many German crazes was to transport and transfer surviving prisoners whenever the opportunities presented itself. Some of the distances involved hundreds and hundreds of miles. And so prisoners from the east were sent westward and from the west to Poland in the east. This penchant for keeping everybody on the move certainly helped in depleting their dwindling rollingstock and scarce fuel. One possible reason for this idiocy might have been that if prisoners were constantly on the move, then mainline railroad tracks would not be bombed or strafed. This strategy, however, was not successful since German railroad yards, lines and bridges were in fact targets in varying degrees for Allied war planes. Accordingly, a second theory might be that these sadists just wanted to add extra misery to the lives of their prisoners. In vacating Auschwitz, a number of German officers were also transferred out and some came to our camp. One of the more notorious of these was Dr. Josef Mengele, Y.S., who was very instrumental in the deaths of hundreds of thousands at

Auschwitz. When he visited our children's barrack, he had very friendly conversations with some ten year olds which belied his reprehensible past. Had his felonious record not been pointed out to us by the Auschwitz survivors then one would never have realized what dirt his immaculate green uniform covered.

IN THE MORNING, BEFORE BREAKFAST, I MADE IT A POINT TO *daven* from my small *siddur* for as long as time permitted. When I took out extra time to *daven,* my piece of breakfast bread, which was covered with jam, always seemed larger. Breakfast consisted of one slice of *kuch* bread covered with some kind of jam, which had more substitute ingredients than real jam should contain. But when one is starving, almost anything will do. For a drink we had some sort of hot imitation coffee without milk.

Breakfast we ate at long, bare, wooden tables placed end to end with hard, wooden benches on each side. The bread was dealt out at one end by *Schwester* Lubah or one of her colleagues and then passed down piece by piece. One morning, I was the last one to come to breakfast since I had been late in finishing my *davening.* As a result, I got the last seat at the end of the tables. My cousin sat next to me. As we were eating, a German inspection team arrived at the scene to observe us. On my head I always wore a navy blue cap, which Mother had purchased at Maison de Bonneterie. The cap had a very narrow, cloth covered, hard visor and a small cloth covered button at the center on top. As I was chewing my bread, one of the *Aufseherinnen,* who now stood behind me, slowly lifted my cap, holding it at the top center button and placed it on the empty bench beside me. As I felt the cap coming off, I stopped chewing and waited till the SS woman passed further down; only then did I put my cap on again and continue eating.

It must be realized that to European non-Jews, eating with a covered head is as impolite as it is for us to eat bareheaded. This episode, of a German removing my cap and the stopping of my chewing, was one of many memorable war events. It was testimony in many ways to my good parents and some of the values they instilled in us. Germans didn't look for good excuses to kill or otherwise harm their victims. Having a hated German stand behind me, single me out and remove an important part of my attire was reason enough for great concern to an eleven year old. Nevertheless, regardless of possible consequences, I did not continue eating, despite the fact that I was starving for food.

For the record, I was, unfortunately, the only boy in our children's group who covered his head and wore *tzitzes*. None of the children or adults paid attention to either of these garbs, as they appeared to be part of my attire.

[From a *halachic* viewpoint, when a Jewish male pronounces a *brocho* prior to and after partaking of food, it is necessary to do so with a covered head. A covering of the bare head can consist of a hat, cap or an equivalent covering. Continuous covering of the head is interpreted by most scholars as a matter of *Chassidus* (piety) and is considered a very laudable custom, which has now become entrenched among many Orthodox Jews. Only under very special and extenuating circumstances is the head kept exposed when consuming food. For an eleven year old youngster to discontinue eating or chewing while not wearing his cap was not a matter of *halacha* but rather a poignant story of *mesieras nefesh* (self sacrifice). For exceptions and details of the *halacha* concerning covering of the head by males, refer to *Mishnah Berurah*,[a] along with the associated commentaries.]

DIGRESSING FOR A MOMENT TO THE FUTURE..., IT WAS FIFTEEN years later, in the year 1960, and I was working as a design engineer for a consulting engineering firm in New York City. Our Chief Engineer was Mr. Rudolf Karoti,[b] a non-Jew with a heavy Hungarian accent, with whom I had a good professional relationship. Mr. Karoti arrived in the States in the early 1950's as part of Europe's "Brain Drain" phenomenon. One day, when we were eating lunch at our respective office desks, Rudi came over and without saying a word removed the hat from my head and placed it on my desk. It brought back a vivid memory of the Bergen Belsen cap episode. Despite the serious nature of this provocation, it was my opinion that not every hostile action need necessarily be anti-Semitic in nature. My rationale in this incident was that there must have been an acute personal stress which triggered this strange conduct since we had always been on good terms. Instead of getting upset, I calmly asked whether he just had some serious disagreement with his wife. Rudi answered in the affirmative and was amazed how I knew. I then requested that he not release his personal frustrations on myself. He apologized and the incident was never repeated.

To be a practicing Jew at home is the correct thing to do. I always considered it a proud hallmark to be known as well in my professional

---

a. 2:6,12 and 91:3,9.
b. The name was changed by the author.

circles as an observant orthodox Jew, who attempted to be consistent and conscientious in his ways. My goal was to approach:

> *"When Hashem accepts a person's ways,*
> *He will even cause his antagonists to make peace with him."*[c]

My professional career was Civil Engineering, which I enjoyed immensely. Nevertheless, my axiom was to be more than just a professional. Thus, I always was considerably involved in non-material aspects of being. The corollary to that axiom is that I didn't live to work but I worked and studied to live. These realities in life always were my guides and parameters in making a career based decision. With the *Ribono Shel Olam's* help, *"Zeh Vezeh Niskaimon Beyodie"*. (With Hashem's help, I practiced Judaism while living in a secular world.)

MOST OF THE *FRAUENLAGER* INMATES WERE ALMOST completely shaven bald. The German excuse for this was probably to avoid hair lice. We children were, however, given ordinary civilian haircuts on several occasions by *Schwester* Lubah. When it came to my turn, I saw that she was using manual clippers, a razor and scissors. In German, I told her that, "My mother does not want my hair to be cut with a razor knife". She considered it peculiar, but complied after discussing it with her colleagues.[d]

In March of 1945, as Pesach approached, I was anxious to at least avoid eating bread. However, without that one daily slice of bread, I would have starved. After discussing it with Erika, we planned to request permission of *Schwester* Lubah to exchange bread for potatoes at the kitchen during those eight days. Of course, such an exchange process would require the "official" sanction of *Schwester* Lubah and would be no easy feat. My German was adequate for simple matters but not for something as important as a food exchange request in a place like Bergen Belsen. To make sure that *Schwester* Lubah would understand my request, it was decided that Erika would teach me to say in good German, "I would like to request permission to exchange my portion of *kuch* for potatoes during the eight days of *Pesach*". I practiced it for at least a week. Then, when I thought my German language request sounded natural, I went over to *Schwester* Lubah when she was not preoccupied with other matters. I made my request and she responded with a few words which I don't remember, but the end result was in the negative. That *Pesach*, I unfortunately had to eat *kuch* – it was a case of *Pikuach*

---

c. Mishlei, 16:7.
d. Vayikra, 19:27, *Maseches Kiddushin,* 35b and *Yoreh De'ah,* 181:2 and 3.

Nefesh. Avoiding bread would only have been symbolic, since the camp's other food rations had enough grain derivatives to render them in violation of the *Pesach* laws.

THE GERMANS MADE IT A POINT TO IMPRESS US CHILDREN WITH their superiority. I remember one day mingling among other children outside our barrack, when an SS officer came along. He showed us a piece of paper with the letter "X" marked on it, and proceeded to post the paper on a low tree branch. Then he yelled over to the guard tower that he was going to do some shooting. He took out his pistol and, from a distance of perhaps fifteen to twenty feet, proceeded to do some target practice. He did puncture the paper. Whether he scored 100%, one could not tell.

THE SETTING WAS DURING THE BLEAK WINTER MONTHS OF 1944-45. We were sheltered in a poorly heated and crowded barrack bedroom, darkness set in very early and the lighting in our barrack was poor. Outside were piles and piles of corpses lining the narrow roadway plus additional piles of bodies further back from the roadway inside the wooded areas. Food was scarce and for the most part not very palatable. We were separated from our parents and no one knew of their fate. There were no telephones, radios, newspapers, mail or other reliable sources of news. Television was not yet commercially available and there were no movies either. Medical needs went unattended, classrooms did not exist and there were no recreational facilities, etc. As one can well imagine, ordinary persons did not have very optimistic attitudes during this period. We knew that the Germans were having a very rough time, being sapped of their strength and resources, we also had great hopes that *Hashem* would take us out of this miserable situation, back to liberty, free from the German yoke.

Seldom did I have dreams, but then, one night, a special dream gave me a great boost in morale. I saw myself climbing up a long ladder, which was leaning against nothing else but the Wailing Wall! *(Kosel Ma'aravi)*. I reached halfway to the top of the ladder, which extended three quarters to the top of the wall. The entire scene was bathed in bright sunlight and there were very few persons present. The meaning of the dream I did not know, but I realized that this was a harbinger of far better times and that we would survive to see freedom again in its full glory as practicing proud Jews, without oppression.

SCHWESTER LUBAH WAS ON GOOD TERMS WITH ONE OF THE German officers. Towards the end of the war, when the Germans were scheming about how to deal with their prisoners, this officer approached *Schwester* Lubah and offered to bring a truck one evening and take all of us Dutch/Russian children along with the three ladies in charge out of camp to a safe location. This strange story was divulged to us by *Schwester* Lubah only after the war. Her response to the officer was that she wanted no favors and whatever would happen to the camp prisoners would be good enough for her charges and herself. I believe that subconsciously there was a second concern in her mind. Too many times the Germans deceived their prisoners, promising them good things only to murder them at the first opportunity. The following euphemisms are typical examples of how the German establishment eroded their credibility:

- ❖ On roads leading to the gas chambers in Auschwitz where one and a half million were murdered, the road signs read "to bath house" in every conceivable language.

- ❖ Victims carried to the gas chambers were frequently transported in trucks with Red Cross markings - implying that the prisoners would not be harmed.

- ❖ Prisoners sent to many labor units or labor camps were sent there for the express purpose of killing them. Thus, the able bodied men left their homes without confrontations and they did not remain behind to form resistance groups, etc. etc.

Towards the end of March, 1945, sanitary conditions at Bergen Belsen worsened by the day. Typhoid fever was rampant and prisoners in the *Frauenlager* died like "flies". Everyday we would walk along the road in front of our barrack and see new piles of bodies added during the night. We were cautioned not to drink the water. That was easier said than done. There were no pots or gas ranges to boil the water before drinking it. Fortunately, the weather was cool and the liquid we got from the watery kitchen soup was sufficient to meet our fluid demands. I did not develop typhoid fever until approximately two weeks after liberation, when I did break out with a very mild case of the disease.

Towards the war's end we developed what was generally referred to in layman's terms as "potato stomachs". These were distended, bloated stomachs attributable to malnutrition and gave us the profile of a giant upright potato, hence the nickname. Potatoes, as well as other vegetables, were in short supply and formed only a small part of our daily meals compared to our watery turnip soup.

Chapter Twenty

BERGEN BELSEN - FINAL DAYS

THE FINAL WAR DAYS IN THE NORTH-WESTERN REGION OF the "European war theater" were eventful. Food was becoming even scarcer than in the meager months to date. The mood in our compound was a combination of being subdued and depressed due to the many prisoners struck by the typhoid epidemic, the countless deaths, the overcrowding and inadequate food. On the other hand there was anxiety as we sensed that our ordeal would soon end on a positive note.

Several days prior to liberation, I took a walk through the shallow woods separating our barrack from the camp's security perimeter. There, I saw a sight never seen before. Directly inside the barbed wire security fence, in front of one of the guard towers - which was only accessible from outside the camp - was a small clearing among the trees. Several blankets had been spread on the grass, on which four German speaking girls in their early to mid-twenties were sunbathing! All four were clad in bathing suits and singing German songs, harmonizing as they sang. I did not approach them and they paid no attention to me, being too involved in talking with and singing love songs to the guard in the tower. Imagine the gall of these beasts in human form, being entirely oblivious to the suffering going on around them and to the piles and piles of dead bodies that reached only a few hundred feet from their sunny perch. May this have been the last nice day these ogresses had in their lives.

During those final days, one could hear explosions and artillery being fired from the distance, probably in connection with the battle to capture the city of Hannover, twenty miles away. The night before liberation, we saw extra military activity outside the camp's security fence. These included many additional German soldiers plus some who were traveling in small security type vehicles that resembled miniature battle tanks.

THE GERMANS KNEW WE WERE ALL STARVED AND DESPERATE for food. They also knew that the state of the camp, with its utter disregard to human suffering, was not the kind of public relations the Germans wanted to be confronted with. And so with typical German hospitality, the camp bakers were directed to bake a double portion of bread for every prisoner. There was only one hitch — the bread was to be laced with lethal poison! A dead prisoner does not tell tales and these beasts had very guilty consciences. To carry their murderous plot to completion, the Germans deprived themselves of badly needed motor fuel and placed barrels of oil in strategic locations throughout the Camp. The plan was first to kill all prisoners with the extra ration of spiked bread and then to destroy all the evidence by fire. With Hashem's help these schemes were foiled. The Allied troops entered camp in the nick of time just before the poisoned bread was distributed. All tainted bread was burned and destroyed and fresh batches were baked.

It was my impression that many of the Jewish prisoners with whom I came in contact were, in former times of peace, capable and willing to emulate the lifestyle of their pious ancestors. Pursuing the path of the faithful can lead to lifesaving Divine miracles. A case in point was the eleventh hour reprieve from an extermination plot as conspired by our benevolent German culinary hosts at Bergen Belsen. This precipitated the following dichotomy: We were taught in Shemos[a] that following the Egyptian exodus, the Jewish people were to prepare double portions of bread every *erev Shabbos*. Partaking of such extra provision at the three *Shabbos* meals throughout the ages continues to shield our people from

---

a. 16:22.

אולי ירחם! ...*Perhaps He will have mercy!*...
A quote from Selichos (a special Tefillah) From the painting by I. Grocholsky
Reprinted from the Israelit,[21] March 1896

three potentially lethal scenarios, including protection from the final war to be fought between Gog and Mogog.[b] Thus the *zechus* of both our historical *double bakings* and the *Shabbos* meals gave wondrous protection and became a Providential antidote that thwarted the lethal *double baking* scheme orchestrated by the wicked Josef Kramer, et. al. and planned for implementation on *Shabbos,* April 14, 1945.

> *"Rabos machashovos b'lev ish v'atzas Hashem he sokum."*
> "There are many schemes in a man's heart,
> but Hashem's plan will prevail."[c]

---

b. Refer to *Maseches Shabbos,* 118a.
c. Mishlei, 19:21.

Chapter Twenty One

LIBERATION!

THE GREAT DAY OF LIBERATION FINALLY ARRIVED. UNFORtunately, it did not come for many poor souls who had already succumbed to disease and hunger and too late for those who were about to leave this world. There were, however, thousands who were fortunate to greet this momentous time in their lives.

It was early Sunday morning, on the fifteenth of April 1945, 2 Iyar, 5705, when a vanguard tank column of British and Canadian troops, serving under the central command of the Supreme Commander of the Allied armies, General Dwight David Eisenhower, rolled into Bergen Belsen. The sun was just above the horizon as they moved slowly down the main camp road. On the lead tank was mounted a loudspeaker. In the Dutch language, it announced!: "You are being liberated in the name of (the Dutch) Queen Wilhelmina". Very few prisoners understood the message of freedom since most of the Dutch prisoners had been transferred several weeks earlier to other camps in Germany and Austria. Those remaining at Bergen Belsen spoke mostly Hungarian, Rumanian, Polish, Russian and Yugoslavian.

Walking along the main road were the high ranking scoundrels, camp *Kommandant* Josef Kramer, with a gun slung over his shoulder, and the *Haupt Aufseherin* (chief German Women's SS soldier) along his side. May they and their kind rot in Hell. Kramer motioned to the prisoners to stay behind the barbed wire fences. It was, however, too late for him. His time had come and he and his companion were immediately taken into custody. Needless to say, the now ex-prisoners were jubilant. The Germans who remained didn't risk public exposure for fear of being torn apart. The guard towers were all miraculously empty and there was practically no resistance to the Allied forces.

I remember standing in front of our barrack that morning, when a familiar S.S. soldier walked past on his way to surrendering. Instead of his usual green uniform, he wore a light beige one, his pistol and bayonet were gone and his head was down. He was mentally beaten.

THE BRITISH PATROLS SPREAD OUT THROUGH THE CAMP TO assess local conditions. Inevitably their scouts stumbled upon the hideous scene of our barrack's road — an open air morgue — a make believe grisly sorceress pantry, a nightmarish sight — not to be believed. Without counting, there were easily more than one thousand emaciated, naked bodies in full view of any passerby. The British became infuriated. They requisitioned an old German truck with the rear cargo section open. Then, eight to ten of the camp's top SS officers, who had been apprehended before they could disappear, were pressed into a mass-body moving detail.

An army tank rode in front of the truck and stopped right in front of our barrack. Body after body was heaved onto the truck.

There was no rigor mortis in these bodies. One German grabbed the ankles, a second the wrists and heaved the bodies face up, the heads bobbing down. They walked in pairs to the truck, in their full green colored officer's uniform, where the bodies were piled onto the flatbed. Another four Germans on the truck neatly piled their hideous cargo, perpendicular to the length of the truck. All along, the British soldiers yelled to the Germans, "Come on!, Come on!..." to speed up their efforts. Every now and then the British would shoot into the air to underscore their point.

While this incredible activity was in progress, I was among the children standing close to the truck who yelled "*Moordenaars!, Moordenaars!...*" ("Murderers!, Murderers!...") and threw small stones at the Germans on the truck. The Germans ducked every now and then. Once I got too close to the truck and when a German pushed one of these stones off the truck it bounced off my knee. My cousin Erika said to me "Why don't you tell the British about that?" I just stepped back, however, and took in the scene.

The Germans were kept loading truck after truck for thirty-six straight hours. Unfortunately, the sight of dead bodies was common and, therefore, the open truck with its appalling load raised few eyebrows as it traveled along the camp roads. The bodies were taken to a temporary morgue where the same officers unloaded their grisly cargo. On one of these short trips, one of the Germans tried to escape by jumping from the truck into a small body of water. He was promptly shot dead in the water by British marksmen in an accompanying truck.

SEVERAL DAYS AFTER ALL THE CORPSES WERE GONE, THERE arrived a strange looking group of men. They appeared to be Hungarian soldiers but their uniforms were oversized. Their equipment consisted of push carts, hand shovels and pick axes. Over the next four to five days, these men dug a huge rectangular shaped pit in front of our barrack on the other side of the roadway. The earth was temporary piled in berms all around this excavation. The depth of the pit was probably eight or nine feet.

Subsequently, the first scene repeated itself. The same truck that had transported the bodies to a temporary storage site now brought all of them back. The German SS officers were again pressed into service, this time joined by SS women soldiers. One by one the bodies were taken off the truck. Then, two Germans grabbed each body as before and heaved it to its final resting ground. Hundreds and hundreds of bodies were thrown into this mass gravesite and neatly laid to rest with steady sounds of thud…thud…thud… as the dead struck bottom in the deep pit.

The scene of over one thousand bodies nonchalantly cast into a mass grave by former SS guards evokes multitudes of impressions and recollections. It was a bizarre setting that few humans ever witnessed. Alas, these cadavers were now devoured in the bowels of a nation once obsessed by their own debauchery. In former years, these deceased represented the elite of their respective societies. Now, their bodies joined the ranks of mankind in humanity's great common destiny the grave.

The entire burial spectacle evinces choking emotions whenever I reminisce of those times.

Here is a litany of mental brushstrokes, painting personal thoughts, emotions and sentiments on this multi-faceted graveside canvas:

Distant Echoes of Those Tragic "Thuds"

Each "thud"	reverberated through worlds of thought.
Each "thud"	stood for worldly hopes and aspirations that were now forever naught.
Each "thud"	denoted another irreplaceable Being to be sorely missed.
Each "thud"	meant more sobbing parents waiting endlessly for a loving daughter's return.
Each "thud"	could mean a lamenting husband never seeing his devoted wife again.
Each "thud"	portrayed a grieving child, needlessly becoming an orphan for life.
Each "thud"	surely meant the loss of a beloved sibling, alas.
Each "thud"	verily bemoaned the loss of a very close friend.
Each "thud"	summoned forth a sigh from generations to come.[a]
Each "thud"	brought a beautiful lifetime abruptly to its end.
Each "thud"	represented another pure *neshomah* that long ago had returned to its source.
Each "thud"	increased the multitudes of friendly accusers in the Heavenly Court.
Each "thud"	multiplied the swollen ranks of advocates in the World to Come.
Each "thud"	hammered another nail in the despicable German coffin.
Each "thud"	represented another innocent victim, succumbing to German-style incarceration.
Each "thud"	alas, brought forth fresh rivers of tears cascading into the Heavenly coffers!
Each "thud"	hallowed more blood soaked soil in a detested land where the creed of Sodom was the vogue.

---

a. *Breishis*, 4:10, *Rashi*

Each "thud"	pierced the air, a marker of sound, where an unknown heroine fell so proud.
Each "thud"	brought an end to being part of the lofty and wondrously serene terrestrial *Shabbos* days.
Each "thud"	bid a strenuous good bye to the delightful and august *Sholosh Regolim, Chanukah* and *Purim* festival-days.
Each "thud"	was counted as another soul given up *Al Kiddush Hashem*.
Each "thud"	ungraciously reminded us mortals: repent we must!, ere we retire to join the immortals at their last resting place.
Each "thud"	was another reason for *Moshiach ben Dovid* to appear quickly.
Each "thud"	meant one less person to be at our *Beis Hamikdosh* when it will soon reappear.[b]

***Ribono Shel Olam,* Guardian of our sanctified people, may Your great Name be exalted and sanctified, speedily and in our days!** *Omein*

According honor to the deceased is a hallmark of our civilized society. Tossing naked dead bodies into a grave is not exactly paying proper last respects. In this case, there was great concern regarding the ongoing typhoid epidemic. To address this important worry without delay, speedy burial was considered to be of the essence.

During this burial activity, one of the Germans who had been nicknamed Pinto because of his short height, collapsed from exhaustion, and he, too, was tossed into this grave, in full uniform. A British woman soldier was there watching when she was thought to have recognized her mother among the dead. Hysterics broke out, as one can well imagine. Shooting into the air and the yelling of "Come on!... Come on!...." accompanied this burial scene as well.

The entire spectacle was inconceivable to the outside world and demonstrated how a so called *civilized* society as existed in Germany could reach its nadir, a society with its poets and famous musical composers, scientists and engineers, its well developed industries, superhighways, modern army, airforce and navy, scientific and medical research teams and development projects, etc. All were harnessed to oppress, to

---

b. *Maseches Rosh Hashonoh,* 30a, last *Rashi*

kill, to murder, to rob, to break every international treaty including the Geneva Convention.

Once all the bodies were laid to rest, the poorly equipped and ill clad Hungarian soldiers reappeared on the scene and covered the mass grave with soil. To the best of my knowledge, this is the site where a monument was erected. At the Holocaust Museum, Yad Veshem in Yerusholayim, there is a replica of this monument. In 1972, while visiting Eretz Yisroel, I photographed the simple rectangular stone. Appropriately, the text reads:

> May G-d, the Jewish People And All Mankind Remember
> Our Sacred Martyrs
> Tortured And Exterminated
> By The Germans
> During The Nazi Regime At
> BERGEN BELSEN
> And All Other Concentration Camps
> EARTH, CONCEAL NOT THE
> BLOOD SHED ON THEE!
> Date of Liberation: April 15, 1945
>
> World Federation of The Bergen Belsen Survivors

This text was repeated on the rectangular stone monument in several other languages including Hebrew, Yiddish and French.

According to information printed in the *Encyclopedia Americana*[8], the following gruesome statistics should place German atrocities at Bergen Belsen in the proper perspective:

"...When the survivors — over 50,000 sick and starving — were liberated by the British Army on April 15, 1945, 10,000 unburied corpses were found. Soon afterwards 13,000 others died of malnutrition, disease and the effects of torture..."

TO ALLEVIATE THE ENORMOUS LEVEL OF SUFFERING DUE TO disease and malnutrition, the neutral Swedish government arranged to take in six thousand Bergen Belsen survivors. Immediately following the liberation, these persons were airlifted to Sweden for recuperation. This was a magnanimous act of true kindness and illustrates how a civilized nation can harness technology for the good of mankind. These Scandinavians surely put the Germans to shame.

MANY OF THE BODIES AT BERGEN BELSEN LAY EXPOSED outdoors, for various durations from the end of the year 1944 until their final burial towards the end of April, 1945. One of the miracles of Bergen Belsen was that there were no flies, vermin or predatory beasts, all of which could have been attracted by the corpses. The deceased almost reached the status of the dead at Betar, who had been murdered by the Romans under King Hadrian, some eighteen hundred years earlier, when Shimon Bar Kochba led an unsuccessful uprising in the year 3896 (135 C.E.). Those bodies at Betar lay exposed for two years until the Romans granted permission for their burial. Yet, Hadrian's victims remained unmolested by beasts or birds of prey until burial.

The sages at Yavneh added a fourth *brocho* to *Birchas Hamozon,* following the mass burial at Betar. In that *brocho,* we are constantly reminded that each generation should not rely on its Bar Kochbas.[c] Instead, we must recognize that it is Hashem who has given, gives and will give all that is good and causes us to "ripen" into a G-d fearing people. The deaths of six million Jews during World War II should cause us to reaffirm this commitment of realization in Hashem's leadership and in His control over all that occurs in our lives. We have faith and trust that Hashem will provide for all our basic daily needs, e.g. the air we breathe, the food we eat, our bodily functions, etc. Therefore we must also have faith and trust in His judgment, despite our lack of knowledge and understanding of the causes and effects of what transpired during this great destruction.

FOLLOWING SEVERAL YEARS OF INADEQUATE FOOD INTAKE and starvation diets, we children just couldn't consume enough food. The Allies accommodated us by making large quantities of food available. This food ranged from army food to the food found in storage outside Bergen Belsen, which had been shipped by the Red Cross but never distributed. The women in charge of our children's group were kept busy making sandwiches to meet our insatiable appetites. The "dining room" tables were emptied of piles of sandwiches soon after we started each meal.

To illustrate our ravenous hunger let me relate the following story. There was an old lady who appeared on the scene in our barrack. That person proceeded to cook kidney beans on our pot belly stove. Since she, too, was famished and accordingly impatient, the beans were only cooked sufficiently so that their insides were soft. Being that this lady had no

---

c. Horav S. R. Hirsch, Siddur

teeth, she therefore began sucking out the bean's inside, one at a time, spitting out each skin. Several of my friends and I then scrambled for these bean skins, picked them up from the barrack floor and immediately ate them!

Wandering around the camp after liberation was interesting, to say the least. Holes had been made in the barbed wire fences, and previously off-limit areas were now swarming with liberated persons. The wooden gallows on the main camp road lay on the ground as if a truck had rammed them. The latter was probably the work of the departing Germans who didn't want any lynchings. Right next to these downed gallows lay the body of an indecently exposed, well fed male. He appeared to be German since no ex-prisoner could have been that well fed. The corpse was dressed in new civilian overalls. These chameleons maintained the well known German army practice of changing to civilian clothes for the purpose of escaping detection.

Many of these SS officers and their partners in crime were bullies in uniform but displayed a large degree of cowardice when it came to publicly acknowledging their unscrupulous practices.

There was some press coverage, and former prisoners were interviewed. On one occasion, the BBC set us children up in a nearby vacant barrack. There we sang many Dutch songs into a microphone. Then I was asked to sing some Hebrew songs. Since, besides my cousin, I was the only one who knew *Zemiros*, I declined because of shyness. Months later we were told that our singing had been broadcast on the radio in England.

Chapter Twenty Two

KAZERNEN

THREE MILES FROM BERGEN BELSEN THE GERMAN SOLDIERS and officers who were part of the concentration camp garrison lived in style, it was probably near the town of Celle. Their barracks, known as *kazernen,* were constructed of stone, brick and concrete, and the rooms were relatively small in size so as to avoid the dormitory/barrack syndrome. There was plenty of light and air around these buildings. The interiors had plastered walls, windows that closed properly and good ceiling lighting. Their hallways even had recessed coal burning fireplaces. In short, they were a far contrast to our flimsy, squalid, wooden barracks.

Arrangements were made for the children's transfer to these *kazernen* after they were cleaned and made ready for our occupancy. Needless to say, we were very appreciative for this improvement in living quarters. Following our stint at the wretched barracks, our coming to the *kazernen* was like being upgraded to "palace" level. There was only one person to a bed and the beds had sheets and proper woolen blankets. The rooms were light and airy.

When we arrived, we found in each room several dark brown crackers on the table. With the memories of the poisoned bread, however, we were suspicious and all the crackers went to the garbage. The first meals were served along long tables in the hallways between the bedrooms. The food was specifically prepared for us and consisted of cooked rice with some fruit compote. Apparently, many of the Russian girls weren't used to eating rice and, therefore, didn't eat much. After the meal was over a group of four or five boys, including myself, went to the unfinished plates and finished the leftovers.

DURING OUR INCARCERATION AT BERGEN BELSEN NONE OF US knew what had happened to our parents, but we were optimistic all along. We children frequently used to sing together one stanza of a popular Dutch song:

Wij gaan nog niet naar huis,

nog lang niet, nog lang niet,

wij gaan nog niet naar huis,

myn moeder is niet thuis!

Translation:

We are not yet going home,

not for a long time, not for a long time,

we are not yet going home,

my mother is not home!

On occasion, some Canadian soldiers would take us on field outings. They knew no Dutch nor German and we knew no English, which made communication difficult; but we sensed their good will and friendship. Riding along a country road, in an open army truck, we sang the above song many times. This was one of many opportunities to sing again.

THE ALLIED ARMIES HAD JEWISH CHAPLAINS FOR THE MANY Jewish soldiers and officers who fought in their ranks. One of these chaplains was an old friend of our family, Rabbi Rodereguez Pereira. He was originally from Amsterdam, Holland. Rabbi Pereira, was of Portugese descent, which accounts for his Hispanic name. His ancestors were among the Jews who the Spanish had banished from the Iberian Peninsula (Spain – Portugal) on *Tisha B'Av* in the year 1492. His niece, Helena, had been engaged to Bob Posen, a son of Father's first cousin. As previously mentioned, Bob subsequently died of malnutrition and hard work in Bergen Belsen. The Levis had contacted Rabbi Pereira and requested him to visit Bergen Belsen so as to inquire and report on our state of well-being. It was exceedingly nice of him to go out of his way and perform a real act of *chesed*. That day, several friends and I, had gone exploring the countryside using the *kazernen* as our home base. When we returned, Rabbi Pereira was waiting. We talked for a short while, and then he went to visit my sisters, who were in a different section of this former garrison.

Upon Rabbi Pereira's return to his headquarters, he dispatched a telegram to the Levis stating that he had met us and found us to be:

Lichamelijk en Geestelijk gezond,

Translation: "physically and emotionally well".

It should be noted that these were the days before direct dialing of transatlantic telephonic communications, and therefore telegrams were the best means of that era for this purpose.

Considering the ordeal we had experienced, it was Hashem's grace, kindness and mercy to us that enabled Rabbi Pereira to make these observations. Indeed, he was correct, we had survived relatively unscathed from one of history's most furious and brutal catastrophes. I had never felt concerned for my life while in the camp. Nevertheless, for years following the war, seeing how many had not returned, the question constantly cropped up in my mind: Why did I survive and not others? The answer to this query is only known to our Creator.

DURING OUR STAY IN THE *KAZERNEN,* I USED TO VISIT MY sisters two or three times a week. They also made forays into the surrounding countryside with their girlfriend roommate and, on occasion, would bring back food to supplement their local meals from the central kitchen. In the immediate weeks following liberation, general lawlessness reigned in the countryside surrounding Bergen Belsen. Food supplies were taken from local villagers by anyone willing to help themselves. Money was not exchanged in these "transactions". Subsequently, the Allies printed and issued German currency in "Marks" for use by the general population.

Our *kazerne* faced a large, open, rectangular shaped parade ground. Camped on three of its sides were British troops in military field tents. The soldiers and officers were extremely friendly to us and even gave us from their meager candy ration. My friends and I would sometimes hang

*German replacement money issued by the Allies.
Shown are half Mark and One Mark denominations.*

around these sites. Under the bushes, behind their artillery guns and tents, the entire area abounded with unspent, loose German machine gun bullets laying scattered on the ground. They were pencil thin and perhaps one and a half inches in length. One of our "entertainments" was to take some of these bullets and throw them in the fires that the soldiers had going to keep warm. Each bullet made quite a pop. To this day, I am not sure how risky that game was, but I would definitely not recommend anyone to try it. It should be stated that burning, torching or heating a mortar or artillery shell has already caused mortal injury.

On May 7, 1945, the Soviet army from the East and the Allied Armies from the West met in Berlin and the Third *Reich* became history. Germany had at long last been defeated, its large cities and industries destroyed and its armed forces taken prisoner. Despite the tremendous toll of human lives and suffering, it was a great day of joy and celebration. Officially, that day was called V.E. day or Victory Europe day. Now began the enormous task of rebuilding the many countries that had been under the heavy yoke of the German fascists, also known as Nazis [National Sozialists].

To celebrate V.E. day, the British assembled some seventy-five artillery guns along three sides of the parade ground perimeter in front of our *Kazerne*. Wooden crates full of artillery shells were delivered to each gun. I was told the shells were dummies, but I always wondered why there were all these dummy shells in a war zone. In the afternoon, a British colonel in full ragalia uniform positioned himself in front of our building and stood at the center of the "U" shaped configuration of the artillery gun layout. With flag in hand, he raised his arm high up and then with a swish he quickly lowered it. Each time the colonel's arm was lowered, we heard a tremendous BOOM!!! All seventy-five artillery pieces discharged in unison. In all, there must have been at least ten salvos per cannon. It was a military salute to V.E. day, the day we had all been impatiently waiting for. The colonel always gave the troops sufficient time to reload their guns and then repeated his signal with a quick downward flag motion. This went on until all the ammunition crates were emptied. We stood within two hundred feet of this scene and even with fingers in our ears the sounds were deafening. This event was another of many occasions to be remembered.

THE TWO MONTHS WE SPENT AT THE *KAZERNEN* WAS A time to recharge our physical batteries. We did a lot of eating, resting, walking and exploring the countryside. The mood of all of us ex-prisoners was mostly positive and we were looking forward to return home again to be with our parents, relatives and friends.

The concentration camp portion of Bergen Belsen was now like a ghost town. My friends and I hiked back to the camp but were stopped at the gate by Allied soldiers. It was strictly off-limits and for good reason. The Allies were concerned that it could be a source of disease, especially typhoid fever, which had been so rampant. One evening, some of the older members of the camp alumni, including my sister Toni and *Schwester* Lubah were invited to observe as the camp was put to the torch and burned to the ground. The German wish of burning down the camp was fulfilled and with Hashem's *chesed,* the roles were now reversed. The former prisoners of those barracks now lived in the comfortable German *kazernen,* and the previous *kazerne* occupants were the post war prisoners of the Allied armies.

THE BRITISH SOLDIERS DEVOTED MUCH TIME WITH US DUTCH children. One of their activities was to build playground swings on the parade grounds. During and immediately following the war there was a shortage of newsprint and newspaper printing equipment. Accordingly, a custom developed to exhibit news stories on special town bulletin boards and in display windows of large stores. During early July of 1945, following our return to Holland, I was walking with a friend through the business district of a medium sized town named Enschede in north eastern Holland. While passing a department store, I suddenly looked up and noticed a whole group of post war pictures in its window. Lo and behold, one of the pictures was of the playground swings erected by the British, and there I was in the background of the photograph watching the activity my favorite past time. We entered the store and talked to the manager, who recognized me on the photograph since I was wearing the same clothing. I then became the proud owner of that news picture. The caption on back of the photograph was typed as follows:

> "Belsen children are happier now. Since the British freed Belsen Concentration Camp, everything possible has been done to make the children forget any horrors that they may have seen there. Most of these children had Jewish blood and many of their parents died in the camp. British soldiers have given up their cigarette rations to the adults and their sweet rations to the children of Belsen camp. Toys have also been requisitioned from nearby towns. Picture taken April 26th. Picture shows:

> Children playing on the swings which were erected by a R.E.M.E. Detachment. A British soldier gives a helping hand."a

On the front of the photograph, the Dutch language caption reads:

> *Kinderen in het concentratiekamp te Belsum*
> *na hun bevrijding.*

Translation:

> Children following their liberation
> at the Bergen Belsen Concentration Camp.

A FLASHBACK TO OLDEN TIMES: BEFORE THE DAYS OF INEXpensive refrigeration, cold storage, controlled temperature storage and importation of out of season fruits and vegetables from distant lands, fruits were available only during their harvest seasons and vegetable availability was usually limited to the summer and fall seasons. Thus, availability of perishable produce during the winter and spring seasons was almost non-existent. One way of preserving items such as potatoes, carrots, turnips, etc., was to dig long trenches in the ground. Those ditches were then lined with straw, which functioned as the bed for the vegetables with another layer of straw placed on top. This was followed by a second layer of those firm tuber/root type vegetables. This layering process was repeated for about three to five strata of vegetables. The entire trench was then backfilled and soil was heaped approximately one and a half foot over the trench, above the ground. In this manner, these vegetables were inexpensively stored below the frostline until used. As the vegetables were needed, the quantity required was dug up, starting at one end of the trench. Many such trenches, partially dug up, were seen near the *kazernen*.

ONE OF MY FRIENDS FROM AMSTERDAM, MEIR PAKTER, HAD also been caught in the German dragnet and he and his family landed up in the Dutch compound at Bergen Belsen. In Amsterdam, we had spent many hours together both in the Pakter house as well as in ours. When we originally arrived at Bergen Belsen in May of 1944, I remember that he was one of the first children whom I spotted in the curiosity crowd

---

a. British Official Photograph No. BU.4525,XL.
 War Office Photograph, Crown Copyright Reserved.

New play swings on the kazerne parade ground. I am seen standing through the portal of the center swing.

that greeted us as we entered. His parents were not in the Diamond Group and I don't know what happened to them. Just prior to returning to Holland, I was told that there was a Dutch Jewish boy who had recently arrived at the *kazernen* but that due to illness was confined to bed. I went to visit him and found the boy to be none other than my old friend Meir. I was shocked by his appearance, he looked like a skeleton with some skin stretched over his bones. He was extremely weak and he hardly spoke but did manage to produce a broad smile. My friend must have been extremely sick but was fortunate enough to have been liberated just in time. When we returned to Holland, Meir had to remain behind due to his extreme weakness and his severe underweight condition. Since then, I lost contact with my boyhood friend.

Section Three

...AND A TIME TO GATHER STONES.

(KOHELES 3,5)

Chapter Twenty Three
RETURN TO HOLLAND

NEAR BERGEN BELSEN WAS A SMALL GERMAN BUILT military airport. During the war, there were times when German planes flew low over the camp, probably to land at that airstrip. In June of 1945, arrangements were finally completed for our return to Holland. Our entire group of Dutch children was trucked to the airport. This contingent consisted of only the younger group. The slightly older group which included my sisters traveled to Holland by truck. Accompanying us was *Schwester* Lubah, who, even though she was Polish, had taken a liking to us and thought anything would be better than returning to her war torn Poland.

This was my first trip on a plane. The airplane was a military craft which had been designed to carry parachutists. The entire interior was bare, with long, narrow, built-in benches along both sides of the fuselage. These were the days before jet engines and the propellers were extremely noisy. The speed of these planes was in the range of two hundred MPH. I remember the weather being pleasant and visibility clear to the horizon. As we flew over the Rhine and the Maas rivers we saw these mighty waterways meander across Holland to the North Sea, a beautiful sight to behold.

Our plane landed at the Southern Dutch city of Eindhoven (home of Philips Electric Co.). From there we went to the nearby town of 's-Hertogenbosch. It was wonderful to be out of Germany and back in Holland but there was much anxiety as to what would happen next.

We ate in classrooms and slept on classroom floors at a local Catholic school. Up until now, the Diamond Group's younger children unit was still intact. *Schwester* Lubah, who had not learned Dutch, communicated with us in German. Being in Holland, she felt very uncomfortable and out of place. The Dutch, rightfully so, hated Germans. Even though many Dutch understood and spoke the German language, their animosity was so deeply ingrained that they refused to communicate in that language then and for many years following the cessation of hostilities. Accordingly, *Schwester* Lubah decided to return east and join the many D.P.s or "Displaced Persons" as they were incorrectly referred to. We all wished her well; it was an emotional departure.

MEANWHILE, MY SISTERS AS PART OF THE DIAMOND GROUP'S older teenage girls, departed Bergen Belsen by truck. Their return trip to Holland took about three days. Everyday they traveled on a different truck or bus and at night they frequently slept on straw or hay in barn lofts. When their group stopped at Enschede, in north eastern Holland, they were met by a group of Jewish women. Among these was the wife of Rabbi de Vries. Mrs. de Vries had recognized our family name as her father was in the diamond business and, after talking to my sisters, asked them to stay in their home. The offer was readily accepted. The de Vries' displayed exceptional hospitality, which lasted until we departed for England on August 30, 1945.

After my cousin and I spent several days in 's-Hertogenbosch, two gentlemen arrived from Enschede. They were Rabbi Aron de Vries and his neighbor. These men had traveled a journey of one hundred miles by car for the express purpose of bringing us back to their homes in Enschede. It was exceedingly kind of them. Both men and their wives had been hidden during the war in Enschede in non-Jewish homes. They now were literally going out of their way to help. Exactly how they knew of our whereabouts is not clear to me but they obtained information probably from a combination of sources like my sisters in Enschede, the Levis in New York and Erica Lunzer (today Mrs. Erica Lawson of London, England), a Jewish lady in the British Army who jointly arranged for this rescue mission.

Being anxious to join my sisters, I gladly accompanied Rabbi de Vries and made the journey to the north. My cousin Erika followed two weeks later after her Enschede accommodations were worked out. In the postwar months there was a general laxity in abiding by strict rules and usual restraints. Therefore, joining two strangers was of little concern. There were no legal transfer documents, all arrangements were strictly by verbal agreement. Traveling by car in those days was difficult. There were almost no civilian automobiles in working order, and the available gasoline was essentially for military use. The European inter-city super-highway network was not to be built until many years later.

POSTWAR CONTINENTAL EUROPE HAD NO FUNCTIONING OIL refineries. To address this handicap, arrangements were made to pump all gasoline from England through a flexible pipeline, across the English Channel. It traversed northwestern Europe via Belgium and then continued to Holland. This six inch diameter pipeline was one of many innovations which the Allies developed and built to speed the war effort. It relieved the transport ships and trucks so they could concentrate on other types of cargoes and made fuel delivery much safer. At the pipe line terminals were literally thousands of five gallon gasoline cans, which were then filled and distributed for use by army jeeps and trucks.

We crossed several major waterways as we traveled north, through eastern Holland. Most, if not all, bridges had been blown up and destroyed by the retreating Germans. The Germans weren't only trained to kill and torture innocent persons, they were also proficient at destroying public and private property. It was therefore not surprising to find that most Dutch people were bent on retribution both against the former occupiers of Dutch soil and against their unscrupulous local collaborators.

To facilitate crossing the rivers, the army's Corps of Engineers had constructed long temporary pontoon bridges, which spanned across a network of floating barges. These were the floating trestles which replaced key blownup bridges of the original arterial highways. Mobile steel bridge sections connected the anchored barges and consisted of modular *Baily* bridge panels, a World War II innovation. The *Baily* trusses were deployed quickly and could carry heavy military loads such as forty ton army tanks. It must be realized that the Corps of Engineers' bridge erectors had to advance ahead of the infantry, thereby making their task extremely hazardous.

Baily bridge panels were a state of the art tool in the Allied arsenal that provided safe roadways for crossing waterways ranging in width from forty feet to a mile. By war's end, seven hundred thousand such panels had been manufactured and placed in use! This ingenious product was just one of many remarkable spinoffs of the battlefront that changed the art of making war. But unlike their German adversaries who manned many war production factories with slave labor working under subhuman conditions, the Allied work forces consisted of positively motivated free individuals.

The part of Holland through which we traveled, had been freed from German occupation several months prior to the liberation of northwest Holland and probably two to three months before Bergen Belsen was liberated. Accordingly, many of the scars of war, such as destroyed vehicles and damaged roads, were no longer in evidence.

I arrived in Enschede late in the day. Mrs. de Vries gave a friendly welcome and made me feel at home. Due to lack of space, my cousin was scheduled to room with the neighbors while my sisters and I stayed with the de Vries'. That night was the first time in over a year and a half that I slept in a civilian bed with a normal mattress. For lack of space my cousin was not as fortunate and had to sleep in the neighbor's bathtub! But since there was no water for baths or showers, this was not as catastrophic as it sounds.

Chapter Twenty Four
ENSCHEDE

THE *SHUL* OF ENSCHEDE AND THE RABBI'S RESIDENCE WERE all in one large brick corner building, built for that purpose at Prinsestraat 18. During the war, the Germans had set up headquarters at this address. The interior of the *shul* building still displayed many scars of German misusage. In the rear of the ground floor, the Germans had built cells for prisoners. These were very small rooms in a dark area with only a small square window in each cell door, measuring six inch square, for "light and ventilation". I was told that before the Germans fled the advancing Allies, they took some of these prisoners, most of whom were from the Dutch underground, into the backyard and shot them dead. There certainly was no love lost between the local populace and the hated Germans.

In the main *shul,* there was fixed seating. Spread across the top of this wooden furniture, for the length of the *shul,* were perhaps one dozen *Sifrei Torah* which were unrolled so that their parchment could dry out. During the German occupation, they had been exposed to excessive moisture. I don't know if the lettering was adversely effected or salvageable.

Following the war, everything was rationed, from food to clothing. The shoes that I wore were still from before we were deported to Westerbork and they showed the effects of wear and aging. They had not been polished in over one and a half years, the heels were missing and the top leather was worn out. In the meantime, I wore Mrs. de Vries' oversized rubber galloshes while we were waiting for town approval to purchase a new pair of shoes. When the shoe inspector arrived to determine my eligibility he did not hesitate and immediately filled out a purchase authorization slip.

One of the more unpleasant things of modern life is to visit a dentist office at least twice a year. We had, however, not gone to any dentist since we left Amsterdam. An appointment was therefore scheduled with the local Enschede dentist. We were more than pleasantly surprised to be told by the lady dentist there that none of us had any cavities and that our teeth were fine. The reason probably was the absence of candy, cake, soft drinks and other sugar products from our meager food intake that had been our staple for the past two years.

After the war, traffic in Holland consisted mostly of bicycles, horse drawn carriages and motorized military vehicles. One day, the de Vries' got a delivery from a horse drawn cart. I became friendly with the carriage driver and he agreed to let me guide the horse. He sat next to me while I sat in the driver's seat which was a pillow at the front of the open flat wagon. He had to return through town which meant that I would have to walk back at the end of his run. Everything went fine until we got to the busy business district when I twisted the reins guiding the horse so that the horse went left instead of making a righthand turn. Traffic "snarled" and I made up my mind that horse carriages were not for me.

TO OBTAIN OUR PAPERS FOR ENGLAND, WE WERE ALL required to go for several days to Amsterdam. Exactly how we traveled I don't remember, but, our stay in the city of our birth was interesting. At that time we applied for Dutch passports.

The province of North Holland, in which Amsterdam is located, was at the time a peninsula. The North Sea was to the west and the potable water Ijsel Meer to its east. Subsequent to World War II, a considerable portion of the Ijsel Meer water was pumped out and large areas dewatered. That body of water, which until May of 1932 used to be a salt water estuary off the North Sea, has since been in part replaced by many highly fertile areas of farmland and some towns. Construction of the twenty eight mile long ocean cutoff dike enabled hundreds of square miles of

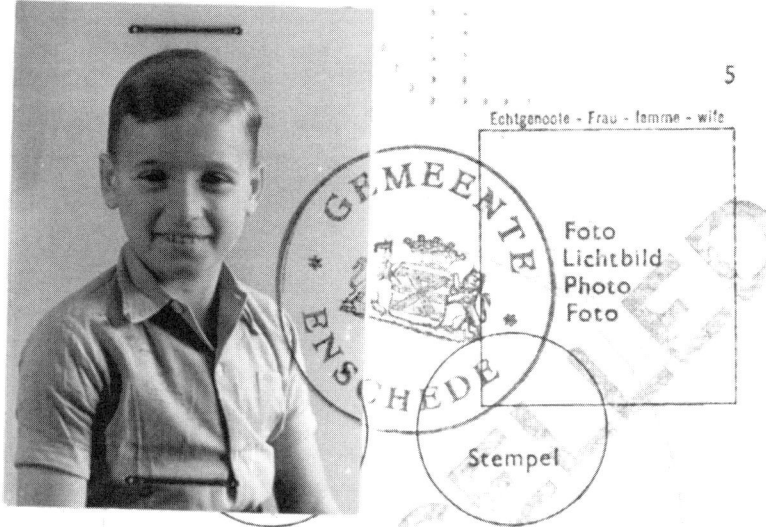

Handteekening van den houder
Unterschrift des Inhabers — Signature du titulaire
Signature of bearer

Oscar Lehmann

en van zijn echtgenoote
und seiner Frau — et de sa femme — and of his wife

*Dutch passport issued to myself while living in Enschede, Holland.
The second photo was added prior to leaving England
and shows the results of improved nutrition.*

ocean bottom to be reclaimed for farmland use. It is one of the engineering marvels for which the Dutch are famous.

The Germans and their Dutch collaborators were holed up in that peninsula and threatened to destroy a good portion of it by undermining and opening the dykes to the ocean water. It was a form of blackmail and the Allied armies therefore bypassed that northwestly portion of Holland including Amsterdam. In the meantime, there was a large hostage population of over a million persons with no food or fuel. The winter of 1944-1945 was exceptionally cold, thereby aggravating the situation. To help out with food, the exiled Dutch government arranged for large shipments of provisions to be parachuted to the population of Amsterdam. The city had many trees and many empty houses, most of which belonged to Jews who had been arrested by the Germans. First, the trees were cut down for firewood. Next, the empty brick houses were taken down brick by brick so that all wooden beams, wood trim, wood lath, window frames, doors, stairs, tar paper, roofing, etc. could be salvaged for heating fuel.

When we arrived in Amsterdam in 1945, we saw large vacant lots where buildings once stood. On the sides of these demolition sites lay neatly stacked, high piles of used bricks. The only remaining structures in these vacant lots were the first floor brick fireplaces and their chimneys. The houses along the famous Joden Breestraat (Jewish Broadway), a very old and narrow street in downtown Amsterdam, where Rembrandt (1606-1669) was said to have made some of his renowned paintings, were completely demolished for purposes of salvaging their wood contents. The street's roadway was now combined with that of an adjoining parallel narrow street to make a literal Jewish "Broadway". In a picture postcard that was dated July 1948, the Levis, on their visit to Amsterdam, described the city. They wrote, "there are trees again along the city's canals but most are still small".

In Amsterdam, we met an old friend by the (first) name of Geraart. He was not Jewish and had been employed by our great aunt, Tante Emma. He had taken care of her house like a superintendent. When Jews were dispossessed of their silver, Geraart volunteered to hide her silver in his house. Geraart's son was a German collaborator and promptly informed the authorities of his father's activities. Because of the son's tattling, Geraart was arrested and imprisoned for about one and a half years!

Mr. Coppenhagen had been a popular third grade elementary school teacher at our Herman Elte School. He and his wife had gone into hiding and now had a small child. A visit with them allowed us to hear fascinating stories of their ordeals while in hiding. Unfortunately, I do not remember any of his experiences.

During our stay in Amsterdam, we ate and slept at the home of a colleague of Father's, the van der Linden family. The van der Lindens were very accommodating and, even though they were not Jewish, prepared their meals in deference to our needs. Several of our belongings were hidden in their attic including an antique clock and Father's gold pocket watch. Amazingly, perhaps ten or fifteen years later, Mr. van der Linden contacted us in New York to announce the discovery of a small envelope of diamonds, which was found in the office safe. They had belonged to Father and were worth about three thousand dollars — a significant amount for those years. Following correspondence, Mr. van der Linden arranged to send us the proceeds of the sale. Trustworthy friends like Father's colleague can teach many of us a lesson in honesty.

We also visited the van Swolle family. Mr. van Swolle had worked at Father's office as a general assistant and trusted messenger. We also had hidden non-personal odds and ends in their house including some Dutch silver prewar coins and stamp albums. My sisters felt sorry for Mr. van Swolle due to his limited income in the postwar months and wanted to give him my entire collection. I, however, prevailed in taking at least one coin of each silver denomination plus some small copper change.

The Dutch minted several interesting coins, which are numismatically unique when compared to those of most other currencies. Both the *Guilder* and the *Rijksdaalder* (which equals $2^1/_2$ *Guilders*) are circular but have no knurled rims. Instead, the smooth circular edge is engraved with the words: *"G-d Zij Met Ons"*, (G-d Be With Us). Their five cent piece, the *Stuiver,* was made of nickel and is stamped into a small square shaped coin.

We also went to Mr. Greco's music store, which was on the corner of Hemonylaan and van Woustraat, diagonally across from our former home. Mr. Greco had agreed to hide our bikes and many of Father's important books. When we entered the store, Mr. Greco looked annoyed at seeing us. Perhaps he was sorry that we had survived our ordeal. When we asked for our items, he said that the books had to be thrown into the Amstel River, because he was afraid of the Germans discovering them and, as for the bikes, he also gave some excuse as to why they were no longer in his possession. We didn't believe a word he said but had little choice as we had to rely on his good will. Mr. Greco did however return my sisters' and cousin's accordion and mandolins. I played no instrument.

The *shul* where we *davened* on Gerard Doustraat was intact but, sadly enough, there were very few attendees. Most members never returned again, victims of German atrocities.

We couldn't leave without dropping in at the Prins family. They had been living incognito in an old apartment along one of the city *grachten*. Their immediate family, including Mr. Prins, their aged father, all survived.[a]

THIS WAS OUR FIRST RETURN TO AMSTERDAM AFTER ALMOST two years. The city of almost one million inhabitants now seemed to me to be only a city of bricks and stones. Our parents, friends and family were nowhere to be seen. The luster and brightness of the city was dulled. Walking down the streets would bring to mind friends and relatives who had lived in various places. We would reminisce on outings our family took. On occasion, we recalled a German atrocity that was committed at a particular location. It was like going on a walk down memory lane. Gone were the friendly greetings from those who never made it back and now lay in some mass grave far away to the east. Houses formerly occupied by friends and family now housed perfect strangers. The *shuls* which still existed were barely able to scrape together a *minyan*. Having been back to Amsterdam for several months following our first stint at Westerbork we knew what a city void of friends was like. This time, however, we came without our parents and many other people we had known. And this time we knew the fate of many others who had perished at the hands of Holland's bully neighbor.

[In August, 1988, Ruth and I spent half a week in Amsterdam as I had made arrangements to *lain* my *Bar Mitzvah sedra* at our old *shul* on Gerard Doustraat. I was again hit by the "emptiness" of this populous city. We visited Diemen to say *Tehillim* at the graves of my Wallerstein grandparents. Seeing familiar names on tombstones gave me greater satisfaction than walking past 26 Sarphatistraat where my great aunt Tante Emma used to live.

Having been one of the last to be deported from Amsterdam meant that some of our books had not been destroyed. Since paper was in short supply, the Germans had removed all the books that were found in vacated Jewish homes. These were then sent to a paper mill for recycling. However, all books were first damaged to assure that the paper mill would not sell or salvage them in lieu of recycling. Introducing "defects"

---
a. Refer to Chapter 8 for other details.

into books involved tearing out a random handful of pages. Some of our books were taken to a beautiful old *Shul* in downtown Amsterdam known as *"The Grote Sjoel"* (the Great Synagogue) where two men were assigned to the task of tearing out pages. Several years later this *shul* was converted into a Jewish museum. My sisters and I took the tram to that *shul,* where we found some forty volumes with our parents' and grandparents' names inside. All books with identification could be taken by their rightful owners. We still have many of these books, some with torn out pages.

We had a neighbor on Hemonylaan, an elderly lady who still lived there at number four. We visited her, and as we sat in her living room, my sister Toni recognized several paintings hanging on her wall as being ours. The lady had "confiscated" them after we were deported. My sister Connie recalls seeing many other belongings of ours in her house as well, none of which were ever returned. To this day, Connie regrets not having thanked the neighbor for "saving" these items and asking for them to be given back.

Amsterdam was full of stores selling used items. In my opinion, most of these were stolen from vacated Jewish homes. [Many years later, in August of 1988, Ruth and I walked down a big shopping street in downtown Amsterdam. There we passed a reputable looking, used silver store with a large, beautiful silver *Esrog* box in the display window. In a city where the Jewish population had dwindled down to fifteen thousand, of which many were non-observant, the presence of a Judaica item like that in a used silver store seemed very suspect. I immediately assumed that it had been stolen during the war, and I again recalled the great plundering that followed Jewish arrests. The thought of entering the store to ask for details was repugnant to me. In fact, the quicker I passed by and distanced myself the better I felt.]

Chapter Twenty Five
POSTWAR TIDINGS

WE RETURNED TO ENSCHEDE AGAIN TO AWAIT FINAL arrangements for our departure to England so we could join the British Lehmanns. While back in Enschede we received word that at a hospital in the nearby town of Hengelo there was a patient who had been part of the Diamond Group. We went to visit the lady, who, we discovered had been with Mother. The hospital was an old building run by a local Catholic order. The patient, was probably Mrs. H. Lopes Cardozo-Rijnvelt. She was extremely weak and could barely talk. She did not have the heart to tell us that Mother had died but she intimated to us not to hold out much hope for her return. Some of the details that we did obtain were that the women of the Diamond Group had been sent to a work camp in the vicinity of Ravensbruck. Subsequently, they were relocated to a camp near a small town named Behndorf (or possibly Behrendorf), which is in the proximity of Hamburg. The ladies had been forced to work in the salt mines! We were shocked at hearing that our Mother, a middle aged Amsterdam homemaker had been forced to do such physically taxing work. How diabolical did the Germans get. We stayed only a short while at the hospital and then returned "home" to Enschede.

During our 1945 summer stay in Enschede, there were good tidings. On August 14, 1945, Japan had capitulated and surrendered to the Allied forces in the Pacific region. Subsequently, General Douglas McArthur, the Allied Supreme Commander of the Pacific War Theatre, went to Tokyo and accepted the Japanese Imperial Government's unconditional surrender. The signing ceremony took place on September 2, 1945 and that day was celebrated as V-J day or Victory Japan day.

The school building next to the *shul* housed Allied soldiers, and music was heard until late into the night. The Axis powers of Germany, Italy and now Japan had unconditionally surrendered and World War II, "the war that ended all wars," had come to an official conclusion. The Dutch had a special interest in the Japanese surrender since the Dutch East Indies, today Indonesia, had been captured by Japan along with many Dutch prisoners of war.

With the ending of hostilities, there was a very subdued and limited euphoria since the casualties of World War II were astronomical. There were well over forty million persons killed in a span of only about five years. Of these over six million were Jews. Millions of casualties were suffered by Germany, Russia and Japan. In addition, there were millions of additional fatalities from among the Americans, British, most European states and from many North African countries, all of whom had been involved in this bitter conflict. So many millions of German soldiers were killed that there was talk in Germany of instituting polygamy. Unfortunately, the governments and peoples of our world did not learn from this global tragedy. Other conflicts in the ensuing four decades probably took similar tolls in human lives, the only difference being that the latter casualties were over a much longer timespan.

PATRIOTISM MANIFESTS ITSELF IN MANY WAYS. ONE SIMPLE way, which is common among many Europeans as well as in many other parts of the world, is to display the flag of one's country. A more basic adaptation of this would be to dress in a national color or to wear a lapel pin or sport a necktie using the national colors, etc. Israel has white and light blue, the Soviets had red, Ireland has light green, Switzerland has red and white, etc. In Holland, the royal family was known as the "House of Orange". During the war, one might see a daring person wear an orange attachment to a broach or lapel pin to show defiance. The Dutch flag consisted of the colors red, white and blue. On occasion, these colors would also be displayed during the war years to show contempt and opposition for the German occupation.

The color combination of the German occupier's standard bearer was black and red. Today, fifty years later, my aversion towards the use of this combination remains. A feeling of repugnance and disbelief creeps over me when I see someone wearing a dress, coat, necktie, yarmulke or any other garment which has a predominance of these two colors. It is, of course, a result of ignorance by the younger generation and disinterest or forgetfulness by some older people, but I still consider it offensive. Such a sight brings back unwanted memories, and I will spend little time with persons so attired. My sister Connie also has a repugnance to a match of those two colors: "When a saleslady tries to convince me to buy such a combination," she once wrote me, "I can only walk out of the store." It is another casualty of the war.

IN THE EARLY 1980'S, MY UNCLE MICHAEL HANDED TO ME A FILE containing old correspondence from Holland. One of the letters therein was written to my aunt, Tante Resi Lehmann on October 8, 1945 by Mrs. de Vries from Enschede. On the back, my aunt had written, "I have not shown this letter to anybody".

Following is a translation from the Dutch:

October 8, 1945
Enschede, Holland

Dear Mrs. Lehmann,

    Last week I was in Amsterdam and I was thinking of following up as to whether anything was known regarding the fate of your brother-in-law. I had the opportunity to talk with Mr. J.van de Kar, someone who the children also know. He came with your brother-in-law to the concentration camp Sachsenhausen and subsequently was sent further to Oranienburg, which is also a concentration camp. From there, your brother-in-law was sent to yet another location and he was unable to maintain contact with him. According to Mr. van de Kar, your brother-in-law was already quite sick when he departed Oranienburg. He suffered seriously from starvation, malnutrition, distention and had badly

A. de Vries
RABBIJN

ENSCHEDE, 8 Oct. 1945.
Holland.

Mrs. Resi Lehmann,
Mulway 53,
LETCHWORTH.
England.

Geachte Mevr. Lehmann,

Ik ben vorige week in Amsterdam geweest en heb daar nog getracht na te gaan of er iets bekend was over het lot van Uw zwager. Ik was in de gelegenheid te spreken met den Heer J.v.d. Kar, iemand die de kinderen ook wel kennen. Hij is met Uw zwager naar het concentratiekamp Sachsenhausen gekomen en met hem verder doorgestuurd naar Oranienburg, eveneens een concentratiekamp. Daar vandaan is Uw zwager verder doorgestuurd en heeft hij het contact met hem niet kunnen houden. Volgens de Heer v.d. Kar was Uw zwager bij het vertrek uit Oranienburg al erg ziek. Hij leed ernstig aan honger-oedeem en had dikke beenen. Helaas heeft men niet veel hoop, dat hij nog in leven is. Op een enkele uitzondering na zijn de mannen van dat z.g. diamant-transport onvindbaar. Ik meende niet langer te moeten wachten, maar U dit te moeten mededeelen. Het is misschien het beste, dat U mondeling de kinderen hiervan iets vertelt.

Wij zijn erg benieuwd hoe het nu met ze gaat, en hoe hun gezondheid en algemeene psychische toestand is. Wij missen hen erg bij ons, maar zijn blij te weten, dat ze bij hun familie zijn.

Heel veel hartelijke groeten,

Dutch language letter by Mrs. de Vries, describing probable demise of Father.

swollen legs. Unfortunately, there is little hope that he is still alive. With very few exceptions, most men from the Diamond transport cannot be located. I did not want to wait any further, but to notify you of this. Perhaps it is best that you pass on some of this information verbally to the children.

We would very much like to know how the children are, (and regarding) their health and their general physical well-being. We miss them very much but are happy, in the knowledge, that they are now with relatives.

Best regards,

Reina de Vries Spier

According to conversations I had in 1990 with my Uncle Jacob Wallerstein (Mother's brother) from Kfar Haro'eh, it was his opinion that all the men in that transport, and Father in particular, were tortured. That was based on various articles and interviews that he had read and heard.

MAY THE ALMIGHTY POUR OUT HIS WRATH ON THE NATIONS that do not recognize Him and on all the despotic powers that have not proclaimed His Name…,".[a] "Pursue them with anger and destroy them from under the Almighty's Heavens".[b] These are quotes that are mentioned at the *Seder* on *Pesach*. Unfortunately, they have not lost their relevance. May we merit to see that these hopes be realized swiftly and in our lifetimes.

The concentration camps of Oranienburg and Sachsenhausen are in the vicinity of Berlin. Father, a person in his prime, was born on 17 Shevat, 5653, (1893) and only 52 years old when he perished at the hands of an insidious and profane German people. We make the assumption that his pure *neshomo* left him on the same date as the one on which Mother passed away, 5 Adar, 5705 (1945). This way, Mother did not die as a widow or Father as a widower.

Our parents, a.h., died as gallant soldiers fighting a formidable, vindictive adversary. Whereas they could have opted for a life of relative comfort had they collaborated with their captors, they and their col-

---

a. Tehillim, 79:6
b. Eichah, 3:66

leagues correctly maintained that giving aid and comfort to a murderous foe was not in the interest of the Jewish people and the civilized world.

Their aspirations were to live a life of respect, based on justice and righteousness, the objective of which superseded their paradigm for survival. Our parents' style was not to go through life solely to increase their material well-being and, in the pursuit of that goal, to possibly step on fellow beings. They did not lead self-indulgent, frivolous lives.

Our parents trained us in the true *Torah* values of life. They set personal examples of self-discipline, examples they were shown by their parents, so as to abide by the *Torah's* lofty rules and Divine ideals. They successfully harnessed and merged these traits of ingrained *Torah* values and self-discipline under circumstances fraught with unbelievable temptation, danger and duress. Most humans are not exposed to such extreme perils that led to their ultimate sacrifice by a *Kiddush Hashem*. Father's and Mother's unwavering and brave defiance, along with that of their colleagues, resulted in a totally successful resistance, denial of achievement to the enemy and a failure of our foe's cause.

May we all glean strength, courage and true life values from their shining examples. May it also be Hashem's Will that we all be spared from being tested in making the supreme and ultimate sacrifice of life. May their descendants and spiritual heirs be worthy of perpetuating their lofty causes and values in a peaceful world.

Chapter Twenty Six
TO ENGLAND

THE PAPERS PERMITTING US TO TRAVEL TO ENGLAND ARRIVED at last. In New York, the Levis had worked extensively behind the scenes for this event to happen so soon. Our aunt, Tante Resi, too, was an unheralded but significant factor in our ability to leave Holland. The Dutch government did not permit its citizens to emigrate. The war had taken a terrible toll on the Dutch population. The Germans never hesitated to kill or deport to labor camps as many Dutchmen as they could handle. Added to this labor drain were the collaborators who had betrayed their countrymen and could not be relied upon to do what was proper for Holland.

To secure the required exit papers, our aunt in England wrote directly to the Dutch queen, Koningin Wilhelmina, in The Hague. She attached to her correspondence our letters, which described some gory war experiences. To assure a "royal" response, our aunt requested the return of these letters (copying machines did not yet exist). The result of all these concerted efforts was that we were the first Dutch citizens to receive permission to emigrate from the Netherlands after the war.

Parallel to the above effort, our aunt, Tante Resi also made contact with the British government's Home Office in London. When that did not produce the needed results, she wrote to King George VI at Buckingham Palace in London. The king must have lit a fire under the Home Office and cut through some cumbersome red tape, for soon the necessary entry papers to the United Kingdom became available.

Despite the short notice, Erica Lunzer was able to arrange for our travel to Amsterdam. Our transportation from Enschede was in an old car with a rumble seat in the rear. Instead of the trunk lid opening from the back, the lid opened backwards, as the latches and hinges were reversed. My sister Connie and I sat on a seat for two inside this rear rumble section. The front portion was a convertible coupe where my sister Toni and the driver sat. Our cousin had to stay behind in Enschede for a few more weeks since she was German born and therefore considered "stateless". England did not recognize former German citizens for immigration purposes. Our luggage was nominal, consisting only of a few small cardboard boxes tied with string. We hardly had any clothing, no spare shoes or other extensive personal articles. Before leaving we thanked Rabbi and Mrs. de Vries for their help and kindness and wished them well. At our young ages we did not fully appreciate the hospitality that the de Vries' had extended to us. Only half a year or so later we were saddened to hear that Mrs. de Vries *o.h.* had died during child birth. Proper medicine was scarce in the post war years and this was certainly the case in a provincial town like Enschede.

In Amsterdam we stayed overnight in Erica Lunzer's apartment which was situated very close to the famous *Concert Gebouw* (Concert Hall). The Germans, however, had dug up large sections of the surrounding meadow and grass parks and constructed integrated underground concrete bunkers in their place. These vacant edifices lay as stark reminders that the enemy had only recently departed.

The Allies had enlisted the assistance of whomever was available to expedite the war effort, so as to bring this world conflict to a successful and rapid conclusion. Accordingly, they recruited a substantial number of men from the *Yishuv* in the Palestine Mandate. This group of men, known as the Jewish Brigade, were trained by the British and wore the khaki colored British army uniforms. They battled valiantly against the Germans, fighting their way up the Italian *"Boot"* (the Italian peninsula is shaped like a "Boot"). When we arrived in Amsterdam, many Jewish Brigade soldiers were temporarily stationed in our vicinity. In later years,

EXTRACT FROM LETTER FROM ERICA LUNZER, dated 30/8/45

Dear Hanne,

I am writing this from the British Consul, The Hague. The Lehman children are leaving in an hour per K.L.M. Am rather proud of the feat. It was not easy. They are travelling on Dutch Military priority papers as envoys for mission Netherland Government. They are the first Belsen children to leave for England and it's good that J.C.R.A. could do it. At the moment I am awaiting the consul to negotiate for a girl whose mother lives in Palestine to leave legally for Marseilles.....

TELEPHONE: EUSTON 7418/9.

Jewish Committee for Relief Abroad

CHAIRMAN:
DR. REDCLIFFE N. SALAMAN, F.R.S.
TREASURER:
HARRY SACHER, ESQ.
HON. SECRETARY:
HBR   MRS. ASENATH PETRIE.

7, ENDSLEIGH PLACE,
TAVISTOCK SQUARE,
LONDON, W.C.1

3rd September, 1945.

Dear Manfred,

I had a letter from Erica Lunzer this morning and am enclosing copy of the part that will interest you and your mother.

A colleague of Erica's has just arrived back here on leave, and she tells me that the children were due to arrive here last Friday; I hope all went well. She says they are delightful and charming. You all will have had a grand reunion.....

Erica has postponed her leave and will now come for Sukot.

I hope you had a good holiday on the farm and had all the conversations and talks you wanted AND that your mother found you looking satisfactory better of all needed by your visit. Best wishes to all the family,

Hanne.

Manfred Lehman, Esq.,
53 Mullway,
Letchworth, Herts.

Two letters of interest: the top letter was sent by Erica Lunzer to Hannah Bernhart-Rath (Mrs. Hannah Landau, Tel-Aviv). The bottom letter was written to our cousin Manny (Professor Meir Lehmann).

the veterans of the Jewish Brigade formed the initial nucleus of the fledgling Israeli armed forces.

The next morning we headed for Schiphol, which nowadays is the major airport near Amsterdam. The flight to England was short and uneventful, but considering that postwar commercial aviation really had not yet developed, it was considered quite a feat to get us children to England by this means of transportation.

WE ARRIVED IN ENGLAND IN LATE AUGUST, 1945. OUR POINT of entry was at London's Croydon Airport, and from there we continued by bus to London. The sprawling Heathrow Airport was only to be built in later years. Our itinerary called for us to stay overnight with our aunt, Tante Else Lehmann. She lived at the time at 190 Lordship Road in the Stamford Hill section of London.

As the bus traveled through London, I noticed a strange sight — ten year old children were playing on the sidewalk! I was totally startled. During the past five to six years, all that I had heard about England was her battles, battle staging grounds, British and American bomber planes using British air bases, German plans to invade England, etc. It never occurred to me that there was a young civilian population, especially in London.

Upon our arrival we received a very warm and loving welcome from our aunts, Tante Resi and Tante Else, who had been waiting for us for several hours. Both ladies were widowed. They were financially not well off and had their own burdens. Despite this, they treated us royally. Naturally, our aunt was very disappointed that her daughter Erika had not come with us, and that it could be another two months until she would arrive. There were many stories to tell and it was late in the evening. The following day Tante Resi and the three of us said good bye to Tante Else and took the L.N.E.R. (London North Eastern Railway, nicknamed the Late, Never Early Railway) to Letchworth, Hertfordshire, which is approximately thirty miles north of London.

I enjoyed the train ride which took me, for the first time, through half a dozen railroad tunnels. The locomotives were coal-fired so as to generate their steam power. Those were the days before Diesel locomotives. The European continent and England did not as yet have high speed intercity highways. Those who had to travel more than ten to fifteen miles usually took the railroad.

ON ACCOUNT OF GERMANY'S INDISCRIMINATE AND RUTHless aerial bombing of London, large segments of the municipal population had sought temporary shelter in the distant suburbs. Letchworth was one of many such towns where refugees from London established themselves. The town was known as "a Garden City", which meant that unlike most towns of that time, it had a planned layout of streets, parks, schools, etc. and zoning was strictly enforced for the various commercial, residential and industrial areas. Every private house had both a front and rear garden. The Jewish population was scattered throughout the town and concentrated in at least three to four neighborhoods.

Letchworth had a relatively small Jewish population but qualitatively and in prominence it was quite significant. The Jewish community was self- sufficient except that it had no *yeshivah.* Everybody pitched in for the *Limudei Kodesh* studies, especially Rabbi Yoseph Yonah Zvi Haleivie Horowitz formerly from Hunsdorf and later from Frankfurt am Main, Rabbi Salman Sassoon and Reb Nachman Dachs who all gave *shiurim* to the older boys, Dr. Heinemann who learned with the younger children, and our aunt, Tante Martha who was Father's youngest sister, taught the very young children. Mr. Sigi Stern was the *kosher* butcher. The younger generation took turns going to a nearby farm to be present while the cows were milked and while the milk was being pasteurized and then bottled for *cholov Yisroel.* It was a close-knit community even though many of us lived far from each other.

The Lehmanns resided at 53 Mullway in a small, two story, fully attached brick house without a basement. It appeared modest and simple on the outside as did the other one hundred or so identical houses on this block. Mullway was half of a development of two "L" shaped streets of almost all similar looking houses. This housing project had been built by a Chassidic Jew, Abba Bornstein, who had left Frankfurt am Main in the mid 1930's. Inside our aunt's 'castle' was the light of a vibrant Jewish home. Of her six children, the eldest daughter Hannah (age twenty-two), lived away from home on a *Hachsharah,* and Joe and Jack learned at the Gateshead *Yeshiva* in northern England. Manny (Manfred) lived at home and worked at an electronics factory several towns away. Shifra and Judith, the youngest (age eleven) also lived at home and attended the local Public Grammar School.

I have many happy memories from the year and a half that we lived with the British Lehmann family. On *Shabbos* we all sat around the large downstairs table in the small living-dining room. The all-pervading *Shabbos* ambiance was *"gezellig"* (Dutch for cozy, which compares with the German, *"gemuetlich")* and conducive to making one forget many of the week's pressures. Frequently, there were local friends who dropped in and joined us after the Friday night meal. We sang beautiful *zemiros* together and when Chanah, Joe and Jack came home between semesters, they taught us new *nigunim.* Late *Shabbos* afternoon, as we sat at the *Seudas shlishis* meal, we talked and sang in a pleasant, warm atmosphere. Then, too, friends came over to join us. Since there was no *Shabbos* clock (timer), the room gradually grew darker until the street lights took over. There we sat, perhaps a dozen of us in the living room, accompanying the *Shabbos* until it was time to go to *Ma'ariv.*

There was little money, but money couldn't buy the warmth, friendship, kindness and *Yiddishkeit* that permeated the home atmosphere. For *Succos,* there was a permanent wood framed structure in the backyard, which was used for bicycles during the remaining part of the year. The *schach* consisted of straw from a nearby farm. To accommodate us three newcomers, Tante Resi moved out of her comfortable second floor bedroom and slept in the dining room, on an old worn couch, which had some damaged springs.

OUR AUNT REGARDED *MITZVOS* AS OPPORTUNITIES. SHE DID not entertain the idea of avoiding and/or passing them on to others. Complaining about the extra work and effort *Mitzvos* might require was not in her vocabulary. The benevolence of the British Lehmanns was exemplary, they were *tzadikim* in every sense of the word for taking us into their cramped, simple quarters, while existing on extremely meager financial resources. The Levis provided the needed monetary assistance for our stay.

The entire house was heated during the winter from a single, small, open wood burning fireplace in the living room. On weekdays, when Manny got up early to go to work, he used to start the fire. By the time I returned from *shul* and we all had breakfast, the fire was already sufficient to provide warmth within five feet of the burning logs. There was no thermal wall or roof insulation and the windows were all single pane glass. This was the typical modest residential construction for this type of structure that was built in the 1938-1939 period. To keep warm at night, I slept for the first time under a down blanket which appeared like a giant feather pillow. For hot water, there was a tank mounted above the bathtub, which was only heated before we took a bath.

The kitchen had a gas meter below the sink which allowed gas to be used for cooking. In the winter, when the gas range was kept on for the entire *Shabbos,* our aunt used to slip about twenty silver *shilling* coins

Festive Succos Meal by B. Picart (1663-1733) Reprinted from the Israelit, 12^[21] October 1894

Chapter Twenty Six: TO ENGLAND 205

(20 *shillings* = 1 *pound sterling*, Note: *Shillings* were used before currency was switched to the decimal system) into the coin slot of the gas meter to assure that both the food and the kitchen would remain warm. It should be noted that the cooking gas was manufactured from coal and only had half the heating power of modern natural gas.

Street lights were also lit by burning this type of manufactured gas. Each street light had a gas pilot light that burned all day. At dusk a city worker came along with a long pole and a special hook at its end. The hook pulled a valve in the street lights' lantern which caused the pilot to ignite the large lamp flame. At dawn another person made the same rounds to douse all the street lights. On occasion, the pilot light was blown out and then there would be a bad gas odor in that vicinity.

Letchworth had an active Salvation Army and frequently, they would come Friday evenings with their troupe of trumpets, clarinets, trombones, etc. to play on the grass mall in the middle of the street, right in front of the house. After playing several minutes of music, a collector would go from door to door for donations. To maintain a peaceful relationship, our aunt always had a few coins prepared. The collector would come into the house, was shown the money on a shelf and departed with it.

After the war there was a chronic shortage of *kosher* wine and what was available was extremely expensive. To address this quandary, the Lehmanns made their own "wine". It consisted of soaking raisins for several days in water. Then, on Friday, the whole container was dumped into a funnel lined with filter paper. That way we had fresh "grape juice" every *Shabbos.*

Being that the Lehmanns moved to Letchworth under emergency war conditions, much of their belongings and furniture could not fit into their small house. Thus, the balance of their furniture plus boxes and many items belonging to friends were all stored in a one car garage about five minutes away from the house. Manny also kept a motorcycle there, which he used for commuting to work.

FOLLOWING EXTENSIVE CORRESPONDENCE WITH NEW YORK, it was decided that the time was ripe to retrieve our belongings that had been placed in safekeeping back in Amsterdam during the German occupation. My uncle arranged for the tickets. And so, after living in Letchworth for perhaps half a year, our aunt and my sister Toni made a trip to Holland. There they made contact with our old time carpenter, Mr. Reusink. Together they went to our former address at Hemonylaan 5, rang the bell and stated that they wanted to pick up some of our property. The residents emphatically stated that nothing was found in the house but they were welcome to check for themselves. Mr. Reusink and his son then proceeded to the ground floor living room and lifted the wooden hatch door, which was right above the watermain shutoff and sewer's housetrap. The young Reusink then slipped through the small hatchway opening and proceeded to crawl on all fours on the sandy ground to the rear of the shallow crawl space below the living room. He uncovered the large crate and proceeded to hand out piece by piece of the silver which he himself had placed there several years earlier. Needless to say, the houses' occupants gawked in astonishment when they saw what had been concealed there and unbeknown to them for all this time.

There was much family history associated with this silver and my aunt and sister were greatly relieved to see these precious heirlooms safely salvaged. It was mind boggling to all of us how these belongings had remained hidden and undisturbed while the world all around had been in devastating turmoil. All the retrieved items were taken to the Reusink carpentry shop. There he added six other wooden crates of personal items which had been placed behind and below his lumber storage. The items included crystal ware, linens, two small crates of old kosher dry Rhine wine of a 1933 vintage plus many other items. The Reusinks were extremely decent people, who showed honesty and kindness, knew how not to divulge secrets and risked their own safety when helping others. They can be counted among the "Righteous of the Nations". To the best of my knowledge, the Reusinks refused extra compensation for their "high risk" efforts.

All retrieved items were properly crated and eventually wound up in New York. Our uncle had an import-export business called The Trans-Caribbean Trading Corp. at 92 Liberty Street in Manhattan, and he arranged to have all items shipped directly to that address.

The recovery of the silver from our house had various parallels. While visiting in Amsterdam during August of 1945, we heard of a less dramatic but similar unfolding scenario from the daughter of the van der Lindens. She was employed as a secretary in a residential neighborhood. Across from her office window was a vacant lot where, during the final 1944-1945 winter siege, empty houses had been demolished for their firewood contents. Only their brick chimneys remained in tact. After the war, a Jewish man arrived with a hammer, mason chisel (cold chisel) and a box. He then proceeded to carefully hammer away at the chimney's masonry near the old fireplace from where he removed several bricks. Then he carefully reached in and removed his belongings, consisting of silver items that had been "stored" in that masonry structure for safekeeping. Half a century after the war, Amsterdam and much of Europe must still have substantial amounts of personal property that was hidden by Jews who alas were murdered and therefore could not reclaim what was rightfully theirs. Our ability to retrieve hidden property was the exception rather than the rule.

Chapter Twenty Seven
AT THE BRITISH LEHMANNS

MUCH MORE SHOULD BE WRITTEN ABOUT THE BRITISH Lehmanns, for my aunt engendered and personified the true Jewish qualities so necessary to build a worthy and lasting house among our people. Indeed, despite having been widowed at a young age and notwithstanding her financial hardships as a result of this loss, my aunt, Tante Resi, was nevertheless a cornerstone for her generation and for those to come. I would like to remember her as:

> "The stone which the builders rejected has become the chief cornerstone," [a]

She skillfully communicated with her own six children and we three newcomers, each on his or her own level. We all received much warmth and attention from her. She was the quintessential committed and dedicated mother and aunt.

---

a. Tehillim, 118:22.

The esprit de corps which imbued the Lehmann home in that small and simple house in Letchworth was the result of strenuous efforts. Only physical factors constrained the construction of their edifice. My aunt, single-handedly raised her family as a true *mater familias*. Her husband Uncle Benno, who passed away in 1935, was no longer there to assist in the many difficult household tasks that fell to his young widow. At the age of thirty-six, she had been left with her six children ranging in age from one to just under twelve years. Her handicaps did not end there. The family was evacuated from London as a result of the war, the house was rented, and there was no discretionary income. Yet, despite these difficult limitations, every child was treated as if he or she were an only child. Memories of kindness, friendship and love far outweigh recollections of hardships. Their remarkable and positive outlook made their home an attraction to all and a magnet for much of the young Jewish crowd in Letchworth.

The Lehmann family made major impressions on whoever saw them in action. There was never a harsh or loud reprimand, since everyone knew their task and needed few reminders. Self pity, because of their status as orphans, never came into question. Their interest in development, self-furtherance and positive outlook was inherited from their energetic mother and mentor who showed them the way on preparing to cope with life.

THE CONGENIAL ATMOSPHERE AT THE LEHMANNS WAS EXPORTED to friends and family alike. When time and school schedules permitted, we packed our bags and traveled to other parts of the country. During the summer of 1946, my sisters joined our aunt, Tante Else, and her two daughters on the southern English sea shore for a short vacation. At the same time, I spent two weeks of my vacation in Gateshead, where I lodged with the family of Rabbi Bamberger. It was a pleasant stay and, with the local *Yeshivah* boys, we made daily trips to both the sea shore and to local factories. We watched glass blowing and bottle making, and we saw the manufacture of light bulbs at the Osram factory, along with various other interesting and skillful trades in action.

Gateshead is an old English industrial town contiguous to the city of Newcastle, which is world famous for its coal shipping facilities. The architecture of Gateshead is drab and plain, with many fully attached, two story, brick, residential dwellings. From a Jewish viewpoint, it has a great *Yeshivah* for boys and young men, plus a famous seminary for girls. With institutions like these, Gateshead attracts many young people from all over Europe and even from America. My cousin Joe Lehmann, spent much time with me both in Gateshead and at home in Letchworth when he came in during his vacation. We took many daily trips together and discussed interesting topics, especially in *Hashkofah*. Today, (1996), Rabbi Joseph Lehmann's Gateshead book business is world renowned. He has been the largest Hebrew Book seller in Europe for many decades.

WHEN I ARRIVED IN ENGLAND, MY ENGLISH VOCABULARY consisted of perhaps ten words in all. The Lehmanns understood a little of our Dutch, but initially the main language of communication was German. Under these circumstances, I was registered in the Pixmore Secondary School, a local Junior High School. To my ears, a more British sounding name than that you can't get. The lower three grades of the Secondary School correspond to the Junior High School level of the American school system. Needless to say, absolutely no one in that school of several hundred students and a staff of twenty-five knew a word of Dutch. It was a case of sink or swim. I had no choice, and after several months, I was already writing long compositions in broken English.

With the exception of English language and grammar, I was near the top of the class. Considering that we missed two years of schooling and, having been only an average student in Amsterdam, it indicates that pre-deportation Dutch schooling standards had been exceptionally high.

In general, I got along well with both my class teacher, Miss Lake, and the school principal (headmaster), Mr. Boorer. The official religion of England is "The Church of England". As a result, religion is taught and prayer sessions are held in British public schools. For the duration of their religious instructions, the few Jewish students at the school were exempt from class and instead were taught by Dr. Heinemann during the school's (Religious) Release Hour. Dr. Benno Heinemann, *o.h.*, the father of Rabbi Moshe Heinemann of Baltimore, MD, authored the book *The Maggid of Dubno and his Parables*.[12] The class prayer sessions were held in a large central lobby area of the school, and the Jewish and Catholic students remained behind in the classrooms. Each class had a glee or singing hour once a week. The entire class would stand in four rows in the large center hall and sing together typical English songs. When it came to November-December time, some of the songs of choice became x-mas carols. The carols were melodious and had very catchy words. Mr. Boorer dropped in every now and then to listen and join in the singing with his deep baritone voice. When he saw that I was just standing there during the carols and not moving my lips, he came over and said, "Why aren't you singing?" I replied, "Because I don't sing carols". He responded in a

<u>Vocabulary Work Abstract Nouns</u>　　　19-2-46

1. A great diversity of nations was gathered in the market place of Paris.
2. The only rain in the holiday came on the day we planned to climb Snowdown; such was the perversity of the weather.
3. The density of the fog made travelling dangerous.
4. The verbosity wearied all her friends.
5. Some Egyptian students are showing great animosity towards the British just now.

<u>Volcanoes</u>

In the ce~~p~~tre [centre] of the earth it is ve~~ry~~[very]ry hot and like with every flamp̄ire to keep it going air must reach it the air comes in through many holes. But something also comes out of the holes. One calls it Lava. Lava comes out by an ~~œ~~ explotion inside the earth. There are about 300 to 400 such holes on the sur~~g~~[f]ace of the earth. One calls them volcanos. The ~~fces~~ [rocks]

Sample from my notebook – February 19, 1946. The distinct cursive writing style was a carry-over from my Dutch schooling.

HERTFORDSHIRE COUNTY COUNCIL
PIXMORE SECONDARY SCHOOL

Report for the **Summer** Term ending **July 26, 1946**
Name **Oscar Lehmann** Form **II A**

SUBJECTS		obtained MARKS	Max.	REMARKS
RELIGIOUS INSTRUCTION		[25]	40	
MATHEMATICS	Arithmetic	58	100	Oscar is quick to understand new methods; sometimes he makes careless mistakes. M.L.
	Algebra	17	30	
	Geometry	31	50	
ENGLISH	Composition	30	50	Remarkable progress has been made, both in understanding English, and in the use of it himself. Written composition shows imagination, and ability to express ideas in very well-chosen phrases. M.L.
	Grammar	-	-	
	Literature	-	-	
	Reading	-	-	
	Spelling	9	20	
	Writing	13	20	
HISTORY		25	50	Very good result. M.L.
GEOGRAPHY		28	50	A most pleasing result in spite of language difficulty. E.
ART		38	50	
HANDICRAFT	Woodwork			
	Metalwork			
	Technical Drawing	41	50	
	Craftwork			
DOMESTIC SUBJECTS	Cookery			
	Laundry			
NEEDLEWORK				
PHYSICAL EXERCISES & GAMES		34	50	
GARDENING				
COMMERCIAL SUBJECTS	Shorthand			
	Typewriting			
SCIENCE		31	50	A very good term's work.

Conduct **Good.** 380 No. of Scholars in Form **38**
No. of Times Absent
No. of Times Late   Position in Form **20th**

.... **M.A. Lake** ..... Form Teacher

Report on General Progress
He is doing very well indeed.
James D. Brown Head Master

Oscar is doing well all-round. He enters keenly into every side of school life. M.L.

My first final report card in four years.

sneering tone, "Because you don't sing carols!" and walked away. That was the only run-in I had with my headmaster.

At an early age I decided not to get involved, even peripherally, with non-Jewish religious philosophies and customs. My priority was to first become very proficient in my own religion's laws, teachings and customs. In fact, I had a thirst for learning about the Jewish way of life. While in a British public school where religion was taught, I became even more conscious of my roots. In my committed ways towards Judaism, the non-Jewish environment only caused me to become more devoted to our ways. This dedication in matters of the Jewish faith negated any tendency towards religious dormancy that resulted from being in a public school system.

FOLLOWING WORLD WAR I, THE LEAGUE OF NATIONS, THE forerunner of the United Nations, assigned the British government the task of administering various geographical areas in the Near East. One of these countries was Palestine, better known to us as Eretz Yisroel.

After World War II, the British were having a rough time in their Palestine Mandate. Three separate Jewish underground groups were vying to fight the British since the latter sided with the Arabs and refused permission for large scale Jewish immigration. Jews from Europe and North Africa, uprooted by German atrocities, were all clamoring to enter their homeland. Unfortunately, many boatloads of these refugees were intercepted by the Royal British Navy. Some boats were returned to Europe. The most famous of these was the "Exodus", which was sent back to Hamburg in northwest Germany with thousands of Jewish passengers. Passengers of other ships were interned on the island of Cyprus in the Mediterranean Sea. There were fatal casualties on both sides due to these naval interceptions.

At Pixmore there was one student whose father had recently been killed in Palestine while serving in the British Army. The boy was burly and a real bully. As I always ate with my cap on, went outdoors in the play yard wearing my cap and had a pronounced foreign accent, the bully singled me out and released some of his energies on me. In my jacket breast pocket, I carried a fountain pen I had inherited from my grandmother, *Oma* Wallerstein. In those years, the advantage of a fountain pen over a regular pen was that its small rubber bladder carried enough ink to write perhaps ten full pages of script. Ordinary pens had to be dipped into an inkwell after every few lines of writing. This meant carrying an ink bottle at all times and exercising caution to prevent its spillage or leakage. Before Grandmother passed away she said that since I would do a lot of writing, I, therefore, should get her pen. The pen was hidden during the war and now I was starting to use it. Once the bully came over to me in the playground and punched me a number of times in the chest thereby breaking the pen. Today, the damaged pen is another memorabilia in our safe deposit box.

TO COMMUTE TO SCHOOL, I USED MY COUSIN'S BICYCLE WHILE he was studying at the Gateshead *Yeshivah*. Life was a little rough during the bitter cold winter months: riding bicycles, wearing short pants and going without gloves, the typical school boy's transportation and attire.

After the war, the British armies were still stationed in the former combat areas of Europe and the Far East. Accordingly, there was a shortage of farm help to assist in routine chores, which was especially pronounced during harvest time. German prisoners of war were still interned in England and were put to work to help the farmers. When potato picking time arrived supplemental labor resources were tapped and schools were given off. The entire student body would then go to various preassigned farmer's fields to fill up potato sacks from morning to night. For this effort, each student would receive at the end of the day a nominal pay, which amounted to approximately five shillings.

On some of our days off from school, our aunt took us to London for the day. There we would stop in at many family friends, including the Goldschmidt family, a brother-in-law of the Levis. Once I spent an entire week at their house and went around town with their son, the late Emil Goldschmidt, who later became a popular Professor of Chemistry and Dean of Sciences at Bar Ilan University. While touring London, one could still note extensive destruction wrought by the German V rockets. Emil had great patience and together we visited many of London's landmarks while also admiring the deep "Underground" railroad system. London was a dreary city which formerly had much pollution. Living conditions in some districts are crowded and several well-known areas have no real natural charm. At low tide the barges in the Thames River lay on exposed mud banks. The city does, however, have great historic significance and boasts many interesting museums and sites. Large portions of the city are indeed beautiful.

[Neither my sisters nor I have visited the British Isles for any extended duration since our departure in 1947. In my opinion, this lack of interest in the U.K. will certainly change with time. Our protracted absence might be explained by the fact that most of the persons whom we knew in England have since moved to either the U.S.A. or to Eretz Yisroel.]

Chapter Twenty Eight
NOTEWORTHY EXPERIENCES

WHILE IN LETCHWORTH, WE RECEIVED A LONG LETTER from Holland. It was written by a member of the Diamond Group who related to us that our mother, *o.h.* passed away on February 18, 1945 which corresponds to 5 Adar, 5705. I am not sure of the name of this person, though it probably was Mrs. Cardozo. Up until now, although we had always suspected the worst, we still maintained a glimmer of hope. Now we knew for sure that the cursed Germans were responsible for yet another asinine killing which should be added to their long and senseless criminal record.

This year (1996), Mother would have been ninety-six years old, not an impossibility considering her two sisters and brother all lived to ripe old ages. Many of her friends lived to their upper eighties, and several friends are now well into their nineties. Our mother was cut down by greedy barbaric butchers at the tender young age of forty-four. She was born on 23 Av, 5660 (1900). May the Almighty take just revenge for her suffering and her precious blood. Thanks to the above letter, I was still able to say *Kaddish* for several months, at the tender age of twelve.

I kept full *aveilus,* which led to an incident which my cousin Manny tells me is still on his mind and conscience fifty years later. Manny loved classical music back then and had recently become familiar with the Beethoven Symphonies and especially the Emperor Piano Concerto. Once he told me that the Emperor Concerto was about to be broadcast on the radio (wireless) and he desperately wanted to listen. Would I mind sitting upstairs (in the unheated bedroom) for about an hour, he asked, since I was in *aveilus* and therefore not permitted to listen to music. Years later he reminded me that I was very "cross" probably not so much because of personal feelings but because Manny did not appear to share my *aveilus.*

MY *BAR MITZVAH* WAS IN THE SUMMER OF 1946. IT WAS A small affair held on *Shabbos Nachamuh,* but, nevertheless, it was beautiful. The practice of making extensive *Bar Mitzvah* celebrations did not start until many years later. I had studied *laining* the entire *sedra* of *Vo'Eschanan* [a] plus the *Haftorah,* all in the Dutch *Nigun,* as I had been taught six years earlier in Amsterdam. As was the Dutch custom, I also pronounced every *ngayin (ayin).* Our cousin, Manny Lehmann taught me the *nigun* for the *Asseres Hadibros* (Decalogue). Today, fifty years later, I still *lain* from the *Torah* with that same *nigun* and am proud of not having changed to one of the many local varieties.

Since the local *shul* of Rabbi Joseph Horowitz was too small, my *Bar Mitzvah* was held in the larger *shul* in "downtown" Letchworth, where Rabbi Epstein and many others *davened.* For the occasion, the London Goldschmidts came for *Shabbos* and brought for me an old *Shabbos* suit with long pants, formerly belonging to their son, Emil. The pants were oversized as I was still quite short (4'-6" 140 cm). Despite the cold weather, English boys in those days wore only short pants, even on *Shabbos.* I still remember walking to *shul* that *Shabbos* with the cuffs of the extra large long pants folded up.

At home, my aunt made a magnificent *Shabbos Seuda,* which was attended by at least twenty-five persons. These days when I attend a local *Bar Mitzvah* and observe how the parents appreciate their son's great efforts in laining a long *sedrah,* I frequently recall how my parents could not enjoy their son's efforts and a tear is wiped away. These are not tears of jealousy but of parental loss.

---

a. Devorim, 3:23-7:11.

Besides the immediate family and the Goldschmidts, we were also privileged to have several other out of town guests join us for *Shabbos*. Mr. Joseph Magnus came from Amsterdam and my aunt, Tante Else arrived from London with her daughters Thea and Erika. Additional family and friends of the family joined us on Sunday when an open house was conducted in the living room. The entire weekend was a memorable event made possible by my aunt's weeks of preparations. It was a labor of love for her sister's sake.

Recently, my sister Connie reminded me of a remarkable story from Letchworth. Meat was rationed, and four weeks prior to my *Bar Mitzvah*, our aunt started saving ration coupons so she would be able to purchase a sizeable roast for the *Seudah*. It was a hot August day that *Shabbos Nachamu*. Since we did not have a refrigerator, the meat was kept Friday night in front of the open kitchen window so as to remain cool. A net covered the roast for protection. The next morning, the meat was found to be fully covered with insect eggs. The entire piece of meat had to be thrown out. Our aunt took it in stride, did not complain and quickly worked out an alternate dish in her small kitchen. She was a true Lady of Valor.

RESIDING DIAGONALLY ACROSS THE STREET FROM THE Lehmanns were my uncle and aunt Sholom and Martha (Lehmann) Hildesheimer. Uncle Sholom was the grandson of Horav Ezriel Hildesheimer from Berlin. Unfortunately, he had vision problems and as a result wore thick lens glasses. Laser eye surgery did not yet exist and contact lenses were not yet used. Frequently, I came to their house to study *Limudei Kodesh* with my uncle, who limited the sessions so as not to strain his eyes. Our aunt Tante Martha was the Hebrew teacher for the young girls of Letchworth. It was always a pleasure to be in their home, which exuded a warm and friendly atmosphere.

Bananas are a subtropical fruit, which were unavailable during the war years. Neither my cousin Judy Lehmann (Mrs. Judith Bloch), who today lives in Kibbutz Sha'alvim, nor I had seen a fresh banana since 1940. We had thus grown up for six years without peeling or eating this treat. When in 1946 my aunt purchased some bananas, everyone in the house was questioned on how one peels this fruit. The youngest were asked first. Neither of us knew the simple procedure of removing the yellow rind!

On December 5, 1946, the Dutch Consul General in London officially designated our aunt Mrs. Resi Lehmann as the Temporary Guardian of my two sisters and myself. This facilitated discharging legal responsibilities in the absence of parental authority.

Several hobbies kept me busy in my spare time. Woodworking was one of my big preoccupations. The Levis sent patterns, which I traced onto thin plywood and then cut out with a fretsaw (similar to a large coping saw). Obtaining thin plywood was not a problem. The English people are prolific tea drinkers. The loose tea was imported from India and packed in large plywood tea-chests. The grocers then used some of these empty chests to deliver orders. Hence, I always had an ample supply of wood. I also made three layered *seder* plates for *Pesach* which were used by various friends in the community. Another hobby I had was stamp collecting. Mail was received from many countries and stamp swapping among friends led to major negotiations. Jack Lehmann had a stamp collection which he gave to me. To this day he won't forget how I swapped his German stamps for Egyptian ones.

Of all the musical instruments that I have heard, the one that, in my opinion, produces the most delicate sound is the violin. As part of our "cultural development", Our aunts, Tante Res. and Tante Alice thought that we should attend a concert. On one of our winter outings to London, they invited us all, including our cousins, to the Royal Albert Hall, one of the world's most prestigious and oldest concert halls. This hall is a landmark building in London and has a similar stature to that of Carnegie Hall in New York. During the war the building had been used for storage, and repairs had just been completed, thereby allowing the hall to be reopened. The program included several symphonies, including the renowned Beethoven Violin Concerto. When, during one of the movements, one of the twenty-five violinists stood alone, playing in front of the large orchestra, I remarked in a whisper, "look he is playing by himself!" It was the soloist, and cousin Manny was aghast at my ignorance of the subject!

One unusual pastime I enjoyed, was going with my friend Sammy Hollander, now a professor of Economics in Toronto, to a distant field by bicycle, sitting alongside the railroad tracks and writing down in our pocket memo pads the serial numbers of the passing steam locomotives. On my occasional trips to London, I would also take down locomotive serial numbers as I saw them pass and then upon my return we would compare which and how many numbers each of us had already seen. These were the years when "modern" streamlined coal fired locomotives were just being introduced and obtaining their serial numbers, e.g. 001, was considered special. Today, this would be equivalent to people who make it a point to recognize different model automobiles, a common preoccupation in some circles.

LETCHWORTH HAD A HUGE PUBLIC SWIMMING POOL WHERE I frequently went to swim. Swimming was mixed and so I stopped using the facility when I became *bar mitzvah.*

THE STREETS OF THE MORE ESTABLISHED NEIGHBORHOODS were lined with Horse Chestnut trees. When it got close to *Succos,* I collected bags and bags of Horse Chestnuts. The chestnuts were inedible but were collected for stringing. The long "necklaces" were then hung in the *succah* for decorations. In the weeks following *Succos,* these chestnuts were fed to deer at a small zoo.

MY MEMORIES OF MANNY LEHMANN ARE DISTINCT. MANNY was a hard working person who put in long hours at his job in the electronics factory. When he was home he helped his mother wherever possible. In his spare time, he studied *Limudei Kodesh* and a profession. As the oldest son and only man at home, he set the religious and secular tone for the household. I learned a lot from him on many matters in which I had little knowledge, especially on Torah subjects concerning science.

Today, Manny has a Ph.D. and is a world authority on computers. He has attended many computer conferences and workshops from Seattle to Moscow to Tokyo. On occasion, he has been requested to organize such affairs worldwide. He has also presented many important research papers at these gatherings. But no matter where he goes, he always studies his *Daf Yomi.* He personifies *Torah im Derech Eretz.* Quite often, "cousin" Manny was able to arrange the itinerary of his consulting conferences and his seminar activities so as to coincide with my sister Toni's and our *simcha* schedules in America. To his accolade, he verily enhanced our *bar mitzvas* and *chassenos.* Manny, or Professor Meir Lehman as he is known, was for many years the Head of the Computer Science Department in London's Imperial College.

In this way, all of Tante Resi's children are prime achievers, despite their early hardships in life. They all displayed qualities worthy of emulation. Today, their children follow in their parent's ways.

My aunt made *aliyah* from England in the 1950's. In Eretz Yisroel she joined the families of her two daughters in the Lower Galil. At Kibbutz Lavi her exceptional character also shone and the entire kibbutz membership affectionately bestowed their lady of valor the title of *Savta.* After a long and productive life, her righteous *neshoma,* surely followed by a great entourage of *mitzvos* and good deeds, ascended to a loftier world on the first day of *Pesach,* 5748 (1988). She was laid to rest in the Lavi *Beis Olam.*

MY FATHER'S FIRST COUSIN, MRS. SELINA SASSOON, known as Lady Sassoon was the oldest daughter of my great aunt, Tante Emma. She was a native of Amsterdam while her late husband David Sassoon came from the large Indian city of Bombay. Now the Sassoons lived at 15 Sollershot East, an exclusive Letchworth street. Residing with her were her son Rabbi Salman Sassoon and her daughter Mrs. Flora Feuchtwanger and their families. Tante Selina, as we addressed her, was congenial and dignified and carried the aristocratic aura of her mother (I had never met her late husband). Edifying our Jewish traditions in their majestic manner was the Sassoon trademark. Visiting them was always a pleasure and invariably this would arouse pre-war memories of the Prins' home on Sarfatistraat. Both Rabbi Salman Sassoon and his brother-in-law Rabbi Osher Feuchtwanger authored scholarly books on the *Torah* and *Chazal* that grace many a Jewish home and *Yeshivah* hall of study.

The Sassoon household had many individuals from different cultural and lingual backgrounds. To assure that the grandchildren became multi-lingual, the various members of the household were only permitted to converse with the children in their own native tongue. In this way, the children learned and became proficient in each foreign language without an accent. Thus, the children learned Dutch, Hindi, Arabic, Hebrew, German and English. [It should be noted that India has twenty states, each with a different language and each of these languages is spoken by an average of forty-five million persons (1994). Every state also has numerous dialects. The languages of choice as used by the Indian Parliament in New Delhi are mostly Hindi and some English, both of which are understood by most of the educated segment of the population. In Bombay, Maharastian is the commonly used language.]

It is not a frequent occurrence that individuals are presented with an opportunity to beautify a *minhag* or a *mitzvah*. *Tu B'Shvat,* our Arbor Day,[b] is an anniversary begging to be honored. Following five years of World War II scarcities, the Sassoon family seized upon the occasion and made a *hiddur* out of this celebration. They channeled all the means at their disposal towards beautifying our Jewish legacy. Assembled from the far reaches of our globe were rare, uncommon and scarce fruits. In the true Sassoon heritage, they conducted a royal banquet in their dining room so as to honor the *Rosh Hashonoh Le Elonos*.

---

b. *Maseches Rosh Hashonoh,* 14b

After the war, exotic fruits were extremely scarce. I was invited to the Sassoons on *Tu B'Shvat,* both in 1946 and 1947. We sat around a large exquisitely set noontime dinner table. Following a tasty and nourishing meal, each person was given a special fruit. There were at least fifteen adults present, each person then made, in turn, a *shehechiyonu brocho* over a different fruit. At the beautifully set tables of the Sassoons there was always an empty chair for Eliyohu HaNovie.

In the 1950's, the Sassoons moved to Bayit Vegan, Yerusholayim. The family has been very active and successful in nurturing the development of the fledgling *Sefardic Yeshivah* movement in Eretz Yisroel. To back up their drive, the late Rabbi Salman Sassoon auctioned off many family owned, valuable Judaica manuscripts and rare books. Many of these prized books were auctioned off in London, since the British government did not permit them to be taken abroad. [On *Succos* 5753 (1992) we visited Flora (Sassoon) Feuchtwanger and Alice Sassoon for the first time since leaving Letchworth. There was much reminiscing and catching up on general news.]

Chapter Twenty Nine
TO NEW YORK

OUR AUNT, TANTE RESI DID HER VERY BEST TO PROVIDE a pleasant home for my two sisters and myself. Despite her lofty intentions, we were nevertheless an added burden to her difficult life. Considering the many pros and cons, the Levis felt that it would be in the best interest for all concerned that now the three of us join their family in New York.

Following World War II, there were literally millions of individuals from Asia, Europe, Africa and Latin America who wanted to immigrate to the U.S.A. America had an immigration quota and it was therefore no simple task to obtain a visa, but thanks to our uncle and aunt's perseverance our American visas came through. Travel arrangements were made and our date of departure was set for March 17, 1947. For some reason, my sister Connie did not want to fly. Mr. and Mrs. Hugo and Lotte Prins (Tante Emma's son) had reservations on the ocean liner Queen Elizabeth just then, but *Oom* Hugo, for business reasons, could not make the journey and so my sister Connie readily accepted to take his place.

The Queen Elizabeth was the largest passenger ship afloat in 1947. This giant ship was the forerunner of the famous QE II (Queen Elizabeth the Second), which was an even larger and more modern luxury liner. The Q.E. had been used during the war as a troop carrier and its conversion to peacetime use had just been completed. It departed from Southampton on *Shabbos* and therefore my sister had to board the Q.E. on Friday. Our aunt, Tante Resi joined her for the weekend so that she should not remain alone in Southhampton. They brought the luggage aboard on Friday and my sister walked to her cabin on *Shabbos* without having to check in. As my sister described it, "our aunt did it with such love, never once did she show me what an imposition it really was for her." The transatlantic journey was extremely stormy with ocean waves eighty feet high! This giant among ships was overpowered, and for one day the Q.E. could not progress, thus delaying their New York arrival.

My sister Toni and I flew with American Airlines. We stopped at Shannon, Ireland for a refueling. There the plane was found to have engine problems and this resulted in a delay for us as well. Planes of those days were all propeller driven. They were noisy and produced much vibration so that one could hardly hear a person talk. In addition, the planes were slow, thereby taking many more hours to cross the Atlantic and requiring frequent refueling stops.

Saying good bye to the Lehmanns was not easy, but we knew we would meet again, hopefully in Eretz Yisroel. It was impossible to thank them for all they had done for us.

Traveling to the *New World* in the western hemisphere now became a reality. While in Amsterdam and during my incarceration by the Germans, I never imagined to one day live in that far away city that was known as *Nieuw Amsterdam* (New Amsterdam, from 1626 to 1664) and subsequently as New York city. This city still has vestiges of its brief Dutch history; Kings county (Brooklyn) states on its official seal the old Dutch phrase: *"eendraght maakt magt"* (unity produces strength) and there are many Dutch street names in the older sections of the borough.

Following what seemed like an endless flight across the Atlantic Ocean, we finally landed in Boston. At the airport I used the lavatory, but alas, I was unable to figure out how to flush the toilet. I was only used to the old European pull chain and overhead water closet [W.C.]. In the United States this type of bathroom fixture had already become obsolete for over a decade.

The huge present day JFK (John F. Kennedy) International Airport of New York was in 1947 only a small domestic airport called Idlewild Airport. It was used exclusively for local air travel.

From Boston we traveled to New York's La Guardia Airport, where we were met by my Uncle Michael and Bram (his son) and my Uncle Fritz (father's brother) and his son Michael. Uncle Fritz was known in America as Dr. Frederick Lehmann M.D. (Ear, Nose and Throat Specialist). This was the first time we met our father's younger brother and his son. Now I had met all my parent's siblings. The flight had been long and tiring and between Boston and New York, I became airsick from all the turbulence due to airpockets caused by flying at a much lower altitude. As we drove from the airport to the Borough Park section of Brooklyn, we used the Belt Parkway. The highway lampposts were of wood and were placed along the center roadway divider. Across the top of these posts was a horizontal board from which hung one lantern on each end. To me, they appeared like a lot of converted gallows.

Before we arrived, I had imagined the Levis living by themselves in a one family house. As we drove up to 49th Street and 15th Avenue, I noticed a six story brick building with many windows. I thought wow, and couldn't believe what a huge house they lived in! It was an apartment building, the likes of which I had never seen before (forty-seven apartments). From the fifth floor, our aunt, Tante Alice and our cousin Bessy (Mrs. Ruth Emanual, Kibbutz Sha'alvim) waved to us, which made me think that the Levis occupied the building's entire fifth floor. When we went up the elevator, I noticed that there were eight apartment doors on that floor. The Levis had only apartment 5B on the corner. They were real *Tzadikim* to take in three children, living in a two bedroom apartment with a small kitchen-dinette and all their four children at home. To accommodate us, my uncle and aunt made the living room their nighttime sleeping quarters, using a highriser bed (pull out bed one bed stored below the other). They squeezed us in by putting one highriser each in the girls' and boys' bedroom. There was only one bathroom for nine persons. The landlord's agent was not happy and objected to this crowding, but then again the sacrifices of the Levis was something seldom duplicated.

RABBI SHMAYE WIESNER HAD A SMALL *ASHKENAZIC MINYAN* on the first floor of his house on 49th Street, off 14th Avenue. In the year 1947, Borough Park had only three or four private *minyonim*. In 1996, there are almost that many on every block. Rabbi Wiesner was a special, humble, unassuming and kind person who had great respect for all who came to him, whether learned or not. His gentle character, discreet insight and noteworthy scholarship made him a shining mentor to many who knew him.

The Levis *davened* at Rabbi Wiesner's *minyan*. Also among the *mispallelim* was my future father-in-law, Morris Rokowsky (Opely). The Rokowskys had many relatives in Europe and frequently their nephews and nieces would be their guests for an extended period of time, sometimes in excess of a year or two! On my first *Shabbos* in America, one of these nephews sat in front of me in *shul*. I recognized him right away and asked him, *"Ben jij Jakie van de Keuke?"* ("Are you Jackie (Yaakov) from the kitchen? at Bergen Belsen".) Jackie Finkel was amazed and didn't expect to hear that question anymore! What a small world. A little over eleven years later, Jackie Finkel's cousin, Ruth Rokowsky, our neighbor of ten years, would become my dear wife!

LIVING AT THE LEVIS WAS PLEASANT DESPITE THE CROWDING. Friday afternoon we would take apart a large heavy wooden table from the boys' bedroom and gingerly manipulate it through the twisting narrow apartment corridor to the living room. There the table was reassembled and served as the *Shabbos* table, where it would comfortably seat ten persons using narrow metal folding chairs.

It should be mentioned that most of the furniture that the Levis owned came from Holland via Paramaribo. My uncle anticipated being frequently on the move and therefore had all furniture made so that it could be readily disassembled. To have built-in furniture was out of the question.

In our highly competitive world with its constant new challenges, our uncle and aunt knew how to foster competence and diligence in the younger generation. This was in contrast to the popular media driven practice of stereotyping as nerds any young person who became enamored with their study of the sciences, professions or religious fields of learning. Being classified as socially disparate will frighten most teenagers, who have a deep fear of not conforming to their peers. Coupled with this potential character stigmatization are the pseudo-intellectuals who taunt and scoff these budding individuals by putting down the sciences and flaunting his or her ignorance thereof. Such attitudes are conducive to stifling personal initiatives and ultimately could result in more non-individuals joining the faceless crowd. Our uncle and aunt avoided this sterile and barren atmosphere by encouraging us to associate with motivated and talent-oriented friends whose backgrounds were not necessarily based on social, financial or business credentials.

Three Moves and it is Mate! by I. Epstein Reprinted from the *Israelit*, [21] April 1895

On *Shabbos,* the table seating was fully occupied with the nine of us and sometimes a guest as well. The atmosphere was warm and pleasant. Some of our cousin's friends were most interesting, such as Herman's (Naftali) friends Johnny (Yisroel) and Peter (Moshe) Auman. Moshe Auman became Vice Consul for Israel in Washington D.C., and Yisroel (Johnny) became a professor in Mathematics, first in Princeton, N.J. and then in Yerusholayim. Herman and Johnny used to walk down the street deeply engrossed, making verbal moves in an imaginary chess game. In 1994, Professor Yisroel Auman was the recipient of the coveted *Prize of Israel* in economic mathematics. This award is the Israeli equivalent of the Nobel prize. Jacob was preoccupied with studying *Tenach, Gemora* and all associated works. Bram (Abraham), who is three months older than I, had many hobbies, including developing films, printing and enlarging photographs. For this, our only bathroom became the "darkroom". We, too, had friends who today are professors, assistant school principals, etc. As for the meals, our appetites were enormous, and our aunt had a rough time keeping up in her small apartment kitchen.

OUR UNCLE WAS A PERSON OF HIGH STANDARDS. HIS HONESTY was impeccable and he expected others to be likewise. His standards on religious principles were high as well. Once four well dressed representatives came to his office from one of the largest New York Jewish philanthropic organizations to collect for a special cause unknown to me. They were asked whether they were wearing a *tallis koton.* When the response was negative, he politely declined to deal with them. Our uncle did not want to cast an aspersion on these individuals, but felt that as representatives of an organization that espouses Jewish causes, the least they could do was to meet the dress code of the culture they advocated. Of course, all other persons who came to his office were not asked regarding their *tallis koton* practices. This query does not imply that all who don such a garment are perfect, while those without this attire are automatically evil. Wearing a *tallis koton* simply means that precept No. 386 of our sacred *Torah* is being implemented, a very worthy act.[a]

On another occasion, a close relative was getting married. The *kallah* decided not to cover her hair after the *chassenah.* In protest, my uncle opted not to attend the ceremony. Nevertheless, they remained on very good terms.

There was so much to learn and emulate, since the Levis practiced what they preached. Their children and grandchildren, moreover, have followed in their paths.

---

a. Bamidbor, 15:38, *Maseches Menochos,* 41a and *Mishnah Berurah,* 24:6

Chapter Thirty
AT THE LEVIS

MANY DETAILS APPEAR ON OTHER PAGES REGARDING the Levis. While often persons preach but don't practice, living with my uncle and aunt was equivalent to experiencing a life course in the *Shulchon Aruch,* and it was done in a matter of fact style, without us even realizing it.

In the course of my stay with them (1947-1957), I heard reminiscing about many past experiences. My uncle was born in 1896 in Frankfurt am Main, Germany. Not being very fond of his native land, he would refer to Germany as "his former birthplace". His family had moved from the town of Nagelsberg to Frankfurt am Main, the city where my aunt was born in 1902. She was my mother's younger sister. During World War I, my uncle was drafted into the German army where he served as a private on the "Western Front" in France. He described his position there as, *Brenzeman,* which translates into "brakeman". Ammunition was transported to the front lines in horsedrawn carriages. The loads were heavy, and when going down steep hills the horses were in danger of becoming overwhelmed by the great load bearing down on them from behind. To alleviate that problem, a soldier was assigned to each carriage's brakes so as to slow down these vehicles. Our uncle had no affection for wars, the military or for army life. His frequent repeating of his *Brenzeman* duties conveyed his distaste for fighting and how he "merited" to put the brakes on the war by slowing down the flow of materiel to the front lines.

After the war, he joined his father in the manufacture of leather goods, such as pocketbooks and purses. Like our father, our uncle was fed up with the German character and he too moved to Holland around 1919. He went back to Frankfurt in January, 1929 to marry our aunt, Tante Alice (Wallerstein), whom he had already known since his school days.

As married sisters living in Amsterdam, our aunt and our mother and their respective families were all very close. This was later enhanced when our grandparents, David and Emma Wallerstein, moved from Frankfurt to Amsterdam. I don't remember my grandfather, since he died in 1934 when I was very young. He is buried in Diemen just outside Amsterdam, near Hilversum, not far from the Amstel train station.

During the summer's school vacation, our families went to the Dutch North Sea resort town of Zandvoort. There, we would rent an apartment or cottage together. The Levis used the unit in the first month and we came for the second month. The children of both families attended the same Herman Elte School. We frequently visited each other and, on such occasions, the discussion between our uncle and Father often gravitated to world politics. There certainly was plenty to discuss on this subject: the saber rattling of the Germans, the German invasion of Sudetenland, the do-nothing and appeasement policies of the British, the Spanish Civil War in which many countries were involved, the arming to the teeth of practically every European country, etc. It was a world time bomb in the making.

OUR UNCLE HAD ABSOLUTELY NO CONFIDENCE IN Holland's ability to both stay out of a probable war and to successfully resist the Germans in a potential invasion from the east. He had sold his leather goods manufacturing business in 1935 because business conditions had changed. Subsequently, he spent most of his time, together with his older brother Albert, *H.Y.D.,* convincing and helping family members and other Jews to leave Germany. When the international political situation worsened, he made plans to leave Holland, should the threat of war increase. When Hitler unilaterally annexed Austria in March of 1938 *(Anschluss)* and his hordes made threatening moves, all six Levis packed up and on short notice flew to England for safety. There they stayed with a sister's family in London and later along the coast in Bournemouth. Four weeks later, after the threat of war had subsided the family was back in Amsterdam. Soon thereafter, the threat of international conflicts took a turn for the worse and that prompted the Levis to depart shortly after *Pesach* 1939, this time for the western hemisphere. They were unable to immigrate to the USA since the quota for native Germans was full and those ahead on the waiting list ensured that the wait would be considerable. Since, however, they were all Dutch citizens, they opted to travel to Paramaribo, the capital of Suriname which sometimes was referred to as Dutch Guiana, and at that time was part of the Dutch West Indie colonies. Today the country is independent and is named Suriname. It is located in the tropics, just north of the equator, east of Venezuela, and north of Brazil.

In Paramaribo, there was a small *Sephardic* community. The climate is very tropical and the lifestyle much more relaxed. In 1939, the Levis sent to us in Amsterdam an 8 mm movie of life near the equator. I remember that the most significant feature of this movie was my uncle and aunt waiting at the boat docks for a weekly mail ship to arrive from Europe. These were the days before regular transatlantic airmail.

The *shul* in Paramaribo had a wooden floor, covered with sand which was replaced annually, a common architectural detail for warm climate *Sephardic shuls*. [In February, 1994, Ruth and I visited Willemstad on the island of Curacao, which is 900 miles northwest of Paramaribo. Curacao is one of the Netherlands Antilles islands. There we toured the large *Sephardic shul,* Mikve Israel. Dedicated in the year 1732, it is the oldest *shul* in the western hemisphere and has been in continuous use from its founding until the present. The floor in this *shul* was also covered with a thick clean carpet of light colored fine sand. The Willemstad Jewish congregation dates back to 1651.]

After fifteen months of exile in Central America and boredom, the Levis moved to New York City, where they settled in Washington Heights, the northerly end of Manhattan. By this time, Holland had fallen to the Germans, but Germany was not yet at war with the United States. Accordingly, we were still able to correspond and send telegrams to America. In one of those letters, my aunt wrote that the children, "had to cross a busy and wide roadway to walk to school, the street was used by many automobiles". That street was Broadway, which, by 1940 European standards, was wide and busy but whose roadway is probably no wider than sixty feet [eighteen meters]. The overseas envelopes and postcards we received were all stamped by a German censor.

My cousin Herman was twelve years old in the year 1941, when his teacher asked the students what their fathers were. Each responded with a different occupation, e.g. carpenter, teacher, lawyer, plumber, etc. When it came to Herman's turn, he said his father was an "optimist". The family was proud of that reply, which expressed the positive attitude with which the Levi family tackled life's challenges.

By 1942, the family settled in the Borough Park section of Brooklyn, an area of New York City which eventually developed into one of the most flourishing Jewish communities America has seen.

Their apartment was a modest two bedroom unit on the fifth floor of a six story elevator building. On *Shabbos* this meant walking up and down four flights of stairs, several times a day. My uncle was the type of person who took nothing for granted and so he insisted that the apartment's lease agreement include a clause giving him permission to build a *Succah* on the building's roof. Though the landlord and the building agent were both observant Jews and, according to them, such a clause was completely unnecessary, after some ado, it was added to the lease. As usual, our uncle's foresight was 20/20. When other upper story tenants wanted to build their *Succah* on the roof as well, they were told to build it in the building's courtyard off the basement. These neighbors now had to carry their food down four or five flights of stairs and all crowd into a common *Succah*.

HAVING BEEN RAISED AND EDUCATED IN FRANKFURT AM Main, our uncle knew the importance of *Torah im Derech Eretz*. He realized well our *Chazal:* "If there is no flour there is no *Torah* and if there is no *Torah*, there is no flour".[a] He therefore, made it a point that every child, including us Lehmanns, had a profession with marketable skills before we left their home. Horav S. R. Hirsch succinctly describes the *Torah* link to *Derech Eretz* when he comments:[b] Studying and practicing *Torah* enhances our purpose in life and causes our livelihood to blossom, family and communal life are elevated and ennobled and as a result of its justice, morality and brotherly love, the Almighty's brochos are deserved.

---

a. *Pirkei Avos,* 3:21
b. Devorim 28:3

Torah im Derech Eretz is the "Trade Mark" of the philosophy of Horav Samson Raphael Hirsch. It implies an uncompromising commitment to the ways of our *Torah,* without rejecting the best that the secular world has to offer, all within *Torah* parameters.

To study a profession or trade meant mingling with non-observant Jews and non-Jews. Our uncle and aunt, however, so strongly imbued the atmosphere at home with Jewish values that the threat of possible assimilating influences were negated.

Out-of-town *yeshivos* for High School and *Beis Hamedrash* were few in number and small in size when compared to those of today (1996). There was no thought of sending anyone of us to such a *yeshivah.* Summer camps in the 40's were in their infancy and not patronized by the Levis. Living at home during those formative years gave our uncle and aunt the opportunity to instill in all of us an important ingredient sometimes overlooked — *halocho leMaase* — a practical application of Jewish values. These included business acumen in the matter of ethics, spousal respect and consideration, manner of spending spare time, etc. Many consider there to be no substitute for parental exposure to these basics. Those youngsters who are entrusted for most of the year to both out-of-town or even out of country institutions of learning and recreation surely do not receive comparable values.

There was no television in their home. The absence of this electronic viewing tube served many positive functions, including the elimination of direct or indirect x-rated entertainment, the avoidance of inactivity *(bittul zeman),* not being exposed to the risk of losing one's sensitivity to the subtleties of our Jewish values and not stifling the imaginative process. The denial of television viewing in no way compromised our ability to remain abreast with current events or other matters of newsworthy interest. Non-tabloid newspapers, current event magazines and informative radio programs provided our necessary coverage.

Coming from Frankfurt am Main made our uncle and aunt great expounders of *"Chanoch lena'ar al pi darko,* "train a child according to his ways…".[c] This was accomplished by encouraging and exposing each child to the various professions that matched their inclinations. The results were just right. Their oldest son Herman (Naftali) became an accountant/economist, his brother Jacob a very popular *Limudei Kodesh* teacher, the youngest son Abraham, a chemical engineer and their daughter Bessy

---

c. Mishlei, 22:16

(Ruth), a teacher. My sister Toni became a secretary/bookkeeper, my sister Connie a clinical laboratory technician and I became a civil engineer. In the mid-1970's, after spending many years teaching at the Yeshivah in Oak Park, Michigan, Jacob wanted to take his family on *aliyah* to Yerusholayim. This prompted the local *Yeshivah* to take him to a *Din Torah* so as to prevent Rabbi Levi from departing. He was extremely popular and has great Torah knowledge. Of course, the *Yeshivah* lost their case.

Jacob Levi is the author of a treatise *Limudei Loshon*.[24] This esoteric work on grammar is a thoroughly researched study of the entire *Tenach*. The first volume broaches the subject of *Tenach's* nominal forms. The fascinating anomalies of the sixth Hebrew letter *vav* and its occasional omission or excess usage is addressed in his second volume. Jacob Levi's entire writings are based on *Rishonim* and *Acharonim,* including the Malbim and Horav Samson Raphael Hirsch. The common thread that binds this work is his veneration and awe towards the *Ribono Shel Olam* and the holiness of the language, as found in our *Tenach*. This is diametrically opposite the *Haskala* grammar works of 100 years ago which considered Hebrew as just another language. Two companion volumes on other interesting aspects of *Tenach* grammar are in an advanced stage of planning (as of 1996).

A favorite quote of my uncle was from the author Samuel Clemens, [pseudonym Mark Twain (1835-1910)]: "I never let my schooling interfere with my education." Following that philosophy, we were programmed to only absorb life's pedagogic kernels and to discard its chaff. To continue our Jewish studies from 1947 to 1951, my cousin Abraham and I were tutored individually by Rabbi Naphtali Wiesner, author of *In His Own Image,*[29]

At the *Shabbos* table, my uncle always expounded on the *Shulchon Aruch* and emphasized what the Rema (Rabbi Moshe Isserles from the Polish city of Krakow) had to say on the subject at hand. Also discussed at the table would be *minhagim* on common daily matters. Frequently, my uncle would turn to one of his favorite *Torah* commentaries, the Ba'al haTurim. He was fascinated with the Ba'al haTurim's *gematrios* and, occasionally, would also derive one himself. On Friday night, after clearing the *Shabbos* table, we sat at the table and took turns *laining* a *parsha* from the week's *Sedrah,* followed by the *Haftorah*. Subsequently, each of us kept ourselves busy with reading or talking. My uncle and aunt, however, would then go over the week's Rashi using the Rabbi Onderwyzer

Shabbos Meal by Sacher Masoch. Reprinted from the Israelit,[21] May 1894

Chumash. Rabbi Onderwyzer was a well-known Chief Rabbi in the Province of North Holland, which included Amsterdam. He had translated the Rashi commentary into the Dutch language. It should be noted that those who engage in this weekly practice of reviewing the *Sedrah* with Rashi merit *Arichas Yomim Veshonim* (longevity in a worthy life). (For specifics of this beautiful tradition, refer to *Mishnah Berurah*.)[d] Both my uncle Michael and my aunt, Tante Alice lived useful lives to a ripe old age.

EVERY ORTHODOX JEW OBSERVES THE LAWS CODIFIED IN the *Shulchon Aruch*. Individuals, however will frequently commit themselves to be more particular and careful in their implementation of selective precepts. Here are some examples of the Levis' good practices which we can all strive to emulate:

On occasion, there would be an appeal in *shul* for a worthy cause. Many would participate and respond by having a pledge announced with their name. My uncle was a great proponent of *matan beseyser* (donating

---

d. 285:1,1 and 2,5.

anonymously).[e] He did not want to violate this requirement despite possible embarrassment or taunting. The fact was that he was probably more prompt and punctual in submitting his contribution than most participants who had their names in the brief spotlight. This modesty was all part and parcel of his inimical attitude towards ostentatious and pretentious lifestyles.

Unfortunately, there are persons who will procrastinate in varying degrees in meeting their fiscal obligations, despite the fact that they are financially able to make payments without delay. In some circles, this social affliction has become such a menace that it has stifled creative entrepreneurial endeavors and bankrupted businesses and institutions of learning. My uncle made it his business to promptly pay all bills. To him, being timely was a natural thing to do and all others who didn't discipline their purse strings were to be pitied. (For an interesting discussion on the laws and importance of punctually paying what is due, refer to the classical commentaries on Devorim.[f])

If our *Yeshivos* would teach the importance and manifestations of *Ma'aser* (tithing) then many of our Jewish institutions would probably be far better off in meeting their financial obligations. The Levis practiced the taking of *Ma'aser* as many others do. Accordingly, they reaped the *brochos* assured to those who observe this law.[g] Once my aunt explained to me that *Ma'aser* is meant for *tzedoko* and not for paying regular bills. Thus, for example, membership dues to an organization, which are obligatory expenses, should not be paid from *Ma'aser* funds. (For a similar example, refer to *Mishna Berurah*.[h] Note: The *Poskim* permit membership dues to a *shul* to be taken from *Ma'aser*.)

Circumventing social norms by use of questionable practices, which may be the type that are seldom followed or which are considered by the general population as improper procedures, were considered as "shtick" or "gimmicks" and were not condoned, to say the least. The Levi's honesty was inimitable and reciprocity by those they dealt with was expected. Their moral standards were also the highest. Thus, they refused to patronize postwar Germany. A product whose label stated, "made in Germany" was not purchased, even if the alternate purchase would be more expensive or of a lower quality. Their high esteem for moral integrity far

---

e. see *Yoreh De'ah*, 249:7 and 8.
f. 24:15.
g. *Malachi*, 3:10 and *Maseches Taanis*, 9a.
h. 694:1,3.

outweighed their regard towards creature comfort. This sensitivity produced true quality in life. On their frequent travels between New York and Eretz Yisrael, they would, whenever possible, avoid airlines that flew over German soil, even where no German landing was scheduled. My aunt loved classical music, but when the radio announcer would state that the next symphony was played by some German symphony orchestra or composed by the Nazi inclined composer Richard Wagner then, of course, the radio station was changed.

My uncle and aunt never attended a parade, even one that was non-military in nature. To them, the impersonal regimented coordination of the participants marching in formation and cadence was robotic and reminiscent of the non-individualism fostered by the military. Individualism in reality, does promote unity and is the basis of strong democracies.

Winning a prize is part of Hashem's *hashgochah*. It is also part of *parnosah*. However, my uncle did not deem it necessary to purchase a raffle or lottery ticket if that was solely for the sake of winning a prize. For as the *Chazal* say: *"Harbei shloechim yesh laMokom"* ("Divine Providence is multifarious"). He frequently would say: "If we are to hit the "jackpot", then *Hakodosh Boruch Hu* (The Holy One blessed be He) has many trusty messengers who will deliver."

Humans are not born as perfect beings. Mortals have a variety of shortfalls. My uncle and aunt were very sensitive to the plight of handicapped and physically impaired persons, whether young or old. Every person entering this world is part of a Divine Master Plan, and, therefore, we have no right to ostracize the incapacitated. Each individual is subjected to *Hashem's* challenges and tested by his or her own custom-fitted program, none are exonerated from hardships. The better the individual's stamina, the more rigorous are the hurdles to which one is exposed. Those with personal flaws are not exempted. It was alien to the Levis to discriminate and hold in lower esteem persons with physical or mental shortcomings. They respected the entire spectrum of the human race, regardless of their disabilities. Intolerance of our Judaic values, lack of proper attributes or character flaws such as arrogance were, however, not condoned.

WHILE STUDYING AT NEW YORK POLYTECHNIC UNIVERSITY, an engineering college, I had to attend a compulsory no-credit swimming course. The school was an all-male institution and female students were not accepted to this college until perhaps twenty-five years after my graduation. The swimming class was to be conducted without donning any swimwear. It was foreign and strange to me and so I discussed it with my uncle. He compared this conduct to the body worship that the ancient heathen Greeks were so well known for. Advocating bodily development in a manner as inspired by the Hellenists was tantamount to institutional heresy. Accordingly, he wrote a note on my behalf, insisting I wear a bathing suit.[i] I was the only class member who swam properly attired. This type of insensitivity and malevolence towards moral degeneration in the citadels of secular learning only led to my increased awareness of our Jewish heritage in this decadent society that we live in.

The free press frequently usurps its power and reports news in a tainted, slanted or euphemistic way. My uncle loved to read between the lines and often refused to accept press coverages at their face value. When a journalist would report a "fact", my uncle would usually add, "and if it is true, then you can believe it". Media accounts of hazardous sports such as scaling formidable mountains, boxing, stunt flying, skydiving and other non-military, life threatening activities were scoffed at and sarcastically classified as *Goyim-Nachas* (enjoyments of the non-Jew).

On *Pesach,* the Levis made beautiful *Sedorim.* To enhance the discussions, my uncle would start each *Seder* by focusing on a different theme as it applied to the *Hagadah,* e.g. assimilation, politics, *Hashkofah,* etc. As is the custom, they also invited guests. One of these guests was a cousin of my aunt (and of Mother's). He was, unfortunately, not an observant Jew and traveled back home on *Yom Tov,* using public transportation. For the following year he would not promise to stay locally until after *Yom Tov.* Not being hypocrites, that individual was never again invited for the *Seder.*

A common approach in some secular circles is to explain many of the miracles we discuss at the *Seder* by alleging that some natural phenomena occurred at the right place and the right time. My uncle considered that a belittlement of Hashem's abilities to conduct His world in any fashion that He desires. His *emunah* (faith) was faultless, and he recognized that the miracles that the world has and will witness do not have to be downgraded to, and excused as freaks in nature. They are specific acts of Hashem to reveal His mighty and merciful ways.

The Levis were proud *Ashkenazic* Jews. When my uncle went to *shul,* it was for the purpose of communicating with our Creator not for socializing or for vocal concerts by *chazanim.* In the 1940's there were, besides

---

i. refer to *Mishnah Berurah,* 2:1 for possible exceptions.

Seder Table
Adapted from a painting by professor Oppenheim and woodcut by S. Benedict.
Reprinted from the Israelit and Jeschurun, [21] April 1891.

the large *shuls,* only three or four small Ashkenazic *shuls* in Boro Park. The latter were the *minyonim* he patronized.

The practice of bad mouthing, commonly referred to as *loshon horah,* was unknown at the Levi home despite many tempting occasions.

AFTER LIVING LONG AND INTERESTING LIVES IN EUROPE and America, my uncle and aunt finally settled in Yerusholayim. They went through four cultures and languages. Their hard efforts on behalf of their children, us Lehmanns, and other members of their family bore fruits for which they can be rightfully proud and is a merit to all their descendants. After long, eventful and productive lives, Hashem took back their pure *neshomos,* laden with *mitzvos.*

My uncle, Uncle Michael departed on 29 Iyar, 5741 and my aunt, Tante Alice left us on 23 Adar, 5750. May their remembrance be a blessing. Even their places of burial were carefully considered and chosen and was consistent with their pure and righteous ways. My uncle and aunt abhorred the whole spectrum of improprieties, from injustice to surfeit permissiveness. They therefore acquired *karkah* (burial ground) next to the sites where children were interred. This fulfilled their wish of being laid to rest next to those who died without sins. On my visits to Yerusholayim I have always made it a practice to recite Tehillim at their *kevarim* (gravesites) which can be found on Har haMenuchos *Gush* 4, *Chelka* 6.

EPILOGUE

Section Four

...AND THE ALMIGHTY SEEKS THE OPPRESSED.
(KOHELES 3,15)

Chapter Thirty One
RETROSPECT

HAVING MIRACULOUSLY SURVIVED ONE OF THE MOST awesome and brutal periods of Jewish and world history has caused many intriguing thoughts to enter my mind. The most common question asked by the fortunate few who survived to tell of the atrocities is, "Why was I saved?" Many of our best, the jewels of our people, perished in the holocaust, that rampage by savage, barbarian beasts. Obviously, it is not for us to judge all the deliberations or to know all that entered into the makings of the Heavenly decrees. We must have faith in our Creator that each individual had his own judgment, as to every detail of his share in the burden and the yoke of this modern day oppression. Similarly, we must believe that our oppressors will have their moment in front of the Heavenly Court.

As a survivor, I am extremely thankful and feel privileged to have had the ability to observe and remember this long and dark night in our history. These recollections are not merely those of a young adventurer oblivious to the realities of that sad period in our people's life. On the contrary, these recollections are those of a hopeful youngster venturing into a melancholy world that was inattentive to the dearth in Divine ideals. My recounting is steeped in stifled emotions of the past, but the tomorrows are faced with faith and optimism. I therefore feel obligated to do my share in rebuilding our people and revitalizing our civilization, following the incredible destruction that we witnessed.

In reviewing some statistics of those massive World War II battle fatalities, it appears to me that it was no accident that Germany, as the main Axis power and as instigator of barbarism, plunder and murder, had three and a half million official battle deaths. The Germans had a peak strength of ten million, two hundred thousand men in their armed forces. This translates to more than **one** out of every **three** uniformed Germans killed. Is it not *hashgochah,* when we compare this to our six million martyrs, we see the same ratio; **one** out of every **three** Jews were murdered by the Germans, et. al., during World War II!!

Furthermore, over one million German civilians were officially killed or seriously maimed as a result of Allied air strikes over Germany. Moreover, there were in excess of a million German soldiers who were very seriously injured. In addition, there were at least two million German civilians killed and/or maimed for life when Soviet troops overran eastern Germany in 1944-1945. This was the Soviet's opportunity to settle the score of German barbarity against their own population. Summing up all the casualties, one can say that there were well over six million Germans who were lost. They lost their "finest" because we lost our "best". In *Tenach* we find:

> Israel is sacred to Hashem, His most favored nation, all that devour him shall incur wrath (and) evil will befall them, saith Hashem[a] (Refer to classical commentaries.)

Premeditated murder is never appreciated or accepted but in this context it gives a small degree of solace that the Germans did not leave this fight unscathed. In short, over six million Germans, masters of — murder, kidnap, plunder, rape, torture, death and destruction all became history by the end of World War II.

---

a. Yirmiyohu, 2:3.

SUMMARY OF GERMAN WAR CASUALTIES[b]

Armed Forces

    Fatalities (official count)   3,500,000

    Seriously Injured   1,000,000 plus

Civilians

    Killed or seriously maimed
    due to Allied air strikes   1,000,000

    Killed or maimed for life
    by Soviet occupation   2,000,000 plus

TOTAL killed/seriously maimed: **7,500,000 plus**

Population of the German Reich, from 1939 census: 69,600,000

Population of Greater Germany from 1939 census: 79,500,000

Greater Germany includes: German Reich, Austria, Sudetenland

In a similar fashion let us now consider the *prima facie* evidence of World War II casualties from the former Soviet Union. The USSR military had a peak strength of twelve and a half million men and women in uniform. Of those, history records that seven and a half million perished during the war! I would like to suggest that this high rate of casualties was also no accident but should be ascribed directly and indirectly to the Soviet Union's blatant anti-Semitic policies prior to and during World War II. The estimated Jewish population in prewar USSR exceeded three million souls.[c] Anti-Jewish acts were implemented by both its government and its various ethnic peoples. The leader of this totalitarian regime was the anti-Semitic tyrant Josef Stalin. The official and enforced state religion was atheism.

Following are some of the Soviet's better known anti-Jewish policies: Following the November 1917 Bolshevik revolution, all *Yeshivos* were closed and the teaching of the Jewish religion was considered a severely punishable subversive activity. Similarly, many *shuls* were closed. Stalin, moreover, conducted various "purges" which targeted many Jews. During

---

b. Source: 1945 *World Almanac* and *Encyclopedia Americana*.

c. Source: 1945 World Almanac.

World War II, as the Germans were nearing the final stages of their systematic murder of millions of deported Jews, including those from the destroyed Warsaw ghetto (original population four hundred thousand!) the Russian army "stalled" east of Warsaw due to "regrouping" requirements. This Russian inactivity gave the Germans enough time and energy to finish their dirty work. In addition, many Russians switched sides and joined the German armed forces. Too many of these traitors became guards at concentration camps and members of murder squads.

[A historical note: Finding appropriate gifts for the person "who has everything" has stumped many a mind. When Germany's chiefs of staff were faced with their *Feuhrer*'s upcoming birthday, these cohorts quickly overcame this dilemma. They settled upon a most fitting present for the celebration – *the annihilation of the Warsaw Ghetto*! So it sadly came to pass that on the eve of April 20, 1943, Hitler's fifty fourth birthday and the first day of *Pesach,* the famed murderous assault began. An arsenal of battle tanks, a flame thrower and elite infantry troops, including Ukrainian-Soviet army defectors, descended upon the innocent Jews of the ghetto. Some two years later, on April 30, 1945, the eve of *Lag B'Omer,* Germany's baneful icon Adolf Hitler, Y.S., nemesis of truth and justice, died of self inflicted wounds and a German malady was eradicated, dawning a new page in Jewish history.

Lag B'Omer commemorates the cessation of the plague that killed thousands of Rabbi Akiva's (15-135 C.E.) students for their lack of mutual respect. Is it not *hashgochah* that Hitler found his end at the time Jews celebrate brotherly love [k] a concept which was the antithisis of the Third *Reich*'s demeanor!!]

Russia's forced assimilation policies, their harassment, imprisonment, torture, forced collectivization, incarceration in labor camps, expedient mass starvation of entire geographical regions and the resultant devastation of millions of Jews are all stains on the former USSR. The result of these despotic policies was that in two or three generations, millions became ignorant of their Jewish values, intermarriage rose to epidemic proportions and countless Jews were destroyed, spiritually and/or physically. It is said that from 1927 to 1953, some *sixty million* Russians and non-Russians, Jews and non-Jews, lost their lives due to the tyrannical policies promulgated by Premier Josef Stalin.

---

k. Vayikra, 19:18

HAVING PERSONALLY GONE THROUGH GERMAN CAPTIVITY, with dead and dying on many sides, I have the feeling of being at the cutting edge of a delicate survival. As a holocaust survivor, I realize how we are constantly in the hands of Hashem and, having come through, I am greatly thankful to our Creator who decided to save me from the German pyres, destruction and hatred.

It is common for all persons to have problems in their everyday lives. These are, however, minimal for the most part when compared to the lifethreatening problems encountered by the martyrs and survivors of World War II. Let us, therefore, be thankful to Hashem for keeping our supposed big problems really minuscule.

Of course, in retrospect, we are thankful to all who helped us survive during the whole epoch of the persecution. Our parents, may they rest in peace, bore the largest burden in this respect. They gave us the physical and mental sensitivity and stability to survive. They, therefore, were instrumental, I feel, in our coming through it all without significant emotional scars. Then, of course, there are the various other groups to whom gratitude is owed: the Allied armies who liberated us in the nick of time and the Jewish relief organizations who helped us leave the continent of Europe. Much thanks go to Ms. Erica Lunzer (Mrs. Erica Lawson) of the British army, who was instrumental in enabling our passage to England. It should be noted that Ms. Lunzer was also very successful in saving many Dutch Jewish children who were hidden in Gentile homes during the war, but alas whose parents did not return from German captivity. We are grateful to Rabbi and Mrs. de Vries for helping us make the transition from Bergen Belsen to normal life.

MAY HASHEM MAKE HIS FACE SHINE UPON AND BE GRACIOUS[d] to the descendants of our aunt, Tante Resi, and the Levis — Uncle Michael and Tante Alice for their many acts of kindness. The British Lehmanns ensured that we again entered the mainstream of daily living, which included everything from learning English to providing a family life and loving care, teaching Jewish values and helping us mature. The Levis continued this task. They spared no effort to normalize and fine tune our lives and values even further. They were in effect foster parents from their sense of duty and love. They were motivated in this task by their close ties to our parents, by the terrible destruction that had been inflicted on the Jewish people and by recognizing their part in furthering Judaism.

---

d. Bamidbor, 6:25.

Frequently I dwell on the altruism of the United States which provided us with refuge and a new environment steeped in personal liberty and equal opportunity. The spirit of personal freedom continues to bless this *medina shel chesed* (benevolent nation). With Divine consent and Providential assistance, the United States will remain a true land of opportunity for as long as the moral climate permits us to strive towards levels of higher ethical postures and whose bottom line allow us to ultimately fulfill our Divine calling.

While I attended college (1951-55), the Levis provided my room and board. My share of the proceeds from our parent's life insurance policy paid for the entire tuition and books. Other expenses were covered by the income I received while working summers for various engineering companies and performing extensive part-time work during the school year.

Frequently, I contrasted myself to some other young men who because of their affluent background avoided serious work and evaded the study of a useful profession or trade. I concluded that with Hashem's help, a useful life, is obtained by immersing oneself at an early age in learning the work and the study ethic,[e] while simultaneously guiding oneself into honest business practices.[f]

IN 1955, MOST OF MY GRADUATING CLASS FROM THE ENGINEERing college accepted employment offers at sites all across the United States. There were few local engineering positions available, and the job market was even more restrictive for me since I had not yet become a U.S. citizen. A meaningful Jewish life at those potential out of town work sites was practically nil. I, therefore, held out to the last moment before graduation in accepting a position of employment. With Hashem's help, I found a most interesting work place at a New York City based consulting engineering design firm. There, I started work in June on a full time basis. As part of my education and to develop the habit of sharing the burden in household expenses, I gave a portion of my biweekly salary to my aunt. Unbeknown to me, that money was set aside and used to cover some of my wedding expenses.

In the mid-1960's, I received a onetime *"Wiedergutmachung"* (restitution) check from the West German government for approximately six and half thousand dollars. This payment was in compensation for our parent's wrongful death and was based on my age and schooling and on father's age and schooling. It was meant to cover my college tuition costs. Since

---

e. Eichah, 3:27.   f. Vayikra, 19:36 and the commentary of Horav Samson Raphael Hirsch.

my sisters were older and had not attended college, the amount they received was considerably smaller. At that time, the Levis were living in the town of Monsey in upstate New York. Ruth and I went to visit them, at which time I offered to give them this check as a small token of appreciation for all their extra expenses on our behalf. To give an idea of the value of the dollar in those years, it must be realized that a new, automatic shift, four-door Chevrolet automobile could be purchased for twenty-nine hundred dollars. A new, modest one family, one floor wood frame, one thousand square foot house, with unfinished basement on a quarter acre of land near the center of Monsey sold for twenty-eight thousand dollars. My uncle and aunt thanked us for our offer but declined to accept the money. The additional costs for the assistance they rendered to us Lehmanns was considered, by them, as a non-compensatory obligation on their part.

To qualify for further monthly stipends of *Wiedergutmachung* would have required myself to claim a degree of extreme financial hardship and/or physical disability, neither of which I could honestly claim. The Germans do not deserve my honorable conduct but my standards in ethics did not permit an insidious demeanor.

AS A SURVIVOR OF LIFE'S MORE DIFFICULT EXPERIENCES, I feel obligated to caution future generations regarding some of the many, many pitfalls of which we all must be aware. Some dangers we can avoid, if only we can recognize them. All dangers can be avoided with the help of Hashem, if only we merit His help. Learning the many lessons from the experiences of our Patriarchs, *Avrohom, Yitzchok* and *Yaacov,* [6] and how they were saved from all types of evil schemes, and by studying *Sefer Breishis* with its numerous classical interpretations will place the learned a major step ahead of the unlearned. Having a proper disposition in matters between individuals is important. Where possible, one must be at peace with all people, since all Jews and many non-Jews, will have an influence on our daily activities at one time or another.[g] This means practicing honesty and Jewish ethics as prescribed and proscribed in our four part *Shulchon Aruch*. Wherever possible, one should not excessively place trust in humans. Their ability to deliver is frequently affected by factors beyond their control. This was aptly illustrated in World War II when Jews were stripped of their citizenship rights in Germany and in every country the Germans occupied.

One must avoid complacency with the social environment and reject influences from the extreme right and left of both secular and religious

---

g. *Pirkei Avos,* 4:3. h. *Koheles,* 7:16.

camps. Beware of those who preach philosophies, secular or religious, that only advance their own interests but, in the end, leave us materially or spiritually poorer.[h] Our way of life is to proceed along the median road, which is *Torah im Derech Eretz,* i.e. study and practice *Torah* on a daily basis and earn a living through a trade or a profession. The profession, of course, could also be in the non-secular field.

Our Jewish people have many great people of their own to emulate. Therefore, there is no need to follow the ways of the world, which are all too frequently the pursuit of "jealousy, lust and fame". Only study these as a medical student would study a disease.

During World War II, the world at large emulated the indifferent, the greedy, the violent, the oppressive and the disrespectful. These non-civilized ways must be exposed for the folly they actually are so that we will not assimilate their ways into our *weltanshauung* (approach to life).

Being a survivor is no cause for self pity. On the contrary, the Jewish people have been survivors since their very beginning. We are, however, accountable for all our deeds. In contrast, the surviving separate entities of the various nations of the world will vanish when their allotted time has come to an end.[i] The Jews, on the other hand, will welcome Moshiach, hopefully soon and in our lifetime.

Following the various war-related trauma to which we were subjected, I found that I was personally affected but not as a stereotype liberated prisoner, touted in the media, as being physically and mentally drained. In describing my state of being, I am, of course, limiting observations to my own feelings, which may or may not coincide with those of my sisters.

As a young inquisitive boy, interested in the world as a whole, I was very much attached to my parents, who saw to my physical and non-material needs. The abrupt loss of parental presence translated into having to face an indifferent and cruel world in an unnatural, accelerated "cold turkey" manner. This shock treatment happened when I was separated from our parents in camp and again after the war, when confirmation was received of their passing. Despite the loving and excellent help and care given by my aunt, Tante Resi, and by my Uncle Michael and my aunt, Tante Alice, there was no substitute to interacting with one's own caring parents. A person never outgrows his orphan status.

In the concentration camp there was hunger, disease, hardships and death all around us. In this context some individuals even made statistical

---

i. Yirmiyohu, 46:28

mental calculations as to when it would be their turn to die. In my own mind, I did think of hunger and deprivations but I was never preoccupied with thoughts of my death and when I would be added to some heap of bodies. I was too busy observing all that transpired.

The ramifications and consequences of parental deprivation were great. Having become an orphan at a young age was something for which I hold the Germans forever accountable. The status of being an orphan was, therefore, nothing that carried a stigma of shame. Nevertheless, among friends or at places of work, I would not freely divulge this information or express my feelings of sadness on this subject to elicit pity. I did not consider myself an object of compassion. On occasion, when completing application forms for employment or forms for medical insurance, where "cause of parental death" had to be indicated, I would usually indicate: "Murdered by the Germans (World War II)", thereby assigning blame where due.

MY CONFIDENCE IN PEOPLE WAS AT AN EBB, SINCE I SAW well-meaning persons having little if any influence in rectifying the shambles that the world was in. This did not, however, place me in a depressed mood. On the contrary, I felt it was an opportunity and obligation for myself, as a member of the new generation, to do my share in the rebuilding process. I was not interested in tagging along with the prevailing crowds. To be self-sufficient was one of my goals. Having been dependent on a shaky, failing world during the war was enough for me, I was not interested in repeat performances.

COMING FROM A COMFORTABLE MIDDLE CLASS BACKground, I frequently noted that as a direct result of my war experiences, my attitude became sensitized and therefore has somewhat mellowed towards the less fortunate. Following are some of these personal points of view which were directly impacted by having been imprisoned and orphaned:

- ❖ Persons who make a serious and honest effort to help themselves and, nevertheless, are in need, obtain my respect and my sympathy.
- ❖ I have little esteem for those who live beyond their means and expect their parents and the world to foot those habits.
- ❖ I have great pity for the havenots; however, the Robin Hood philosophy of transferring wealth by robbing the rich is foreign to me. This was one of the triggers which detonated World War II, where Germany expected to absorb their neighbors' wealth.

- Similarly, I experienced enough sorrow and want and therefore will not recommend to the havenots Marie Antoinette's proverbial "pastries" ("let them eat cake").
- I respect those who have to work to earn a living more than those who don't have to work because of their wealthy financial status.
- Bedecking one's self with excessive jewelry, etc., is just losing track of our station in life. Our goal should not be too materialistic; humans are far too frail for that. My constant reminder of our mortal feebleness is to focus back on the many bodies piled in front of our barrack.
- Watching holocaust movies and wartime documentaries stir up old memories. Therefore, I prefer to avoid them.

In contrast, I find my peers who did not experience the holocaust to be in varying degrees oblivious to many of the above. A case in point was when I worked for the New York City Transit Authority as a Project Engineer/Manager, and for many years, was in charge of a large group of engineers and administrative personnel. Within organizational guidelines, I frequently found myself to be the buffer between our front office and my charges on matters of seeming robotically decreed directives. As a result, there were frequent requests from individuals in colleagues' offices to transfer to my group. This, despite the more demanding type of work that I had. The question was always raised in the organization, why are those engineers attracted to Lehmann's group? I never went into my past history, so no satisfactory response was given. However, the answer was that I treated everyone just as I had expected to be treated in earlier years, when I worked for strict individuals or was in stressful situations. I considered all these subordinates as humans and gave respect in accordance to their needs and abilities — an administrative attitude that bore fruit for the organization and was highly appreciated by all involved.

Contractors who did capital construction work (as opposed to routine maintenance) for the Transit Authority were also beneficiaries of my attitude. I remember one contractor who was awarded a very large [$45.0 million] and difficult construction contract, to be administered by my project office. His superintendent was irate and had scheduled a showdown meeting with my boss. In that office he confronted me and proceeded to yell and scream. It was my policy never to yell at colleagues or contractors. So when this man finished with his shouting, I calmly said: "You yell very nicely". That disarmed him and it was the last time that person raised his voice at me. Subsequently, that superintendent cooperated so that all goals for his project were achieved safely, on schedule and within budget. All this, despite the contractor's lack of experience in building complicated train tracks and switches and repairing large steel substructures on a very active segment of railroad — Brooklyn's West End Line.

BEING LIBERATED FROM OPPRESSION CARRIED WITH IT THE responsibility of standing up for one's basic rights and principles. In my early professional career days, especially in the 1950's and 1960's, I noticed that the agnosticism of some Jews led them to be excessively intolerant of religious practices of both their fellow Jews and non-Jews. That older and bitter generation, which gave me some extra and unsolicited challenges, has since mellowed or passed away. In contrast, I found many of my non-Jewish professional colleagues to be extremely tolerant of those who sincerely practiced religious beliefs. I remember an incident in the 1960's, at the New York City Transit Authority which occurred prior to the enactment of certain federal anti-discrimination laws.

A group of Sabbath observers, including myself, were informed by the Chief Engineer's office that on Friday afternoons, especially in the winter, we would no longer be permitted to depart the office early to be home in time for the start of the Sabbath. In December, the local time for the commencement of the *Shabbos* is as early as 4:10 P.M. Commuting time ranged from half an hour to one and a half hours depending on the weather and where one lived. The office closed at 5:00 P.M.

Leaving work at an earlier hour was by no means a bonanza, since the missed time was either deducted from one's vacation allowance or was made up by working extra hours on other days. The ruling by the Chief's office was therefore considered nothing short of harassment directed against hard working individuals within the Engineering Department.

Working in the Transit Authority's Engineering department was a Roman Catholic Engineer, the late Richard Izzo, who was the president of the Technical Guild. Ric Izzo interceded on our behalf and sadly enough met with our Jewish Chief Engineer, Nathan D. Zrotkin.[j] He successfully argued our case and the anti-Sabbath directive was rescinded. To my knowledge, there were no further anti-religious rulings from the Chief Engineer's office following that historic meeting. Richard Izzo practiced tolerance; may this deed be a merit to his soul. A short while later, Mr. Zrotkin was traveling on the subway to attend a function scheduled for early Friday afternoon. At the DeKalb Avenue station, while still on the train, he suffered a fatal heart attack. May his soul rest in peace.

---

j. The name was changed by the author.

Chapter Thirty Two

EPITAPH: SURVIVAL FROM A FAILED "CIVILIZATION"

I T WAS IN THE 1880'S IN IMPERIAL GERMANY WHEN MY GREAT grandfather, Horav Meir Lehmann, commented on the *Pesach Hagadah* song *Chad Gadyoh* [20] ...In contemporary civilized circles it would no longer be suggested that Jews be murdered simply as victims of intolerance...(!!) Implicit in *civilized circles* is a society with the ability to live in harmony through the practice of equal justice, mutual respect and tolerance of diversity. Furthermore, a *civilization* reaches its apogee when the proverbial lion coexists with the lamb. That concept is diametric to the law of the jungle where *might is right*. Reflecting on the Third *Reich:* My great grandfather did not envision a social retrogression where the masses failed to remain subservient to civility. Consequently, German society harnessed the *might* of technology to murder whole segments of a population on the altar of *intolerance.*

A nation's *cultural* characteristics are usually equated to the level of *civilization* popularly practiced within its borders. According to the

Webster's New Collegiate Dictionary, one of the measuring sticks for gauging *culture* is a people's "acquaintance with taste in fine arts, humanities and broad aspects of science as distinguished from vocational and technical skills." During the Holocaust period the Germans perversely contaminated their *culture* and subsequently their *civilization*. Pluralism, a crucial ingredient of traditional *culture* was banished from their *apartheid* style society. In addition, the Berlin government switched national priorities and demanded the subservience of its citizens through emphasis of ancillary, autonomic and robotic lifestyles. Alas, abandoned were the humanities, the traits which distinguish civilized man from the primitive. Thus, slowly but steadily, German civility regressed to savagery.

Ode To Survival From A Failed "Civilization"

COUNTLESS SURVIVORS disembarking from a torturous journey through the rugged years of World War II had to discard all their residual feelings of mental anguish, stress, trauma and self pity.

FOR SURVIVORS to face the future, required picking up the pieces of a now splintered world and a shattered society which once had nourished each of them. Communities that had taken centuries to develop and blossom, emerged with branches severed and luscious fruits culled by an untimely modern day, unimaginably barbaric tempest.

COUNTLESS SURVIVORS had roots that stretched out far and wide, to nurture from the wells of our *Torah*. These roots served as tenacious anchors for many a stately tree, their trunks were thus well secured and strong enough to withstand the raging unforgettable unforgivable Teutonic storm. Destabilization was therefore kept to a minimum, and with Divine providence, the healing of bruised lives and wounds commenced, realization of visions and resources flowed again in a timely fashion.

FOR SURVIVORS it remained an obligation but for some alas a difficult task, to rejoin the remnants of society's main stream. They were compelled to rebuild their lives, establish families when possible, and be infected with joy and happiness, culminating in our People's long awaited rebirth.[a] May we ultimately achieve and witness the restoration of our genuine *Torah* heritage to its original prominence as in the years of yore.

SURVIVORS IMBUED with and committed to our religious values graduated with a degree in "Life Experiences, *Extraordinaire*". They learned to better discern and differentiate between the ostentatious and falsely veneered and the sincere, between the ignoble masses and the nobly devout, between the wicked and the pure. Their maturing process was compressed and accelerated.

AS A SURVIVOR, I pray for the Supreme Judge to harken in our days to the cries of the murdered. Let the spilled blood of our six million immortal brethren remain revered. Their perishing is a stark epitaph to a vain, bygone make believe German "civilization" that was cowardly, greedy, deceitful, robotic and inhuman.

FOR SURVIVORS, the harmony of life's orchestrated experiences of: affliction, positive yearnings and complete trust in the Almighty, has led to a symphony of *faith at the brink*. These repatriates arduously departed from the "faithfulness in the nights" phase and sojourned to witness the ushering in of "to proclaim Thy loving kindness in the morning!"[b] With Divine mercy, they will greet the arrival of the long awaited and enduring salvation.

---

a. Tehillim, 126:2
b. Tehillim, 92:3

Chapter Thirty Three
PSYCHOSIS – GERMAN STYLE

IN THE YEAR 1887, LORD ACTON COINED THE PHRASE "POWER tends to corrupt and absolute power corrupts absolutely". The fascist minded people of Germany, under their despotic *Fuehrer* (Leader) Adolf Hitler, abandoned all semblances of democratic norms and did as they pleased, regardless of whether that involved breaking international conventions, agreements, treaties, covenants or just plain standards of decent and normal human behavior.

In August of 1939, Adolf Hitler signed a Friendship Treaty with Josef Stalin of the Soviet Union that included the breakup of their common neighbor, the sovereign state of Poland, which is geographically sandwiched between Germany and the Soviet Union. Under that agreement, Germany conspired to carve out Poland's western portion, while the Soviets schemed to take possession of the eastern part. Both the Germans and the Soviets had a propensity for expansion and coveting contiguous turf. It was a case of political immorality by two fascist governments, whose tyrannical leaders were bent on implementing the law of the jungle and swallowing a weaker neighbor. Of course, Poland was not consulted and one sorrowful day, in September 1939, that pathetic country was simultaneously invaded across both its eastern and western borders. There was no Polish provocation and suddenly, without notice, its cities were intensely bombarded by the German *Luftwaffe* (airforce).

Poland was "digested" by these two bully nations, and both Hitler and Stalin saw to it that the Polish military was crushed. The conquering of Poland led to the next step in Hitler's greedy agenda and that eventually became one more nail in his charred coffin.

Now that Poland was disposed of, Hitler broke his "Friendship Treaty" with the U.S.S.R. In June, 1941, the Germans proceeded to invade their "friend", the U.S.S.R. As the saying goes, "there is no honor among thieves".[a]

THE GUILELESS GERMANS CONSIDERED THEMSELVES AN ARYAN super-race and imagined their people to be superior over all fellow humans. Of course, there were Germans who did not fit that mold and were frail, invalid, mentally handicapped, etc. All these ailing fellow citizens were a contradiction to the theory of the Master race. Besides, these persons were filling the hospitals and other institutions, which was a drain on national resources and manpower. Physicians represented one of a series of defective links in Germany's long chain of worthless social virtues. At the behest of the Berlin hierarchy, these fratricidal intellectuals did not hesitate to break their Hippocratic oath. Their intellect was tainted by subservience to corrupted societal values. Accordingly, the German doctors, beyond the ken of a stunned world, emptied health institutions by murdering their feeble kin. It is said that close to half the Third *Reich's* medical staffs have blood on their filthy sleeves.

Most Germans were familiar with their icon composer Ludwig van-Beethoven (1770-1827) and the words of his ninth symphony,

>...Alle Menschen werden Brueder...

Translation:

>...all mankind are destined brothers....

German mentality apparently did not recognize non-Aryans as part of mankind. A famous story was told of a German firing squad gunner humming these words of brotherhood while pumping lead into his lined up victims!

In their quest to build an Aryan nation, the Germans became obsessed with their passion for pursuing bodily and material perfection. Human

---

a. Refer to Appendix A for a saga of deliverance involving the "Friendship Treaty".

THE NEW YORK TIMES **MEDICAL**

Exhibition Examines Scientists' Complicity In Nazi-Era Atrocities

Medical historians trace loss of ethics to devaluation of life.

By WARREN E. LEARY

Special to The New York Times

WASHINGTON — It is a question that few have been willing to face or to debate for decades. Why were so many doctors and scientists so intimately involved in some of the greatest atrocities of Nazi Germany?

There is a tendency to see these atrocities, from the deliberate extermination of millions of people to barbaric medical experiments on thousands of innocents, as isolated occurrences during a period of madness more than a half century ago.

Many people, including some historians, have attributed these acts to the perversions of a few sadists and madmen who, through coercion, forced others to become unwilling participants in these programs.

But that view, particularly as it pertains to doctors, nurses and other health workers in Germany before and during World War II, is being challenged by medical historians and ethicists who say that there was more at work than people being forced into compromise and crime at the barrel of a gun.

Devaluation of Human Life

A disturbing exhibit that opened here last week at the National Museum of Health and Medicine argues that something happened to German science and medicine after World War I as attempts to expand health care and to improve society were turned into a system that devalued human beings and allowed doctors to abandon their ethical responsibilities.

Modern medicine, which faces such ethical questions as rationing of health care, using genetic engineering to identify or treat disease, testing experimental treatments with human subjects, or doctor-assisted suicide for the terminally ill, must never forget what happened in Germany and how easily ethics can be eaten away by expedience, the exhibit's organizers said.

The exhibit, "The Value of The Human Being: Medicine in Germany, 1918-1945," was commissioned by the Berlin Medical Association and was first shown in 1989. The current exhibit is co-sponsored by the American Medical Association.

Dr. Christian Pross and Dr. Gotz Aly, members of a group of young German doctors and historians who began searching archives in the early 1980's to uncover the role of the medical establishment before and during the war, said doctors in their country had developed a "collective amnesia" when the era was over.

"No one wanted to admit to what extent they profited under the system and how none of this could have happened without the direct complicity of the German medical establishment," Dr. Pross said in a telephone interview. "It was more than just a few doctors who were involved," he said. "The medical establishment knew what was happening and lended a credibility to it through its direct and indirect involvement."

Agents of the State

Dr. Marc Micozzi, the physician who directs the museum that is showing the exhibit through Dec. 9, said many people, including doctors, would like to believe that what happened in Nazi Germany can never happen again. However, he said, the exhibit of 45 panels of text and photos illustrates how changes in how doctors view their relationship with patients can lead to disaster. "If we don't understand how it happened in the first place, how can we assure it won't happen again?," Dr. Micozzi asked.

The groundwork for atrocity was paved with good intentions, said Dr. Pross and other experts. After World War I, Germany's Weimar Republic tried to use scientific principles to build a better, more orderly society, including establishing the first true system of universal access to health care. This system emphasized using the best medical technology for treatment and research into the causes of disease, coupled with a strong emphasis on preventive medicine.

Seeking Superior Genes

This new interest in improving Germany's health, which produced substantial decreases in infant mortality, tuberculosis and venereal disease through expanded use of public clinics and hospitals, shifted the emphasis of medicine from helping each individual to improving the health of the community at large, experts said. Many doctors became agents of the state instead of advocates of the patient, they said, and began viewing people as impersonal statistics in-

Some of the worst torturers were German medical doctors.

The German experience raises profound questions for modern medicine.

stead of individuals.

In addition, theories of genetic inequality among races and the idea that some people had greater value than others to society were gaining popularity worldwide and particularly in Germany. Numerous genetic institutes were established to study racial differences and to prove the superiority of "Caucasians of non-Jewish origin."

When Western economies were hit with the Great Depression in 1929, the Weimar Republic had much less money for health care and began cutting back on services. Limited resources were used to help people of greatest value — nnon-Jewish whites in the workforce. This cost-benefit approach worked against people who were poor or who were considered an expression of genetic inferiority, and those who suffered from mental illness, deformity and inherited diseases or conditions.

Adolf Hitler and his followers embraced the idea that the right to life must be earned and justified, not assumed, and this became an excuse for eliminating the genetically deficient, who consumed valuable resources. Among those considered deficient were Jews, gypsies, people of mixed blood and those with inherited illnesses.

The exhibit suggests that doctors, more than any other professional group in Germany, accepted the new order. More than 38,000 doctors, almost half of Germany's total, joined the Nazi Party. Being part of this system allowed doctors and scientists to get research grants, receive promotions at universities and take over the jobs and practices of thousands of Jews who were no longer allowed to practice medicine.

It was hard for doctors who did not go along with the system to advance their careers, Dr. Pross said, but he added that there was little evidence that physicians who refused to take part were killed or sent to prison unless they also actively worked against the party or supported the underground.

Fewer than 100 doctors and scientists were found guilty of war crimes in Allied courts after the war, said Dr. Arthur L. Caplan, director of the Center for Biomedical Ethics at the University of Minnesota. But he said many more had helped to conduct research on prisoners and to organize the death camps by assisting in designing and reviewing the "research" or by offering technical assistance.

Dr. Caplan, who edited the book "When Medicine Went Mad: Bioethics and the Holocaust," (1992, Humana Press), said the role of mainstream medicine and science in the atrocities had been underplayed.

"A relatively small number of doctors and scientists took a direct role in killing and torture," Dr. Caplan said. "But a large number, many in universities and prestigious institutions, provided intellectual and professional support for the policies of the Nazis."

'An Awesome Potential'

Dr. James S. Todd, executive vice-president of the American Medical Association, said there is always a moral hazard when powerful individuals achieve such dominance over ordinary people. Doctors, he said, have a special responsibility because people entrust them with their privacy as well as with their lives. The museum, which is located on the campus of Walter Reed Army Medical Center at the Armed Forces Institute of Pathology.

"The great concern of American physicians is the Government increasingly interfering with the doctor-patient relationship," Dr. Todd said. "One of our biggest challenges today is balancing medicine and health against the resources available. But we have to strive to do this without forgetting about the patients we serve."

The issues that faced German doctors still exist, and modern biomedical science has given people the tools to manipulate human genetics in ways the Nazis could never have dreamed of, Dr. Todd said. "Genetic manipulation gives us an awesome potential to use it for good, to detect and treat disease and deformity," he said. "But we must learn to use it morally and ethically, without stepping over the line."

The exhibit, which shows what can happen when doctors stop following the Hippocratic Oath with its admonitions to "give no deadly medicine to any one if asked" and to "abstain from every voluntary act of mischief and corruption," teaches that human beings cannot be devalued below the sum of their parts.

"These were our brothers and sisters," Dr. Todd said of those depicted in the exhibit, "The ones who suffered so, and the ones who inflicted the suffering upon them."

b. New York Times, November 10, 1992

values and religion became secondary, and along with their abandonment of cherished ideals, arose hatred and inconsideration for others, all were the spinoffs of their defunct and arrogant national policy. Ultimately, German callowness led to an attitude of international belligerency which then ushered in mass murder of civilians and prisoners of war.

THE GENEVA CONVENTION OF 1929 AND THE HAGUE Conventions of 1899 and 1907 all dealt with rules of war. Every West European country and the U.S.A. were signatories to these international agreements. The rules of these conventions were very specific and detailed. The Germans broke all tenets of conduct in very big ways:

During World War I, Holland, like Switzerland, was a neutral country. When war started in 1939, Holland again declared its neutrality. Nevertheless, Germany invaded Holland in May, 1940 opting thereby to not respect Dutch neutrality — a major breach of the Hague Convention. When Holland was invaded, many German troops entered the country, disguised in Dutch army uniforms — another violation of the Geneva Convention.

The Germans degraded, kidnapped, tortured, murdered much of the civilian populations in the countries they conquered all without local provocation. These victims included men, women, children, the aged and infants. The Geneva Convention states that both combatants and non-combatants, etc. are to be humanely treated and protected against undue violence and insult. Women in particular are to be treated with due regard to their sex. Other convention provisions include prohibitions against bad treatment, the retention of personal effects (except arms), accountability for civilian wealth, and protection against needless exposure to danger. The convention rules provide extensive details on internment of prisoners of war which include health care, safeguards for hygiene, and provisions for clothing, heating and lighting. Food rations of prisoners of war should be equal in quantity and quality to those of one's own troops at base camps. Prisoners should be afforded recreation, religious freedom, medical care, etc. All these and many more requirements of the Geneva Convention were completely disrespected, ignored and broken by the Germans.

Allied prisoners of war were frequently executed by the Germans and those who had Jewish sounding names were singled out for harsh treatment including death — all in violation of the conventions.

Interestingly and typically, German prisoners of war in American or British custody were all treated according to the rules of the Convention. Germans fared poorly in Russian prisoner of war camps, as did the Russians in German camps. This was due to their mutual hate, with poor treatment the norm, and executions of captured soldiers a usual occurrence. On the other side of the coin, a Russian soldier was considered a traitor to his country if he had allowed himself to be captured. This harsh attitude resulted in imprisonment and worse for many repatriates returning to Soviet rule from former German prisoner of war camps.

The Japanese had similar negative attitudes towards international conduct. When the Japanese struck at the American navy in their sneak attack on Pearl Harbor in Hawaii on December 7, 1941, it was termed "a day of infamy", because they gave no advance declaration of war, as is required by the Geneva Convention. Germany and Japan were allies and, as the saying goes, "birds of a feather flock together".

The Germans, conducted their *Blitzkrieg* on the Dutch port city of Rotterdam from the air without provocation, leveling many buildings and causing unnecessary civilian casualties and damage. This was another breach of the international conventions.

AFTER THE WAR, MANY TERRIBLE STORIES OF GERMAN shamelessness emerged. Most are too grisly to repeat but the common denominator to all these tales of woe was that the Germans considered themselves superior to others and therefore permitted themselves to destroy anything non-German.

The Germans even desecrated their victims after they were dead. There are many ways to make soap. Ingredients range from animal derivatives to vegetable byproducts. The Germans decided to manufacture soap from the dead bodies of their murdered victims. The late Shmuel Sommerfeld, an old family friend, remembered attending a "funeral" after liberation, where these soap bars were buried with full honors and eulogies. After the war, there was extensive media coverage of a German army S.S. woman who had made lamp shades of prisoners' skins!

German army photographers were proud to frequently photograph scenes of prisoners before and after execution, maltreatment of prisoners and general photographs of how heroic the German soldiers were in oppressing the helpless. When German soldiers were frequently shown pointing the barrel of a gun at their victims, these despised killers invariably displayed a smiling face. Incredibly, they enjoyed their dastard "sport".

It can be said that the Germans used any and all products of modern science to perform their primeval animal acts. Germany was a country that promoted cultural and technological development for the purpose of advancing a robot type non-civilization. Their decadent society was entirely void of the ability to deal, communicate, socialize and abide by decent laws, as civilized humans do.

The German population as a whole allowed themselves to be mesmerized and duped by opulent parades, pomp and glitter. This in effect amounted to their people becoming totally oblivious to everything but their evil pied pipers. For that reason, I find all types of parades distasteful whether by friends or foes. I cringe from old memories, each time I see mindless regimented masses of humans marching in synchronous format with metronomic regularity in lock step, whether in movies or in real life.

Unfortunately, there were only a miniscule percentage of Germans who showed evidence of having uncorrupted minds and who were sensible enough not to succumb and be beguiled by Berlin propagandists. With few exceptions, all Germans bear responsibility for World War II and its atrocities. The vast majority had their hands in its appalling barbarism and must share in the guilt and its consequences.

In summation, German style psychosis led to a World War II bottom line that counted millions upon millions of casualties. Persons were willfully murdered, killed, mutilated or maimed either physically or mentally by shooting, hangman's rope, torture, medical experiments, gas chambers, truck exhausts, malnutrition, starvation, disease, hard labor, knifings, live burials, stompings, lack of heat, lack of water, etc. All these sadistical derivatives were the result of a paranoidal nation sunk into an abyss of irrationality. The Third *Reich* had lost complete touch with reality and their vast population permitted all this government condoned insanity to transpire in varying degrees for twelve long years. The carnage ceased when law and order was imposed on Germany from without. Decency did not develop from within this psychopathic nation.

By May, 1945, the once invincible Aryans were routed, thoroughly defeated and joined the dust heap of history. Their military industrial complex lay in shambles and utter ruin. The hulks of their pernicious war machines dotted millions of square miles of land, river and ocean bottom, while the sublime stench of countless German carcasses sent to oblivion became metaphorical tranquilizers to a liberated world.

ND# New York Times

Late Edition

New York: Today, clouds yielding to sunshine. High 52. Tonight, clear, not as chilly. Low 39. Tomorrow, cloudy, a few showers late. High 56. Yesterday, high 54, low 38. Details, page A20.

FRIDAY, APRIL 13, 1990 — 50 cents beyond 75 miles from New York City, except on Long Island. — 40 CENTS

THE EAST GERMANS ISSUE AN APOLOGY FOR NAZIS' CRIMES

NEW CABINET INSTALLED

Parliament Says It Is Willing to Pay Reparations and to Seek Ties With Israel

By FERDINAND PROTZMAN
Special to The New York Times

WEST BERLIN, April 12 — As it formally installed the country's first democratic Government, the East German Parliament also ended 40 years of official denial today by accepting joint responsibility for Nazi crimes and expressing willingness to pay reparations to victims and seek diplomatic ties with Israel.

Lothar de Maizière, head of the Christian Democratic Union, was elected Prime Minister, and his 24-member "grand coalition" Government was officially approved in a nationally televised vote by the 400-member Parliament.

Mr. de Maizière's predecessor, Hans Modrow, said in a February letter to the head of a Jewish organization that his Government recognized "the responsibility of the entire German people for the past" and stood ready to "provide material support" for those who were persecuted. But today's action was the first formal acknowledgement by a freely elected government.

Western Border Reaffirmed

The new policy was approved as part of a statement that also reaffirmed the "inviolability" of Poland's western border and condemned East Germany's participation in the Warsaw Pact's 1968 invasion of Czechoslovakia, which crushed the "Prague Spring" reforms.

The statement included the admission that genocide was carried out against "the Jews in all European countries, the people of the Soviet Union, the Polish people and the Gypsy

Prime Minister Lothar de Maizière of East Germany, left, being congratulated yesterday in East Berlin by his predecessor, Hans Modrow. — Reuters

Soviets Admit Blame in Massacre Of Polish Officers in World War II

By Reuters

LONDON, April 12 — Moscow admitted for the first time today that the Soviet secret police, not the Nazis, carried out the massacre of 15,000 Polish Army prisoners in the early months of World War II.

Moscow radio, quoting the official Soviet press agency, Tass, said the Soviet broadcast said that recently discovered evidence pointed to N.K.V.D. responsibility.

This evidence was not specified. However, Moscow News, an unorthodox weekly, reported three weeks ago that official records indicated that the Polish officers were killed in the spring

---

Mea culpa no longer an aberration!
East Germans admit responsibility for past atrocities against the Jewish people
45 years later! Russia admits killing 15,000 P.O.W. Polish army officers
in the Katin forest 50 years later!
c. N.Y. Times, April 13, 1990

ONE WOULD THINK THAT THE GERMAN SPIRIT OF HATRED AND killing was a thing of the dark past and that the human spirit of respect for others has again resurfaced. Not so. On August 2, 1993, the newspapers reported that the German commander of Treblinka, the Polish death camp, where some nine hundred thousand persons were murdered, was freed from prison! Kurt Franz Y.S., who was responsible for three hundred thousand deaths, including one hundred and ninety-three killed with his own hands, was freed from the German prison in Remscheid!

There is an American proverb: "You can't teach an old dog new tricks!". While on April 22, 1993, America opened a large museum in the heart of Washington, D.C. to memorialize the Holocaust atrocities, their contemporary German allies followed up by mocking it all, snubbing their noses and contemptuously spitting at the world.

I interpret the German release of a high ranking war criminal as a blatant insult to the civilized world. It implies that the responsible parole officers are a pack of canines, guilty of malfeasance, and by seemingly treating as insignificant the bloody pursuits of a mass murderer of helpless prisoners, they showed no signs of civility or morality. It furthermore indicates that many Germans in this generation are still under the spell of the hate policies spouted by their former war propaganda machine.

To further underscore the reality that many Germans have yet to repent, consider the cases of their atypical soldiers who refused to do Hitler's dirty work. It is astonishing to some but to me it is telling and alas not surprising, that fifty years after cessation of hostilities, these anomalous German soldiers are still considered felons under their country's laws! The Bonn government has consistently refused to vindicate, pardon or at least reduce the harsh charges and associated stigma against twenty-two thousand five hundred Third *Reich* army defectors of record. Of those who escaped execution by guillotine or firing squad, all but a few hundred died in the five decades since the war ended.

In contrast, German magnanimity has pardoned those East German servicemen who fled to the west while Germany was divided. Incredibly, and in apparent contradiction, they have also lionized as heroes the army officers who attempted to assassinate Hitler in the bomb plot of July 20, 1944.

The enduring stature of court-martial convictions meted out by the former Third *Reich* reflects the lingering and ill-founded myth that Hitler's army was apolitical. Furthermore, by enjoining their derelict parliament from granting a general deserters' amnesty, the Germans have, by

Herald International Tribune

Published With The New York Times and The Washington Post

ZURICH, MONDAY, AUGUST 2, 1993

Germany Sets Treblinka Chief Free After 34 Years

Reuters

BONN — Kurt Franz, convicted for his role as commandant of the Treblinka Nazi death camp, was recently released from prison, authorities said.

A spokesman for the Justice Ministry in North Rhine-Westphalia, where Mr. Franz, 79, spent 34 years in prison, said Friday in response to a query that he had been released "quite a few weeks ago, maybe in May" from a jail in the western town of Remscheid.

He was set free under a law that allows a prisoner's release at any time after a minimum 15 years of a life sentence, despite an appeal from state prosecutors who argued his crimes were too severe to justify release.

Mr. Franz, was sentenced to life imprisonment in 1965 at a war-crimes trial in Dusseldorf for his part in the murder of "at least 300,000 people," including 193 with his own hands, in the gas chambers of Treblinka.

About 1 million people were killed in Treblinka, the overwhelming majority of them Jews.

Words have not yet been developed to describe this specie

implication, silenced history and thus avoided the casting of evil aspersions on the blood smeared hides of their former comrades in arms.

A point to ponder: German veterans of the Third *Reich* still receive veteran's benefits. Indeed, some former career personnel even receive very large government pensions. German standards for prosecuting perpetrators of World War II atrocities are, with the exception of Austria, entirely different from most, if not all, the nations of the world. Germany has no laws of capital punishment, and murderers and criminals are freed from confinement. As long as these German war veterans and their support groups are alive, pension and health benefits will continue to be accrued by them, despite the fact that recipients are stained with the blood of innocent victims. Buying goods that are "Made in Germany" support those programs.

Section Five

...AND A TIME TO PRAISE.

(KOHELES 3,7)

Chapter Thirty Four

TECHNOLOGICAL CHANGES – ECLECTIC PERSPECTIVES

IN MY FIRST SIXTY YEARS, MY GENERATION HAS EXPERIENCED unparalleled technological advancements and breakthroughs. In these few years, I witnessed humanity leap a scientific octave beyond the previous generation in the symphony of Hashem's wondrous creation. Mankind's giant advances in technology have accelerated the process of harnessing our world's potentials. In the non-material spheres, however, our societies have unfortunately regressed and deteriorated.

In Breishis,[a] Hashem blessed mankind: "...be fruitful and multiply... and subdue *(Vechivshuho)* the (planet) earth..." According to the Ramban and Horav S. R. Hirsch, "and subdue" is interpreted to mean mastering, appropriating and transforming the earth and its products for human usages. Rashi interprets "...and subdue..." that man was commanded to be fruitful and multiply.

---

a. 1:28

When the German government of the 1930's announced to the world that they required more land for *"Lebensraum"* (space to live), their agnostics obviously did not trust that Hashem, the Creator, would provide the needed sustenance for their expanding population within Germany's existing recognized international borders. The Germans maintained the theory of Thomas R. Malthus (1766-1834), the English economist who preached some one hundred and fifty years ago, that the world would soon run out of food. Malthus maintained that the world population would increase geometrically (a geometric progression increases in a constant multiple of its previous number, e.g. 2, 4, 8, 16, 32, 64…) while the food supply would only increase arithmetically (an arithmetic progression increases in a constant addition to the previous number, e.g. 2, 4, 6, 8, 10, 12…). With Providential guidance, these skeptics and preachers of impending calamity were relegated to the historical bizarre. By our fascinating technological advancements, the human race has made ever accelerating strides in "subduing" our world.

LET ME DESCRIBE SOME OF THESE MATERIAL BETTERMENTS which have affected us all and which I witnessed to date (1996). When I started in first grade (1939), we wrote our school notes by three separate means – pencil, *griffel* and pen. The *griffel* was a thin rod approximately five inches long and about half the diameter of a pencil. It consisted of a brittle slate type material and was the writing instrument used for copying notes and numbers on our small portable blackboards. In our briefcases we carried: a wooden case that had striated grooves to hold *griffels,* a small blackboard and a container with a damp, soft, pliant leather chamois *(zeemlap)* used for erasing and wiping the blackboard clean. We also carried a small bottle of navy blue ink, into which we frequently dipped our pen. The pen's metal nib was replaced in its nib holder after it became too worn or rusty. Subsequently, we used fountain pens, which held a reservoir of ink in a small rubber bladder. To prevent ink smudging, thick absorbent blotting paper was pressed on the writing to dry the ink while still moist. A crude and expensive version of today's ball point pens arrived on the scene in the late 1940's.

Up to the 1950's, telephones were mostly used for local calls. Intercity and international long distance calls were rare and extremely difficult to make. Such calls were expensive and time consuming to arrange. It could take hours or even days to get through to the second party. Before the advent of transistors and communication satellites, the volume of the phone call's sound and quality of its voice transmission left much to be desired. A mechanical, automatic central switching system for phone calls within large cities came into use by the late 1930's. This state of the art approach became obsolete with the advent of "electronic switching" of the 1960's. The far superior "digital switching" of the 1980's supersedes all previous methods and allows for exceptionally rapid connections to most phones in the world. Direct long distance dialing on a limited scale did not exist until the late 1950's. In the late 1960's an additional dimension was added by permitting remote computer manipulation through the use of the twelve button telephones. Portable cellular telephones came into use on a very limited scale in the 1980's.

Shortly after World War II, my mother-in-law, "ordered a three minute phone connection" from New York to talk to her mother, *Oma* Bollag, in Switzerland. Overseas phone calls were seldom made and this was the first time mother and daughter had an opportunity to talk since the Rokowsky family departed from Switzerland in May of 1941. After many hours, the overseas operator was able to make the connection. This conversation was extremely emotional as they had not talked to each other for five years. Half of those three minutes was taken up by crying on both sides of the Atlantic.

The few automotive passenger vehicles that were used in the 1930's and the 1940's were extremely heavy and inefficient, consuming a gallon of gasoline per six or seven miles. In the 1930's, prior to the introduction of car batteries, engine ignition was accomplished by cranking the motor manually. In the event the crank handle had a defective release mechanism or in case it was not released quickly enough then the engine would "kick back" and an arm injury to the cranker could result. Advances in the science of road building allowed for the development and introduction of superhighways in the 1950's. The constant stop and go traffic so typical of urban and many rural roadways was virtually eliminated. The improved traffic flow cut down roadside air pollution and reduced per mile fuel consumption. A spinoff beneficiary of the latter is the public's diet; we can now receive fruits and vegetables year round, shipped over thousands of miles by inexpensive refrigerated trucks. The gradual elimination of leaded gasoline in the 1970's has relegated that toxic air pollutant to history.

Airplanes of the 1950's that were used for international travel were small and slow. Two hundred M.P.H. was considered the top speed. Their range between refueling was two and a half thousand miles and a filled-to-capacity, large plane carried but one hundred and fifty to two hundred passengers. Compare that to the current speed of five hundred and fifty M.P.H., flying seven thousand miles non stop and carrying four hundred and fifty passengers. Today's jet engines are also quiet when compared to the former propeller engines that were so noisy that passengers could hardly hold a conversation.

Trains were slow and railroad cars were shaky. Tracks were built with poor tolerances and had bolted instead of welded rail joints, so that high speed travel was not practical. Locomotives burned coal to produce steam, which in turn powered their engines. The locomotive's fire chambers were manually loaded by a stoker's coal shovel. Thus, on a warm day when passing through a railroad tunnel, passengers had to quickly close all windows to prevent the cabin from filling up with suffocating, foul smelling locomotive smoke. In the year 1939, we visited a train exhibit in Amsterdam commemorating one hundred years of railroads in Holland. The more recently built railroad cars of the 1930's appeared "re-packaged" and nicer than those of 1839 but technologically, they had changed little. Subsequently, since the late 1940's, we have had diesel and electric powered inter-city trains that were able to attain speeds of two hundred to three hundred M.P.H. The most recent development is the Mag-Lev train, which is electrically propelled and needs no wheels for support since the train hovers above the ground by a vertical magnetic repelling force or "Magnetic Levitation". Locomotion is provided by a linear induction motor. These type trains can travel extremely fast and are whisper quiet.

Food has been a major beneficiary of research and development. Thanks to less expensive refrigeration, it is now possible to purchase fresh fruits and vegetables all year round from farms half way around our globe. Compare this to the 1930's when "fresh" winter food in northern Europe and the northern USA was limited to potatoes, cabbage, carrots, turnips, onions and a few apples. In some areas, oranges were also sent north using the railroads. Improvements in refrigeration and cold storage in the 1950's and 1960's has permitted the freezing of many fruit juices and vegetables, thereby making many local summer crops available out of season.

Recent advances in bio-engineering has increased food supplies so dramatically that countries that used to be chronic importers now export their surplus food. This was accomplished by development of new disease and drought resistant crops and crops that require a reduced growing season. This reduction in maturation time has resulted in the American cornbelt being pushed northward by two hundred and fifty miles, where the growing season is considerably shorter. Larger size grains and bigger fruits are now produced and some marginal soils as found in certain arid areas and deserts, are able to yield crops. Not frequently considered a food production factor is the development of artificial fibers since the 1940's. As a result of woven materials made from man-made yarns, millions of acres of farm land have become available for additional food production.

Energy sources used to be essentially limited to wood, coal and oil. Today we make extensive use of atomic power, renewable solar energy, ocean tides, huge hydroelectric power projects, geothermal heat from the earth and natural gas. It is estimated that in the state of Texas alone there is enough wind power to provide electrical energy for the entire USA! Furthermore, there is one thousand times more known geothermal energy than the combined energies of all the discovered reserves of oil, coal, gas and uranium!

By making fuel consuming and power equipment two to three times more efficient than in former years, by cogeneration and by insulating buildings, the national fuel consumption has steadily declined by several percent a year per capita. This has contributed greatly toward improving air quality in the chronically polluted smog cities like Los Angeles, London, New York and Pittsburgh where air pollution problems are no longer a major issue.

I never cease to marvel at the radical and swift changes brought about by technological advancements. Some early manifestations of this rapid obsolescence process can be noted in New York City where many residential buildings predate the electrification of the 1920's. In the 1990's, I still come across small and large buildings which conceal within their walls intricate gas piping for the obsolete gas lamps and special kitchen drain lines that provided runoff for the former iceboxes.

Types of materials in use have changed drastically. Steel has in many cases been replaced by plastic, glass and aluminum alloys. Communications are improved by replacing copper wires with fiber optic cables made of thin glass fibers that transmit laser beams. "Laser" is the acronym for Light Amplification by Stimulated Emission of Radiation. Many newly developed metal alloys can take more extremes in both hotter and colder temperatures and are much stronger than their pure parent metal or than former alloys. A large number of these improvements are a spinoff of the costly space programs and have greatly benefitted the global economy.

In 1956 electronic computers were bulky and their magnetic disk drive had a limited storage capacity of only two thousand bits per square inch. Forty years later, portable laptop computers have drives with 1.3 billion bits[b] in the same square inch area, far more miniaturization of data storage than was ever imagined to be possible.

In the mid 1950's, when electronic computers were just being developed, the speed of each operation was measured in milliseconds, or thousands of a second. By the late 1950's, the speed was increased to micro seconds or millionths of a second. Currently, computers have activities that are measured in parts of nano seconds or fractions of a billionth of a second. In the 1990's, industry is heading towards a speed of pico seconds, where one pico second is a trillionth of a second. Combining increased data storage with high speeds and large microchips, can readily lead one to understand how a giant computer of the 1950's, which required a very large room and air conditioning to cool the multitude of hot diode tubes, can now be replaced by a battery operated model that is far superior, miniaturized and can fit in a briefcase!

I FIND IT FASCINATING THAT COMPUTER ACTIVITIES HAVE become asymptotic to a zero second duration! (Asymptotes are tangents that meet a curve at infinity.) Extrapolating this remarkable phenomenon of duration-shrinkage to the creation of our world *[yesh mayesh]*, provides an interesting concept in reconciling the supposedly astronomical number of years required to develop the universe to its current state of being. The secularists postulate an aged universe by using the present pace of nature as their measuring stick in arriving at billions of years for timing of apparent sequential activities. By reverting to a creation phase where the current pace of nature was shrunk to a highly accelerated mode and like our computer, approaches zero seconds per activity, one can begin to comprehend a time miniaturization process. This compaction of total duration permits the juxtaposing of aeons of activities into the six days of creation as taught in the *Torah*.[c]

DIODE AND TRIODE TUBES WERE TYPICALLY ASSOCIATED WITH radios up to the 1950's. These were replaced with transistors and other semi-conductors and have permitted miniaturization of everything electronic, such as computers, radios, televisions and military equipment.

Computers are used in more industries every year. They allow orderly planning of very large projects having thousands of interrelated

---

b. or 1.3 giga bytes   c. Shemos, 31:7.

activities (CPM: Critical Path Method). They are also used for rapid information retrieval, difficult engineering designs, making complicated engineering drawings, typing correspondence and publishing. Computers greatly help the space exploration program and the military could not do without them. Since the mid-1980's, an entire *Sefer Torah,* which took half a year to a year to write and several weeks to check, can now be fully examined in less than an hour for errors in spelling and defects in writing by the use of computerized character recognition or scanners. Since the 1990's, voice recognition has become a reality for typing documents and dialing telephones, etc. Computers allow more work to be done in offices and factories by far fewer persons and in a small fraction of the original pre-computer time. As a result of computers, overall quality and quantity of production are greatly enhanced.

Medicine has advanced so extensively that practically every major medicine and virtually all medical equipment and procedure currently in use was not even heard of forty to fifty years ago. Research and development have augmented numerous so-called new "wonder" drugs. Even the so called orthodox medical schools, which until recently considered vitamin supplements and antioxidants as quackery, are now slowly starting to recognize the importance of nutrients such as vitamins, minerals, enzymes, antioxidants, etc. New equipment include many non-invasive body monitors such as: sophisticated miniaturized remotely controlled organ and vital-signs monitors, which are spinoffs from the space program, ultrasound and magnetic resonance imaging (MRI). Other electronic equipment include the pacemaker for the heart, hearing aids, electron microscope, laser and ultrasound for surgery, etc. Surgery and procedures unheard of years ago now include bypass heart surgery, organ transplants, DNA identification, gene splicing, genetic screening, gene correction, laser cataract surgery, hemodialysis to assist weak kidneys, etc. Detoxification of excessive lead levels, and reversing both hardening of the arteries and gangrene are now routinely performed in doctor's offices by the chelation process. This procedure can correct some elevated blood pressure conditions and greatly reduce the number of bypass heart surgeries and limb amputations due to gangrene complications. Hospital stays have in many cases been safely reduced from many weeks to only a few days, thereby allowing downsizing of needed bed capacities. It is not unusual for a monitoring or analysis procedure to be completed in a matter of minutes at outpatient facilities or decentralized satellite clinics and instantly interpreted at a Medical Center thousands of miles away, using advanced communication devices.

The use of space satellites over the last thirty five years has changed every phase of life. There are weather satellites which, with high speed computers, can accurately forecast difficult weather scenarios. Satellites are used extensively for communication and several of these units are "parked" over the Atlantic and the Pacific Oceans. Satellites are used for agricultural planning and raw material discoveries. They were recently very successful in archeological finds. Other uses for satellites include military spying, space testing laboratories, land surveying and astronomy.

Many technical developments have updated the home. Houses are now economically heated and cooled with electrical heat pumps and cooled with extremely efficient air conditioning. These important appliances came into use by the early 1950's and have been improved steadily and dramatically. Sizes and capacities of this equipment were reduced by the advent of house insulation and storm windows in the 1950's. In the 1980's, further energy savings were realized by the use of insulated glass window panes. Various types of light bulbs that last five times longer and use one third the electrical power of the incandescent bulbs came into use during the 70's, 80's and early 90's. Besides the commonly used ballast control, 60 cycle fluorescent light bulbs, which are very damaging to the eyes, there are now healthier mercury vapor bulbs, sodium vapor bulbs, electronically controlled bulbs and solid state ballasts with high frequency (25,000 cycles per second) fluorescent bulbs. As a result of electronic equipment improvements, there are now millions of people who work locally instead of commuting long distances. This is due in part to the fax machines, computer work stations, personal computers and many improved communication devices. In the early 1990's global communications took on a new dimension with the use of *cyberspace.*

Cooking in the home can now be done at a fraction of the time it took in the 1940's. Cooking gas was formerly manufactured from coal and was known as coke-oven gas, it had a much smaller heating value than the currently used methane based natural gas. Furthermore, the pressure cooker and the microwave oven both reduce cooking time and fuel consumption. The need for hot water is reduced by the use of electric home dishwashers.

Offices were updated in the late 1950's with the introduction of instant office copiers, like the type introduced by the Xerox Corporation. Some copiers even collate pages. Prior to such copiers, there were carbon paper and messy mimeographing. In the 1980's, manual and electric typewriters became obsolete when electronic word processors were introduced. In the 1980's, it also became possible to copy and rearrange printed materials by the use of computer scanners. A scourge of the 1980's — computer viruses, a product of electronically oriented pranksters, can now be addressed in routine fashion. High speed laser printers joined the office arsenal in the early 1990's.

In the late 1930's, radar was developed. It has since played a major role in guiding planes safely at night, in situations where visibility is restricted and at crowded airports. Militarily, it also had a significant impact on early warning capability and enemy plane detection. The U.S.A. now has military planes which elude radar detection (Stealth bombers and fighters).

Since the 1950's, the science of seismic monitoring has been steadily improved. As a result, the exact location of an earthquake anywhere on earth can be readily determined. A spinoff of this procedure was the ability to detect, monitor and locate secret underground nuclear blasts.

Helicopters were developed for both military and civilian use during the late 1940's. Had these type aircraft been available during World War II then all strategies would have been different, e.g. capturing a strategic bridge, beachhead or airport, etc. Fewer paratroopers would have had to be used while allowing for more sophisticated leapfrogging techniques and the war could have ended much sooner.

The following is an impressive array of many additional and miscellaneous developments and discoveries: FM (Frequency Modulation) radio, efficient solar batteries that can power a small town, supersonic passenger planes like the Concorde, atomic powered submarines and surface navy ships, fusion energy, accurate and speedy surface-to-air and air-to-air missiles, automatic automobile transmissions, tape recorders, compact digital disc records, an optical multi-layered digital CD disk that can hold 6.5 billion bytes and is able to store many thousands of typewritten pages, synthetic rubber, home movies, which were subsequently made obsolete by home videos, which in turn were made again obsolete by digital videos, interactive and virtual reality T.V., interplanetary spacecrafts, moon landing module and spacecraft, re-usable space shuttles, the orbiting space telescope which may be rendered obsolete by the development of the far more sensitive telescopes that use radio and optical interferometry, discovery in outer space of the invisible non-baryonic matter that forms much of the cosmic mass, discovery of dozens of subatomic type particles, fish farms, pipe line networks to pump water, oil or natural gas for thousands of miles, cryogenic gas storage, contact lenses, tooth implants, infra-red scanning, accurate computerized electronic fingerprinting, automobile traction control for anti-skid braking, videoing interior of small diameter sewer lines, hover-craft ferry boats, gyroscope, computerized chess games, electronic pocket dictionaries, supermarket checkout by electronic scanners, artificial heart valves, reverse osmosis desalinization of water, nuclear medicine *(isotopics),* angiographics, numerous vaccines including the salk polio vaccine, etc...

It is most unfortunate that many of the above innovations had to be initially developed for purposes of war. Following declassification by the military and the Space Administration (NASA) of many of these discoveries, spinoffs became popularly available for civilian use.

WE ARE NOW WITNESSING A NEW PHENOMENON IN OUR daily lives which is the result of steady outpourings of new discoveries and changes in scientific knowledge. Lifestyles that remained unchanged for generations are now being touched by miraculous scientific developments and technological break-throughs. As a result of those constant changes, textbooks in these fields become quickly outdated and are continuously being revised. It is estimated that in the 1990's half of a technical discipline's non-fundamental subject-matter as taught in engineering, medical and other scientific fields becomes obsolete and is relegated to historical status within *five* to *ten* years! (half life)

During my first sixty years, the world population has almost tripled and despite many ravages now approaches the threshold of the *six billion* mark! Thus the apparent disparate interpretations of Rashi and Horav S. R. Hirsch for the 'subduing' process are seen to be complementing each other and reconciled: Appropriating the earth's yields to mankind's benefit has allowed world society to become *fruitful and multiply* at a raised and sustained level.

Hashem's *Torah* is considered the abstract blueprint of His Master Plan by which He created the universe. It is therefore no coincidence that over the last two hundred years, the world has experienced an ever increasing proliferation of technological and scientific knowledge: An amazing prediction was outlined some nineteen centuries ago by the *Tannah,* Rabbi Shimon bar Yochai regarding Breishis 21:1[d] where he states that six hundred years into the sixth millennium from creation of the universe, the heavenly gates and the terrestrial wells will open to gush

---

d. Zohar, 117.

wisdom for the benefit of humanity. Amazingly, that year corresponds to 1840 C.E. when the Industrial Revolution was in the midst of ushering in mankind's ascent on the technological ladder! Refer to *Ma'aseh Avos Simmon Lahbonim*,[e] by Rabbi David Cohen [6], As a result of this blossoming wisdom, recent generations have been privileged to witness the unraveling of much abstruse knowledge and reap the benefits of improved quality of life.

As Hashem continues to open for us the well springs of material wisdom, we will be catapulted beyond our present horizons of knowledge. Whilst each element of wisdom reaches fruition, mankind marvels further at the many features He has programmed into His magnificent creation.[f] According to some of our Talmudic sages, a summit in the "subduing" process of our world will be reached in two and a half centuries hence, when by the year six thousand from creation, the seventh millennium will commence. At that time, these sages expect the world to become fallow and there will come a thousand years of total *Shabbos*.[g]

It is mankind's challenge to direct all these newly found material benefits in ethical and virtuous ways. As we find in Hosheah;[h] "...the just walk in the ways of Hashem but the iniquitous stumble through them".

The crown of the "subduing" synthesis and the universal realization of this goal will occur when the world shall witness the knowledge and understanding of Hashem permeating the whole of mankind, thereby joining humans into a harmonious unity where everyone will contribute to the prosperity of the whole.

"....For the earth shall be full of the knowledge of Hashem as the waters cover the oceanic spans."[i]

The climax for mankind will be achieved when "On that day shall Hashem be (acknowledged as) One, and His Name will be One".[j]

---

e. page 3
f. Breishis, 2:4 commentary by Horav S. R. Hirsch.
g. *Maseches Sanhedrin,* 97a and *Maseches Rosh Hashona,* 31a.
h. 14:10.
i. Yeshayohu, 11:9. Refer also to commentary by Horav Mendel Hirsch on the *Haftorah,* 8th day *Pesach,* [13].
j. Zechariah, 14:9.

Chapter Thirty Five

APPENDICES

TABLE OF CONTENTS

	PAGE NOS.
Appendix A	281
Four Vignettes of Providential Guidance/ Divine Deliverance Sagas	
❖ A Sage's Sage Will	282
❖ Expressed to the Orient	285
❖ A Nanny is Punctually Late	288
❖ They Should Have Fired a Boomerang!	290
Appendix B	292
Ancestral Primacy	
❖ Horav Meir and Tirza Lehmann/Paternal Forebears	293
❖ Hachover, Reb Osher and Toni Lehmann	306
❖ Chaim Boaz & Tzipora Chana Mindel Rabinowitz	310
❖ Hirsch and Johana Oppenheimer/Maternal Forebears	315
❖ David and Emma Wallerstein	321
❖ End of a Namesake	323
❖ Continuum ad Infinitum	324
Appendix C - The *Chover* Title	326
Appendix D - B-17 Flying Fortress Bombers	330
Appendix E - A Sordid German Folktale	333

Appendix A:

Four Vignettes of Providential Guidance - Divine Deliverance Sagas

IN OUR LARGER FAMILY, MANY OF MY PEERS HAVE MIRACULOUS accounts of survival. In gratitude and for the sake of posterity, I will recount some of these awesome experiences.

"Come, hear, so I may tell to all who fear Hashem, what He has done for my soul."[a] These succinct words of King David were interpreted by Horav Samson Raphael Hirsch as the relating of stirring experiences that occurred to Jews in exile and which are now recorded, in gratitude, as a testament for all times to come.

The above verse is very apropos to the following episodes:

---

a. Tehillim, 66:16.

A Sage's Sage Will

CONTEMPORARY ANTI-SEMITISM REARED ITS UGLY HEAD in the deep German countryside as early as the year 1934. My brother-in-law, Moses L. Schwab, related the following interesting and fascinating story regarding his father:

> In the year 1933, Rabbi Shimon Schwab, *Zatsal* (of New York) moved his family to a very small country town named Ichenhausen, which was located in the Bavarian section of southern Germany. Schwaben was the name of the local district. In Ichenhausen, Rabbi Schwab made detailed and extensive arrangements to open a local *yeshivah* for out of town boys. Permission for this project had been granted by the *Gestapo*.
>
> The doors opened up in May of 1934. It was, however, not many hours before Rabbi Schwab was advised by a friendly non-Nazi local police chief that the Hitler Youth were preparing a pogrom against the y*eshivah* that night. Rabbi Schwab then requested a meeting with the *Gestapo* to avert a tragedy. When Rabbi Schwab arrived at their local office, he found a brawly Nazi officer behind a desk and a growling dog next to him. Rabbi Schwab sized up the situation, gathered his courage and looked the German straight in the eyes. "I have come to discuss the safety of my students", Rabbi Schwab said. He was told that the presence of out-of-town *yeshivah* students was considered a provocation to the local population. "The only way to stop a pogrom and

bloodshed is for the boys to leave today, before nightfall. Otherwise, we will not be responsible for what happens tonight." The officer continued, "I have already telegraphed *Gestapo* headquarters in Munich that we will not be responsible for what happens tonight."

It was the first day of *yeshivah*. When Rabbi Schwab returned to the boys an hour later, they were prepared to ask a whole list of questions on various *Rashis*. Unfortunately, they were directed by Rabbi Schwab to close their books, pack their belongings and immediately head for the train station. Each student was given the fare for his ticket from the *yeshivah* account to return home. On the way to the station they were jeered by the local hoodlums but were not harmed. With the boys returning home, a local pogrom was averted and almost a year's work of preparing for the *yeshivah* came to an abrupt halt.

RABBI SCHWAB REALIZED THE SORRY STATE OF AFFAIRS in Germany and how matters were becoming more and more hopeless. He then authored his first book in German, titled *Heimkehr ins Judentum* (Returning to Judaism's Roots), the crux of which conveyed the message that all German culture *(Kultur)*, German Humanism, etc., was corrupt and that Jews have only the *Torah* to hold on to. In the following years, Rabbi Schwab investigated ways to relocate abroad. He received offers from Haifa, London and elsewhere. In December of 1936, he made his choice and accepted a *shtelle* (position) in Baltimore, MD.

Several years later, while perusing through *Sefer Chasidim*[10] and the *Tzavo'oh* of Rabbi Yehuda Hachosid (born in the year 4910), Rabbi Schwab was amazed at what he found. There in item No. 56 the will stated:

"A man from the land of Schwaben will not be able to raise boys to learn in a (local) Yeshivah." [!!!]

Rabbi Schwab considered that section, without a doubt, to have been directly targeted at him.

Rabbi Schwab was the world renowned Rav Emeritus of Khal Adas Yeshurun in New York. Less than a year before his passing away, he published his Magnum Opus, the *Torah* commentary *Ma'ayon Beis Hashoayvoh*.[28] This magnificent work climaxed his many other literary works in Hebrew, English and German.

The circumstances surrounding the untimely and rude closure of the Ichenhausen *Yeshivah,* led Rav Schwab to realize in the early 1930's that Germany was not where he and his family should remain. This early warning gave the Schwab family an ample opportunity to emigrate in an orderly fashion from their native land.Thus, the will of that pious sage, uttered some seven hundred and fifty years earlier, contributed significantly towards saving the Schwab family from becoming Holocaust victims.

נו. איש מארץ שוואבין לא יגדל
נערים שיזכו לישיבה

Hebrew text of terse statement No. 56 by
Rabbi Yehudah Hachasid

It is noteworthy to mention that on 7 Mar Cheshvan, 5719 (1958) Ruth and I were honored to have Horav Shimon Schwab officiate at our *chassenah (Messader Kiddushin).*

Expressed To The Orient

FREQUENTLY WE HAVE 20/20 HINDSIGHT IN RECOGNIZING silver linings to our dark clouds. Soviet Russia's invasion of Poland under its "Friendship Treaty" with Germany was a case in point. That treachery by both the Soviet Union and their German friends set off a chain of events that had positive ramifications to a select group of Polish Jews.

Following the invasion of Poland in the year 1939 and with determination to increase his "friends", Josef Stalin of the Soviet Union ceded the entire Polish enclave of Vilna to the neighboring Lithuanians. This international transfer of jurisdiction resulted in thousands of Polish Jews becoming refugees in an expanded Lithuania. The Mirrer *Yeshivah* with its four hundred member staff and student body plus their dependents were among these new immigrants. Had Vilna remained under Soviet domain then their public teaching and studying of *Torah* would have ceased, since religion was not condoned under Soviet rule.

By the year 1940, the Soviet Politburo in Moscow could no longer restrain its greed and promptly proceeded to swallow the three small Baltic states — Lithuania, Latvia and Estonia. With Lithuania now occupied by the Soviets, *Torah* learning at the Mirrer *Yeshivah* became an illegal operation. The *Yeshivah's* escape route to the west was cut off by the Germans. Accordingly, their sights were now trained on America, and they immediately proceeded to obtain papers from the Dutch Consul in Sweden for traveling to the Caribbean island of Curacao in the

Netherlands Antilles. The only viable option for reaching their goal was by heading east. They traveled for six thousand miles, through eight time zones, using the famous Trans-Siberian railroad and an ocean liner. At Vladivostok the group boarded a ship to cross the Sea of Japan with the Japanese city of Kobe as their temporary destination. Obtaining Polish passports, Japanese transit visas and Soviet Russian passage in hostile environments was no mean feat. These were all overt miracles.

In the meantime, war had broken out with America and that made crossing the Pacific Ocean no longer feasible. Since they couldn't remain in Japan, the group was sent twelve hundred miles west, across the Yellow Sea, to Shanghai, in Japanese occupied China.

ANOTHER OUTRIGHT MIRACLE WAS AWAITING IN SHANGHAI. Mr. Sassoon, a Shanghai philanthropist who probably never heard of the *Yeshivah,* had recently completed construction of a large new *shul* in the heart of a light commercial district that was in the city's International Zone. It was in an area of Shanghai which had practically no Jews to use the building. Its seating capacity was just equal to those learning in the *Yeshivah!* Hashem had His messengers complete the needed groundwork ahead of the *Yeshivah's* arrival. For many months that *shul* became the *Yeshivah's Beis Medrash.*

Neither in Japan nor in China were Jews persecuted, since the Japanese respected religions and considered Jews as Asians. Tokyo's slogan was: "Asia for the Asians". While World War II was escalating and dimming Europe's lights, the Mirrer *Yeshivah* was enlightening Shanghai with *Torah.*

Rabbi Akivah the Tannah recommended that persons acquaint themselves with the saying: *"Kol d'ovid Rachmonah letav ovid".*[a] ("Everything that the All-Merciful does is done for the good".)

Traveling to a remote section of our globe, away from the European Jewish center of gravity, amidst all the chaos and anti-Semitism was perceived to be devastating. In reality, the *yeshivah's* exile became a lifesaving event, as the adage of Rabbi Akivah stated.

Among the many brilliant scholars of the Mirrer *Yeshivah* was Horav Joseph Pinchas Levinson with his wife and young son Zvi Hirsch. In later years, Rabbi Levinson became a prominent contributing editor to the *Encyclopedia Talmudis,* cf volume No. 10. In the year 1962, Zvi Hirsch married my sister-in-law Deborah Rokowsky. Most who know Harry

---

a. *Maseches Brochos,* 60b.

Levinson, Esq. of Monsey, New York don't realize that he trekked more than a quarter way around the world, across mountains, deserts and oceans, and so escaped the German claws. To the Levinsons and all their Mirrer *Yeshivah chaverim,* the perceived tragedy of the "Friendship Treaty" proved to have been Divine salvation.

Helping to bring this series of miracles to fruition was an inspirational lesson. It illustrated how a handful of hardworking and sincere Jews and non-Jews of various races from around the globe, each in their own spheres, effectively strived to rescue a large group of individuals from falling prey to German chaos.

The diplomats who issued the needed visas and thereby allowed the Levinson family and thousands of other Jews to flee from Soviet occupied Lithuania, included the honorary Dutch consul Jan Zwartendijk and his Japanese counterpart, consul Chiune Sugihara. The latter's humanitarian action was considered insubordination and resulted in his dismissal from the Japanese diplomatic corps. These benefactors are commended for their exemplary show of selflessness and kindness and are among the Righteous of the Nations.

A Nanny Is Punctually Late

THE FOLLOWING IS A REMARKABLE STORY OF SURVIVAL. Edmund Stern's (see chapter 15) brother and sister-in-law, Mr. and Mrs. Joseph Stern, lived in Budapest, Hungary with their three young children. Their daughter, Tziporah, had just been born. By mid-1943, many doomed Jews from Hungary had already been deported to Polish death camps. Like an uncontrollable plague, the country was rife with anti-Semitism. To avoid becoming victims of German atrocities, the Stern family arranged to escape to the neighboring country of Rumania. Conditions across the border were not much better, but at least the Rumanian Government was not deporting their people to the gas chambers or exposing them to death squads. To avoid attention, the various members of the Stern family were to head for an inconspicuously parked truck on a side street and approach the vehicle from different directions at separate times. For the truck to make it safely across the border, departure was carefully calculated and scheduled at a particular hour. It was impressed on all prospective passengers to be on board this truck by a designated time. The driver would not wait, not even a minute.

When the hour and minute arrived, the entire Stern family had arrived at their rendezvous and all had climbed on board. Only little Tziporah was missing. Mr. Stern begged the driver to wait, but to no avail. The truck slowly drove off. In the distance and to the utter dismay of the family, they saw Tziporah's baby nurse approaching the appointment site, pushing Tziporah's baby carriage!

RABBI AKIVA'S TEACHER WAS NACHUM ISH GAM ZU.[a] IT WAS Reb Nachum who gave fame to the cliche "Gam zu lctovah" — "whatever happens is for the good". Tziporah's separation from her family, considered an apparent catastrophe, turned out to be her salvation, precisely as Reb Nachum preached. The Stern family was intercepted and arrested at the Rumanian border and sent to the infamous Auschwitz concentration camp. There, the two older children were senselessly murdered. Meanwhile, the non-Jewish baby nurse took Tziporah to her own home and raised the baby as if she were her own child. To avoid possible snitching by neighbors, Tziporah was henceforth called by the name "Marika" — meaning "little Marie".

Following liberation, Mr. and Mrs. Joseph Stern returned to Budapcst. They were fortunate and thankful to find their youngest child alive and well. Subsequently, the Sterns moved to Geneva, Switzerland, where they raised a new and beautiful family of which Marika was now the oldest of her new siblings. For years, the Sterns sent "Care" packages to the now elderly woman who took such special care of Marika.

In 1964, Marika Tziporah Stern and my brother-in-law Yitzchok Rokowsky were married. They now reside in Monsey, New York. Few persons realize the dramatic story behind Marika's non-Jewish given name, which has remained with her. The name is a living testament and statement to the kindness of a Gentile Hungarian nanny which was in contrast to the utter wantonness of the low German character.

---

a. *Maseches Taanis,* 21a.

They Should Have Fired A Boomerang!

MY PARENTS-IN-LAW, MEIR ROKOWSKY AND *L.B.* RACHEL Rokowsky, were born and lived in Switzerland. There they were very active in extricating literally hundreds of Jews from Germany, Austria and Czechoslovakia. In some cases, my father-in-law even crossed the German border at the city of Basel to save these people. Due to inflexible statutes of Swiss law regarding these rescue missions and the potential danger of arrest by the Swiss Authorities, the Rokowsky family found it unsafe to remain in Switzerland. Thus, my parents-in-law and their four children emigrated to the United States in June, 1941.

International events were developing at an ever increasing tempo. There was even talk of a possible German invasion of neutral Switzerland. As a result, the Rokowsky family's departure from their native land had to be made in great haste. Making the huge Atlantic ocean a German domain was one of Berlin's priorities, and implementing that evil plan was an additional factor that contributed towards relegating the German nation to renegade status. As a result of that policy, the ocean liner, which brought the family to New York was torpedoed and sunk by a *U-boat* (German submarine) on its return voyage to Spain. The fact that the ship was not a military transport, had a neutral country's registry and war had not yet been declared between the United States and Germany meant nothing to these unscrupulous predators of the sea. By sinking dozens of ships, these assassins displayed absolutely no compunctions and were responsible for taking thousands of civilian lives. Many of their victims floundered mercilessly in the ocean waves before succumbing to overexposure, starvation, thirst and drowning.

The family's arrival in New York was not a bit too soon. By September, 1941, when the Rokowsky family had barely settled down in the Borough Park section of Brooklyn, their youngest son Yisroel was born. Today, hardly a person who knows the *Rosh HaYeshivah* of Ohr Somayach in Monsey, Rabbi Yisroel Rokowsky, realizes the close call he had with some unsavory German sponsored sea mail.

Appendix B:
Ancestral Primacy

IN THE TURBULENT YESTERYEARS, MANY OF MY ANCESTORS were eminent in the struggle to maintain authentic Judaism. Our forebears mustered all material and spiritual means at their disposal to inspire upcoming generations with loyalty and enthusiasm towards *Torah* values. They remain the pride and protective shadows for many of their progenies.

It is my fervent hope that our daily conduct will not fall below the high *Torah* standards these *patres familias* instilled and cultivated. Those generations represent a bygone splendor in the *Torah* world of which I am extremely proud. Their influence remains a great motivating force in my philosophical approach to life. It is therefore fitting to briefly trace several of these recently formed roots and describe a few of their attributes.

"Children's children are the crown of the aged, and the glory of children are their forebears." [a]

---

a. Mishlei, 17:6.

Horav Meir & Tirza Lehmann

Paternal Forebears

OUR PATERNAL GREAT GRANDFATHER, *HORAV* DR. MEIR Lehmann, was born to Oscher Lemuel and Roeschen Lehmann in the northwestern German town of Verden, Niedersachsen, on 25 *Teves,* 5591 (1831). Meir was the youngest of eight children.

His father, who lived from 1769 to 1858, wrote a diary in the old Jewish German vernacular, which was printed in 1936 under the title *Urgrossvaters Tagebuch;* [14] the appended family tree depicts a lineage dating as far back as 1685. Of the one hundred and thirty-two direct descendants listed, I was the fourth youngest entry and the youngest Lehmann shown. Many of Oscher Lemuel's forebears were described as *rabbonim* in important cities and districts.

This diary was reprinted in a hard cover edition with addended family dates by the non-Jewish city government of Verden, Germany in 1989,[15] in deference to one of their former famous sons.

It is a great pity that the German authorities only realized the significance of the Jewish people and the prominence of our family fifty years too late — after they orphaned us needlessly at a tender young age.

In his bachelor years, Oscher Lemuel traveled to Prague, where he practiced *Torah im Derech Eretz*. He attended the *shiurim* of Rabbi Yecheskel Landau, known as the Noda BeYehudah, while also studying at the local university. Subsequently in the year 1792 he returned to Germany and his home town of Bamberg.

Our great uncle, Jonas Lehmann, wrote a very interesting biography of his father, Horav Meir Lehmann.[17] It reveals many interesting details of his times and life.

HORAV MEIR WAS BORN AT A TIME WHEN JEWS HAD RECENTLY been emancipated and were now considered regular German citizens with full rights and privileges. These were the years when committed and sincere Jews showed their mettle. Assimilation of religious practices ran rampant. Despite the false religious philosophies that permeated Western Europe, young Meir received a good, basic orthodox Jewish education at a small *yeshivah* in Verden. He was extremely bright and was reputed to have had a photographic memory. It is told that on one occasion he read an article to his parents in fluent German, which was the national tongue. When his parents looked at the book later, they noticed the text was entirely in French!

Following completion of his studies at the Verden *Yeshivah,* young Meir went to a *yeshivah* in Halberstadt, Germany and from there to Prague to follow in his father's footsteps. At the university, he studied philosophy, history, Hebrew, Arabic and Theory of Law. While in Prague, he also studied at the *yeshivah* and subsequently received *semichah* on 19 Av, 5612 (1852), from Horav Shlomo Yehudah Leib Cohen Rappaport (1790-1867), *Rav* and *Rosh Beth Din* of Prague. In part, the *semichah* document stated that he is to be called to the *Torah* and referred to henceforth by the name and title of *Moreinu Horav* Rabbi Meir ben *Hachover* Rabbi Oscher.[b]

Wherever Horav Meir Lehmann settled, whether in Prague, Berlin or Mainz, he always established *Talmud Torah* organizations for the local college students. These were institutions which continued to exist for many decades, with some remaining in existence up to World War II.

In Berlin, Horav Meir Lehmann established a *Chevrah Shas,* which lasted for more than sixty years. It was in Berlin that Horav Meir Lehmann received his doctorate in philosophy (Ph.D.). He was also very much interested in classical literature and drama, the involvement of which was almost to his Rabbinical detriment. Having written a classical play of special quality, Rav Meir was approached by a prestigious producer-critic who encouraged him to henceforth devote all his professional

---

b. For an explanation of the *Hachover* title, refer to Appendix C.

Horav Meir Lehmann Zatsal as printed in the Israelit, [21] *issue April 16, 1890*

energies to the theater. There was to be a meeting one evening at which Horav Meir was to present his work. That afternoon, Horav Meir made a *Cheshbon Hanefesh* (conducted an introspection). He was in a serious dilemma — should he become a playwright or use his G-d given energies and talents for better things. These thoughts echoed in his mind while sitting at the local student lounge. Suddenly he jumped up and cried out, "What do I need this for, I have better aspirations!" With that, he took the play's manuscript and threw it in its entirety into the burning fireplace. The young Rav Meir then cried aloud, "Create for me a clean heart, O Hashem, and renew a steadfast spirit within me!" [c] That evening, the playwright producer, et. al., waited in vain for the young writer. They never met again.

Rav Meir was relieved after his great sacrifice and now set out to pursue the Rabbinate in earnest. He continued his studies at the Adas Yisroel Rabbinical Seminary of Berlin, which was founded and under the constant leadership and tutelage of Horav Ezriel Hildesheimer (1820-1899). At this institution of higher learning, many of Europe's Orthodox *rabbonim* received their training.

While Rav Meir was heroically climbing the Judaic ladder, the Jews of Mainz stumbled into the lamentable Reform movement. They built a temple with an organ, installed a women's choir and neglected the *Shabbos*, etc. It was a pathetic state of affairs for a city steeped in so much Jewish tradition. This was the city where Rabbeinu Gershom lived a thousand years before. In this city lived and was martyred Horav Amnon the composer of the *Unesaneh Tokef* that we recite on the *Yomim Noroim*.

Rabbi Shmuel Bondi, a prominent citizen of Mainz, resisted peer pressures and took no part in this destructive assimilation. He also had an eligible daughter Tirza, in whom Rav Meir Lehmann was interested. And so the *shidduch* came about with Tirza Bondi becoming his *rebbetzin* and homemaker the day after *Succos* on 24 *Tishrei*, 5617 (October 23, 1856).

Since Mainz was governed at the time by Napoleanic law, it became a necessary prerequisite for all individuals who moved there to take on a secular given name. That name had to be one that was commonly used or frequently found in the annals of secular world history. Accordingly, Rav Meir took on the German name of Markus on September 29, 1854. One of the guidelines used by German Jewry in choosing a non-Jewish given name was to use a secular one with the same initial as the Hebrew name.

---

c. Tehillim, 51:12.

IN EUROPE, IT WAS THE CUSTOM IN MANY CONGREGATIONS FOR the rabbi to wear special vestments while officiating. In Rav Meir's letter of acceptance for the Rabbinical position at Mainz, he wrote from Berlin that he wanted only "a small apartment with, if possible, a small garden". He also stipulated that he "not have to wear any special Rabbinical garment, ...since the *tallis* is the most beautiful attire for all Jews and that applies equally to rabbis."

Becoming rabbi of the Orthodox congregation in Mainz in the year 1856 became an uphill battle as the appointment was bitterly contested by the Reform congregants. The latter had the only certification in town for a Jewish house of worship. However, using his statesmanship, connections and talents, Horav Meir was able to finally have an officially recognized orthodox community. The *Israelitische Religions Gesellschaft* now became the forum for many celebrated causes. Their general impetus was to oppose the disintegration of the Orthodox community and to strengthen *Yiddishkeit*.

My great grandfather was a prototype in his time, who with brazen boldness jumped into the breach, scoured out by the tides of assimilation and secularization. He pursued his mission through creative writings, speeches, scholarly works and community leadership.

Horav Meir also opened up a Jewish school, which existed close to eighty years. The curriculum consisted of both *Limudei Kodesh* and secular studies.

Unfortunately, there were too many individuals whose sole goal was to destroy the Jewish religion from within. The assimilationists despised orthodoxy and wanted to estrange and alienate Jews from everything sacred. Eminent contemporary *rabbonim* assisted in confronting the assimilationists in this cause-celebre, these included Horav Yitschok Dov Bamburger of Wuerzburg, Horav Samson Raphael Hirsch, Dr. R. Adler and Horav Ezriel Hildesheimer.

DUE TO A CLANDESTINE CENSORSHIP MANY ARTICLES written by Horav Meir to strengthen *Yiddishkeit* never reached their intended readership. Therefore, in May, 1860, Horav Meir founded *Der Israelit*.[21] It was a weekly magazine-type publication that was mailed throughout Europe and even to America. The *Israelit* was edited by Horav Meir Lehmann until his passing in the year 1890. It was rightfully called, "A Central Voice for Orthodox Judaism" up to its demise in the year 1938. [4] In it were found *Divrei Torah* on the weekly *Sedrah* and Jewish news from local and foreign cities. In those years there were numerous small Jewish communities in the outlying farm country where there existed little, if any, formal Jewish education. I am told by my brother-in-law, Moses Schwab, originally from Darmstadt, Germany, that in some of these small communities, the *Dvar Torah* from the *Israelit* was read aloud in their *shuls* and then followed by a *Kaddish D'Rabbonon* (special prayer)!

In the year 1867, Horav Meir continued to utilize his literary talents *leshem Shomayim* by authoring historical novels with educational, Jewish and anti-assimilationist themes. These stories were then serialized in the *Israelit* one chapter at a time.

Frequently, he was stopped in the street by avid readers who wanted to know the sequel to a story and couldn't wait for the next chapter to be published. His standard response was, "I don't even know myself what will happen". These novels had settings in a variety of time frames spanning eighteen hundred years. The subjects included Rabbi Akivah the Tannah, Roman slavery, Rabbeinu Gershom, the Crusades, the Spanish Inquisition, a Jewish Pope, the period of the Protestant Reformation, the daughter of the Shach and many more. Each story became a classical historical novel, meticulously researched and based on *Medroshim, Chazal,* documents, etc. These sagas involve former Jewish leaders and heroes. Our repertoire of Judaic literature was certainly embellished by the addition of these classics. Their themes are spun into webs of intrigue and adventure, always complimented with accurate historical backgrounds. Readers, both young and old, are rewarded with profound and lasting impressions in *hashkofah*. Many a non-German speaking person studied the German language for the sole purpose of reading these literary works. The stories were subsequently translated into many languages including Hebrew, English, Yiddish, French, Spanish, Russian and more. Some stories were excerpted or abridged, which did not do them proper justice.

Following are the German language titles of Horav Meir Lehmann's historical novels and the year in which they appeared. Those which were translated to English have their titles shown in parenthesis.

1867 Rabbi Elchanan
 Des Koenigs Eidam —(Faith and Courage the Shach's daughter)
 Die Verlassene
1869 Das Licht der Diaspora
 Graf oder Jude — (Del Monte)

II. Jahres-Bericht.

I. Der Unterricht.

a. Tabellarische Uebersicht der Fächer und Lehrstunden.

1. Mädchen.

Klasse.	Religionslehre u. bibl. Geschichte.	Deutsche Sprache.	Französisch.	Englisch.	Hebräisch.	Geographie und Geschichte.	Mathematik.	Naturlehre und Naturgeschichte.	Zeichnen.	Schönschreiben.	Schriftl. gram. Uebungen.	Weibliche Arbeiten.	Gesang.	Insgesammt.
V.	2	5	—	—	6	—	5	—	—	4	3	4	—	29
IV.	2	4	4	—	4	2	4	—	2	2	1	5	2	32
III.	2	3	3	3	4	4	3	2	2*	2	—	6	2	36

2. Knaben.

Klasse.	Religionslehre u. bibl. Geschichte.	Deutsche Sprache.	Französisch.	Englisch.	Hebräisch.	Geographie und Geschichte.	Mathematik.	Handelswissenschaft.	Naturlehre und Naturgeschichte.	Zeichnen.	Schönschreiben.	Schriftl. gram. Uebungen.	Hebräisch Schreiben.	Gesang.	Insgesammt.
V.	2	5	3	—	6	—	5	—	—	—	2	3	2	—	28
IV.	2	4	4	—	6	2	3	—	—	—	2	3	2	1	29
III.	2	3	3	2	8	4	5	—	2	2	2	—	2	2	37
II.	2	3	4	2	9	4	6	2	2	2	3	—	2	2	44

Am französischen Unterrichte in der V. Klasse nimmt nur die erste Abtheilung Theil; dazu befähigte Schüler der II. Klasse genossen noch wöchentlich einen zehnstündigen Unterricht im Talmud; ebenso dazu befähigte Schüler der III. und IV. Klasse wöchentlich einen fünfstündigen Unterricht in demselben Gegenstande, so daß die Stundenzahl derselben sich auf 40 und 51 belief; sie waren nämlich theilweise dafür vom Hebräisch-Schreiben dispensirt.

Curriculum of Mainz's Orthodox elementary school for boys and girls, third, fourth and fifth grades for religious and secular subjects, September 1863.

1870	Bostanai — (Bostanai)
	Saeen und Ernten
1871	Zur rechten Zeit — (Just in Time)
1872	Suess Oppenheim
	Der Fuerst von Coucy — (The Count of Coucy)
1873	Die Familie y Aguilar — (The Family y Aguilar)
1876	Binjamin
1877	Der Koenigliche Resident — (The Royal Resident)
1878	Ester Chiera
1878-79-80	Rabbi Joselmann von Rosheim — (Rabbi Joselman of Rosheim, parts 1 and 2)
1880	Vor Hundert Jahren — (The Penknife)
	Zwei Schwestern — (Portrait of Two Families)
1881	Akiba — (Rabbi Akiba and His Times)
1882	Parthenope
	Der Sohn der Witwe
	Aus der Zeit der Reaktion
1883	Spurlos verschwunden
	Nur Standhaft
1886	Nechamah
1888	Ithamar — (Ithamar)

(Many descendants of Horav Meir had bound copies of the *Israelit*. Our father's set was lost during World War II. When my aunt, Tante Else moved in the 1970's from London, to Melbourne she offered me the *Israelit*, bound in annual volumes for the years 1860 to 1907. I readily and gladly accepted them and was proud of the honor to be the keeper of this family heirloom.)

Besides extensive international correspondence and his articles in the *Israelit*, Horav Meir also published in the year 5635 a *peirush* on the *Talmud Yerushalmi, Zeroim* [22] by Moreinu Horav Shlomo Sierielieoh, who was one of the *M'Gorshei Sforad* (Spanish Expulsion, 1492). To this commentary he added his own *peirush, "Meir Nesiv"*. The edition has on each page the *Talmud Yerushalmi* and both *perushim*.

Approbations *(Haskomos)* were given for the *peirush* by many great Rabbonim: Horav Meir Auerbach of Yerusholayim, Horav Avrohom Ashkenazi of Yerusholayim, Horav Yitzchok Elchonon, Horav Meir Leibush Malbim, Rabbi Ezriel Hildesheimer, Rabbi Reuven Cohen Rappaport, Rabbi Naftoli Zvi Yehudah Berlin and many more.

Title page from the Talmud Yerushalmi, Brochos [22] with the commentary Meir Nesiv

ALSO PUBLISHED WERE HIS *PEIRUSHIM* ON THE *HAGADAH Shel Pesach*[19] and *Pirkei Avos*.[18] The *peirush* on *Avos* included extensive historical background for each *Tannah* there, and some of the linkage thereof to his particular teachings in ethics. Unfortunately, Horav Meir Lehmann was unable to complete these two works, as he passed away in the middle of his efforts on 24 Nissan, 5650 at the age of 59. With the exception of the second half of the sixth chapter, the *peirush* on *Avos* was posthumously completed by his *mechutan,* Eliezer Liepman Prins, from Amsterdam.[2] The style of Eliezer Prins was such that it blended in with Horav Meir's work and provided a perfect continuity.

On the title page of the 1906 edition [19] of the *Lehmann Hagadah,* it states that the *peirush* was: *"beendet von dessen Mitarbeitern"* (completed by his (Rabbi M. Lehmann's) colleagues).

Subsequently, the *peirush* of the *Lehmann Hagadah* was significantly embellished. On the title page of the 1914 edition [20] it states: *"Zweite, durchgesehene und aus dem Nachlasse des Verfassers erweiterte Auslage"* (second edition, reviewed and expanded with writings from the Author's collection) It is assumed that Horav Meir Lehmann's son, Reb Osher Lehmann was instrumental in producing this revised and augmented edition.

Horav Meir Lehmann was very active in helping his fellow Jews in need. Especially close to his heart was the *Yishuv* in Eretz Yisroel. In the Founder's Hall of the famous Shaare Zedek Medical Center in Yerusholayim one can still find, over one hundred and twenty years later, the name of Rabbi Marcus Lehmann as one of the hospital's founders. The other contemporary founders inscribed on the same plaque are Rabbi Seligman Bamberger of Wuerzburg, Rabbi Samson R. Hirsch of Frankfurt am Main, Mr. Akiba Lehren of Amsterdam and Rabbi Anshel Stern of Hamburg.

HORAV MEIR LEHMANN'S WIFE, TIRZA (BONDI), WAS BORN ON 17 Kislev, 5589 (1828). She survived her husband and passed away on 22 Shevat, 5659 (1899). Her father, Shmuel Bondi of Mainz, descended from an illustrious family. In July 1966, Reiner Auman a descendant of the Bondi family, assembled and edited *The Family Bondi and their Ancestors*.[1] It describes a lineage which certainly is worthwhile studying. The family Bondi derives its name from *Buenos Dias,* which is Spanish for "good day" or *Yom Tov.*

XXV. Jahrgang.

Zweite Beilage zu Nr. 55 des Israelit.

Leitender Artikel.

Literarischer Bericht.

Ein lieber Gast ist der uns jährlich besuchende „Illustr. Jüd. Familien-Kalender" Herausgegeben von H. Meyer, Halberstadt. Abgesehen von dem schönen und sauber hergestellten Kalendarium, der מנהגי בתי הכנסת, Regententafel 2c. 2c. bietet das Büchlein noch so viel des Unterhaltenden und Wissenswerthen, daß es des ermäßigten Preises von 50 Pf. nicht bedurft hätte, ihm auch dieses Jahr einen Platz auf dem jüd. Familientisch zu sichern. Den Glanzpunkt des diesjährigen bildet eine reizend erzählte historische Novelle des geistig ewig jungen Verfassers des „Gabriel", S. Cohn, betitelt „Ein Anderes". Bis zum Schlusse derselben wird man in Spannung gehalten und auch die echt jüdische Tendenz, die bei so vielen anderen Schilderern jüdischen Lebens vermißt wird, findet hier beredten Ausdruck. Von einigen Arbeiten des gewandten jüd. Journalisten Ludw. A. Rosenthal seien hier erwähnt: „Lied des Kalenders," „Einfluß des Judenthums und seines Schriftthums auf die außerjüdische Kunst und Wissenschaft," „Lied des Kalenders," „Samuel Nagrela," „Romanzen" 2c. Als Titelblatt ziert den Kalender ein durch künstlerische Ausführung wie sauberen Druck sich gleich vortheilhaft auszeichnender Holzschnitt, darstellend das Portrait des berühmten Rabbi Dr. B. H. Auerbach ז"ל, Rabbiner der Synagogen-Gemeinde in Halberstadt, an welches Bild sich eine gut geschriebene Biographie des bedeutenden Mannes anschließt. Damit sich unsre Leser ein Urtheil über die Vorzüglichkeit der Meyer'schen Illustrationen bilden können, wurde uns von genanntem Verlag ein Bild des vorjährigen Kalenders zur Verfügung gestellt, das in dieser kurzen Besprechung nicht Abdruck bringen. Es ist das Brustbild des weit über die Grenzen Deutschlands gekannten Rabbiner Samson Raphael Hirsch, des Nestors der deutsch-jüd. Orthodoxie. Auf das Wirken dieses Mannes näher einzugehen, ist in dieser kurzen Besprechung nicht der Ort. Sein Leben und Thaten ist auch zur Genüge bekannt.*) Mit einem Anhang gemeinnütziger Mittheilungen schließt das Jahrbuch, dem wir eine recht große Verbreitung wünschen.

Ө

Samson Raphael Hirsch,
Rabbiner der israel. Religions-Gesellschaft zu Frankfurt a. M.
(Illustrationsprobe aus „Illustrirter Jüd. Familienkalender" pro 5644 von Julius Meyer,
Verlag von H. Meyer's Buchdruckerei, Halberstadt.)

*) Samson Raphael Hirsch wurde im Jahre 1808 in Hamburg geboren, bezog später die Jeschibah zu Mannheim und machte in Bonn seine Universitätsstudien. 1830 wurde er zum Großherzogl. Oldenburgischen Land-Rabbiner ernannt, eine Stelle, die er einige Jahre nachher mit der eines Königl. Hannover'schen Land-Rabbiners zu Emden vertauschte. 1845 wurde er als Kaiserl. Oesterreichischer Ober-Rabbiner von Mähren nach Nicolsburg berufen, von wo er 1851 nach Frankfurt übersiedelte, um daselbst das Rabbinat der soeben in's Leben gerufenen Israelitischen Religions-Gesellschaft orthodoxer Richtung zu übernehmen. Möge der um das Judenthum hochverdiente Mann noch eine lange Reihe von Jahren segensreich wirken!

A bust portrait of Horav Samson Raphael Hirsch (1808-1888) in the literary column of the Israelit, Reprinted from the Israelit, [21] July 1884.

The Bondi family can trace their ancestry all the way back to Rabbi Shlomo Yitzchaki, more commonly referred to as Rashi (1040-1105), the leading commentator on *Tenach* and the *Talmud*. He was born in the French city of Troyes and later studied in the German *Yeshivos* of Mainz and Worms.

Rabbi Shmuel Bondi was extremely correct and devout. Thanks to him and two *chaverim,* the Jewish tradition of the city of Mainz was rescued from oblivion, following the Reform movement's taking hold of a large segment of that community. Part of his normal routine during the course of a year was to fast every Monday and Thursday. At the age of seventeen years, he performed his first *bris*. After thousands of *bris milos* and sixty-seven years later, he performed his last *bris* just twelve days prior to departing from this world. He completed his last *bris* with "unflinching strength, speed and skill". On *Yom Tov* he only talked in *Loshon Hakodesh* (Hebrew or literally "Sacred Language") at the family table so that no profane words should spoil the festive atmosphere. During his last thirty years, he dedicated his time exclusively to the study of *Torah* and the performance of *mitzvos* from the 'crack of dawn until close to midnight'. His brother, Horav Teveleh Bondi of Frankfurt am Main, wrote a commentary on the *Pesach Hagadah,* which was published in the year 5658.[5] [Eighty-nine years later, George Auman of Brooklyn, a descendant of the Bondi family, made a Bondi *Hagadah* available so we could reprint it for the occasion of the *chassenah* of our children Yocheved and Yitzchok Jacobs.]

Shmuel Bondi never *paskened sha'alos,* even in his own home. However, in later years, he obtained *Hatoras Haroa* (accredited to adjudicate whether meat is kosher) from Rabbi Dr. Auerbach in Darmstadt and Rabbi Dr. Bamberger of Worms. This occurred after the Conservative board of directors of Mainz deposed the Orthodox Rav, Rabbi Loeb Ellinger. In the year 5635 (1875), Rabbi Shmuel Bondi published the sefer, *"Torei Zohov"*.[3] It contained writings of both his grandfather, Horav Herz Naftali Scheuer, as well as his own.

Torei Zohov [3] *title page, published by Horav Shmuel Bondi*

Hachover Osher & Toni Lehmann

OUR GRANDFATHER REB OSHER LEHMANN FOLLOWED IN the ways of his father. He was born on 3 Tamuz, 5618 (1858) in Mainz where he lived most of his life. In the year 1885, our grandfather married Toni Rabinowitz of Bobrujsk, Russia who became his *Eishes Chayil* and lifelong partner. Grandfather passed away in Mainz on 25 Tishrei, 5689 (1928). He was involved with the local Jewish school, was president of the Mainz Book Publishers' Guild and continued publishing the weekly *Israelit*. [21] According to Mordechai Breuer, "He strove to give the paper a less petit-bourgeois appearance by bringing in numerous book reviews, artistic and other supplements. He also paid more attention to the propagation of Torah study and Jewish knowledge…". [4] In the year 1906, the *Israelit* was sold and the editorial offices were relocated to Frankfurt am Main. Our grandfather also authored several historical novels written in a style similar to that of his father. One was titled, *Shmuel HaNagid*. Another, which depicts Moshe Rabeinu as he grew up, was titled *Die Leiden des jungen Mose*. Information for both books was carefully researched.

Reb Osher Lehmann's life was not as tranquil as he had hoped it to be. The Franco-Prussian War took place in the 1870's. World War I, with all its hardships, broke out in 1914. His three sons were drafted into the Kaiser's Imperial army and served on both the eastern and western fronts. Later in the 1920's, he lived through a period of hyper-inflation, when ordinary German postage stamps had denominations of several million Marks. His wife predeceased him by three years. Despite all hardships, he

Mazeivos of Hachover Osher and Toni Lehmann, Mainz, Germany

remained a well-liked leader in his community and, with the help of his dear wife, Toni (Chaya Toiva), raised a worthy family of six children.

On our grandfather's *matzeivah* it is stated that the Chover, Reb Osher, *Zatsal,* was a wise and respected elder (of the Orthodox Community), eminent in his knowledge of Torah and in his fear of Heaven. He was the spiritual heir to his father, Horav *HaGoan* Reb Meir Lehmann *Zatsal...* He disseminated *Torah* and wisdom to many, was modest in all his dealings, respected Hashem by his liberal contributions to worthy causes as well as by leading a devout lifestyle. He revered his Creator and held Him in great awe.

THE JEWISH COMMUNITY OF FRANKFURT AM MAIN WAS internationally renowned for its reputable and knowledgeable medical practitioners. Obstetrics in Bobrujsk and elsewhere in Russia and

Poland was still very crude. To assure a safe childbirth, our great grandmother, Tzipora Chana Mindel, traveled some one thousand miles to the west so that Toni Rabinowitz, our grandmother could be born in Frankfurt am Main. This major trip involving a combination of trains and boats was taken in the year 1869 and must have taken at least one week, assuming an average speed of twenty MPH plus various overnight rest stops along circuitous routes.

Regarding our grandmother, Toni Rabinowitz, I know very little. Judging, however, by her children, most of whom I knew well, she must have been an exceptional person with aristocratic qualities and tendencies. Our grandparents, the Lehmanns, imbued their six children with honesty, integrity, love for family and the Jewish people, plus many other exceptional qualities and character traits.

Toni Rabinowitz was born on 1 Iyar 5629 (1869) in Frankfurt am Main but was raised in Bobrujsk, Russia. She passed away on 1 Iyar, 5686 (1926) and is buried next to her husband in Mainz. Her date of birth and departure coincide. She lived her last year therefore completely and fully, thereby giving testimony of her exceptional piety.[a] On her *matzeivah* it is inscribed that she was from the *"Gezah of"* (descendant of) both the Tosafos Yom Tov and the Noda BeYehudah. In addition, it describes her as having been devout, modest, pleasant, full of grace, intelligent and caring for the sick and poor. To me it seems that she must have been the family queen in her generation.

THE CITY OF MAINZ HAS TWO JEWISH *BOTEI OLAM*. BOTH were spared destruction during World War II. Part of the explanation to this respect and consideration on the part of the Germans might be that this section of the country is known as the "Bible Belt" and, therefore, there was less atheism as compared to most of Germany (eighty percent). This does not, however, mean that local Jews or their property were spared from deportation, murder and destruction. A second explanation, possibly more plausible, is that Adolf Hitler, *Y.S.*, wanted to establish Jewish museums, so that after his proposed "final solution" by genocide would be implemented, there would remain extensive evidence of his "achievement". These *Botei Olam* are being maintained by the post-war government of Germany and are in excellent condition. The office of the Mainz Jewish community maintains an index card for every individual buried in the new *Beis Olam*. Horav Meir Lehmann and his wife Tirza are buried in Section II, row five, number ten and number

---

a. *Maseches Kiddushin*, 38a.

eleven respectively. Reb Osher Lehmann and his wife Toni are buried in Section IX, row seven, numbers one and two respectively. None of their four *matzeivos* contain a single non-Hebrew letter or number. It should be realized that the "new" *Beis Olam* is already several hundred years in use. The "old" *Beis Olam* dates back well over one thousand years and is the final resting place of both Rabbeinu Gershom and Horav Amnon.

Rabbeinu Gershom ben Yehudah (960-1028 C.E.) was *Rosh HaYeshivah* in Mainz and the teacher of Rashi's teacher. Years later, Rashi described this luminary as the one "who enlightened the eyes of the exile". Henceforth, Rabbeinu Gershom was known as the *"Me'or HaGoloh"* or "the Light of the Exile".

Horav Amnon was probably a contemporary of Rabbeinu Gershom. Three days after his untimely demise, he appeared in a dream to Rabbi Klonimos ben Meshullam, a worthy Talmudic and Kabbalistic scholar of Mainz, and taught him the text of the *Unesaneh Tokef*.[b] Rav Amnon's legendary demise inspired many to martyrdom during the grim days of the Crusades.

---

b. *Ohr Zoruah*

Chaim Boaz & Tzipora Chana Mindel Rabinowitz

ZISLA MERETSKI (RABINOWITZ) WAS THE YOUNGER SISTER of our grandmother Toni Lehmann. In her brief German language memoirs she provides some interesting insights regarding the Rabinowitz branch of our family. [25b]

The family lived in the town of Bobrujsk, Russia, which is approximately sixty miles or one hundred kilometers southeast of the city of Minsk and two hundred and ten miles southeast of Vilna (Vilnius). Family memories indicate that the Rabinowitz's were established in that location from at least the turn of the nineteenth century. They continued to reside in Bobrujsk until after the infamous and devastating Russian revolution of 1917. While Jews were oppressed under most of the Russian Czarists regimes, Lenin's communist revolution of 1917 visited mass destruction on Jewish religious practices in the new Soviet Union. The result was that most of the generations born and raised subsequent to that revolution knew and practiced almost no *Torah* and *Mitzvos*. It was one of the major Jewish tragedies of the twentieth century.

IN THE YEAR 1847, BOAZ WAS BORN TO YITZCHOK AND REBECCA Rabinowitz. Rebecca came from the famous town of Rogatschow. Boaz was renamed Chaim Boaz following a serious illness. Shortly prior to his eighteenth birthday, he married Tzipora Chana Mindel, the daughter of Yehudah Landau. Her family came from Brody (Galicia) and they were direct descendants of Rabbi Yecheskel Landau, also known as the Nodah BeYehudah. Horav HaGoan Yecheskel Landau lived until 17 Iyar, 5553 (1793).

One of the Rabinowitz family traditions was to annually kindle a *yahrzeit* light on 6 Elul for Rabbi Yom Tov Lipmann Heller (1579-1654), also known as the Tosefos Yom Tov, an ancestor of the family, who passed away in the year 5414.

Needless to say, the Rabinowitz family made *Torah* and appropriate secular knowledge a high priority in the education of their children. For this purpose they hired highly qualified *Talmidei Chachomim* and *Yorei Shomayim* from Holland and Germany to lodge with the family and tutor their children. To facilitate the studying, the house had a large fully stocked library. Secular subjects such as the sciences and foreign languages were studied by attending local non-Jewish schools. Our grandfather, Reb Osher Lehmann, was one of those who taught the Rabinowitz children. Thus, in the *zechus* of *Torah,* the *Ribono Shel Olam* caused two fine families one thousand miles apart but with similar lofty aspirations to meet and create an everlasting bond.

Chaim Boaz was a non-conformist with progressive views in the positive sense. Universal education, as we know it today, had not yet arrived in eastern Europe. On a formal basis, Jewish education for boys was usually provided up until the age of eleven. This age was sometimes extended to fourteen in the case where the boy was exceptionally gifted. For girls, such formal religious education was totally non-existent until years later, when in the year 1917, Soro Schenierer appeared on the academic arena and founded the successful Bais Yaakov movement in the City of Krakow, Poland.

CHAIM BOAZ RABINOWITZ'S FATHER WAS GRANTED THE monopoly for the production of brandy from the local government of Minsk. Subsequently, with the help of his father, Chaim Boaz became well established in the lumber business and used the local forests as his source of timber.

With the lumber enterprise prospering, Chaim Boaz acquired a bank and was even said to have been appointed as honorary Consul of Persia. He was a very devout Jew and extremely knowledgeable in matters involving the world's current events. The poor, as well as the Jewish soldiers in Bobrujsk, found Chaim Boaz to be very philanthropic.

Every *Pesach,* he distributed *Pesach* meals twice daily to Jewish soldiers who had been disciplined in and heedful of their observance of

Jewish traditions and laws. He maintained a *yeshivah* in his house for twelve young men, which included room and board, and also maintained a home that was entirely dedicated for the use of the elderly and handicapped. The latter housed twelve men and twelve women, all of whom were provided with all their needs, including medical attention.

At the marriages of their children, Chaim Boaz and his wife did not forget the poor. Six hundred poor persons were invited to the wedding of our grandmother Toni, and were fully served by family members. Family members were also requested to regularly visit the old age home, to inquire about the welfare of the elderly and address any possible complaints.

In honor of the marriage of our grandparents, Reb Osher Lehmann and Toni, Chaim Boaz and his wife presented the young couple with a beautiful *menorah* and a pair of *Shabbos* candlesticks. [This *Menorah* was used by our grandfather and Father. Presently, it is used by myself. Occasional offers or suggestions to sell this *menorah,* of course, fall on deaf ears. Family Judaica should, in my opinion, not be equated with profit and belongs in the home and not in a museum. The candlesticks are used by my sister Toni.]

In a part of Europe where the havenots far outnumbered the haves, it is a fascinating testament to the determination of Chaim Boaz and his wife Tzipora to have dedicated so large a segment of their material resources towards the family's and community's Jewish welfare. This family of mavericks shone out as bright stars in the dark morass of the Russian spiritual and material poverty. Their efforts were truly a *Kiddush Hashem.*

IN THE YEAR 1903, CHAIM BOAZ PASSED AWAY. ON OUR GRANDmother's *matzeivah,* he is referred to as *Moreinu Horav.* Following the passing of Chaim Boaz, dark clouds drifted over Russia. First, Russia lost the naval war with Japan in connection with Port Arthur. Then came World War I, in which Russia and Germany were bitter foes. This was followed immediately by the Communist Revolution in the year 1917. During that revolution privately owned property in Bobrujsk was confiscated. All three sons of Chaim Boaz remained in Russia. Their daughter, Zisla lost contact with her brothers in the year 1934. They were not heard from again. In later years our great aunt, Tante Zisla, lived in Nahariya. Her children and grandchildren all settled in Eretz Yisroel.

Bobrujsk, at the end of the nineteenth century had a population of several hundred thousand persons. It was strategically located near

...וראה בטוב ירושלים...
Beis Hamedrash at the Home for the Aged, Sholom Ho'Oretz Yerusholayim
Reprinted from the Israelit, [21] July 1895

international borders of that time and was considered a garrison town. Rabbi Chaim Mordechai Wainkrantz, who learned in the pre-World War II Beth Joseph *Yeshivah* in Bialystok (Lithuanian Poland) and with whom I have had a regular *Shiur* now for some forty years, indicated that Bobrujsk had an excellent reputation in the Orthodox Jewish world. He stated that, in his time, there was even a student from Bobrujsk studying at the Bialystok *Yeshivah.*

[In October of 1993, I met, with Hashem's *hashgochah,* a very old, Yiddish speaking, Russian man in Brooklyn at the same time that I had finished writing about the family Rabinowitz. When I inquired from which city he hailed in Russia, I couldn't believe what I heard! He was from the city of Bobrujsk! He then told me that there is a large Jewish *Beis Olam* attached to the town. A second cemetery is used by both Jews and non-Jews. Both places of burial survived the revolution and World War II. The city itself, however, sustained considerable damage during the war.]

Hirsch & Johana Oppenheimer

Maternal Forebears

FROM OUR MOTHER'S SIDE, THERE IS MUCH LESS AVAILABLE information regarding former generations. Our mother's maternal great-grandfather was Hirsch Oppenheimer, born on 11 Tamuz, 5565 (1805) in Gronau, in the Kingdom of Westfalen, Prussia (Germany). He passed away on 30 Shevat, 5644 (1884) in Hannover, Germany. A short biography [27] written by his youngest son, Levy (Louis) Oppenheimer, describes him as an energetic person who was a Jew with a capital "J". He was meticulous in keeping the *Torah* and its *Mitzvos* and practiced what he preached.

Hyronimus Napoleon decreed that all Jews must take family names rather than being called the son of their father. In this way, the three sons of our *pater familias*, Israel Oppenheimer (1778-1813) became Levi Steinberg, Samson Rothschild and Hirsch Oppenheimer.

Following completion of his schooling at an out of town *Yeshivah*, Hirsch returned to his mother and stepfather to celebrate his *bar mitzvah* and start in the business world. His father had died in an accident as a young man while crossing a local river by horse. The river was frozen and the treacherously thin ice was snow covered. The day after his *bar mitzvah*, Hirsch was given one *thaler* (dollar) by his stepfather "to start earning a livelihood!" Hashem gave him a *brocho* and that *thaler* soon became two. In several years, he was able to open a local general store. Because of his honesty, modesty and energy, everybody was eager to do business with him. When the city of Hamburg had a large fire, Hirsch was the only person who was willing to start a viable salvage operation. His enterprising game plan and bid were accepted by the Hamburg municipality, and this was the start and basis of his fortune. Hirsch met Johana Enoch from Celle, near Hannover (Celle is very close to Bergen Belsen) and they were married in the year 1834. Medical standards and knowledge were extremely limited. With Hirsch's strenuous schedule, both in business and for the community at large, his health failed him. Whatever he tried, from spending time at a spa to medicine, was to no avail. He then made a *neder* and vowed to become a *mohel* as soon as his health was restored. This promise he fulfilled. He performed his first *bris* at the age of twenty-five.

THE TOWNS OF THAT ERA HAD SMALL POPULATIONS, WERE FAR apart and the roads between were rough, narrow and unpaved. Communication was either by telegraph — using the Morse code — or by mail. The railroads, if they existed, were slow, and many times Hirsch had to travel by horse with or without coach. Despite all these handicaps, Hirsch was able to perform nineteen hundred and fourteen *bris milos,* over a span of more than fifty years, no small feat for those days.

As a *mohel,* Reb Hirsch experienced some strange scenarios. On one occasion, his cousin from Lemford sent a telegram, which read *"Mazel Tov* on the birth of a boy, *bris mechabed* to you" i.e. the honor of performing the circumcision is accorded to you. After traveling for two days on horseback, Reb Hirsch arrived and received a warm welcome. But when it came time to examine the newborn, it turned out to be a girl! His cousin hadn't seen him for so long and this was the only way to prompt a visit.

Another interesting situation took place some years later. Reb Hirsch arrived at a small town to be the *mohel.* Upon examination, he determined that the baby was not considered fit to be *mahled* (circumcised). In spite of repeated statements from the local doctor that the child was healthy and strong enough to be circumcised, the *mohel* departed without performing the *bris.* While still en route, a telegram arrived stating, "child died suddenly". Reb Hirsch was content in having diagnosed the baby's health properly and relieved for not having acquiesced to the doctor's wishes, though saddened of the infant's death.

Meanwhile, the Oppenheimers moved thirty miles to the north, from Gronau to Hannover. There, they had many friends and admirers.

Two golden bris miloh cups presented in 1873 to Hirsch Oppenheimer on performing his one thousandth bris

On January 4, 1873, Reb Hirsch performed his thousandth *bris*. To celebrate that major achievement, the local community presented him with two golden bris *miloh* cups. One was inscribed *"kos shel m'tzitza"* and the other *"kos shel b'rachah"*. Each cup measures six inches (15.2 cm) in height. [Recently (1994), these cups were on display in the Bar Ilan Jewish Museum near Tel Aviv. The cups are presently the property of the Dr. Floersheim family residing in Zurich, Switzerland.]

As an additional act of appreciation, the Jews of Hannover established a fund in his honor with the huge endowment of five thousand five hundred thalers. (To place this amount in the right perspective, I checked the "help wanted ads" in the *Israelit* of the year 1873. There, I found that the Jewish community of Luebeck, Germany was willing to pay an annual salary of five hundred thalers for an excellent *shochet* who must also be an experienced educator to teach at their *yeshivah*.) The principle of the Hannover *Gemach* fund (Relief fund) was not to be touched. Only the interest was to be used to underwrite assistance for needy new mothers, to provide for *bris milos* and to teach and train new *Mohelim*. In western Europe, it was the custom to celebrate *simchos (semachot)* by giving *tzedoko* (charity) in lieu of or in addition to lavish parties. It was also customary to give contributions to worthy causes during *aveilus* and at a *yahrzeit*. Our family made it a special matter to contribute towards this foundation. And so it was that in a few short years, the funding had reached twenty-five thousand *thalers*.

JOHANA WAS A HELPFUL AND HAPPY HOMEMAKER AND WIFE. She assisted her husband and backed him up through thick and thin. It was a long and happy marriage. In the year 1870, the Franco Prussian war broke out between France and Germany and, with the strain of war and stress of a recent illness, Johana occasionally went out of town for recuperation. On Friday, March 25, 1870, Reb Hirsch went out of town for a *Shabbos bris*. When he returned on Sunday by train, his oldest son, Yisroel, walked into his train coupe at a distant train station. His Father asked in astonishment, "Where are you heading?" "To Hannover," the son responded. Reb Hirsch said immediately, "You don't have to tell me. I dreamed Mother passed away yesterday. She was brought from the dining room to the bedroom. I saw it all clearly." This is the way it actually had occurred.

ON THE DAY BEFORE HIS DEATH, REB HIRSCH HAD TO request another *mohel* to substitute for him. Even though his hands were still steady, he felt ill. That evening, he summoned his youngest son to his bedroom. The father said, "I feel my death is approaching, please go and settle my accounts with the *chevrah* and with the relief committee, bring the credit books up to date and place them in order. Then bring paper and ink." After several items were dictated, Reb Hirsch said, "Call all the children and grandchildren, I want to *bench* them all." This, too, was done. One daughter-in-law, Shifra (Sophie), my great grandmother, was out of town visiting her father in Hamburg. Reb Hirsch requested that a telegram be dispatched for her to return home at once. He then placed his hands on each person individually and *benched* everyone.

His four sons got special admonitions, especially: "to keep in good standing their father's excellent reputation which had taken much effort to acquire, to be honest in business and to remain good Jews." (in that order)

The rationale for the sequence of these three demands eluded me for a long time. From an ethical viewpoint, I would have arranged the order so that the second or third admonition would be first, and the first would then be in the third position. Reb Hirsch was a learned person and extremely devoted to the ways of our *Torah*. Therefore, a deeper meaning was obviously involved. I offer the following explanation:

A portion of the Sifra's introduction is recited daily, prior to *shacharis*.[a.] There, we note that Rabbi Yishmoel taught, in the sixth of his thirteen hermeneutic rules for studying *Torah,* that:

> *(klal, prat uklal)* When three categories are listed and the first and the third of these are general statements, but the middle (sandwiched) item is a specific stipulation, then we are limited to infer from the two general statements only to what is similar in them with respect to the specific stipulation.

To apply this rule to the above admonishments, Reb Hirsch left to his sons and to posterity the important *Halochoh Lema'aseh,* that in order to maintain an excellent (business) reputation (item a) and to remain a good Jew (item c), requires that the practice of a proper and honest business acumen (item b) be upheld. In other words, one cannot maintain a good

---

a. *Bereisah d'Rabbi Yishmoel*

reputation and be a good Jew at heart while simultaneously indulging in improprieties in one's business dealings. Deception in business conduct reflects lack of faith in Hashem, our Provider. Ultimately, this demeanor may lead to profaning His Name. This cryptic and noble lesson from Reb Hirsch encompasses the cardinal goal of sanctifying Hashem's Name.

It is my belief and conviction that universal implementation by our people of Reb Hirsch's lofty last will "…will cause the Jewish people to become a living testimonial to Divine sovereignty among all the peoples of the earth."[b]

Reb Hirsch rested till the evening, but then became restless in anticipation of his daughter-in-law's return. When she finally arrived, he put his hands on her head as well and *benched* her. He then said, "this is the last". His pure *neshomo* departed an hour later. He had instructed his children on every last detail including the text on his stone and who should drive the hearse to the *Beis Olam* — "He drove me while I was alive, he should also drive my hearse…

---

b. Refer to commentary in the Rav Samson Raphael Hirsch *siddur* in the section prior to *Shacharis*.

David & Emma Wallerstein

LITTLE IS KNOWN TO ME REGARDING MY GREAT GRANDFATHER, Shmuel (Semmi) Oppenheimer. My aunt, Tante Alice, the family historian constantly updated the records of our branch of the Oppenheimer family tree. From her meticulous records [23] I was able to glean the following key dates. Shmuel Oppenheimer was born in Gronau in the year 1844 and passed away in Hannover in the year 1899. In 1870, he married our great grandmother, Shifra (Sophie) Blumenthal, who lived from 1849 to 1928. Emma Oppenheimer (our grandmother) was the third of eight children. She was born in Hannover on 13 Adar II, 5635 (1875) and passed away in our house in Amsterdam on 29 Adar, 5702 (1942). Our grandmother was married in Frankfurt am Main in 1896 with *"Grootvader"* David Wallerstein, who was born in Frankfurt am Main on 25 Iyar, 5622 (1862). He passed away in Amsterdam, 20 Tamuz, 5694 (1934), five days before my first birthday.

RECENTLY, DURING *SUCCOS* OF 5754, WE VISITED A GOOD FAMILY friend, Mrs. Rosa Onderwyzer. Her father-in-law was the well known Chief Rabbi of the Province of Noord Holland in the Netherlands during the period of 1917-1934. Her father was Rabbi Dunner, who was our Rav in the Gerard Dou Straat *shul*. Mrs. Onderwyzer was a native of Cologne, Germany, lived many years in Amsterdam, subsequently resided in New York and is today retired in Yerusholayim. One of our favorite pastime topics of discussion is the subject of our grandchildren, especially their progress in character development. To this end, we always bring along recent photographs and amazingly, Mrs. Onderwyzer,

Mazeivos of my grandparents David and Emma Wallerstein in Amsterdam (Old field B 36, 57 Diemen) Holland. The author standing in the rear, July 1988.

even though she never met most of them, is consistently accurate in describing each child's individual traits. This *Succos* we also asked her what she remembered of the Wallersteins in Frankfurt am Main. She answered that the Wallersteins were known for their high standards of Jewish quality and for their good character. We accepted her memories as they came from a person whom we have personally seen to be an excellent judge of personality and character traits. Our grandparent's pious qualities, suitably spiced with Jewish etiquette were not achieved through casual habits but rather by serious daily application of lofty principles espoused by the devout segment of their Frankfurt am Main community.

I find it interesting that most of the Wallerstein's children and grandchildren went into professional types of livelihoods; very few were in retail or wholesale businesses.

Two "Lehmanns", Two "Tirzas"
Explanation — End of a Namesake

MY MATERNAL GREAT GRANDMOTHER, THE WIFE OF JACOB Wallerstein, was named *Tirza Wallerstein*. Mother's sister, my aunt, Tante Resi *(Tirza Wallerstein)* Lehmann, was named after her grandmother, *Tirza Wallerstein*. (Note: Her husband came from a small town near the city of Karlsruhe, Germany and was no relation to our Lehmann family from Mainz, Germany i.e. two sisters married two unrelated Lehmanns.)

Remarkably, my maternal great grandmother *Tirza Wallerstein* and my aunt Tante Resi were both widowed at a very young age. Subsequent research of family records, by my cousin Naftali Levi, revealed that my great-grandmother *Tirza Wallerstein,* was named after her grandmother who had also lost her husband at a young age. Thus, my aunt, Tante Resi was the third of three alternate, direct lineage generations where each *Tirza Wallerstein* had become a widow at a young age. For these reasons my aunt told her children that she does not want any of her descendants to be her namesake. My sister Tirza (Connie) Rubinstein of Yerusholayim, our daughter, Tirza Goldschmidt of Zurich, Switzerland and our granddaughter, Tirza Kassai of Brooklyn, New York were each named after Tirza (Bondi) Lehmann, my paternal great-grandmother. May they all emulate that tzadekes' deeds and be *Ma'arich Yomim Veshonim* along with their respective husbands and husband to be.

Continuum Ad Infinitum

"P ROPERLY WEIGH YOUR PLANS, AND ALL YOUR WAYS WILL BE FIRMLY ESTABLISHED".[a]

From my recent ancestry, I came to various observations. The great material wealth possessed by both the Rabinowitz and Oppenheimer families did not last. It could be generalized that seldom does inherited material wealth last more than four or five generations. One to three generations is more of the norm.

In contrast, non-material wealth does perpetuate, provided each generation renews its lofty commitment and efforts. The descendants of the Rabinowitz and Oppenheimer families, who chose to continue in the devout ways of their forebears, certainly benefitted from their sacred heritage as passed on by these predecessors and countless other less affluent ancestors. It is therefore logical to place far greater emphasis in allotting time and energies toward promoting and propagating non-material legacies to our descendants, as that endures and provides a superior meaning and quality to life.

A MASSING EXCESSIVE PERSONAL WEALTH DOES NOT necessarily assure survival. All too often, the initial rationalization for being preoccupied in the pursuit of wealth is to justify obtaining creature comfort for oneself and for generations to come, i.e. it is the means to the end. Those good intentions are all too frequently lost. Entering the

---

a. Mishlei, 4:26.

wealth accrual mode unfortunately then becomes "the end" and no longer "the means".

Fostering survival of the generations is addressed by *Chazal,* who obligate a parent towards his child(ren) "to teach them *Torah* (so they can live a Torah style Jewish life); to help them get married (to a worthy partner, who will assist in living a Torah type life); to teach them a useful profession or trade (that will allow ample time for *limudei kodesh* and its implementation,[b] and to assure that they know how to swim (to survive water accidents)".[c] Survival from the cradle to the grave requires dedication of all phases of human existence to life's common denominator — the *Torah.*

Thus, to consecrate the mundane requires that it be subservient to the non-material. Throughout history, various civilizations and cultures have dawned and waned. Our sanctified *Torah*-oriented culture is the exception and is the prototype of a prime civilized society that defied the forces of obsolescence. With Divine assistance it survived, despite the onslaught of affluence, poverty, plagues, emancipation, assimilation, scientific and technological advancements, persecutions, wars, famines and revolutions.

---

b. *Maseches Brochos,* 35b.
c. Maseches Kiddushin, 29a.

Appendix C:

The "Chover" or "Hachover" Title:

NON-RABBINIC LIFETIME TITLES OF ESTEEM WERE NOT easy to come by. Several such titles that were sparingly bestowed by the Orthodox community included *Chover, Moreinu* and *Parness*.

We find in *Chazal* that a person known as a *Chover* is considered trustworthy and could be relied upon to implement his obligations without delay, especially regarding matters of *Taharos, Terumos* and *Ma'aseros*.

A person takes on the obligation of a *Chover* and becomes a *Chover* in the presence of three *Chaverim* of equal or higher stature.

The wife of a *Chover* is considered as reliable as the *Chover*. Should the latter pass away, then the wife and the members of his family retain their trustworthy status until there is reason to consider otherwise.[a]

---
a. For a full discussion refer to *Maseches Bechoros,* 30b, *Rambam Hilchos Ma'aser Perek* 10, etc.)

The concept of the *Chover* title was exhumed and adapted in recent generations by the West European *Ashkenazic Kehillos* so as to show recognition for an individual's scholarship, community service and other noteworthy religious reasons. However, the title was only conferred on persons fully observant and trustworthy.

The qualifications required for receiving this honorable and highly valued title of distinction varied with the era and with the standards of the community where it was presented. In contemporary times, the determination of title eligibility was made by the *Morah D'Asrah,* and formal bestowals were made by incorporating the title in a *kesuvah* prior to one's *chassenah* or at special personal or *kehilloh* anniversaries, functions, etc.

Having a *Chover* title implies belonging to the elite of the observant in the Orthodox Jewish community. It is almost a prerequisite to the *"Moreinu"* title that was bestowed by *rabbonim* on exceptional *talmidei chachomim* who were married, had high ethical standards and were beyond reproach in all their conduct. One opportunity for the use of these titles is on the occasion of being called up to the *Torah.*

Section Six

...AND A TIME TO DESTROY...
(KOHELES 3,6)

Appendix D:
B-17 Flying Fortress Bombers Described

IN 1989, THE WELL KNOWN PUBLISHER MCGRAW HILL INC. printed a book [26] which describes many of the B-17 characteristics in vivid detail and the difficulties of flying these bombers in combat over occupied Europe and Germany. Various personal accounts provide many particulars of the Axis powers' nemesis, i.e. the Allies' Eighth Air Force, which, with their heroic crews and supporting groups, were instrumental in breaking the *Luftwaffe's* back by April, 1944.

The B-17 bomber was an American designed and manufactured product. It came into being only thirty-nine years after the Wright brothers flew the world's first successful, heavier than air, powered flying machine for a distance of one hundred and twenty feet at Kitty Hawk, North Carolina. The B-17 plane incorporated all the latest technologies known by the year 1942.

The bomber had a 75 foot (23 meters) long fuselage and a 104 foot (31.70 meters) wingspan. There were four propeller driven engines mounted on its wings. Traveling at two hundred MPH, the range of these

"Flying Fortresses" in the early war years of 1942 was twelve hundred miles. This enormous distance made striking of targets deep within Germany's heartland a reality. Cruising altitude was twenty-five thousand to twenty-seven thousand feet (7,600 to 8,200 meters), which enabled these planes to avoid most ground anti-aircraft fire, as that became inaccurate at high elevations. The B-17 had six unique plexiglass bubbles for the gunners. Gunmounts were located at the bombers' front, rear, top, bottom and on both sides. Each of these positions was manned by a gunner operating two 0.50 caliber machine guns to shoot down or ward off enemy fighter planes. These six gunners joined the pilot, copilot, bombardier and radioman as the "eyes and ears of the plane", since these planes usually traveled under "radio silence".

IT MUST BE NOTED THAT BOMBERS LEAVING ENGLAND WERE accompanied by Allied fighter planes for a very limited distance toward their mission targets, due to a highly restricted fighter plane range. Following removal of that "protective fighter plane umbrella", the bombers had to fend for themselves. Bomber ordnance included four thousand pounds of bombs. Depending on the targets, these bombs weighed from one hundred to two thousand pounds each. Machine gun ammunition for the entire plane consisted of fourteen thousand rounds. On some of the more hazardous and difficult assignments, this ammunition was entirely spent upon the bombers' return to their home base. Fighter escorts consisted mostly of the British Spitfire or the American Mustang P-47, P-49 or P-51 one or two engined planes which had speeds of up to 350 MPH.

Accuracy of bombing was enhanced by the visual Nordon Bomb Sight and the electronic Radar Scope, which took into account the plane's height above target and its air to ground speed. In general, the bombing missions were conducted both in broad daylight and at night.

Massive bombing raids on enemy targets commenced in August of 1943 and involved as many as two hundred and fifty to three hundred B-17s per target city or factory complex. The number of bombers and frequency of missions increased steadily as more planes and personnel became available. For example, on February 24, 1945 there was a coordinated American and British bombing effort against numerous German aircraft manufacturing plants and other important industrial installations. It was one of the severest bombing raids the world had ever witnessed and involved eight hundred and nine bombers escorted by seven hundred and sixty-seven fighter planes! This followed raids of similar magnitudes on February 21 and 22.

To have assembled such a formidable number of planes, despite unfortunate losses on numerous past missions, says much about the U.S. and British war efforts in manufacturing capabilities and capacity, training of manpower, maintenance and repair crews' ability to provide fast turn around time and quality service. Along with these were the efforts of countless associated trades, crews and missions needed for backup purposes. On the flip side, these numbers unfortunately reveal how the world's isolationist policies of the 1930's allowed Germany to expand its military prowess and manufacturing base to such a degree that a gargantuan effort was required to remove their stranglehold from the free world.

Appendix E:

The Pied Piper of Hamelin — A Sordid German Folk-Tale

MOST COUNTRIES HAVE THEIR MEDIEVAL FOLK HEROES. As a youngster in Amsterdam, I frequently read sagas of past Dutch heroes who defeated pirates or overcame the aggressive Spaniards, e.g. Piet Hein, Admiral de Ruyter, etc. In contrast, I find that too much of the German folk-lore has a common thread of inordinate violence against the innocent. Since I refer in this book to the Picd Piper, let me relate the sordid details of this legend, which probably is standard fare for most German story telling hours.

It was the year 1284 in the beautiful town of Hamelin, nestled along the Weser River. The town elders had reached an understanding with a magician to rid the area of its burgeoning rat population for a stipulated sum of money. As tradition goes, this wizard achieved his goal by playing on his tuneful pipe as he walked towards the river. The rats, following the captivating music, were entranced and charmed into the river where they all met their demise. When the townspeople refused to pay the piper's bill, the magician once again played his melodious pipe. The piper walked out of Hamelin, but this time he was followed by no less than one hundred and thirty of the town children. Upon arriving at a hill named *Koppenberg,* the piper and his young entourage entered the hill and vanished from sight, never to reappear.

MY COMMENT TO THIS TALE OF WOE IS THAT IRRATIONAL AND subtle violence is an ancient evil that has sealed many destinies. Lauded conduct in these gruesome varieties of enigmatic fables has regretfully contributed towards numbing German compunctions and elevated their levels of social dysfunction. I consider these legends to be precursors of the modern "humane murder" schemes as developed and practiced by members of the avaricious German military-industrial complex at such infamous sites as the Auschwitz gas chambers.

GLOSSARY

A.H.	may their souls dwell in peace (acronym)
Aishes Chayil	valiant wife
Aliyah	emigrate to Eretz Yisroel
Atzei Chaim	plural for *Etz Chaim*
Aveilus	mourning
Ba'al Midos	excellent character
Bamidbor	Numbers, fourth book of the *Torah*
Beis Hamedrash	post graduate *yeshivah*
Beis Olam/Botei Olam	burial ground(s)
Bench	to give a blessing
Benching	grace after meals
Bimah	platform in the center of *shul*
Breishis	Genesis, first book of the *Torah*
Bris Miloh	circumcision
Brocho	blessing
C.E.	Common Era
Chag	holiday
Chassenah	wedding
Chaverim	colleagues
Chazal	Our Sages of Blessed Memory (Acronym)
Chesed	kindness
Chevrah Shass	study group formed to understand the Talmud
Cholov Yisroel	milk that was milked under Jewish supervision
Choson	bridegroom
Chover	devout trusted colleague
Churban	destruction, holocaust
Daf Yomi	the study of one page (both sides) of the Talmud daily
Devorim	Deuteronomy, fifth book of the *Torah*
Din Torah	Rabbinical Court
Droshos	sermons on religious subjects
Eichah	the Book of Lamentations
Eitz Chaim	wooden rods on which the *Torah* scroll is wound
Eretz Yisroel	the Land of Israel or Israel
Erev Shabbos	Sabbath eve or Friday
Eruv	rabbinic demarcation around a city or district inside which one is permitted to carry on Shabbos.
Gepo	(Jewish) Ghetto Police (acronym)
Gestapo	*Geheime Staats Polizei* (German) or Secret State Police (Acronym)
Ge'ulah	redemption from exile
Golus	exile
Grootmoeder	grandmother (Dutch)
Grootvader	grandfather (Dutch)
Hagaon	Highness, title of the Jewish princes in the Babylonian exile, devout scholar

Halacha/Halachic	Jewish law
Halochoh LeMa'ase	practical application of Jewish law to daily living
Hashem	code name for the Creator of the Universe Who alone made makes and will make everything in creation
Hashgochah	Providence
Hashkofah	perspective from a religious viewpoint
Haster Ponim	Hashem will figuratively hide His Face
Hatzola work	relief work
Hiddur	beautification
Horav	the eminent rabbi
H.Y.D.	Hashem will avenge his/her/their blood (Acronym)
Isru Chag	the day following a holiday
Jahrzeit, Yahrzeit	anniversary of when deceased passed away
Kaddish	prayer sanctifying Hashem
Kapo	(Jewish) camp police (acronym)
Kehillah	congregation
Kesuvah	written religious marriage contract
Kibbud	honor
Kiddush Hashem	sanctifying Hashem's Name
Koheles	the *Book of Ecclesiastes*
Kosel Ma'aravi	the western wall along the Temple mound in Yerusholayim
Lain	to read from the *Torah*
L.B.	to differentiate between the living and the deceased (Acronym)
L'shem Shomayim	in the name of Heaven
Levaya	escorting the deceased prior to burial, funeral cortege
Limudei Kodesh	non-secular studies
Luach	Jewish calendar
Luftwaffe	German Air Force
Ma'amar Chazal	a saying of our Sages of Blessed Memory
Ma'arich Yomim Veshonim	to live to a ripe old age (literally, to live long days and years)
Mallachim	Angels
Maseches	a tractate in the Talmud
Matzeivah	tombstone
Matzo	unleavened bread
Mechutan	relationship between the two father's of a married couple
Medrash/Medroshim	perspective(s) of the Talmud
Megillah	The book of... (e.g. Esther)
Meilitz Yoshor	a Heavenly advocate
Minchah	afternoon prayers
Minhag	a religious custom
Minyan	quorum of ten men who are thirteen years and older
Mishlei	the Book of Proverbs
Mishnah	forerunner of the Talmud
Mishnah Berurah	an expounding commentary of the Jewish Code of Law
Mispallelim	worshippers
Mitzvos	commandments from the *Torah*
Mohel	person performing circumcision

Morah D'Asrah	rabbi of the community
Moreinu	our teacher in *Torah*
Nachamu Ami, Yomar Elokeichem	"Comfort ye comfort ye My people, says Hashem."
Neder	oath
Nachas	enjoyment
Neshomo	soul
Nigunim	tunes
n.y.	may his/their light shine bright (Acronym)
o.h	may his, her soul dwell in peace (Acronym)
Oma	grandmother (German) affectionate, grandma
Omein	Amen
Oom	uncle (Dutch)
Opa	grandfather (German) affectionate, grandpa
Parness	benefactor
Parnosah	livelihood
Paskened Sha'alos	ruled on rabbinical queries
Parve	food being neither of meat or dairy products
Peirush	commentary
Pesach	Passover holiday
Pikuach Nefesh	life threatening
Pisukim	verses, sentences
Poskim	those who rule on halachic matters
Protectia	connection for obtaining favors
Rabbonim	Rabbis
Rav	eminent Rabbi
Reb	Sir
Ribono Shel Olam	Master of the Universe
Rosh Bes Din	Head of the Rabbinical Court
Rosh haYeshivah	dean of the *yeshivah*
Savta	Grandma (Hebrew)
S'chach	roof shade covering for a *Succah*
Sedrah	weekly section of the *Torah, Parsha*
Sefer	book with religious contents
Semichah, Musmach	ordination, one who was ordained
Se'uda	meal
Se'udas Sh'lishis	third Shabbos meal
Shabbos	Sabbath/Saturday, starts at sundown Friday
Shacharis	Morning prayers
Shemos	Exodus, second book of the *Torah*
Shidduch	marital match
Shiur/Shiurim	study period/s
Shlita	may he live a long and good life (Acronym)
Shavuous	Pentecost, holiday celebrating the giving of the *Torah*
Shochet	ritual slaughterer
Shofar	ram's horn
Sh.t, Shetichyeh	may she live a good long life. (Acronym)
Shulchon Aruch	Code of Jewish law.

Siddur	prayer book
Simchas Torah	Additional holiday following the *Succos* festival
S.S.	(German) elite security guard or soldier (Acronym)
Shul	synagogue
Succah	temporary abode built for eating or sleeping during the Feast of Tabernacles or *Succos* festival.
Tahara	ritual washing of the deceased
Tallis Koton	special undergarment worn over the undershirt by Jewish males
Talmidei Chachomim	learned students of the *Torah,* Talmud and associated works
Talmud Torah	Jewish day school
Tante	aunt (Dutch, German)
Techiyas Hameisim	resurrection of the dead
Tefillah	prayer
Tefillin	phylacteries
Tehillim	the Book of Psalms
Tenach	the 24 books of the Jewish Scriptures (Acronym)
Torah	the five books of Moses
Torah im Derech Eretz	an observant Jew who studies Torah on a daily basis and also practices a trade or profession
Tzavo'oh	last will
Tzadikim	righteous people
Tzitzes	unique fringes worn on a special four cornered garment worn by Jewish boys and men
Vayikra	Leviticus, third book of the *Torah*
Yeshayohu	the book of Isaiah
Yesh may-yesh	its literal translation: something (created) from something (that was previously created). This teaching also postulates that in the initial moment of creation, when time started, Hashem created from nothing: all that is spiritual and non-material, and simultaneously and also out of nothing, the cosmos, by summoning into being all the universe's physical and non-physical aspects. [A parallel, but not necessarily identical secular aphorism that would correspond to the latter is one aspect of the Big Bang Theory when, just after time zero, all the universe's matter and energy came into sudden existence.] Creation through *yesh may yesh* was completed in the six days that followed the start of time, by the unfolding of all mundane through Hashem's nine progressive commands.[a]

Yirei Hashem	G-d fearing
Yishuv	settled areas in Eretz Yisroel
Yirmiyohu	the book of Jeremiah
Yiddishkeit	the practice of true Orthodox Judaism
Yom Tov	Jewish holidays
Y.S.	may his name be obliterated (Acronym)
Zatsal	may the remembrance of the righteous be a blessing (Acronym)
Zechus/Zechusim	merit(s)
Zechus Avos	ancestral merits

---

a. Refer to *Breishis,* Chapter 1, and to *Malbim's* commentary on *Breishis,* 1:1.

BIBLIOGRAPHY

1. Auman, Reiner J., compiler and editor, *The Family Bondi and their Ancestors,* Queens, New York, July, 1966.

2. Bendheim, Els, General Editor: *Liepman Philip Prins 1835-1915. Parnes Ledoro His Scholarly Correspondence.* Ktav Publishing House Inc., Hoboken N.J., 1992."

3. Bondi, Rabbi Shmuel, author and editor *Torei Zohov* Mainz, Germany, Yechiel Brill Publishers, 1875.

4. Breuer, Mordechai, *Modernity Within Tradition,* translated by Elizabeth Petuchowski, Columbia University Press, New York, 1992.

5. Bondi, Horav Teveleh, *Hagadah Shel Pesach,* Frankfurt am Main, Germany, 1898, reprinted by Osher and Ruth Lehmann, Publisher Jacob Goldman, Otzar Hasefarim Inc., Brooklyn, New York, 1987.

6. Cohen, Rabbi David, *Ma'aseh Avos Simmon Lahbonim,* Mesorah Publications Ltd., Brooklyn, New York, 1995.

7. Emanuel, Yonah, *Yesoepar Lahdor*, Mosad Yitschok Breuer, Yerusholayim, Israel, 5754.

8. *Encyclopedia Americana,* Grolier Incorporated, Sherman Turnpike, Danbury, Connecticut, 1993.

9. Finkel, Yehoshua Mattisyahu, *To My Dear Children from Max Finkel,* Max Finkel, Brooklyn, N.Y., 1992.

10. Hachasid, Rabbi Yehudah, *Sefer Chasidim,* Mosad Horav Kook, Yerusholayim, Israel, 5720.

11. Hecht, Ben, *Perfidy*, Julian Messner Inc. New York, 1961.

12. Heinemann, Dr. Benno, *The Maggid of Dubno and his Parables,* Philipp Feldheim Inc., New York, 1967.

13. Hirsch, Rabbi Dr. Mendel, eldest son of Rabbi Samson Raphael Hirsch, *Haphtoroth,* Translator and Publisher Isaac Levy, Honig and Sons Ltd., London, England, 1966.

14. Lehmann, Oscher Lemuel, *Urgrossvaters Tagebuch* published by Max Lehmann, Magdeburg, Germany, December, 1936.

15. Lehmann, Oscher Lemuel, *Urgrossvaters Tagebuch* updated by Jurgen Weidemann, reprinted and published by the City of Verden (Aller), Germany, July, 1989.

16. Lehmann, Osher and Ruth, *In Memory of Morris Rokowsky,* Flatbush, New York, June 1992.

17. Lehmann, Jonas, *Biography of Dr. Markus Lehmann,* Verlag von I. Kauffmann, Frankfurt am Main, Germany, 1910.

18. Lehmann, Rabbi Dr. M., *Spruche Der Vater* reprinted by Victor Goldschmidt Verlag, Basel, Switzerland, 1963.

19. Lehmann, Rabbi Dr. M., *Hagadah Schel Pesach,* Joh. Wirth'sehen Hofbuch druckerei, H.S., Mainz, Germany, 1906.

20. Lehmann, Rabbi Dr. M., *Hagadah Schel Pesach* second Edition, Verlag von I. Kauffmann, Frankfurt am Main, Germany, 1914.

21. Lehmann, Horav Meir and (after the year 1890) his son Osher, the *Israelit* and in some years the *Israelit and Jeschurun,* weekly magazine, Mainz, Germany from 1860 to 1906.

22. Lehmann, Horav Meir, *Talmud Yerushalmi, Zeroim,* with commentary *Meir Nesiv*, first edition, Verlag von I. Kauffmann Frankfurt am Main, Germany, 1875.

23. Levi, Alice, *Oppenheimer Family Tree and Dates, from 1778 to 1978,* Kibbutz Sha'alvim, Eretz Yisroel, 1988.

24. Levi, Rabbi Yaakov, *Sefer Limudei Loshon,* Yaakov Levi Publishing, 9 Divrei Yerucham, Bayit Vegan, Jerusalem, 96429, Israel, 5750.

25a. Meisels, Rabbi Zvi Hirsch, *Mekadshei Hashem,* International Printing Co., Chicago Illinois, 1955.

25b. Miretzki, Zisla, *Erinnerungen der Frau Zisla Miretzki (Rabinowitz) Biographical notes on Chaim Boaz and Tzipora Chana Mindel Rabinowitz,* Nahariya, Eretz Yisroel, circa 1963.

26. O'Neill, Brian D., *Half a Wing, Three Engines and a Prayer, B-17s over Germany,* TAB Books, Division of McGraw Hill Inc., 1989.

27. Oppenheimer, Levy, *Biography of Our Late Father Hirsch Oppenheimer* Hannover, Germany, May 15, 1922.

28. Schwab, Rabbi Shimon, *Ma'ayon Beis Hashoayvoh,* Mesora Publications, Ltd., Brooklyn, New York, 1994.

29. Wiesner, Rabbi Naphtali, *In His Own Image,* Mesorah Publications Ltd., Brooklyn, New York, 1992.